INTERNATIONAL HANDBOOK OF
PARTICIPATION IN ORGANIZATIONS

VOLUME I

INTERNATIONAL HANDBOOK OF PARTICIPATION IN ORGANIZATIONS

For the Study of Organizational Democracy, Co-operation, and Self-Management

Volume I

Organizational Democracy: Taking Stock

We are very pleased to announce that the planning of the *International Handbook of Participation in Organizations* series is supported by the Maison des Sciences de l'Homme, Paris.

INTERNATIONAL HANDBOOK OF PARTICIPATION IN ORGANIZATIONS

For the Study of Organizational Democracy, Co-operation, and Self-Management

Volume I

ORGANIZATIONAL DEMOCRACY:
TAKING STOCK

Edited by

CORNELIS J. LAMMERS

and

GYÖRGY SZÉLL

OXFORD UNIVERSITY PRESS

1989

Oxford University Press, Walton Street, Oxford OX2 6DP

Oxford New York Toronto
Delhi Bombay Calcutta Madras Karachi
Petaling Jaya Singapore Hong Kong Tokyo
Nairobi Dar es Salaam Cape Town
Melbourne Auckland
and associated companies in
Berlin Ibadan

Oxford is a trade mark of Oxford University Press

Published in the United States
by Oxford University Press, New York

British Library Cataloguing in Publication Data
International handbook of participation in
organizations.
Vol. 1, Organizational democracy
1. Management. Participation of personnel
I. Lammers, Cornelis J.   II. Széll, György
III. Series
658.3'152
ISBN 0–19–877259–9

Library of Congress Cataloging in Publication Data
Organizational democracy: taking stock/edited by Cornelis J.
Lammers, György Széll.
p.   cm.—(International handbook of participation in
organizations; v. 1)
1. Management—Employee participation. I. Lammers, C. J.
(Cornelis Jacobus), 1928– . II. Széll, György. III. Series.
HD5650.068 1989   658.3'152—dc19   89–3041
ISBN 0–19–877259–9

Typeset by Cotswold Typesetting Limited, Gloucester

Printed in Great Britain
by Bookcraft Ltd.
Midsomer Norton, Bath

Foreword

This is the first volume in a new series of International Handbooks of Participation in Organizations published by Oxford University Press. It follows a previous series of three books published by John Wiley & Sons in 1983, 1984, and 1986.[1] The two series have the same Editorial Board and the same broad objectives: that is, to provide policy makers, practitioners, and academics with books of reference on significant developments in participative practice in organizations.

The field covers organizational democracy, co-operatives, employee share ownership, job involvement, aspects of job design, semi-autonomous work groups, joint consultation, self-management, co-determination, and the participative part of Quality of Work Life schemes. The forms of behaviour described under these headings overlap—and every few years different words are coined to accommodate changing socio-political realities. For instance, the term 'human resource management' has recently become popular and includes practices within our frame of reference.

The literature of research and practice is dispersed over a large number of journals and books so that even specialists have difficulty in keeping up to date and, inevitably, quality varies from excellent to indifferent. We have therefore brought together in accessible form the work of people with considerable expertise in these diverse fields.

Each volume is designed by two editors, who collaborate with the Editorial Board to invite experts to submit chapters under five headings: evaluation of current and recent seminal work; assessing what has become of well-known landmarks of the past; theoretical developments; description of recent research findings; and country studies. In addition, each editorial group can choose a theme to provide a focus for some of the contributions. We have covered work from East European, Asian, and Third World countries, but most of the literature on national and organizational experiments comes from Western Europe and the United States. This may change in the future.

We have changed the name from Yearbook to Handbook to stress that the content of each volume is chosen for its general importance and has no direct relation to the year of publication. The term 'participation' has replaced

---

[1] International Yearbooks of Organizational Democracy: for the study of participation, co-operation, and power. Published by John Wiley & Sons, Chichester, UK. Vol. i: edited by Colin Crouch (then London School of Economics, London) and Frank Heller (Tavistock Institute of Human Relations, London), 1983. Vol. ii: edited by Bernhard Wilpert (Technische Universität, Berlin) and Arndt Sorge (Wissenschaftszentrum, Berlin), 1984. Vol. iii: edited by Robert Stern (New York State School of Industrial and Labor Relations, Cornell University, Ithaca, NY) and Sharon McCarthy (Samuel Curtis Johnson Graduate School of Management, Cornell University, Ithaca, NY), 1986.

'organizational democracy', because over the years the latter term has, in the eyes of some people, taken on a different value. The series of reference books will continue to present a balanced picture.

On behalf of the Board, I warmly recommend this new series of Handbooks to a wide audience of responsible decision makers and scholars.

FRANK HELLER

Acknowledgements

To compose a book on participation in organizations entails a rather complicated process of organizing the participation of authors, reviewers, secretaries, assistants, and last but not least—in the case of two editors—of organizing themselves.

We want to express our gratitude to all those involved in the project and regret that we cannot mention them all by name. Therefore, let us single out those who contributed to this Handbook a bit more (in some cases quite a bit more) than others.

First of all, we are grateful to Pamela Hattingh, who corrected and improved the English of all those authors (and the two editors) whose mother tongue is not English. If Pamela performed the role of 'co-editor', Frank Heller turned out to be a 'super-editor' who valiantly and patiently helped us in all phases of the production process, from designing the book and recruiting contributors, to finalizing the manuscript and delivering it to the publisher.

Of the secretaries in Leiden and Osnabrück who handled the flow of communication between all the (sometimes not too well-organized) participants in the project, we want to thank especially Mw. Verschuur in Leiden and Frau Stürenberg in Osnabrück for the skilful and diligent ways in which they helped us perform the editorial tasks. Winfried Matthes prepared the list of abbreviations and Jan de Groot assisted in various ways the processing of the manuscript.

The laborious and not always rewarding work of reviewing the first (and sometimes second) drafts of contributions was done competently and efficiently by: Prof. K. R. Chaudhuri, Sergio Contreras Villa, Prof. Colin Crouch, Prof. Steven Deutsch, Prof. F. R. FitzRoy, Dr Frank Heller, Dr Peter Jansen, Prof. Richard J. Long, Prof. Burkart Lutz, Prof. Hans G. Nutzinger, Dr Michael Poole, Prof. Eugen Pusić, Dr Veljko Rus, Prof. Raymond Russell, Prof. András Sajo, Prof. Eberhard Schmidt, Prof. W. Scholl, Prof. Robert N. Stern, Prof. George Strauss, Prof. A. W. M. Teulings, Prof. Malcolm Warner, Prof. Bernhard Wilpert.

We are grateful to the Maison des Sciences de l'Homme, Paris, for supporting various editorial planning meetings.

Finally, we want to mention our indebtedness to the publisher, and the desk-editor, Enid Barker, and copy-editor, Laurien Berkeley, who lived up to the positive stereotype many on the Continent have of the British: tolerant, courteous, understanding, and pragmatic (in spite of all the inexcusable delays and technical imperfections in the end-product we delivered).

C.J.L.
G.S.

Leiden and Osnabrück
March 1988

Contents

Abstracts of Papers

Part I

EVALUATION AND REVIEW OF THE FIELD

1 Participation: Its Contradictions, Paradoxes, and Promises
(Marcel Bolle de Bal)

'Participation' as a theoretical concept and as a practical policy gives rise simultaneously to satisfied and frustrated reactions and is subject to ambiguous interpretations.

By looking at the different dimensions of the concept, at the contradictions within its practice, at the paradoxes linked to the desire for participation, and at the promises such policies hold out—that is to say, by combining a sociological, a psycho-sociological, and a socio-political approach—this paper attempts to clarify these ambiguities and to show under which conditions 'participation' could be a positive and synergetic programme.

2 The Labour Movement and Post-rational Models of Organization: A French Case or a Trend in Western Societies? *(Pierre Eric Tixier)*

Western societies have developed on the basis of rational models of organization: the Taylorian one in industry and the rational–legal model in bureaucracies. These models, in which trade unionism evolved, have been disappearing in recent years. New forms of organization have come into being, adapted to the values of creativity and participation. How can unions react to these post-rational models of organization, which short-circuit their influence and reduce opportunities for direct opposition? The article emphasizes how union strategies, collective identities, and structures of unions built up during economic growth are destabilized by the changes in organizations, and shows how unions at the level of the firm are trying to adapt to this new challenge.

3 Worker Co-operatives in the UK: Temporary Phenomenon or Growing Trend? *(Chris Cornforth)*

Historically the formation rate of worker co-operatives in the UK and the USA has followed a cyclical pattern where periodic waves of formations have been followed by periods where the formation rate drops to zero and the sector declines. In contrast, in countries like Italy and Spain the worker co-operative sectors, although also subject to cyclical variations, have become well established so that they are a significant economic force. Drawing on recent theoretical and empirical studies, the paper identifies various barriers that worker co-operatives face which limit their formation rate relative to capitalist business and their ability to grow and compete with large capitalist firms. The relative success of the co-operative sectors in countries like Italy and Spain is attributed to the actions of the co-operative movement and the State in overcoming these barriers. The paper concludes by outlining the actions that will be necessary to overcome the barriers to co-operative development in countries like the UK and the USA.

4 Taking Stock of the ESOPs *(Raymond Russell)*

Since 1974 researchers on workplace democracy in the United States have been increasingly fascinated by the nation's Employee Stock Ownership Plans, or 'ESOPs', but have had few reliable data about them. This gap in our knowledge is now rapidly being filled as a result of a major study of the ESOPs being carried out by the US General Accounting Office. The GAO estimates that by 1986 the US had more than 7,000 ESOPs and ESOP-like plans, of which nearly a third (32 per cent) were in the process of acquiring a majority of the stock in their firms. Already by 1983 the ESOPs had made stockholders of more than seven million American employees, with a median account balance of $5,226 per employee. By 1985 nearly a fifth (19 per cent) of the ESOPs had acquired 25 per cent or more of their firms' voting stock, but the GAO data indicate that the ESOPs' voting strength has so far done little to increase the influence of rank and file employees. For the present these plans, therefore, remain the major American instance of something that has been seen previously only in other parts of the world—that is, a form of worker ownership that is unaccompanied by any meaningful form of workers' control.

Part II
LANDMARKS REVISITED

5 Co-determination in British-Occupied Germany 1945–1949
(Ian Turner)

This contribution looks at how the military government in British-occupied Germany, imbued with the traditions of British industrial relations—the separation of management and work-force interests, the emphasis on collective bargaining, and the commitment to voluntarism—responded to German demands for co-determination. It traces the various developments during the occupation period after the Second World War and illustrates clearly how difficult it is to transplant institutions from one society to another when their respective histories and outlooks are very different.

6 Co-determination Research in the Federal Republic of Germany: A Review *(Leo Kissler)*

Co-determination (i.e. employee participation in management decisions) ranks among the central projects of post-war economic and social policy in the Federal Republic of Germany (FRG). In the 1950s and again in the first half of the 1970s, co-determination provided the battlefield for the furious skirmishes over the reorganization of post-war German society and its economy in which the political parties and the various economic interest groups and social forces engaged. But co-determination has now been widely accepted and has become a mainstay of the Federal German economic system. The view is now clear over a field which not only represented an arena of political conflict in the past, but has also provided an important area of scientific research for the last thirty-five years. This review is an attempt to draw up a balance sheet of empirical research into co-determination in the FRG.

7 Participative Management in the United States: Three Classics Revisited *(Edward E. Lawler III)*

Three classic books by Argyris, Likert, and McGregor are reviewed. Their contribution to introducing participative management to the United States is assessed. Although their ideas are seen as seminal, a number of reasons are given to explain why adoption of participation did not quickly follow their writings. The reasons include the lack of any compelling reason to change, the lack of knowledge about how to produce change, and the negative impact of participative management on the individuals who manage large organizations. The situation changed dramatically in the late 1970s when widespread adoption of participation began, primarily because a reason to change appeared: world competition. At the present time, a number of large corporations are publicly committed to operating in a participative management style that is based on the ideas of Argyris, Likert, and McGregor.

8 A New Milestone in the Development of Industrial Democracy in Norway? *(Thoralf Ulrik Qvale)*

The author describes the background to a major policy speech by the Prime Minister of Norway during which she announced an important new phase of democratization of work life in her country. He sketches in the historical background to this policy, which has been in operation since 1960 and inspired collaboration between the Norwegian Work Research Institute and the Tavistock Institute in London.

9 The Scandinavian Challenge: Strategies for Work and Learning *(Gro Harlem Brundtland)*

This chapter by the Norwegian Prime Minister is based on her speech to the opening session of a conference in memory of Einar Thorsrud, who was one of the most influential social scientists in the field of organizational democracy. Through a series of important action projects he had built up an international reputation, and Mrs Brundtland explains how this pioneering work established itself as a central pillar of the Norwegian labour movement. It led to the adaptation of technology to human needs through the use of the Tavistock Institute's socio-technical model and, on a wider plane, played a part in the overall strengthening of democracy in Norwegian society with the full co-operation of trade unions. These ideas made a considerable impact on Sweden and later diffused to other countries.

Part III
RECENT THEORETICAL DEVELOPMENTS

10 The Dilemma of Non-participation *(Sharon McCarthy)*

The term 'non-participation' is defined, and various levels of non-participation are described. Greenberg (1975) and Dachler and Wilpert (1978) provide four 'schools of thought' on participation, and these are used as a framework for a review of the literature relevant to non-participation. It is hypothesized that each school would explain non-participation slightly differently. Researchers from the 'management school' might feel non-participation is a result of individual differences or inefficiencies of participation. 'Humanist' researchers might suggest that non-participation occurs when participation is not genuine or when individuals are not developmentally ready to deal with participation.

Researchers from the 'democratic theory' school of thought consider participation a learned behaviour and would suggest that non-participation occurs when individuals have not had the opportunity to learn how to participate. Finally, research from the 'participatory left' perspective suggests that non participation will continue until substantial changes occur in the structure of ownership in corporations. Each of these hypotheses is examined using relevant research from the literature. Non-participation is presented as a dilemma of theory and practice where theoretical perspectives do little to explain the continuing prevalence of non-participation in employee participation initiatives.

11 Participation: A French Perspective   *(Anni Borzeix and Danièle Linhart)*

Rather than comment on the present state of organizational democracy in France, this contribution highlights the political and economic framework in which sociological discourse on participation has recently emerged. What are the main epistemological foundations to be found behind theories of social change affecting firms today?

Evidence from recent field-work leads the authors to differentiate revealed and concealed forms of worker participation at the workplace. Beyond ideological discourse the recent trend toward what can be seen as an increase in democracy or in citizenship in the firm via participative arrangements seems to aim at something more subtle: at shifting the boundaries between formal and informal activities, at converting covert into overt involvement, at reorganizing, through joint discussions and initiatives, the interface between two central rationales—prescription and protest—at work within companies. This might help to explain employees' reservation (shown by most studies on the subject) about becoming actively engaged in participative schemes.

12 Industrial Relations Theory and Employee Participation   *(Gerd Schienstock)*

In contrast to prescriptively orientated neo–human relations, industrial relations research is concerned with the explanation of business organization structures. This transfers the debate on the humanization and democratization of work into the broader framework of an analysis of organizational change. In industrial relations research a differentiation is made between systems theory, the Marxist approach, and the actor-centred approach. Approaches orientated towards systems theory point out the transition to post-industrial social structures, technological development, and the dynamics of the market as central determinators of organizational change. Expectations tend to be in the direction of integral work roles, new forms of professionalization, group labour, and expansion of autonomous decision making. From a Marxist viewpoint the striving of capital for control of the labour process is decisive for the development of industrial and decision making structures. The clear trend towards Taylorist and Fordist organizational concepts is confirmed. The third approach regards organizational structures as the result of strategic considerations and of a struggle between social actors. The relative openness of coalitions between various actors, even over and above the class barriers, scarcely permits the establishment of a clear-cut trend of organizational change. It is therefore to be expected that a process of structural differentiation will take place both at the level of individual enterprises and at departmental level.

13 Industrial Democracy and Organizational Symbolism
(Silvia Gherardi, Antonio Strati, and Barry A. Turner)

A remarkable development of the past decade has been the upsurge of interest in the cultural features of industrial and administrative organizations, both from a managerial point of view and from other perspectives. This development is reviewed, and its future implications for the study of industrial democracy are considered. The new managerial emphasis upon 'corporate culture' may be seen as potentially inimical to the further development of industrial democracy, in so far as it seeks to replace earlier attempts to control through social psychology by control through the application of social anthropology. Against these concerns the sketchy treatment of power in the cultural literature calls for exploration. On the other hand, cultural and symbolic studies are seen by some of their protagonists as pointing to alternative ways of enhancing and fulfilling the possibilities of industrial democracy. In this perspective, organizational culture is seen as something continually created and recreated by the active membership of the organization. A series of studies of Italian co-operatives are used to examine in more detail a number of the issues which this review highlights.

Part IV
RECENT RESEARCH FINDINGS

14 Factory Occupation and Industrial Democracy *(Joop C. Visser)*

The extensive use which has been made of factory occupation in industrial conflicts in most industrialized countries over the last fifteen years has received little attention. One of the explanations for this is that most authors see scarcely any difference between this form of action and the classical weapon of the strike. Based on the assumption that it has always, or almost always, been used in an attempt to prevent the closing down of factories and mass redundancy, factory occupation is viewed as a tactical alternative to a strike. It is not considered to give a special meaning to industrial conflicts. In these analyses historical perspective is almost entirely lacking. The author intends to demonstrate by means of a historical comparison that the aforementioned view is ill-founded. This comparison concerns the wave-like pattern with striking concentration occurring in the periods 1917–21, 1935–7, and 1968–83 and is restricted to factory occupations which take place within the framework of the industrial revolution. It will be argued that the relation between the phenomenon of factory occupation and that of industrial democracy can be made clear by looking less at the instrumental function of such actions and more at their expressive function.

15 From Co-determination to Co-management: The Dilemma Confronting Works Councils in the Introduction of New Technologies in the Machine-Building Industry *(Eckart Hildebrandt)*

At present a new generation of production and organization technologies known as Computer-Integrated Manufacturing (CIM) is being introduced in industry. The most important components of this type of rationalization are Computer-Aided Production

Planning and Control systems (CAPPS). Top management expects much more flexibility in connection with market needs, smoother handling of orders, higher efficiency and control in administrative and production departments. On the other hand, some leading managers declare that these technologies mean skilled and integrated jobs for the workers and more influence on a 'social system design' for the workers' representatives.

The presented paper refers to the latter thesis. Does this new type of integrative rationalization really include a professional and political strengthening of the works councils? An empirical study in the machine-building industry of the Federal Republic of Germany suggests very different results. Worker representatives are not equipped to meet the demands implicit in these systems and fear substitution by a new technological élite in factories.

16 In Search of Workers' Participation: Implementation of New Technologies in GDR Firms *(Artur Meier)*

Information technology (IT), which represents the major trend of technological change, can be used for better or worse depending on the economic, political, and social interests it primarily serves. Thus the search for democratic control of technology with its implications for work organization and job security becomes highly important. Under socialist conditions IT has not only to contribute to economic efficiency but also to follow socio-cultural imperatives.

From a socio-technical point of view 'weaker' forms of employees' representation are increasing, such as users' participation, influence on job design due to greater competence for meaningful participation based on information and enskilling, and participation in employment matters and necessary changes in working regimes broadly based—in the GDR—on labour legislation and legally binding collective agreements at company level. Unthreatened by unemployed workers and other groups of employees in the GDR, firms are powerful enough to safeguard their interests when more and more rationalization induced by IT implementation comes into being.

Sociological action research proves itself able to advocate the interests of the social groups involved, to point out opportunities for democratic participation, and, finally, to formulate socially compatible or advantageous solutions connected with the introduction of IT. However, there is a special need for comparative sociological research into different types of technology applied in different kinds of organization with a variety of participatory possibilities located in different societies and implying a wide range of national peculiarities.

17 Designing Support Organizations for Industrial Co-operatives in Developing Countries *(Peter Abell)*

On the basis of research conducted in Tanzania, Sri Lanka, and Fiji, the author details some of the problems in establishing a support and promotion organization for industrial producer co-operatives. The main conclusion of the research is that established agricultural and consumer movements are antipathetic to producer co-operation and, as a consequence, promotion cannot be put in their hands.

Part V
COUNTRY STUDIES

18 Workers' Participation and US Collective Bargaining *(George Strauss)*

New forms of worker participation have spread rapidly among unionized US firms. These range from job enrichment to stock ownership and union membership on company boards of directors. Many of these new, presumably co-operative, relations have been accepted (with various degrees of enthusiasm) by unions are quid pro quos for wage and work rule concessions. The new relations are inconsistent with traditional US collective bargaining and have contributed to considerable intra-union conflict, especially between union leaders who see their roles as adversarial and those who see their roles as participative. Nevertheless, enough individuals have gained vested interests in these schemes to make them likely to persist. They are not just fads.

19 Firms in Transition: Towards Industrial Democracy? The Case of Reforms in France since the End of the Second World War
(Philippe Bernoux)

Reforms in French firms since the end of the Second World War are examined. After a short description of the socio-economic context and technical evolution, managerial policies are presented. Several types of managerial policy have succeeded one another: the American model and the period of rationalization, then the Scandinavian model and the humanization of work, the Japanese model and mobilization. Is there a meaning to these changes? Researchers give explanations in terms of fashion, in terms of workers' social movement and social control, or in terms of economic realism. All these explanations are discussed. The author rules out a recourse to any one single explanation. On the contrary, it is a question of combining traditional factors (economic, technical, professional relations, etc.). But such combinations are illuminating only if they are predicated on the manner in which they are present in people's minds.

20 The Recent Growth in Employees' Representation in The Netherlands: Defying the Times? *(Jan C. Looise)*

In The Netherlands there seems to be a considerable growth in employees' representation, both formally and in terms of quantity and quality. This article deals with the question of whether this impression is correct and, if so, what the causes of this development may be and what effect they will have on the future development of the Dutch system of employees' representation.

One of the major conclusions of the research is that the recent growth of employees' representation corresponds with the trend towards decentralization occurring in Dutch industrial relations. Further decentralization, however, can lead to the opposite: participation through representation being replaced by forms of direct participation.

21 Does the 38.5-Hour Week Collective Agreement Change the West German System of Co-determination?
(Rudi Schmidt and Rainer Trinczek)

The 38.5-hour week collective agreement signed in 1984 after a major strike in the metal industry gave rise to a widespread discussion about the future of the West German system of industrial relations. The possible effects of flexible working hours and of the partial decentralization of the bargaining structure, associated with the delegation of some negotiating authority from national bargaining to plant level, became the particular subject of much speculation.

The main argument of the paper is that, although there is enough evidence to speak of a critical phase or even a turning-point in the history of West German industrial relations, until now the existing structures were able to integrate the new developments to a suprisingly large extent. However, taking into account the emerging trends of increasingly flexible working conditions and of further deregulation, destandardization, and differentiation, together with the growing dependence of plants on company groups and the lack of workers' representation at that level, it seems uncertain whether the West German system of industrial relations will be able to absorb the growing pressure on it without major restructuring in the future.

22 Organizational Democracy in West Malaysia: A Case-Study *(Hing Ai Yun)*

This study looks at a specific model of participation with the intention of exploring various constraints faced by members and the strategies adopted to overcome obstacles raised by an organizational structure which offers only limited opportunities for participation. This case was chosen for study particularly for its wide impact as about 20 per cent of Malaysia's rural smallholders now operate and live within its confines. Despite its many limitations, this alternative mode of participation has not only raised the standard of living of its participants, moulding them into more disciplined and progressive farmers, but members have also managed to augment their political power to achieve their goals, albeit by indirect means. This may be only a case-study but the lessons learnt will surely have wider ramifications.

Concluding Reflections. Organizational Democracy: Taking Stock
(Cornelis J. Lammers and György Széll)

On the basis of the findings reported in the foregoing chapters the editors conclude that—contrary to their expectations—the 'ground swell' of democratization in work organizations in the Western world is not subsiding. Furthermore, there is considerable evidence of successive 'waves' in the form of varying fashions in participation, co-determination, and co-operative undertakings. To explain the 'ground swell' the authors point to the operation of economic, technological, political (legislative), and cultural developments, which tend to counterbalance each other, and above all to processes of institutionalization. The 'waves' are interpreted primarily in terms of changes in industrial relations and general social values. Finally, the authors arrive at a fairly optimistic prognosis for the future of organizational democracy. They emphasize the role that social research could play in enlightening managers and other practitioners of the benefits of a 'functional' type of democratization in organizations.

Biographical Details of Contributors

PETER ABELL is Professor of Sociology at the University of Surrey, Guildford, UK. Previously Professor of Sociology at the University of Birmingham and Director of Research, Industrial Sociology Unit, Imperial College, London. Recent books: *The Syntax of Social Life* (Oxford, 1987), *Small-Scale Industrial Co-operatives in Developing Countries* (with Mahoney; Oxford, 1988), *Establishing Support Systems for Industrial Co-operatives: Case Studies from the Third World* (Aldershot, 1988).

PHILIPPE BERNOUX, Docteur d'État, is Director of Research at the Centre National de la Recherche Scientifique. Head of the Groupe Lyonnais de Sociologie Industrielle. Previously lecturer in industrial and organizational sociology at the Institut National des Sciences Appliquées de Lyon. Author of *Les Nouveaux Patrons* (1974), *Un travail à soi* (Toulouse 1981), *Sociologie des Organisations* (Paris, 1983), *Trois ateliers d'OS* (with Motte and Saglio, Paris, 1973), and a number of other books and articles.

MARCEL BOLLE DE BAL is Professor of Sociology and Psycho-sociology at the Free University of Brussels. In this capacity he is President of the Scientific Board of the Institute of Sociology, Director of the Centre of the Sociology of Work, and Head of the Social Psychology Department. He is also Honorary President of the International Association of French-speaking Sociologists and has published fifteen books in the field of industrial sociology and more than eighty articles, many of them on participation problems.

ANNI BORZEIX is a *chargé de recherche* at the Centre National de la Recherche Scientifique (CNRS) and belongs to the Laboratoire de Sociologie du Travail et des Relations Professionnelles (CNAM), Paris. Main interests concern the French labour movement's attitudes towards the organization of work, participation at the grassroots, self-management, collective action and identities. She has published *Syndicalisme et organisation du travail* (Paris, 1980) and *Le Temps des chemises* (with Maruani, Paris, 1982).

GRO HARLEM BRUNDTLAND was Prime Minister of Norway from February 1981 until the general election in October the same year. First elected to Parliament in 1974 when she became Minister of the Environment. Served as deputy leader of the Labour Party from 1975 until she took over as leader in 1981. Became Prime Minister again in May 1986. Vice-President of the Socialist International and member of the Independent Commission on Disarmament and Security. Chairman of the World Commission on Environment and Development.

CHRIS CORNFORTH is a lecturer in the School of Management of the Open University, Milton Keynes, UK. Vice-President of Research Committee 10 of the International Sociological Association on 'Participation, Workers' Control and Self-Management' and a member of the editorial board of *Economic and Industrial Democracy*. Recently co-directed a three-year project aimed at examining the factors and processes affecting the development of worker co-operatives in the UK. The results of the project are published in a book entitled 'Developing Successful Worker Co-operatives' (Beverly Hills, Calif., 1988).

SILVIA GHERARDI is a researcher in the Department of Social Policy, University of Trento, Italy. Specializes in the Sociology of Work and Organizations. She has published accounts of research on the female labour market, industrial relations in small firms, innovation and organizational decision making, temporal strategies among clerks in the public sector, and organizational culture and the life cycles of newborn co-operatives.

ECKHART HILDEBRANDT is a research co-ordinator at the Labour Policy Research Unit in the Science Centre, Berlin. Trained as an engineer and taught political sciences at the Free University, Berlin. For the last ten years he has been doing empirical research on rationalization in the automobile and machine-building industries, on trade union politics, and the introduction of information technologies. He has published *Internationale Beschäftigungskonkurrenz* (1986) and a range of research reports, and is co-editor of the year-book *Kritisches Gewerkschaftsjahrbuch*.

HING AI YUN is currently a senior lecturer in the Department of Sociology, National University of Singapore. Research interests focus on new technology and its impact on the labour process. Also working on job-related stress and strategies for coping with stress.

LEO KISSLER is Professor in the Department of Educational and Social Sciences at the Open University, Hagen, FRG. His major fields of research are political sociology and the sociology of work. Publications include *Partizipation als Lernprozeß* (Frankfurt and New York, 1980), *Arbeitshumanisierung und empirische Sozialforschung* (with Georg; Baden-Baden, 1981), *Arbeitspolitik: Ein deutsch-französischer Vergleich* (with Lasserre, Mothé-Gautrat, and Sattel; Frankfurt and New York, 1986), and *Tarifpolitik: Ein deutsch–französischer Vergleich* (with Lasserre; Frankfurt and New York, 1987).

CORNELIS J. LAMMERS holds a Chair in the Sociology of Organization in the Faculty of Social Sciences at the University of Leiden, The Netherlands. He is a member of the international Industrial Democracy in Europe (IDE) research team, and engaged at present in research on intermediary organizations, especially their role in the control system operated by the Germans in the occupied countries of Western Europe during the Second World War. Edited *Organizations Alike and Unlike* (with Hickson; London, 1979); author of a treatise on the development and relevance of sociological thinking on organizations, *Organisaties Vergelijkenderwijs* (Utrecht, 1983), and of other books and articles, many of which concern problems of organizational democracy.

EDWARD E. LAWLER III is a professor of management and organization in the Business School at the University of Southern California. In 1972 he joined the University of Michigan as Professor of Psychology and Program Director in the Survey Research Center at the Institute for Social Research. In 1978 he moved to USC. Founded and became the Director of the university's Center for Effective Organizations in 1979. In 1982 named Research Professor at USC. Dr. Lawler is a member of many professional organizations in his field and is on the editorial board of five major journals. Author and co-author of over 150 articles and fifteen books including *Pay and Organization Development* (Reading, Mass., 1981), *Managing Creation* (New York, 1983), and *High Involvement Management* (San Francisco, Calif., 1986).

DANIÈLE LINHART is a *chargé de recherche* at the Centre National de la Recherche Scientifique (CNRS), at the Laboratoire de Sociologie du Travail (CNAM), Paris. Has specialized in employer and trade union strategies concerning labour organization and work-force management, as well as the manual worker's experience of work (*L'Appel de la sirène*, Paris, 1981). She is now undertaking new research on trade unionism and youth, and is taking part in the co-ordination of the PIRTTEM, an interdisciplinary programme of the CNRS on technology, work, employment, and lifestyle.

JAN CORNELIS LOOISE is a lecturer on organizational sociology and industrial relations at the Faculty of Management of the University of Twente, The Netherlands. Previously worked for nearly ten years for Dutch trade unions as a research officer and policy adviser. At present he is also the leader of an extensive research project commissioned by the Ministry of Social Affairs and Employment on the functioning of works councils in The Netherlands.

SHARON MCCARTHY received her MBA (1983) and Ph.D (1987) from the Johnson Graduate School of Management, Cornell University, Ithaca, NY. Her dissertation evaluates the decision not to participate in Quality Circles in an aerospace manufacturing plant. She is also involved in research on managerial ethics and cross-cultural and gender-related questions of non-participation.

ARTUR MEIER is ISA Vice-President (1986–90) in charge of the publications and programme committees; has served before on the ISA executive committee (1982–6), publications committee (1977–86), research committee on sociology of education (Vice-President, 1978–86). At present he is Director and professor at the Institute of Sociology of Humboldt University, Berlin, GDR. Research and publication areas: sociological theory, sociology of education, sociological problems of new technologies, sociological aspects of peace research.

THORALF ULRIK QVALE was from 1967 to 1970 research assistant at the Norwegian Technical University working with Professor Einar Thorsrud on several field experiments in phase B of the Norwegian Industrial Democracy Programme (IDP). From 1970 to 1973 research fellow at the Work Research Institute in Oslo continuing work with the IDP. Since 1974 senior research fellow at the Work Research Institute working both with socio-technical theory and action research to promote participative forms of work organization, and with empirical studies of employee participation in Norway and internationally. Since 1978 Director of the newly formed programme, Safety and Offshore Working Conditions. Member of the Government's Commission on the further development of industrial democracy (1983–5) and Director of the Work Research Institute (1983–5).

RAYMOND RUSSELL is an associate professor of sociology at the University of California, Riverside. He has written a number of articles on the subjects of employee ownership and workplace democracy, and is the author of *Sharing Ownership in the Workplace* (Albany, NY, 1985). He was also a member of the team that designed the GAO study of ESOPs, and has subsequently served as a consultant to the project.

GERD SCHIENSTOCK is Head of the Department of Sociology at the Institute for Advanced Studies and Scientific Research in Vienna. The main emphasis of his work is on labour market and career, industrial labour relations, and innovative research. At the present time he is working on research projects concerning the introduction of new technologies and the efficacy of business training and job creation measures.

RUDI SCHMIDT is a research fellow at the Institute of Sociology at the University of Erlangen–Nuremberg. He has published on workers' consciousness, white-collar workers, and on some aspects of industrial relations. Currently working on new industrial production strategies and their consequences for the work-force.

ANTONIO STRATI is a researcher in the Department of Social Policy, University of Trento, Italy. His research and publications have been concerned with labour and productivity, latent skills and ergonomics in sawmills, models of bargaining relations and the labour market at a local level, local employment policies, the temporal dimension in organizations, and symbolic and cultural analyses of work and organizations. He is a founder-member of the Standing Conference on Organizational Symbolism (EGOS) and Editor of *SCOS Note-Work*.

GEORGE STRAUSS is a professor of business administration and former Director, Institute of Industrial Relations, University of California at Berkeley. He is also a former editor of *Industrial Relations*. He has had a life-long interest in workers' participation in management.

GYÖRGY SZÉLL is Professor of Sociology at the University of Osnabrück, FRG. Currently President of the Research Committee 10 of the International Sociological Association 'Participation, Workers' Control and Self-Management'. Main fields of research: new technologies, arms conversion and alternative production, trade unions, Third World countries. Main publications: *Rüstungskonversion und Alternativproduktion* (West Berlin, 1987), *Participation, Workers' Control and Self-Management* (London, 1988), *The State, Trade Unions and Self-Management* (Berlin and New York, 1989).

PIERRE ERIC TIXIER is a senior lecturer at the University of Paris, Nanterre, and a member of the Centre National de la Recherche Scientifique (CNRS) at the Laboratoire de Sociologie du Changement des Institutions. He has made a particular study of the problems of democracy and self-management in organizations: see, for instance, *La Démocratie en organisation* (with Sainsaulieu and Marty, 1983). He is at present working on the French trade union movement and is writing a book on the Confédération Française Démocratique du Travail (CFDT).

RAINER TRINCZEK is a lecturer and research fellow at the Institute of Sociology at the University of Erlangen–Nuremberg. He has specialized in industrial relations studies and industrial sociology and is currently working on new industrial production strategies and their consequences for the work-force.

BARRY TURNER is Reader in the Sociology of Organizations and Head of the Department of Sociology at Exeter University, UK. In addition to his interest in organizational culture, he has been studying the organizational features of disasters and crises for the past ten years and his book *Man-Made Disasters* (London, 1978) was one of the first to deal with such topics from an organizational point of view.

IAN TURNER is research fellow and lecturer at Henley, The Management College. His doctoral thesis was on the British occupation of Germany after the Second World War with special reference to the Volkswagen works. More recently he has been working on a major research project examining relations between the government and the pharmaceutical industry in Britain and West Germany.

JOOP VISSER is a historian, Doctor in Social Sciences (thesis: 'Factory Occupation: The History of a 'New' Form of Industrial Action'), lecturer in social aspects of the history of industrial societies at the Department of History, Erasmus University of Rotterdam, The Netherlands.

Abbreviations Used in the Text

AT&T	American Telephone & Telegraph Company (USA)
CAD	Computer-Aided Design
CAM	Computer-Aided Manufacturing
C&P	Customs and Practice
CAP	Computer-Aided Planning
CAPPM	Computer-Aided Production Planning and Management
CAQ	Computer-Aided Quality Assurance
CCG	Control Commission for Germany (British, in occupied Germany, 1945–9)
CDU	Christian Democratic Union (West Germany)
CFDT	Confédération Française Démocratique du Travail (French Federation of Socialist Trade Unions, focusing on self-management
CFTC	Confédération Française des Travailleurs Chrétiens (small, French trade union)
CGC	Confédération Générale des Cadres (French union for executives only)
CGT	Confédération Générale du Travail (the largest French trade union federation)
CIM	Computer-Integrated Manufacturing
CNAM	Centre National des Arts et Métiers (French polytechnic)
CNRS	Centre National de Recherche Scientifique (France)
CSO	Co-operative support organization (esp. in France and the UK)
DGB	Deutscher Gewerkschaftsbund (West German Trade Union Federation)
DIO	Democracy in Organizations (research project)
DRUPA	IG Druck und Papier (West German printers' union)
E(E)C	European (Economic) Community
EGOS	European Group for Organization Studies
ESOP	Employee Stock Ownership Plan (USA)
EVA	Europäische Verlagsanstalt, Frankfurt-on-Main (publisher)
Exco	Executive committee (selected regularly at the annual general meeting of the JKKR, Malaysia)

FELDA	Federal Land Development Authority (Malaysia)
FIAB	Forschungsinstitut für Arbeiterbildung (research institute for worker's education)
FIOM	Federazione Italiano dei Operai Metalmeccanici (communist Italian metal-workers' union)
FO	Force Ouvrière (in full, Confédération Générale du Travail—Force Ouvrière; French anti-communist trade union)
FRG	Federal Republic of Germany
GAO	General Accounting Office (USA)
GDP	Gross Domestic Product
GDR	German Democratic Republic
GM	General Motors (USA)
GRID	Method of organizational development
IDE	Industrial Democracy in Europe (research project)
IDP	Industrial Democracy Programme (Norway)
IG Druck	Industriegewerkschaft Druck und Papier (DRUPA; West German printers' union)
IGM(etall)	Industriegewerkschaft Metall (West German metal-workers' union)
IHPO	International Handbook of Participation in Organizations
ILO	International Labour Office
IMSF	Institut für Marxistische Studien und Forschung (Institute for Marxist Studies and Research, Frankfurt-on-Main, FRG)
IPC	Industrial producer co-operative
IRWWH	Individual regular weekly working hours
IRS	Internal Revenue Service (USA)
ISA	International Sociological Association
ISO	Institut zur Erforschung sozialer Chancen (Research Institute for Social Opportunity, FRG)
IT	Information technology/ies
IYOD	International Yearbook of Organizational Democracy
JKKR	Scheme development committee (see FELDA; Malaysia)
LDC	Less/least developed country
LO	Landesorganisationen (Norwegian federation of trade unions)
LOS	Norwegian social science research programme
NAF	Norwegian Confederation of Industry

NGISC	North German Iron and Steel Control (1945–9)
NKV	Federation of Dutch Catholic trade unions
NOU	Norges Offentlige Utredninger (Norwegian Commission on Industrial Democracy)
OD	Organization development
PIRTTEM	Programme Interdisciplinaire de Recherche sur le Travail, les Technologies et l'Emploi (France)
PRO	Public Record Office
QC	Quality Circle(s)
QWL	Quality of Working Life
STS	Socio-technical system
UAW	United Automobile Workers (union, USA)
UCS	Upper Clyde Shipbuilders (union, Glasgow, UK)
WRI	Work Research Institute, Oslo
WSI	Wirtschafts- und Sozialwissenschaftliches Institut des DGB (Düsseldorf, FRG)

Introduction

CORNELIS J. LAMMERS AND GYÖRGY SZÉLL

The main object of this volume is to evaluate trends in participation, co-determination, self-management, and co-operatives as these developed in the last decade under the impact of economic, technological, political, and socio-cultural forces. What ideas, forms, and processes of organizational democracy were thwarted or stopped? What trends were furthered or initiated under the influence of these macro-developments? What prospects for the future of organizational democracy can one infer from the analysis of recent developments and the present state of organizational democracy?

In the 1950s, 1960s, and early 1970s the literature on organizational democracy had an *evolutionary perspective*. Many authors took it for granted that due to rising levels of welfare and education and nearly full employment, in most Western countries people had become gradually less and less willing to comply with paternalistic and authoritarian regimes in the family and the community, in schools and churches, in firms and offices, in unions and other voluntary associations, in the armed forces, and even in correctional institutions. In other words, there was thought to be a growing 'demand' for participation, co-determination, semi-autonomous work groups, and even for forms of self-management, in organizational life.

At the same time, to many observers it looked as if the 'supply' of participative management, decentralization, and other more or less democratic ways of governance had increased as a result of the 'functional requirements' of organizations which tended to become larger, more complex, more intertwined with one another, and more continuously confronted with the need to adapt to fast rates of environmental change. 'Democracy is inevitable,' proclaimed Slater and Bennis in a much-quoted article in the *Harvard Business Review* in 1964.

In the late 1960s, particularly in Europe and the USA, but also to some extent in Latin America and many Third World countries (in the wake of decolonization and national emancipation movements), efforts towards democratizing organizations received new impetus. In the worlds of work, education, politics, religion, and other spheres of life, so it seemed at the time, unprecedented levels of co-determination if not self-determination could be reached. The 'many', who had always been ruled by the 'few', appeared finally to be gaining their rightful place in the sun.

However, this rather optimistic view of the progress of organizational democracy became seriously undermined by a variety of trends in the 1970s and

1980s. Already in 1970 the very same Bennis who six years earlier had hailed the 'inevitability' of organizational democracy noticed that 'A Funny Thing Happened on the Way to the Future' (Bennis, 1970) and had a serious look at a number of forces militating against the spread of more egalitarian and humane forms of organization.

Other authors who had never been convinced by the predictions of a rosy post-industrial future started to emphasize the dialectics of the democratization process, and so gradually a *cyclical perspective* emerged and came to replace the former evolutionary vision.

During the last decade it has become clear that various developments may slow down, halt, or even reverse trends towards increased participation, co-determination, and self-management. First of all, the *economic recession* which set in in the second half of the 1970s probably undermined the zeal and force of democratic opposition 'from below' as well as 'top down' initiatives. This affected students, workers, and ordinary citizens in decisions about their organizational settings. In the wake of the downward trend in the business cycle, unions often had to give priority to protecting the rights of their members in declining industries, to preventing deterioration in the conditions of employment elsewhere, and in general to keeping going in the face of loss of members and of public status. On the whole, this implied that some (if not many) of the unions which had raised the banner of industrial democracy in the 1960s and promoted efforts to humanize, if not democratize, work relations in firms and public agencies had to put aside such demands for 'immaterial gains' for the time being.

Moreover, many work organizations, in order to improve their levels of competitiveness and flexibility, had recourse much more often than before to hiring employees on a temporary or part-time basis or to contracting out work as much as possible. This increase in the demand on the secondary sector of the labour market at the expense of the demand for 'primary' labour, may also have had hitherto seldom explored repercussions on the state of organizational democracy in developed countries. Institutionalized forms of participation and representation are in all likelihood attuned mainly to the interests and perspectives of the stable ('primary') labour force. Therefore, one suspects that this tendency towards greater reliance on auxiliary labour exerted a heavy toll on the sphere of influence, if not the viability, of works councils, experiments with semi-autonomous groups, consultancy practices of first-line supervisors, and the like.

New technologies may be designed, introduced, and incorporated in work organizations as part and parcel of neo-Tayloristic or 'Fordist' methods of centralized planning and programming. On the whole, it looks as if managements have developed earlier and more consistent strategies with respect to these *technological developments* than unions have. As pointed out already, unions are in a difficult position to start new lines of activity anyhow, and in addition they are faced with the problem of engaging and keeping the manpower needed as 'counter-expertise' to match managerial resources.

Finally, one should not underestimate the effect of *socio-cultural and political changes* occurring in the wake of these macro-trends. In the course of the 1970s, the dominant climate of values changed, and the ideal of a more egalitarian society was replaced by revaluation of entrepreneurship, élite-formation, no-nonsense policies, and 'strong' leadership. A great many politicians and their publics reacted swiftly to these economic and socio-cultural changes. In several countries centre right parties or coalitions pushed centre left governments out of office and many advocates of leftist politics became less assured of the desirability and feasibility of organizational democracy.

Given these set-backs to what Mannheim (1940: 44–9) long ago called the process of 'fundamental democratization', it is small wonder that in recent years authors like Ramsay (1983) started to elaborate a cyclical instead of an evolutionary view of processes of democratization. This trend in theory-formation concerning democracy is of interest not just from the scholarly but also from the practical point of view, for obviously the evolutionary perspective is no longer a useful tool for prognosis.

Of course, the somewhat gloomy prospects for organizational democracy contained in the above sketch of forces hindering the maintenance of further diffusion of ways and means for the rank and file to have a say in decision and policy making in their organizations are to some extent offset by developments countering these trends. In some countries the laborious process of preparing and enacting new laws meant that legislation often lagged behind alterations in the *Zeitgeist*, and, consequently, new forms of participation were introduced in spite of the outgoing tide of organizational democracy.

Not only can new technologies provide options for new forms of Taylorism or Fordism, but they may also contribute towards employee involvement in the context of more participative approaches, like Organizational Development, Quality Circles, GRID, etc. In several nations there are also noticeable tendencies towards decentralization of collective bargaining. Although this often undermines union power, it may enlarge the role of works councils in negotiating collective agreements with the managements of their firms. Particularly if they have acquired new powers through legislation and are quick to seize chances to promote participation in decisions about the installation and utilization of new technology, works councils may be in a better position than unions alone to assert themselves as forces to be reckoned with.

We are aware of the dangers of sweeping generalizations, purportedly applying to ubiquitous developments everywhere. It goes almost without saying that countries—and usually also sectors within a country—exhibit enormous variations in the 'mix' of trends and countertrends summed up here. Depending on the peculiarities of national systems of industrial relations, economic conditions, political alignments, cultural traditions, and social composition of the populace, one may find even in adjacent countries—and again even in different industries within one country—that organizational democracy is moving in divergent directions.

Therefore, in our efforts to 'take stock' of these trends and countertrends we wanted to obtain as many contributions as possible from authors knowledgeable about a great variety of forms and processes of participation, co-determination, and self-management in quite different parts of the world. Alas, we found it hard to locate scholars in the Second or Third World who had made professional studies of organizational democracy. Moreover, in a number of cases the colleagues contacted were unable to produce a paper of the format required within the time limits set.

Consequently, the collection presented here, much to our chagrin, contains only two contributions on non-Western countries and one on Eastern Europe. Thus, in spite of all our good intentions, we can take stock only of organizational democracy in North America and Europe. However, we feel privileged to have received many excellent pieces from European authors who, because many publishers only accept work written in English, see themselves deprived of the right to express themselves in their mother tongue. In fact, this volume includes five chapters written by authors from Germany and Austria, four written by French-writing colleagues, two produced by Norwegians, and another two by Dutchmen, and 'only' seven by UK and US authors. Finally, one chapter is co-written by Italian and British sociologists, so that, all in all, we offer the reader a survey of the state of the art of organizational democracy in continental Europe, Great Britain, and North America.

As in the *International Yearbook of Organizational Democracy* (the predecessor of the present series, as explained in the Foreword by Frank Heller), the chapters are grouped into five different parts: Evaluation and Review of the Field (Part I), Landmarks Revisited (Part II), Recent Theoretical Developments (Part III), Recent Research Findings (Part IV), and Country Studies (Part V). We have written separate comments for each of these sections.

In a final chapter we offer an evaluation of some of the main findings of the contributions against the background of the assumptions and hypotheses in this introduction.

References

Bennis, W. G. (1972), 'A Funny Thing Happened on the Way to the Future', *American Psychologist*, 25 (1970), 595–608,; reprinted in J. M. Thomas and W. G. Bennis (eds.), *Management of Change and Conflict* (Harmondsworth: Penguin Books).

Mannheim, K. (1940), *Man and Society in an Age of Reconstruction* (Studies in Modern Social Structure; London: Routledge & Kegan Paul).

Ramsay, H. (1983), 'Evolution or Cycle? Worker Participation in the 1970s and 1980s', in C. Crouch and F. Heller (eds.), *International Yearbook of Organizational Democracy*, i (Chichester: Wiley).

Slater, P. E. and Bennis, W. G. (1964), 'Democracy is Inevitable', *Harvard Business Review*, 42 (Mar.–Apr.), pp. 51–9.

PART I

EVALUATION AND REVIEW OF THE FIELD

Outline of Part I

SINCE the purpose of this volume is to 'take stock', all sections contain evaluations and reviews of the field. In Part I we group those contributions which provide a critical assessment of research, theory, and practice of forms of organizational democracy. It may be noted in passing that our way of classifying the chapters has a somewhat arbitrary character. Many, if not most, of the studies collected in this Handbook fit into more than one category. Scholarly work, like any other kind of socio-cultural product, can be viewed from different angles and, therefore, always defies efforts to devise an all-encompassing classification which allows the allocation of each 'object' to one class and one class only, beyond any reasonable doubt!

The first four contributions question traditional approaches to organizational democracy against the background of long experience and/or extensive investigation in the field.

The contribution of Marcel Bolle de Bal elaborates an integrative approach, which helps to clarify the inherent contradictions, paradoxes, and promises of various forms of participation and co-determination in work organizations. The author combines in a thoughtful and original manner two theoretical perspectives often conceived of as rather incompatible, and distinguishes three paradoxes for the employers and workers, and four levels of participation. He ends with a socio-political view. Certainly the rigour of this Cartesian think-piece from somebody from the Latin world might seem a little strange to an Anglo-Saxon reader at first sight, but we are convinced that its provocative nature gives new insights to all those who are active in the field, either as researchers or as practitioners.

Using the same line of argument Pierre Eric Tixier draws conclusions from a study of one of the most important trade unions in France and tries to develop some generalizations out of this case-study which might have an impact on the whole field of organizational democracy. The unions seem very appropriate organizations to investigate, because they claim to be democratically structured and wish to introduce more democracy into society and into the economy. The problems encountered by the French unions are not peculiar to France: the new work organization and management strategies tend to incorporate the workers' demands instead of opposing them as in Taylorian or Fordist models. The unions are therefore confronted with the need to revise their whole concept and even their *raison d'être*. Another issue affecting unions is the current fashion for the development of a company identity, which becomes a cultural problem. Some French researchers already speak of *post-rational* models of organization. Whether these models are really non-rational or are based on another kind of rationality while keeping the same objectives has to be established by further research.

Chris Cornforth concentrates on another form of organizational democracy which has generated much interest over recent years: worker co-operatives. His reflections are based on research in this field, both within and beyond Britain. Certainly co-operatives currently exhibit the most widespread and 'complete' model of organizational democracy, although, of course, they vary a great deal in the extent to which rank and file members have a decisive say in policy matters. In Italy and Spain co-operatives play an important role in society and the economy, whereas in the United States, the United Kingdom, and the Federal Republic of Germany they are more marginal. How far social movements and/or the State form support organizations which help co-operatives cope with the manifold problems they face constitutes the core of the article.

Raymond Russell treats the role of 'Employee Stock Ownership Plans' as a phenomenon specific to the United States. Since their creation in 1974 they have aroused intense debate about the extent to which they are able to offer a viable democratic alternative to the conventional hierarchical type of enterprise within a free market system. Several contributions in the *International Yearbook of Organizational Democracy* document the ongoing debate. The data recently gathered by a US government agency provide the basis for evaluation of ESOPs. Russell's account of the findings in question do not give rise to high expectations with regard to the democratic potential of this form of economic democracy. For example, in only 39 per cent of the ESOPs do the owners of stocks have voting rights. This seems to be in complete contradiction to the principles of capitalism itself! The debate is far from over and the data presented here will be discussed in some detail in Volume II of this series, with its emphasis on ownership and participation.

1

Participation: Its Contradictions, Paradoxes, and Promises

MARCEL BOLLE DE BAL

PARTICIPATION is an old concept, but an ever-renewed socio-political goal, a modern 'must' for managers of private enterprises and public institutions today. Many publications and research reports deal with the subject, many speeches advocate its use, and a great deal of experience reveals its misuses and abuses. Reading, hearing, or looking at these sources of information we must admit that 'participation' as a theoretical concept and as a practical policy is the source simultaneously of satisfaction and frustration, and of ambiguous interpretations. How could we clarify them? By looking at the different dimensions of the concept, at the contradictions apparent in the practice, at the paradoxes linked to the desire for participation and at the promises of such policies: in other words, by combining a sociological, a psycho-sociological, and a socio-political approach.

The contradictions of participation: a sociological analysis

In order to interpret the divergent information given by many research reports, I suggest adopting a sociological perspective, using and combining two classical types of interpretation: a functionalist approach and an actionalist approach.

A functionalist approach . . .

From this perspective one should theoretically distinguish

- *the theoretical functions* of participation policies and structures (i.e. those assigned to them by specialized literature or interested persons: for example, 'motivation', 'efficiency', 'integration', 'industrial democracy', etc.);
- *the real functions* (i.e. their practical impact: for example, 'debureaucratization', 'power gains', etc.). Among these (and in reference to the general functionalist theory, Merton, 1957) one should also distinguish between the subjective goal and the objective effect, tracing the actual coincidence between project and result;
- *the manifest functions*, which coincide with the project, i.e. with the theoretical functions (for example, 'productivity', 'co-operation', etc.);

- *the latent functions*, which do not correspond to the expressed intention (for example, 'power bargaining', 'regulation', 'social control', etc.).

Too often these distinctions are not made, and this does not help the interpretation and comparison of research results. We badly need empirical investigations based on such fundamental concepts: they should help the debate to progress in both theoretical and practical ways. Let us hope that a national or, even better, an international institution will sponsor such an investigation. At this stage, while waiting for such information, we may—as sociologists—notice, as a strong hypothesis to be tested, that there is often some difference between the theoretical functions (the official statements) and the real ones (the concrete practices).

Moreover, in order to avoid the danger of a too 'positive' interpretation (everything that happens is what should happen, is justified, functional because it exists), we shall complete the study of the functions (the consequences which help the system to realize its goals) with a study of the dysfunctions (the consequences which disturb its functioning).

. . . and an actionalist approach . . .

However, an analysis in terms of functions and dysfunctions does not take sufficiently into account human actions, feelings, struggles for power. Man as an individual or as a member of an organization is represented as a passive element, conditioned by organizational structures and the industrial relations system. Such a mechanistic and incomplete model does not facilitate the understanding of change.

Therefore, I believe it is necessary to complete the analysis in terms of functions and dysfunctions with another type of analysis derived from an 'actionalist' approach, i.e. in terms of social action (Touraine, 1966), of struggle for power, struggle to share economic results, struggle for social change. From that perspective, a participation policy and participation structures should be interpreted less as the answer to the functional requirements of a specific socio-technical system than the result of power confrontation in the field of industrial relations, of strategies developed by diverse and adverse social forces, as a means to more equal distribution of power and therefore of democratization (Clegg, 1983).

. . . lead to a synthetic approach . . .

How could we mix these two apparently opposed approaches?

I would like to formulate the following proposition: let us start from the most common model—the functionalist one—but let us enrich it by distinguishing the diverse 'reference units' (or structures)—the employer, the worker, the union, the macro-social institutions (government, State, the EEC)—for which participation could be functional or dysfunctional. Actually, 'participation', when it appears functional for one unit, can often, but not always, be dysfunctional for another one:

that is when power relations, strategies, and bargaining develop and open the way to compromise; this is when specific 'actionalist' analyses should be elaborated, taking into account the development of specific actions adapted to the particular interest of social actors and also the evolution of society as a whole.

... but also a diversified approach ...

Besides that, we must avoid two common confusions: one between direct and indirect participation and one between *de facto* and voluntaristic participation. I shall make a distinction between

- *direct* participation, which is the one experienced by individual workers through personal and small groups opportunities,
- *indirect* participation (or participation through representation, (Poole, 1986)), which is the one offered to workers by collective bargaining or institutional structures (workers' councils, for instance).

Following one British colleague (Cressey *et al.*, 1987), I think we have also to make a distinction between

- *de facto* participation, which is based on the fact that a worker, just by working on the assembly line or in a team, 'participates' (takes part) in a collective activity. This participation is of a technical and objective nature;
- *voluntaristic* participation, which is based on a structured policy of managers of the organization and on workers' needs and desires.

The first distinction is necessary since the functions and dysfunctions of direct and indirect forms of participation are different in many respects, and so are the attitudes and strategies of the social actors towards them. Therefore, I will present a specific functionalist–actionalist interpretation for direct participation on the one hand, and one for indirect participation (so-called by Poole, 1986: 253) on the other. The second distinction will help me to clarify my own definition of participation—at least the one I will use in this paper.

... based on a restricted definition

Defining 'participation' is a difficult problem since this term does have specific meanings within different languages and within different national human and industrial relations systems. Because the task is not easy, many researchers and writers talk about participation without defining the concept and use it, more or less consciously, in different senses. This, of course, contributes to making a complex matter still more complex.

For instance, by 'participation' one could understand

- participation in the sharing of economic results of the production unit or of the enterprise (profit-sharing in English, *participation aux bénéfices* in French), which we could call *'financial participation'*;

- participation in the life of the group or of the enterprise, in the activities of the social system, which we could call *'social participation'*;
- participation in the decision-making process at group, departmental, or enterprise level, which we could call *'political participation'*.

In order to avoid common confusions of interpretation, I will, unless otherwise specified, restrict the use of the term 'participation', in this paper, to two dimensions of that complex reality: its voluntaristic and its political ones. My main concern will, therefore, be with institutional policies and practices aiming at more participation by the individual worker (direct participation) and/or of workers' organizations (indirect participation) in the decision-making process at group, departmental, and/or enterprise level. In that respect I follow the conceptual and methodological choice of Cressey *et al.* (1987). To discuss the specific problems of financial, social, and *de facto* (technical) participation would need more space than that allotted to this paper.

Functions and dysfunctions of direct participation

For the employer a strategy of direct participation can have five main functions: an ideological one (work humanization, worker integration, union weakening), an economic one (improvement of work-force and management efficiency), a psychological one (motivation, reduction of stress), an organizational one (debureaucratization, modernization, decision emergence, training), and a sociological one (social regulation, co-operation, and control).

On the other hand, it could present some dysfunctions in the same five dimensions: ideological (criticism of managerial authority or capitalist property), economic (cost), psychological (tensions and frustrations), organizational (bureaucracy, slowness, disorganization), sociological (middle management frustration, union opposition).

For the worker direct participation can have also five main functions: an ideological one (recognition, achievement, promotion), an economic one (profit-sharing, acquisition, and use of skills), a psychological one (job enrichment, stress reduction), an organizational one (decentralization, delegation), and a sociological one (integration).

On the other hand, it has also some dysfunctions in four of these dimensions: ideological (manipulation, managerial reassertion of influence), economic (cost: time and energy), psychological (responsibilities, loss of freedom), and sociological (alienation).

Even *for the union* direct participation can have some functions: it offers the occasion for exercising counter-power in the ideological, economic, psychological, organizational, and sociological fields.

However, its dysfunctions are often considered as more important: paternalism, manipulation, atomization, individualization, exclusion (of the union).

The macro-social institutions (governmental or supragovernmental) can pursue, through a participation policy, some ideological goals in their own interests: social justice, industrial democracy, institutional change, and social peace. The only possible dysfunction, for them, could be the cumulative opposition of the social actors.

Functions and dysfunctions of indirect participation

For the employer, indirect participation has different functions: improvement of social relations, integration of the union into the enterprise, social peace and its economic benefits, and negotiation of organizational or technological changes.

But, of course, there are also some dysfunctions: challenge to managerial authority and to property privileges, cost (time and energy), mistrust by foreign investors, social tension, bureaucratization.

For the worker indirect participation has indirect functions: collective recognition and promotion, and protection of material (financial) and non-material (statutory, sociological) interests.

Its only possible dysfunction is his exclusion from the *jeu à deux* (game played by the employer's and union's representatives) and a growing feeling of double alienation.

To the union indirect participation offers the possibility of acting as a counter-power, of fighting the employer's arbitrary decision to move towards another socio-economic system, to fight excessive economic rationality, to defend purchasing power, to prevent unfair dismissal, to negotiate technological and organizational changes, to reinforce union power, and to force necessary compromises.

But of course, there are for the union some dysfunctions too: the risk of integration into the capitalist system, the cost (time and energy), the possible gap between leaders and the rank and file.

For the macro-social institutions indirect participation has the same functions as direct participation: social justice, industrial democracy, socio-economic transformation, an answer to social struggle, social peace, improvement of industrial relations.

The only possible dysfunction is the risk of corporatism: agreement of particular interests against the common good.

From this rapid inventory of the main functions and dysfunctions of participation for the social actors, there appear to be great differences between the functions (and dysfunctions) of direct participation and those of indirect participation.

These differences probably explain the ambiguities of certain attitudes, the contradictions of certain practices, the difficulties encountered in the application and evaluation of participation policies, and the evolution of the latter due to changes in the power relations between social forces.

Table 1.1 Functions of individual participation

Type	Units of reference			
	Employer	Worker	Trade union	State
Ideological	Humanization Integration Power	Appreciation Development Promotion	Ideological counter-power	Social justice Industrial democracy Transformation of structures Reform of enterprise Counter-protest
Economic	Efficiency of work force • productivity • Utilization of qualifications • cost reduction • flexibility Efficiency of management • communication • planning	Material interest Productivity Utilization of qualifications Development New qualifications	Economic counter-power	
Psychological	Motivation • sense of initiative • sense of responsibility • resistance to introduction of new technology • compensation for wage freezing Reduction of stress	Psychological interest • job-enlargement and -enrichment • compensation for wage freezing Reduction of stress		
Organizational	Debureaucratization Modernization Maturation Education	Decentralization • of authority • of power	Information	
Sociological	Regulation Co-operation Control	Integration	Social counter-power	Improvement of social relations

Table 1.2 Dysfunctions of individual participation

Type	Units of reference			
	Employer	Worker	Trade union	State
Ideological	Protest Subversion Revolution	Integration		
Economic	Cost	Cost		
Psychological	Tensions	Compromise Engagement	Paternalism Manipulation	
Organizational	Bureaucratization Disorganization			
Sociological	Malaise of middle management Union distrust	Alienation	Atomization De-solidarization Exclusion	Cumulative resistance of parties

Table 1.3 Functions of collective participation

Type	Units of reference			
	Employer	Worker	Trade union	State
Ideological	Improvement of social relations Integration of union	Promotion (collective) Recognition (collective)	Counter-power Transformation of structures	Social justice Industrial democracy Reform of enterprise Counter-protest
Economic	Efficiency of work-force • overcome resistance • reduce breaks • avoid strikes	Defence of material interests	Fight against excess rationalization Defence of income Prevention of redundancies	
Organizational	Negotiation of organizational changes		Negotiation of organizational changes Control of management	
Sociological	Regulation (Social peace) Negotiation (compromise)	Defence of social status and conduction	Strengthening of union Negotiation (compromise)	Improvement of social relations

Table 1.4 Dysfunctions of collective participation

Type	Units of reference			
	Employer	Worker	Trade union	State
Ideological	Social protest	'Game for two' Double alienation	Integration	Corporatism
Economic	Costs (time, energy) Mistrust by foreign investors		Cost (time, energy)	
Psychological	Tensions • expression of complaints • creation of new needs			
Organizational	Bureaucratization Disorganization		Rupture base/top	
Sociological	Dissatisfaction of middle management • short circuit • unionization		Compromise Integration	

For instance, it appears that unions would be interested in giving priority to indirect participation: this seems quite natural, because for them direct participation has many important dysfunctions (manipulation of individuals, atomization of claims, exclusion of the union), while indirect participation has many important functions (reinforcement of its counter-power, bargaining of technological and organizational changes, etc.). On the other hand, and for opposite reasons, employers will favour direct participation. Intermediately, the worker will be more interested in direct participation but should not ignore the advantages—either preventive or defensive—of indirect participation.

The result of these contradictory forces will depend largely upon the socio-economic context and its influence on the balance of power. The socio-cultural environment may also play a role in that respect: attitudes of unions may be somewhat different in southern and northern European countries due to their historical, sociological, and cultural backgrounds. Practically, the most common solution is to combine both types of participation. We may suppose it could be the most efficient in the long run. However, there is at present a move from indirect to direct formulas of participation (Cressey *et al.*, 1987). This move is the result of a new balance of social powers more favourable to the employer in a period of economic difficulty and of a deeper socio-cultural evolution (towards individualization, deregulation, flexibility, and debureaucratization). In the light of this, one could foresee, along with the evolution of political—institutional forms of particiption, a renewed interest in different kinds of financial participation (like profit-sharing, for example).

Strategies of participation

As we have seen, participation is advantageous (functional) to all the parties concerned. But their interests are contradictory. The main general function (social and organizational utility) of 'participation' is that it offers the possibility of solving, through individual and/or collective bargaining, these contradictions. It helps to fight against what Michel Crozier has called 'the bureaucratic phenomenon' (1965) or 'the blocked society' (1970) by democratization of decisions, humanization of interpersonal relations, and negotiating what some scholars would call today 'all-win' solutions.

There are many studies, reports, and books—written and spoken—on the various systems of participation. But, as far as I know, we lack sufficient results from empirical sociological research exploring ways in which different models of participation tackle these social contradictions, how the social actors negotiate their part in the participation process, and what their attitudes are—usually ambivalent and ambiguous—towards participation.

Very often the participation process is felt by the social actors to be at once unsatisfactory and satisfactory. Participation is a *complex* process with a double *strategic* meaning: it is strategic for the development of our industrialized and computerized socio-economic system, and it needs strategic capabilities from the different actors in order to be successful. (By 'strategic' capabilities, I mean what Crozier and Friedberg (1977) have called the 'relational' abilities of the social actors, that is, their capacity to handle the human system of social interaction, or what Touraine (1978) has called the 'institutional' abilities of the social actors, that is, their capacity to express themselves, to act in such a way as to realize what they feel to be necessary social change; in other words, I mean the capacity to have a political vision of the economic and social system which they have to manage, to understand the contradictory values and interests at stake, and to build up and apply a dialectical approach to the development of the socio-technical system.)

Participation is complex not only because of the complexity of its functions/dysfunctions, but also because it is the source of new contradictions between social actors. For example,

- *indirect participation* could develop such a complicity between employers and union representatives that it would be to the detriment of the other social actors: the short-circuited middle managers, the workers cut off from contact with their representatives and thus feeling alienated from both the enterprise and the union, and the State, defender of the common good, which sees the latter threatened by a kind of neo-corporatism;
- *direct participation*, as encouraged by the employer and appreciated by the worker, could be the source of new collective tensions or conflicts. The union, threatened by this new managerial 'gimmick', could be the source of tension, with middle management insufficiently prepared for the necessary new attitudes and new ways of exercising authority (founded on consultation, participation, and negotiation, and no longer on traditional statutory, hierarchical power).

But beyond these new social contradictions, the policies of participation reveal some *psycho-sociological* contradictions and paradoxes linked to individual characteristics and social situations.

The paradoxes of participation: a psycho-sociological approach

Indeed, three basic psycho-sociological paradoxes are hidden by the recognized need and desire for participation:

1. *We wish for participation without risk* but there is no participation without risk; participation is neither a gift (in contrast to what some employers believe), nor a feast (in contrast to the hopes of many workers). It is a necessity (against the obstructions of the bureaucratic system) and a risk (for the contested employer and the engaged worker). To obtain workers' participation, one ought to pay a fair price which is that of risk and necessity.

2. *We wish for participation for us, not for the other* (our collaborators): we claim it

from upstairs, we are unwilling to give it downstairs (a classic attitude amongst many managers).

3. Our desire for participation is ambivalent: we desire, it and at the same time, more or less consciously, we desire that it will be refused so that our opposition will still have a basis. *We desire and fear participation* at the same time, because it forces us into compromises which are felt to be imposed rather than voluntary.

These paradoxes nourish a kind of double bind, which makes the analysis of participation very difficult: participation is at the same time an individual aspiration and a systemic necessity, which implies individual anxiety and systemic disorganization.

Beyond these paradoxes, there is another source of complexity: the diversity of motivations. For individuals do not always have the same kind of desire for participations. Four types or levels of desire for participation amongst workers can be distinguished:

- level 0 (the retreat): workers not at all interested in the enterprise as a productive system;
- level 1 (the individual project): workers seeing the enterprise as a structure through which they could realize their personal aspirations, which ultimately lie outside the enterprise;
- level 2 (participation in the social system): workers interested in social interactions within the enterprise;
- level 3 (participation in the decision-making process): workers interested in the management of their work situation.

Most international reports[1] have studied level 3 in particular. But, because of its cost (in energy and time) and their own lack of expertise, that level does not seem to attract the support of the bulk of the work-force (Cressey *et al.*, 1987). A practical conclusion appears to be that a multidimensional policy of participation is the only solution to the variety of workers' expectations:

- for those at level 0: no participation policy could motivate them;
- for those at level 1: a policy of financial participation could motivate them;
- for those at level 2: a policy of direct participation could be effective;
- for those at level 3: a policy of direct and indirect participation could fulfil the

[1] Among so much research and so many publications on participation—so many that it is impossible to quote all of them and unfair to quote only some of them—let us mention two sponsoring organizations, the ILO in Geneva and the Foundation for the Improvement of Living and Working Conditions in Dublin, which have supported international comparative research programmes on the subject. See e.g. International Labour Office, *Workers' Participation in Decisions within Undertakings* (Geneva: ILO, 1981), and J. Monat and H. Safarti (eds.) *Workers' Participation: A Voice in Decisions, 1981–1985* (Geneva: ILO, 1986). The ILO, through its International Institute for Labour Studies, intends to publish two other reference books on worker participation in 1987 and 1988. In addition, the Dublin Foundation has appointed a team co-ordinated by Vittorio di Martino and composed of Peter Cressey, *rapporteur*, Tiziano Treu and Marcel Bolle de Bal, *co-rapporteurs*, and Kevin Traynor, assistant, to prepare a collection of more than fifty of its reports dealing at least in part with participation. This collection was published in 1987.

needs of these highly motivated workers (who are the most productive—and the most difficult to satisfy)

As participation is a strategic tool and needs strategic abilities, the first condition of its smooth functioning is a good strategy for initiation and implementation, taking advantage of the flexibility of the concept to ensure its efficiency. But there is a second condition, which should not be ignored: a participation policy should be implemented carefully, taking into account the psychological paradoxes which have been described, and also a sociological paradox which I would call 'bureaucratizing debureaucratization'. Experience reveals that 'participation', which by many is conceived of as a means of fighting what has been called 'the bureaucratic phenomenon' (which is, as one knows, an institutional system aimed at avoiding face-to-face relations), very often becomes the source of new bureaucratic procedures or structures. When that happens people are frustrated and the idea of participation quickly loses its psycho-social support.

But opposition to participation is sometimes paradoxical too. Much of the criticism against participation comes from those who regret that they do not get *complete* power, but only a *part* of it. They do not take into consideration that participation means, by definition, that 'participants' should give up the infantile desire to get *complete* power.

The promises of participation: a socio-political perspective

Participation responds to people's needs but needs people's support. It is, as we have seen, neither a gift, nor an easy, agreeable social venture. To be successful, it requires mature individuals with psychological, social, and strategic capacities. For them it appears to be a promising solution to many problems in the fields of management and politics. It constitutes one way of fighting authoritarianism and bureaucracy, one way of stimulating motivation and self-actualization. It will also become increasingly necessary because of the growing size of socio-economic organizations in industrial society and the need for network co-operation in post-industrial society. Finally, it is a possible solution to the aspiration of people to be reunited in an atomized society based on separation, isolation, and disconnectedness—a society characterized by the breaking of traditional communities (*Gemeinschaft*) and the tendency towards what has been called the 'lonely crowd', developed society (*Gesellschaft*).

In that respect, one could remark that different types of participation could be an answer to different types of need:

- the primary, physiological and economic needs (lodging, food, etc.), could be taken into account by formulas of indirect participation;
- the secondary, psycho-social needs (security, justice, solidarity) could be taken into account by formulas of indirect participation;

- the tertiary, cultural needs (autonomy, initiative, development, achievement) could be taken into account by formulas of direct participation.

Conclusion

In conclusion, it seems to me that this analysis—sociological and psychological, functionalist and actionalist—of the contradictions, paradoxes, promises, and difficulties of the participation process helps us to understand, from a socio-political point of view, why a cyclical perspective tends to emerge and replace the former evolutionary vision of the process and theory of organizational democracy.

Of course, participation has a promising future and constitutes a real challenge to management, unions, and workers. It could be a positive sum game where both sides win if certain conditions are realized (Cressey *et al.*, 1987):

- a 'mature' climate of industrial relations,
- a renunciation of definitive and global solutions,
- an acceptance of the slowness of the process (of changing ideas, values, attitudes, structures),
- an understanding of the cyclical nature of the process (it will always be necessary to re-evaluate, redefine, and adapt to the changing and conflictual needs of the social actors).

In this last respect, national and supranational bodies (like the EEC) should encourage programmes of social experiment, sociological intervention, and action research aimed at testing, initiating, implementing, and developing participation structures: this kind of experiment and action research implies the *participation* of the social actors in the conception, realization, and exploitation of the research, in the production of knowledge, and in the use of the accumulated knowledge.

References

Clegg, S. (1983), 'Organizational Democracy, Power and Participation', in C. Crouch and F. Heller (eds.), *International Yearbook of Organizational Democracy*, i (Chichester: Wiley).

Cressey, P., di Martino, V., Bolle de Bal, M., Treu, T., and Traynor, K. (1987), Participation Review: A Review of Foundation Studies on Participation (Dublin: European Foundation for the Improvement of Living and Working Conditions).

Crozier, M. (1965), *Le Phénomène bureaucratique* (Paris: Seuil).

—— (1970), *La Société bloquée* (Paris: Seuil).

—— and Friedberg, E. (1977), *L'Acteur et le Système* (Paris: Seuil).

Merton, R. K. (1957), *Social Theory and Social Structure* (Glencoe, Ill.: Free Press).

Poole, M. (1986), 'Participation through Representation: A Review of Constraints and

Conflicting Pressures', in R. Stern and S. McCarthy (eds.), *International Yearbook of Organizational Democracy*, iii (Chichester: Wiley).
Touraine, A. (1966), *Sociologie de l'action* (Paris: Seuil).
—— (1978), *La Voix et le regard* (Paris: Seuil).

2

The Labour Movement and Post-rational Models of Organization: A French Case or a Trend in Western Societies?[1]

SEVERAL factors have been proposed to explain the crisis of the union movement. Among the most frequently mentioned are: managerial policies (Smith, 1987); the over-politicization of unions in certain countries, in particular France; and the transformation of Western economies (Piore and Sabel, 1984) resulting in a loss of jobs, a reduction of economic activity, and a shift of employment from strongly unionized industries toward the much less unionized service sector. While not denying the importance of any of these factors, or of some combination of them, this article seeks to shed light upon the consequences for union action of the profound changes in the models of firm-level organization with regard to rationality and social domination (Morgan, 1986).

Western societies have developed on the basis of rational models of organization: the Taylorian one in industry as well as the rational–legal one in bureaucracies. These models have in common a major characteristic, namely, that they enclose human activities within a set of rules that social actors are supposed to obey. Taylor postulated a man–machine to be paid at a piece-rate; and Weber (1963) a person who fills a job or function that he disinterestedly performs out of a sense of duty and that, alone, defines his status. The creativity and subjectivity of wage-earners were thus excluded from consideration.

Given the oppressive situation that arose from the application of these models, the labour movement set itself the task of forcing those who were imposing them to recognize the subjectivity and creativity denied to the social actors by the rational organization of work. Its aim was as much to create an identity for the working

[1] This article is the result of research carried out at the request of the French trade union, the CFDT. The survey, conducted with the assistance of Sophie Lecorre, Michel Oriel, and Barbara Jankowsky, is an analysis of the functioning of this union from executive to local branch levels involving 430 interviews, observations of union meetings, and analysis of leaflets and texts. Systematic feedback has begun in order to validate the working hypotheses. The model presented here is based on the analysis of various company monographs: two car accessory plants in the same industrial group, one insurance company, and one hypermarket. It was translated from the French by Noal Mellott, CNRS, Paris. The author wishes to thank Stephen Bornstein of McGill University for his advice and editorial suggestions.

class as to struggle for its material improvement. Union strategies were, first of all, aimed at controlling the set of work rules instituted by these models (rules that were, of course, formulated differently depending on the national situation). Secondly, union actions would be—under what certain economists have called the Fordist compromise—directed at redistributing the benefits of economic growth. Labour–management interactions took place along these lines from 1950 until 1965–70; but, since then, these stable forms of interaction have been undermined owing to factors, which are internal as well as external to firms, that have changed the constraints conditioning organizational models (Peters and Waterman, 1983) and union actions (Kochan *et al.*, 1984).

A twofold constraint

Since the late 1960s, companies and administrations have been faced with cultural as well as technical and economic factors that have forced them to undergo change. Let us review these two sets of factors.

At the cultural level, during the period from 1965 to 1980, demands for autonomy from authoritarian models of social organization were often expressed and forcefully pressed. In firms, wage-earners manifested their opposition through union actions via resistance to production quotas, absenteeism, or personnel turnover. Coming out of a period of prosperity, these social actors had a higher level of education than had prevailed at the time when rational models of organization had been conceived, and their resistance demonstrated their capacity and desire for models founded upon the recognition of their autonomy. This sort of demand was simultaneously being expressed in challenges to other large-scale institutions, such as schools and the army.

At the same time, the socialist myth was wearing away. Along with rational models (Taylorism and bureaucracy) had come the belief of part of the working class in a socialist dream (bread and roses) to be brought about by the seizure of State power and the dictatorship of the proletariat. The discovery of alienation in the socialist countries of Eastern Europe shattered this structure of beliefs. Effecting radical change by taking over the State was no longer a convincing means of transforming society. Social change came to be seen in more immediate, smaller-scale terms. Qualitative, and no longer merely quantitative, demands were being asserted about working life.

Technical and economic factors have also had an impact upon organizational structures. The pressure of international competition upon firms, the insistence upon product quality, and the increasing segmentation of markets necessitate making organizations more flexible than under rational models. Information must circulate more freely and openly and wage-earners must be actively involved in operations. This flexibility, which enables firms to react more effectively to market conditions, is now a possibility owing to new, computer-based technology.

A new organizational rationality

Given this twofold constraint, firms have carried out experiments in reorganizing work—Quality Circles, progress circles, or 'direct expression groups' of the sort instituted by the 1982 Auroux Laws[2] in France. These new structures, which tend to become permanent, seem to be in the process of gradually displacing the models that, from the earlier period of industrialization in Western societies, insisted upon obedience to set rules and refused to recognize social actors' creativity and subjectivity.

This new 'post-rational' model of organization, often called 'participative management' (Sainsaulieu *et al.*, 1983; Tixier, 1983), constitutes an objective rationality adapted to the values of creativity, self-expression, and participation, a rationality that can be formulated as the following set of principles:

- job hierarchy is narrowed and the workers regain a number of tasks that the Taylorian model had hived off to the technical staff;
- supervision based on authority is replaced by supervision based on competency and performing two functions: technical consultancy and small-group human relations;
- negotiations become possible at the rank and file level over production goals, product quality, working conditions, and job assignments;
- hiring and promotion are done as a function of a person's technical capacities, but also of his degree of involvement, or participation, in company life. Line management and staff mutually evaluate each other using a system for measuring satisfaction and increasing mobility;
- mixed decision-making models are developed in which the hierarchy sets general objectives while leaving many questions open to negotiation at lower levels;
- 'islands' of production are created where small groups of wage-earners are responsible for a complicated set of maintenance, production, and quality control tasks;
- employees' activities are all linked to the firm's objectives through the overriding concern about product quality; on management's initiative, participative groups are formed, and cultural operations (information, communication, and 'company charters') are launched.

The overall model that emerges introduces a new type of rationality of human action within the organization, a model pivoting around the attempt to match people, structures, and human creativity. It has two important consequences for the patterns of work relations and for the types of culture and management linked to these patterns.

---

[2] For more details see Appendix to Ch. 19.

Toward a new social order in the firm

This reorganization of both productive structures and cultural systems leads to the emergence of new forms of social domination. In the Taylorian and bureaucratic models, social domination was based on eliminating the subjectivity and the creativity of social actors, who were expected to follow rules. In the new social order that is in the process of developing, social domination operates by taking advantage of this subjectivity and creativity. Management's problem is no longer to make actors obey external rules linked to a legalistic or scientistic vision, for the myths of industrial society that once legitimized these rules are now being challenged.

In the face of the dual constraints (technical–economic and cultural) discussed above, management seeks rather to control interactions among the subgroups that make up the firm, after having emptied them of any real strategic import or political significance by manipulating small groups through what Bauer and Cohen call 'the principle of domination' (Bauer and Cohen, 1984; Bauer, 1985). The development of microgroups and of company charters can thus serve to have the organization's goals internalized at the individual level.

Under rational models, wage-earners expressed their desire for autonomy through resistance or withdrawal. The new forms of domination, while providing some scope for controlled self-expression, tend to make the individual bear the model's constraints. Since everyone may vent his feelings and make his contribution to what is presented as a shared undertaking, employees no longer feel that it is the organization that is oppressing them.

Social domination is thus internalized, creating a sense of personal responsibility and even guilt concerning the goals of the organization, and eliminating any possibility of blaming the management or the supervisors for whatever problems are encountered. Because his creative capacities are brought into the production process, each employee is pushed to his limits, and a special type of psychological stress is generated. This shift in rationality that we are witnessing tends to displace the logic of domination of the old model: wage-earners have no longer to obey but to participate, and everyone must accept a world of bargaining and face-to-face confrontation. Thus, the social life of the new 'islands of production' requires co-operation and managerial interaction; working life no longer requires only the use of a repertoire of gestures, but also the expression of feelings. Group life based on compromise among workers implies that they vent limited feelings of love and hate. This expression of emotions, avoided (because it was forbidden) in rational models of organizational behaviour, now becomes an issue. The result is new problems of social regulation and control since the new model demands not only the ability to work, but also the ability to express oneself and to relate to others. This new social order in the firm thus tends to exclude employees who cannot or do not want to play this face-to-face game.

This new organizational model also has social and political effects in that it proposes, through company charters, a conception of the 'community', but a conception that hides differences in position, power, and pay. By resorting to the unifying logic of a community identity that transcends the particularisms of the microgroups and their cultures but no longer refers clearly to notions of social class (which used to provide an escape from the particularisms of trades), the firm sets about manipulating the meaning and symbols of community. Managerial know-how, drawn from the social sciences, serves to search out and capture commonly held conceptions that refer to occupations, crafts, or cultural frames of references such as social class. These ideological makeshifts function to create a sense of belonging, and the company charter, this new founding myth, offers symbolic protection, thus gaining a new hold on the employee.

Towards a redefinition of the labour movement

How can a union react to these organizational changes that short-circuit it and reduce the opportunities for direct opposition? Traditionally, the union movement was based on the existence of a sort of mass collective entity: the union set itself the task of protecting workers who were alienated by their work—an alienation that was as much organizational as economic because they were unable to make themselves heard. The participative model has taken the unions unawares, for it has created another type of group that generates an internal kind of competition, and a different form of alienation and domination that has become horizontally rather than vertically structured, and decentralized to the level of the peer group. Local union branches have responded to these changes by negotiating over secondary issues (for instance, who should lead the workers' self-expression groups) or by letting supposedly experimental agreements be drawn up without having any control over them. The fundamental characteristics of participative management interest but, at the same time, deeply threaten them. This model has taken shape in response to the pressure brought to bear by workers or, more generally, employees; but its effects have gone beyond what the unions expected.

Does this mean that the labour movement will become extinct in Western societies? A similar question was asked about the human relations approach, which sought to satisfy individuals in place of the unions by advocating a purely motivational, psychologistic conception of labour action as the satisfaction of individual needs. The unions could indeed disappear if they insist upon ignoring the workplace situations in which the participative model originated and has developed. Some multinational firms, in particular American and Japanese ones, when they set up new plants under participative management, also create substitutes for the unions in the form of councils for settling disputes (Cressey, 1985).

The unions could thus fall victim to an organizational system that now allows for individual and collective aspirations, whereas they previously flourished because such aspirations were not allowed. This vision is not ineluctable. However, because the systems of interaction at the workplace have been transformed, the labour movement must redefine its strategies, its structures, and the self-conceptions of its activists (Tixier, 1986).

Obsolete union strategies

Union strategies have, in general, been ineffectual in dealing with these organizational changes. The refusal to play the new game within the firm,[3] even where most of the personnel are union members, has turned out to be a losing strategy; for the workers generally prefer working under this new model, which allows them more autonomy and recognizes their abilities. Certain strata, notably skilled workers, may oppose the new model, but their opposition is usually outweighed by the more favourable attitude of the rest of the work-force. The most frequently adopted strategy of *laisser-faire* (firm-level union organizers have determined that the issue did not concern them so long as there was no direct breach of the work rules) has also turned out to be a failure. The unions have sometimes found room for manœuvre when participative structures were set up hastily and without the personnel's consent or when the pattern of authority has not changed. In such cases, employees, after playing the participative game without having their expectations met, have returned to using the union mechanisms they had abandoned.

These new forms of organization, if they are intelligently established, undermine the bases of union action by altering the social relations of work, the shaping of collective identities, and the patterns of collective bargaining, and they do so even where management did not necessarily have anti-union motivations. They threaten the very foundations on which the previous period's union strategy was constructed. The union strategy that prevailed during the period of economic growth—quantitative demands, upgrading job categories, and controlling work rules—loses much of its effectiveness in the new organizational context. Quantitative demands do not necessarily vanish, but they must now take into account the firm's situation. Moreover, the job classification schemes based upon skills as defined under the Taylorian and bureaucratic models become obsolete. The new work groups, even though they do not perform all tasks, tend to develop collective skills, the internal development of which are left up to the wage-earners themselves, and which are based on their co-operation and confrontations (Groux, 1985). What counts is the work groups' aptitude for informal co-operation, and this is hard to measure, rather than an individual's skill in transforming raw materials. This collective skill is thus a highly complex phenomenon subject to local differences. It is also more difficult to enforce a set of work rules: it is no

---

[3] For the use of the term 'firm' see Ch. 11.

longer an issue of making management abide by a body of rules that define a specific job, but rather that there is a set of tasks connected to a work group whose members manage their own internal job assignments.

These participative models require a redefinition of union strategies in two ways. Firstly, the application of a participative policy may mobilize the better-trained employees, who are more conscious of their abilities and of the economic as well as technical constraints within which they function. As a consequence, these workers, who are best able to evaluate the possibilities of their environment, may produce new demands for control over work or over pay and employment conditions. This amounts to trying to beat participative management at its own game, namely, through bargaining and making credible economic proposals. Such a strategy requires an offensive approach from within the logic of the participative mechanisms. Union members must give up stances of *laisser-faire* and withdrawal to take an active role in the setting up of participative policies (Kochan *et al.*, 1984) so as to control them or, at least, to intervene effectively during company-level negotiations and thus to avoid the splintering of microgroups and the fragmentation of negotiations at a level beneath the reach of the law. This calls no longer for negotiating or enforcing strict rules about individual job qualifications but for constant surveillance of the activities of the basic work groups.

Secondly, the unions can fight against the negative effects—stress, the requirement to be creative, etc.—that wage-earners experience under this new model. They can have a regulatory and protective role for those employees who find it hard to take this new way of working and who end up isolated or rejected by the microgroups. The unions would thus assume the same role of defending the individual against the work group that they now play in co-operatives and self-managed firms.

This twofold redefinition of union strategies can hope to succeed only under certain conditions: the national labour confederations must take a clear position; safeguards must be sought in the participative game; and union representatives must be trained in how these new structures work and how to lead them.

The unions and group identities

Under rational models of organization, a necessary relationship links a person's position in production to his identity as a union activist. At the deepest level, participative management undermines this identity-making process based upon the similarity between positions and experiences at work (Sainsaulieu, 1977) and focused on opposition to supervisors and management. Under the Taylorian and bureaucratic models, the unions provide the possibility for solidarity within a work situation that fragments communication between workers and allows only an informal counterorganization. In contrast, the participative model brings into being microgroups which the unions themselves have to deal with.

By simplifying the command structure, by creating work collectivities in which individual roles are assigned by the group and production quotas negotiated and internalized by the workers, these groups become the locus of the creation of collective identities. The identity-making process no longer works through wage-earners' feelings of being dominated, for their creative capacities are now partly recognized. The unions are no longer able to constitute themselves in opposition to the other, whether the representative of the 'bourgeois order' or the 'class enemy'. There are, at least for the time being, no pre-existing group identities. The social class identity that served as a frame of reference for workers, that permitted them to give meaning to every gesture and action and to establish a constant connection between individual experience and collective experience, life at work and life outside work, no longer works in this new context. Identities are no longer predetermined but have to be constructed through daily interactions at work.

Since these microgroups create their own frames of reference and norms, it is difficult to homogenize actors' strategies, for each employee has a personalized relationship with every other person in his work group. The identity-making process takes place in a lilliputian social world where relationships are 'psychologized' because of the very size of the structure in which interactions occur. Above all, however, it is the relationship between the collective identities and organizational structures that is the most profoundly transformed. However, the process of forging a group identity is a lengthy one. It necessitates a continuity and repetition of interactions that become ritualized and make action meaningful. Because they create constantly evolving structures into which wage-earners' innovative capacities are continuously fed back, participative models prevent the formation of identities out of the similarity between workers' positions.

The unions thus may be said to fall victim to an organizational system that allows for individual and collective aspirations where previously they fed on the system's non-recognition of such aspirations. The unions are squeezed out by 'fraternities' that form in the microgroups and that are legitimated by the workers as a means of leading a more sociable life at the workplace.

Among the other effects of post-rational models are the acceptance of the firm's economic goals, the legitimization of the firm's authority structure, and the internalization of production norms. But these integrative effects hold only as long as employees' creativity is recognized; this is the corner-stone of the system's social legitimacy. The risk for employers, and the opportunity for the unions, is that this movement can go beyond what these models can stand and call into question the basic social and economic relations in the firm. Certain observers have considered this risk; for instance, AFCERQ (1983) has envisaged the risks of collectivization and union domination if management does not develop the skills needed to run the groups, if Quality Circles do not function on a voluntary basis, or if tasks are not distributed according to the workers' abilities. In France, the application of the Auroux Laws' provisions concerning employees' self-expression has, in a few cases, increased the power of the unions because management was not up to the job of managing employees' creativity. How paradoxical if a policy of integration were—the possibility cannot be ruled out—to arouse the desire for self-management.

Can these microgroups be the basis for new collective identities? This is the essence of what is at stake. Because so many participative structures have been set up at the same time, stable groups have not yet been formed, and the individual is among a multitude of groups, none of which is really autonomous. But can this situation last for long? The permanent utilization of employees' creativity may, in the long run, create so great a stress that stable participative groups have to be formed that are defined, as in the Japanese model, as much by their autonomy as by their integration. But how to link these microgroups together? How to co-ordinate them? This is not a merely tactical problem, but one that also involves culture and identity.

From social class to the company community

Under rational models, the company was thought to be divided in two: on one side, management representing shareholders and on the other, wage-earners represented by unions, meeting around the bargaining table to negotiate a collective agreement. This conception has lost its symbolic potency. The creation of company charters and, more generally, the emergence of ideologically sophisticated management offers workers a locus of symbolic identification based on the sense of belonging to a community and runs counter to a vision of society as opposition and conflict. In these circumstances, on what symbolic structures can the labour movement found a new identity (Segrestin, 1984)?

Inasmuch as the company charter appeals to a set of values shared by the personnel, the unions can intervene as guardian of these values if supervisors or management do not respect them. The appeal to the organization as a community can be a two-edged sword. Recently, some local union branches in France have begun intervening to insist that management respects the values contained in the company charter.

During the past few years, management has taken considerable advantage of the fact that union identities forged under rational models have fallen out of phase with the new participative systems of work relations, cutting off union representatives, both national and local, from the rank and file. To be sure, this situation is changing (CFDT, 1987). Some unions, in Europe as well as in North America, are changing their strategies. Some new strategies must, however, be accompanied by an effort to reshape the identities of their members. The unions must thus serve as the midwives of new collective identities adapted to these participative systems. They can do this by relying on new strata of employees and union activists who are employed in the new style of firms and who can serve as the core for new networks of organizers.

Reorganizing the unions

While Western societies were developing economically, unions, considered to be an emanation of the workers' movement, helped establish systems of indirect democracy and collective bargaining based on the principle of voluntary membership. Today, these structures are fundamentally destabilized by the participative model. By making possible perhaps not direct democracy but at least direct expression (Mothé-Gautrat, 1986), the new model has allowed certain problems in daily working life to be settled on the spot by the workers instead of being referred to arbitration or collective bargaining at company level. The operation of the participative groups leads to on-the-job, subjuridical negotiations. Union representatives in the firm must find a way to take hold of these fragmented issues that do not fit into the traditional bargaining mechanisms. The activity of shop stewards has also lost much of its meaning, since many employee demands are now treated outside the command structure by the microgroups themselves.

The revolt against authority and the criticism of management's objectives no longer provide enough material for the delegates, for it is the work groups themselves that are the source of the normative pressure that weighs upon their members. The union's duty of representing collective interests—its central duty under Taylorism—no longer has a basis since, within the new model, some of these interests can now be expressed not as resistance to hierarchical authority, but through mobilization around shared objectives defined in the company charter. Peripheral loci of union action, such as health and safety committees, may also be destabilized since work groups are empowered to make proposals concerning working conditions and the organization of work. Unions can still use established institutions such as the *comités d'entreprise* (works councils) as a tool, but this type of intervention will tend to produce a union movement centred on services rendered to members, rather than on militancy, with the workers becoming consumers of what the unions offer, rather than participants in an organizational effort. The unions can also continue to utilize the institution of shop stewards, but only if they can manage to find new functions for them as their traditional role of settling the daily grievances of workers is increasingly taken over by the internal regulation mechanisms of the microgroups. Within the new participative firms, shop stewards can serve as links between the microgroups and firm-level collective bargaining by generalizing and funnelling upward demands and complaints emerging from the operation of a large number of diverse, small work groups.

Membership-based unionism at stake

Even if the labour movement moves on the various fronts described above, the result will not necessarily be a revival of membership-based unionism. The shift in France from a unionism of militants to an institutionalized unionism of elected officials (Adam, 1983) has not made it any easier for the unions to recruit members.

Previously, membership of a union not only made possible the acquisition of individual and collective benefits, but also signified membership of a community and provided a mode of self-expression in a world of work where the means of such self-expression was severely limited. Inasmuch as the new, participative models of organization allow employees to vent, even incompletely, their creativity and to represent themselves, being a union member loses part of its symbolic importance. This change ought to lead the unions to rethink their relationship with the workers.

General remarks: the national contexts

We can assume that in Western societies characterized by representative democracy, individualism, and high levels of economic development, greater flexibility (Alter, 1986) can only be achieved by firms which involve their permanent employees in the management of their work and use their social creativity. This in turn is bound to bring about changes in trade union strategies. But the expansion of these new organizational forms can be brought about in differing conditions, according to the different national contexts.

The new challenge of post-rational models of organization in Western countries such as the USA (Coriat 1987), Canada (Wells, 1986), or France (Groux, 1985), where the compromise between labour and management is fragile, is that the unions are most destabilized by these new forms of organization. The labour movements in socio-democratic countries seem to be able to resist the effects of these new policies—as in Germany (Pornschlegel, 1987)—by wielding greater control over their implementation process and by setting safeguards. The tradition of negotiation makes it less necessary to transform the organizational structure of those firms which have in most cases been integrating their employees' creative capacity.

References

Adam, G. (1983), *Le Pouvoir syndical* (Paris: Dunod).
AFCERQ (1983), *Bulletin de l'Association* (Paris).
Alter, N. (1986), *Informatique et management: La Crise* (Paris: La Documentation Française).
Bauer, M. (1985), Le Patronat face au nouveau droit d'expression', *Démocratie et entreprise*, 2(3).
—— and Cohen, E. (1984), 'Les Limites du pouvoir des cadres, l'organisation de la négociation comme moyen d'exercer la domination', *Sociologie du travail*, 3.
CFDT (1987), *CFDT Aujourd'hui* (Special Issue Devoted to Participative Management and the Labour Movement).
Coriat, B. (1987), 'Modèles contractuels et rapport salarial: La Variante américaine', in

P. Bourvier and O. Kourchid (eds.), *France–USA vie de travail et de la production* (Paris: Méridiens-Klincksieck).

Cressey, P. (1985), 'Recasting Collectivism: Non-unionism in Two American Branch Plants', paper presented to the Conference of 'The Role of Trade Unions in the Coming Decade', Maastricht (20–2 Nov.).

Groux, G. (1985), 'Mobilisation collective et productivité économique: Le Cas des cercles de qualité dans la sidérurgie', *Revue française de sociologie*, 26.

Kimberley, J. (1980), 'Initiation, Innovation and Institutionalization in the Creation Process', in J. Kimberley *et al.*, *The Organizational Life Cycle* (San Francisco, Calif.: Jossey-Bass).

Kochan, A. T., Katz, H., and Mower, N. (1984), *Worker Participation and American Unions* (Kalamazoo, Mich.: Upjohn Institute).

Morgan, G. (1986), *Images of Organization* (Beverly Hills, Calif.: Sage Publications).

Mothé-Gautrat, D. (1986), *Pour une nouvelle culture de l'entreprise* (Paris: La Découverte).

Peters, T. and Waterman, P. (1983), *Le Prix de l'excellence* (Paris: Interédition).

Piore, M. J. and Sabel, C. F. (1984), *The Second Industrial Divide: Possibilities for Prosperity* (New York: Basic Books).

Pornschlegel, H. (1987), 'Trade Unions' Response' in G. Spyropoulos (ed.), *Trade Unions Today and Tomorrow*, ii (Maastricht: Presses Universitaires Européennes).

Sainsaulieu, R. (1977), *L'Identité au travail* (Paris: Presses de la Fondation Nationale des Sciences Politiques).

—— Tixier, P. E., and Marty, M. O. (1983), *La Démocratie en organisation* (Paris: Méridiens-Klincksieck).

Segrestin, D. (1984), 'Pratiques syndicales et politique revendicative', in G. Groux and M. Kesselman (eds.), *Le Mouvement ouvrier français 1968–1982* (Paris: Éditions Ouvrières).

Smith, W. R. (1987), *Crisis in the French Labour Movement* (London: Macmillan).

Tixier, P. E. (1983), 'Démocratie directe et organisation: Pour une théorie du fonctionnement collectif', *L'Année sociologique*, 33.

—— (1986), 'Management participatif et syndicalisme', *Sociologie du travail*, 3.

Weber, M. (1963), *Économie et société* (Paris: Plon).

Wells, D. (1986), 'Soft sell: Quality of Working Life Programs and the Productivity Race' (Ottawa: Canadian Centre for Policy Alternatives).

3

Worker Co-operatives in the UK: Temporary Phenomenon or Growing Trend?

CHRIS CORNFORTH

Introduction

This paper is concerned with the development of worker co-operatives in various countries in Western Europe and the USA, with particular attention to the UK. The number of co-operatives in these countries varies considerably, from countries such as Denmark with a handful of worker co-operatives to Italy where it is estimated that there were over 14,000 producer co-operatives in 1984 (Paton *et al.*, 1987). However, even in countries with strong worker co-operative movements they tend to be concentrated in a few industrial sectors. Historically, the formation rate of worker co-operatives has varied cyclically. This is most apparent in the UK (Thornley, 1981; Cornforth *et al.*, 1988) and the USA (Shirom, 1972; Aldrich and Stern, 1983) where periodic waves of formations have been followed by periods where the formation rate has dropped to zero. Even in countries with more established sectors such as France and Italy there is also a strong cyclical element in the formation rates (Thornley, 1981). Since the early 1970s the formation rate in many Western countries has again increased dramatically.

These variations in the development of worker co-operatives raise a series of interesting questions. Why do the formation rates of co-operatives have a strong cyclical component? Why does the success of the worker co-operative sectors in different countries vary so dramatically? Can the present upsurge in co-operative formation be sustained? Can worker co-operative sectors grow in countries like the UK and USA from their present small size to become a significant sector of the economy as in Italy and Spain?

This paper seeks to answer these questions by drawing upon recent theoretical and empirical studies. The paper adopts the view that worker co-operatives face various barriers which inhibit both their formation rate relative to capitalist businesses and their ability to grow and compete on equal terms with large capitalist companies. However, the strength of these barriers varies in different social, political, and economic contexts. In addition, there are actions that can be taken by bodies such as governments and the co-operative movements themselves to counteract these barriers.

The next section of the paper presents the framework that is used to conceptualize the various pressures and forces that inhibit co-operative development. The paper then goes on to examine how these factors affect the formation rate of worker co-operatives and the ability of co-operatives to grow and compete with large capitalist companies. The paper draws on experiences to promote co-operatives in various countries to suggest how some of these barriers to co-operative development may be overcome.

Framework

Any firm is caught up in a web of social and economic relations that extend beyond the workplace (Weber, 1968; Marx, 1966). As a result, it is not possible to understand fully the performance and development of the firm in isolation from its wider social and economic context. In the West co-operatives have had to develop within what are essentially capitalist economies. As a result, we must examine how this environment affects the ability of co-operatives to compete (not just economically, but ideologically) with capitalist forms of enterprise during the various stages of development.

The framework also assumes that four factors are crucial in the formation and development of a business: motivation, resources, organizational capability, and the opportunities open to the firm. So if the worker co-operative sector is to grow to challenge the capitalist sector it must be able to attract and motivate people to form co-operatives in similar numbers to capitalist enterprises; it must have access to similar human and financial resources to enable formation and growth to take place; it must have the same organizational capacity to grow and develop, and finally it must have similar opportunities for growth.

Co-operative formation

The majority of investigators of worker co-operatives have concentrated on examining the social and economic performance of established co-operatives (see e.g. Vanek, 1970; Meister, 1974, 1984; Oakeshott, 1978; Thornley, 1981; Jones and Svejnar, 1982; Gunn, 1984; Jackall and Levin, 1984). However, a number of writers have recently suggested that the formation process of worker co-operatives requires greater attention. They suggest that it is the low rate of co-operative formation that is most significant in explaining the relatively small size of worker co-operative sectors in most capitalist countries (Abell, 1983; Aldrich and Stern, 1983).

Why then is the formation rate of worker co-operatives relatively low and inclined to vary cyclically? Our model suggests that the answer is to be found by examining how changes in the wider social and economic structure affect the motivations of potential entrepreneurs and entrepreneurial groups to choose between different business forms, and the resources and opportunities available to these individuals and groups to form businesses.

Historically, the co-operative form of enterprise emerged as a reaction to the development of capitalism during the industrial revolution and the social and economic dislocations that resulted (Bonner, 1961; Pollard, 1967; Thornley, 1981). As a result, co-operatives have had to grow within a capitalist system. One possible reason for the low formation rate of worker co-operatives is that the co-operative form was not well known in comparison to other forms of business. This argument has been largely dismissed by both Abell, and Aldrich and Stern, who point to the widespread and recurring political interest in co-operatives. However, knowledge of co-operatives at a political level does not mean that people have a widespread knowledge or experience of how co-operatives are formed or work. While the point should not be over-stressed, it does appear that they both underestimate the costs in time and resources of finding out about a relatively unusual form of enterprise. A recent survey of co-operative support organizations in the UK (Cornforth and Lewis, 1985) shows that they have to spend a good deal of time and effort familiarizing people with the co-operative form of business.

Abell, and Aldrich and Stern lay greatest stress on the lack of incentives that worker co-operatives can offer their founders in comparison to other forms of business to explain the low formation rate. Three different sorts of incentive can be distinguished (Clark and Wilson, 1961): material, i.e. money, wealth, and prestige; purposive, i.e. incentives that stem from pursuing broader social and political goals in which one believes; and solidarity, i.e. incentives that arise from associating with people who share similar attitudes and beliefs. They argue that in capitalist society material incentives of wealth and power, and self-interested motivations dominate. Any person or group forming a co-operative will have to share the economic rewards that come from developing a successful enterprise, and will have to share control. As a result, they argue that it will only be under exceptional circumstances that potential entrepreneurs will form co-operatives. Abell concludes: 'Only in the exceptional circumstances where individuals are roughly equal in capital endowment and hold a marketable idea in common will a co-operative begin to prove at all attractive' (1983: 88).

Aldrich and Stern also envisage other material circumstances when co-operatives might appear attractive, for instance when workers lack other opportunities to realize the gains from their labour during periods of industrial restructuring or as a tactic during strikes. In addition, they suggest that co-operatives might be formed when purposive and solidarity incentives are considered more important than material incentives. 'If people are committed to co-operation as an ideal, or if they believe co-operation is a means to some larger political objective, they might be willing to ignore the obvious disincentives involved in creating co-operatives and instead provide the resources required' (1983: 387). They draw on empirical evidence from the USA for the period 1875–1935 to support their analysis. They show that many co-operatives arose as workers reacted against the 'loss of craft status and the institution of impersonal administrative hierarchies'. These ventures gained ideological (and often financial) support from radical movements such as Kellogism and a variety of trade unions.

In Britain a similar pattern emerges. Workers formed producer co-operatives in response to the appalling conditions that often prevailed as traditional craft industries were brought under the factory system. Some were a response to lock-outs, others were an attempt to break free from economic exploitation or an attempt to retain craft status (Jones, 1894 describes many examples). Ideological support came from Owenism, and groups like the Christian Socialists and the emerging trade union and consumer co-operative movements, who also helped to finance many of the new co-operatives (Cole, 1944; Bonner, 1961, Pollard, 1967).

The cyclical nature of the formation rate of worker co-operatives can be explained, at least in part, as a reaction to periodic social and economic crises. The current wave of co-operative formations is again a reaction to prevailing social and economic circumstances, with people being drawn to co-operatives by a mixture of 'material' and 'purposive' or 'idealistic' motives. In the early and mid-1970s many co-operatives were formed by young people inspired by the alternative movements of the 1960s and early 1970s who were seeking to find new non-authoritarian ways of working and to produce for need and not for profit. As the economic conditions deteriorated during the late 1970s and the 1980s co-operatives began to be formed for more pragmatic reasons to save or create new jobs. Ideological support for these ventures has come from across the political spectrum, although most practical support has come from the left. For example, in Britain most support has come from Labour-controlled local authorities, and in Italy the trade union movement has promoted co-operatives as a way of rescuing failing enterprises.

Another factor limiting formation rates concerns resources. Historically, many co-operatives faced considerable hostility from capitalist employers, who would often refuse to deal with producer co-operatives (Jones, 1894; Bonner, 1961). As a result, producer co-operatives were often dependent on their ideological supporters in the co-operative and trade union movements to supply both finance and markets for their products. However, in Britain and the USA the producer co-operative movements were unable to sustain this support. Trade unions and consumer co-operative societies often did not themselves have large financial reserves. The spectacular failure of some producer co-operatives led many co-operative societies and trade unions to be much more reluctant to finance producer co-operatives (Thornley, 1981; Aldrich and Stern, 1983). In addition, and more importantly, producer co-operatives gradually lost the ideological support of these movements. Increasingly, trade unionists saw collective bargaining as the most effective means to protect their members' interests, while in the co-operative movement there was a debate whether consumer societies should support independent producer co-operatives or set up their own factories. It was frequently argued that producer co-operatives would act in the interests of workers and not consumers, and eventually producer co-operatives lost the support of consumer societies. These arguments were crystallized and given renewed force by Sidney and Beatrice Webb (1914, 1920, 1921) in Britain. Without ideological and financial support producer co-operatives ceased to be formed in Britain from about 1915 onwards. In contrast, in Italy and France, where producer co-operatives never completely lost the support of the State and political and trade union bodies, they continued to be formed.

Another limitation on the formation of new co-operatives concerns the interrelationship between the opportunities available to potential entrepreneurs, their motivations, and the various domestic, social, and economic constraints on their activities. Many new businesses are formed by people working alone. Curran (1987) estimates that there are 1.7 million self-employed in the UK. Sometimes these businesses are formed out of preference for independence and the desire to avoid the responsibility of employing other workers. However, others are contrained to this form of business by lack of resources, domestic constraints, or because they perceive it as a less risky way of starting a new business. Obviously, it is difficult for a worker co-operative to start with only one employee. This alone may mean that many entrepreneurs do not consider forming co-operatives, and having started their own business it seems most unlikely that at a later date they would want to share it with others.

The growth and competitiveness of co-operatives

There has been a good deal of theoretical debate concerning the relative economic performance of co-operative and capitalist firms. On the one hand it is argued that the financial and organizational structure of co-operatives will lead to difficulties of raising finance, underinvestment, and poor management and discipline, which will lead to co-operatives having inferior performance to capitalist businesses (Fanning and McCarthy, 1986: 23–9). On the other hand it is argued that co-operation will lead to increased worker motivation and commitment and subsequently to greater efficiency (Abell, 1983: 75–7). Although it is often difficult to make meaningful comparisons of the performance of co-operatives with capitalist businesses, the results of empirical research so far do not appear to suggest a strong difference in performance either way (Jones and Svejnar, 1982; Abell 1983), although Abell expresses some concern about the small size of most co-operatives compared with large capitalist companies.

However, a weakness of the majority of these empirical studies is that they fail to examine the performance and development of co-operatives in relation to changes in the industrial sectors in which they are located. Instead, analysis is usually restricted to comparing performance with sector averages or with similar conventional firms of comparable size. An exception is the work of Bennett (1984), and her analysis suggests the value of this approach. She carried out an analysis of the performance of thirty-two long-established producer co-operatives in the UK between 1950 and 1979. These co-operatives were concentrated in the printing and shoe-manufacturing sectors. Her analysis revealed that, although co-operatives did not perform badly, they still got squeezed out of the market by large capitalist competitors:

The evidence suggests that co-operatives have not failed because of their inefficiency. Rather they have been squeezed out of the market because their potential outlets have been acquired by competitors, and because they are unable to grow to a sufficient size (being unable to acquire other firms) either to (i) set up their own outlets, (ii) have the strength to obtain a decent bargain with monopolistic buyers, (iii) provide the range and flexibility of production available from large competitors. (Bennett, 1984: 25)

Bennett overstates the case in suggesting that co-operatives cannot take over other firms. However, there are clearly organizational and ideological difficulties for co-operatives in absorbing capitalist firms. In addition, the restriction on external shareholding removes an important means of raising the capital for financing take-overs. Because of these limitations on growth Bennett suggests that co-operatives get squeezed out of sectors like shoemaking as they become dominated by a few large firms. In terms of our model the analysis suggests that the structure and ideology of co-operatives and their access to external resources limits their opportunities for gaining dominance in any industrial sector. As a result, they will be dominated by capitalist firms.

Bennett advocates some form of market protection for co-operatives as a way to resolve this problem. (It is interesting that in the construction industry in France and Italy, where the State has treated co-operatives favourably, they have thrived, Thornley, 1981: 146.) In the absence of State intervention she advocates that co-operatives should be promoted only in sectors which 'serve a broad and fragmented market', for example, printing and specialist retailing such as whole foods. Declining industries or those dominated by large organizations should be avoided. Another potential solution that Bennett does not mention is that co-operatives might be able to overcome the problems of growth by developing federal structures, secondary support organizations, and intertrading. This can allow both vertical and horizontal integration without individual co-operatives having to grow too large. This is a feature of both the successful Mondragon system of co-operatives (Thomas and Logan, 1982) and the Italian co-operative sector (Thornley, 1981: 160).

The position of new co-operatives today also has to be understood in relation to developments in the wider economy. The opportunities open to new businesses are often highly constrained by existing large public and private companies. As a result, many of the opportunities for new businesses are in marginal sectors of the economy with low levels of profitability and poor prospects for growth (Schutt and Whittington, 1984; Rainie, 1985). The establishment of co-operatives in marginal sectors of the economy is reinforced by the fact that many co-operatives are formed by the unemployed, by workers with traditional skills that are now less in demand, and by workers who are unskilled or have had few opportunities to develop their skills.

The development of new co-operatives is further limited by two other factors: the availability of finance and the shortage of management skills within co-operatives.

The problem of obtaining finance has several aspects. Many new co-operators, coming as they often do from the ranks of the unemployed, have little to invest and few personal assets that could be used to secure bank loans. In Britain, at least, some co-operative development workers also report a bias against co-operatives by banks and other financial institutions. In addition, the restrictions placed on shareholding in co-operatives limits the amount of external capital that can be raised in this way and causes problems of high gearing. It is perhaps significant that in Italy, France, and Mondragon, Spain, where the worker co-operative sectors are more developed, they have better access to finance either through developing their own financial infra-structure or from the State than in countries with smaller worker co-operative sectors. In France various banks and funds, going back as far as 1893, have been established in order to help finance producer and other forms of co-operatives (Thornley, 1981: 133). In Mondragon the bank has been able to attract capital from the local community for investment in the co-operative system (Oakeshott, 1978; Thomas and Logan, 1982; Weiner, 1987). Although the co-operative movement in Italy does not have a central source of finance, as in France, it has been quite successful in raising finance from a variety of external sources. Government loans have been available for certain types of construction work. Two of the co-operative federations have set up their own financial institutions to negotiate on behalf of co-operatives with banks and government agencies.

A further problem stems from a shortage of staff with managerial skills and a commitment to and understanding of co-operative working. Again, this problem has a number of aspects. First, many co-operatives because of their size and commitment to low wage differentials cannot offer the same material incentives to those with management skills as private firms. Secondly, because the co-operative sector in many countries is small the majority of managers do not have experience of co-operatives, and the business education system does not usually consider the co-operative option. Third, the small size of the sector inhibits the development of a managerial labour market for co-operative managers.

To some extent these problems will tend to diminish as the co-operative sector grows and a labour market for co-operative managers develops, as in Italy. It is also interesting that in larger co-operatives some form of wage differential nearly always has to be introduced in order to attract and retain managerial staff, although these differentials are usually less than for private firms.

Overcoming barriers to co-operative development

This section of the paper briefly examines how some of the barriers to co-operative development already identified might be overcome in countries such as the UK and the USA with relatively undeveloped co-operative sectors. Clearly, in a short paper it is not possible to present proposals in any detail, to assess their relative merits or their applicability to different situations. The intention is to suggest the broad directions that policy makers and practitioners might follow to encourage co-operative development.

It was suggested that the main reason for the relatively small size of worker co-operative sectors in capitalist economies was the low formation rate of worker co-operatives. Various barriers to co-operative formation were identified: lack of knowledge of co-operatives; discrimination against co-operatives; lack of 'ideological' and financial resources for co-operatives; the fact that co-operatives did not meet the needs of individuals wanting to form one-person businesses; but most importantly of all the ascendancy of materialistic and individualistic values in Western cultures, which makes co-operatives an unattractive option to many potential entrepreneurs.

How can these limitations on co-operative formation be overcome or reduced? One way in which the cultural barriers to co-operative development can be reduced is if a strong social movement that supports co-operative principles can be established. In Italy the worker co-operative movement has managed to maintain strong links with other political movements and with bodies such as the trade unions that share some common beliefs (Thornley, 1981). In Mondragon it is probable that Basque nationalism has provided a powerful ideological bond between the community and the co-operatives, which has helped to sustain support for the co-operative system (Thomas and Logan, 1982). The message for countries like Britain and the USA is that their worker co-operative sectors need to build ideological and practical alliances with other movements and organizations that share similar values.

In addition, policy makers need to consider how new co-operatives can be spawned from existing co-operatives and how co-operatives can be established to save businesses. It is significant that in Italy much of the recent growth of the co-operative sector has come from the take-over of ailing firms (Thornley, 1981; Paton *et al.*, 1987).

The development of a support structure to promote and develop co-operatives is also vital to increase the formation rate of co-operatives. Co-operative support organizations (CSOs) can increase awareness about the co-operative option, and help to reduce discrimination against co-operatives by negotiating with key institutions such as banks and educational and government bodies on their behalf. In addition, they can help to facilitate or possibly institutionalize the entrepreneurial process and so encourage or even initiate co-operative formations. In Britain CSOs play an important role in assisting groups to form co-operatives (Cornforth and Lewis, 1985). In Mondragon the co-operatives' bank has further institutionalized the entrepreneurial process (Cornforth, 1988). It has the expertise to thoroughly research and evaluate new proposals for co-operatives, and if satisfied with the proposal to finance the venture on an appropriate scale.

When a co-operative sector is small and new it is likely that the development of a support structure will be greatly facilitated by the availability of public money. Public money has certainly played a vital role in the development of CSO's in France and the UK. Once the co-operative sector becomes more established it may be able to develop its own supporting structure through the formation of federations and joint ventures, which are characteristics of the strong Italian co-operative sector.

As well as barriers to formation, the paper has argued that co-operatives face various constraints which limit their ability to grow and compete with large capitalist firms. Many new co-operatives are constrained to operate in marginal sectors of the economy with poor potential for growth. Those co-operatives that do show the potential for growth face other barriers. They frequently face difficulties raising external capital and recruiting appropriate managerial staff. Growth is also constrained because it is difficult for co-operatives to acquire and take over other firms.

There are a number of ways in which these barriers to co-operative development might be lessened or overcome. One option is some form of market protection for co-operatives. This can be done without encouraging inefficiency, for example by reserving a certain proportion of State contracts for co-operatives as long as their tenders are competitive. In France and Italy such practices have enabled a strong worker co-operative sector to develop in the construction industry. Another option is for co-operatives to try to achieve horizontal and vertical integration through intertrading between co-operatives, or to achieve economies of scale by establishing joint ventures. Perhaps the best-developed examples here are the consortia established by Italian co-operatives. Among other things, consortia have been established to enable co-operatives to bid jointly for large contracts and to undertake joint marketing and purchasing.

Secondary co-operatives or support organizations can also be used to help provide the managerial and technical expertise and finance that co-operatives need to grow and prosper. At Mondragon the co-operatives first established their own bank to provide finance and a management consultancy service. Later, they established a joint research and development co-operative, a facility that individual co-operatives would have found difficult to finance themselves. In Italy some consortia also provide a management consultancy service for co-operatives and have been able to act on behalf of a group of co-operatives to obtain finance.

Conclusions

This paper set out to examine why the worker co-operative sectors in countries like Britain and the USA are relatively small and weak in comparison to countries like Italy and Spain, and whether the current wave of worker co-operative formations could be sustained rather than decline as it has in the past.

It was argued that an important reason for the small size of the co-operative sectors in Britain and the USA was that historically they were unable to sustain the support of other powerful social movements, such as the Labour movement, and of the State. If the co-operative movement in countries like the UK and the USA is to continue to grow then it needs to regain the support of other, broader social movements that share similar values, and of the State, both to secure the resources necessary for co-operative development and to ensure that there are people who want to form and work in co-operatives. It has to be recognized that co-operatives are likely to be unattractive to many entrepreneurs. As a result, it may be necessary for co-operative support organizations to assist or even to take over parts of the entrepreneurial function.

Co-operatives today are being formed in established economies where capital is highly concentrated. They face various barriers which limit their potential for growth. As a result, they are likely to be restricted to marginal sectors of the economy unless ways are found of overcoming these barriers. It was suggested that co-operatives will need to find new ways of working together, as in the case of Mondragon or the Italian consortia, if they are to gain the economic strength to compete with larger capitalist firms. The State can play a vital role in encouraging co-operative development by providing market protection for co-operatives, and by ensuring that they have adequate access to finance and are not discriminated against in legislation.

References

Abell, P. (1983), 'The Viability of Industrial Producer Co-operation', in C. Crouch and F. Heller (eds.), *International Yearbook of Organizational Democracy*, i (Chichester: Wiley).

Aldrich, H. and Stern, R. (1983), 'Resource Mobilization and the Creation of US Producer's Co-operatives, 1835–1935', *Economic and Industrial Democracy*, 4(3): 371–406.

Bennett, J. (1984), 'Producer Co-operatives: A Case for Market Protection', occasional paper, Centre for Research in Industrial Democracy and Participation, University of Glasgow.

Bonner, A. (1961), *British Co-operation: The History, Principles, and Organisation of the British Co-operative Movement* (Manchester: Co-operative Union Ltd.).

Clark, P. and Wilson, J. (1961), 'Incentive Systems: A Theory of Organizations', *Administrative Science Quarterly*, 6: 129–66.

Cole, G. D. H. (1944), *A Century of Co-operation* (London: George Allen & Unwin).

Cornforth, C. (1988), 'Can Entrepreneurship be Institutionalized? The Case of Worker Co-operatives', *International Small Business Journal*, 6, 4, 10–19.

—— and Lewis, J. (1985), *The Role and Impact of Local Co-operative Support Organizations*, Monograph 7, Co-operatives Research Unit, Open University, Milton Keynes.

Thomas, A., Lewis, J., and Spear, R. (1988), *Developing Successful Worker Co-operatives* (London: Sage).

Curran, J. (1987), 'Small Business and Industrial Strategy', paper presented to the Seminar on Small Business Policy, House of Commons, London (Feb.).

Fanning, C. and McCarthy, T. (1986), 'A Survey of Economic Hypotheses Concerning the Non-viability of Labour-Directed Firms in Capitalist Economies', in S. Jansson and A. Hellmark (eds.), *Labour-Directed Firms and Worker Co-operatives* (Aldershot: Gower).

Gunn, C. E. (1984), *Workers' Self-Management in the United States* (Ithaca, NY: Cornell University Press).

Jackall, R. and Levin, H. (1984), *Worker Co-operatives in America* (Berkeley: University of California Press).

Jones, B. (1894), *Co-operative Production* (Oxford: Clarendon Press).

Jones, D. and Svejnar, J. (eds.) (1982), *Participatory and Self-Managed Firms* (Lexington, Mass.: Lexington Books).

Marx, K. (1966), *Capital* (Moscow: Progress Publishers).

Meister, A. (1974), *La Participation dans les associations* (Paris: Éditions Ouvrières).

—— (1984), *Participation, Associations, Development, and Change* (New Brunswick, NJ: Transaction Inc.).

Oakeshott, R. (1978), *The Case for Workers' Co-ops* (London: Routledge & Kegan Paul).

Paton, R. *et al.* (1987), *Analysis of the Experiences of and Problems Encountered by Worker Take-Overs of Companies in Difficulty or Bankrupt*, Report to the Commission of the European Communities (Study 85/4).

Pollard, S. (1967), 'Nineteenth Century Co-operation: From Community Building to Shopkeeping', in A. Briggs and J. Saville (eds.), *Essays in Labour History in Memory of G. D. H. Cole* (London: Macmillan).

Rainie, A. (1985), 'Small Firms Big Problems: The Political Economy of Small Businesses', *Capital and Class*, 24.

Schutt, J. and Whittington, R. (1984), 'Large Firm Strategies and the Rise of Small Units', paper presented to the National Small Firms Policy and Research Conference, Trent Polytechnic, Nottingham (Sept.).

Shirom, A. (1972), 'The Industrial Relations System of Industrial Co-operatives in the United States: 1890–1935', *Labour History*, (Fall), 533–51.

Thomas, H. and Logan, C. (1982), *Mondragon: An Economic Analysis*, (London: Allen & Unwin).

Thornley, J. (1981), *Workers' Co-operatives: Jobs and Dreams* (London: Heinemann Educational Books).

Vanek, J. (1970), *The General Theory of Labour-Managed Market Economies* (Ithaca, NY: Cornell University Press).

Webb, S. and Webb, B. (1914), 'Co-operative Production and Profit Sharing', *New Statesman* (special supplement).

—— —— (1920), *A Constitution for the Socialist Commonwealth of Great Britain* (London: Longman).

—— —— (1921), *Consumers' Co-operative Movement* (London: pub. by the authors).

Weber, M. (1968), *Economy and Society*, i–iii, ed. G. Roth and C. Wittich (New York: Bedminster Press).

Weiner, H. (1987), *Worker Owners: Mondragon Revisited* (London: Anglo-German Foundation).

4

Taking Stock of the ESOPs

RAYMOND RUSSELL

SINCE 1974, it has been difficult to write about prospects for employee ownership or workplace democracy in the United States without devoting most of one's attention to the federally mandated 'Employee Stock Ownership Plans', or 'ESOPs'. Thanks to the wide range of tax incentives for forming ESOPs that the federal government has offered to corporations beginning in that year, the ESOPs have proliferated rapidly, and in a number of prominent instances have acquired a majority of the stock in their firms. But ten years after the initiation of the federal ESOP programme researchers and policy makers were still largely ignorant of what the actual impact of the ESOPs on the firms that had adopted them had been. It was at this point that Senator Russell Long, the chief legislative sponsor of the ESOPs, requested the US General Accounting Office (GAO) to conduct a thorough study of these plans.

Long asked the GAO to begin by conducting a complete census of the ESOPs, providing the best estimates ever generated of the number of ESOPs that had been established, the number of employees who owned stock in these plans, and the total amount of stock that they owned. Long also asked the GAO to collect a good deal of additional information about the impact of the ESOPs on their firms, and to prepare detailed estimates of what the impact of the plans on the federal budget had been.

As this article is finalized in the summer of 1987, the GAO has so far released a total of three reports on its study of the ESOPs (US General Accounting Office, 1985, 1986a, and 1986b), with a fourth and final report likely to be issued late in 1987 or early in 1988. While certain quite interesting issues remain to be explored in the final report, the reports previously issued have already provided the GAO's final answers to such major questions as how numerous and large the ESOPs have grown to be and what the impact of the ESOPs on employees' participation in decision making has been.

The number and size of the ESOPs

In many ways the most challenging part of the GAO's task was what might appear to have been the easiest—finding out how many ESOPs there are. The main problem here is that the federal government does not maintain an official list of ESOPs and has no unambiguous way of differentiating ESOPs from a number of similar plans. The Internal Revenue Service does, however, require all employee benefit plans to let it know whether they have 'ESOP features' or not. The question that the IRS uses is in fact deliberately vague, as it is used to identify not only ESOPs, but all other benefit plans that invest significant portions of their assets in the securities of their employer and that therefore require special scrutiny from the IRS. This meant that, before the GAO could do any other research on ESOPs, it would first have had to write to a sample of plans with ESOP features to find out how many were actually ESOPs and how many were not.

By the autumn of 1984, a total of 8,891 employee benefit plans had reported having ESOP features to the IRS. That listing is believed to have included all or almost all ESOPs that had been established by the end of 1983; plans formed in 1984 would not yet have submitted their first returns to the IRS. Early in 1985, the GAO sent brief questionnaires to 2,004 plans from this IRS list. This survey produced responses from 1,616 plans, a response rate of nearly 81 per cent.

Based on the responses received from this survey, the GAO arrived at an estimate that the IRS list of plans with ESOP features formed through 1983 contained a total of 4,174 ESOPs that were still active in 1985, plus another 719 ESOPs that had been terminated by that time. This figure is lower than some other estimates, but the GAO's December 1986 report suggests that it should be supplemented in a couple of important ways. First, the IRS reports that an additional 625 newly formed benefit plans had requested letters of determination explicitly identifying them as ESOPs between the beginning of 1984 and March 1986. Secondly, the GAO estimates that as from March 1986 there were another 2,405 'stock bonus plans' in the nation that were virtually identical to the ESOPs in all but name. Adding these plans to the ESOP total as such other authorities as the National Center for Employee Ownership customarily do would bring the GAO estimate for the total number of ESOPs and ESOP-like plans active in 1986 to well over 7,000.

In addition to estimating the number of ESOPs, the GAO has also provided data on the size of the plans. Through the end of 1983, the GAO calculates that the total population of ESOPs had accumulated $18.66 billion in assets in the names of more than seven million employees. Because these figures are strongly influenced by a small number of very large plans the GAO notes that the median ESOP had 54 participating employees and held an average of $5,226's worth of stock in each employee's account (US General Accounting Office, 1986*a*: 23).

Why do firms form ESOPs?

In addition to giving us our most reliable estimates of the number and size of the ESOPs, the GAO study has also provided a wealth of information about both the causes and the consequences of these plans. Much of this information comes from responses to a lengthy questionnaire that the GAO mailed out in the summer of 1985 to each of the 1,113 plans that it had identified as ESOPs in the first phase of its study. Fully 860 plans responded to this second-wave survey, another remarkably high response rate of 77 per cent. Some of the most interesting of these responses are those having to do with why the ESOPs were formed.

The GAO's second-wave questionnaire included a question that asked respondents to indicate which, out of a long list of potential reasons for forming an ESOP, were considered to be 'major reasons'. The frequency of responses to this question is shown in Table 4.1.

Table 4.1 Why firms form ESOPs

Reasons given	%
To provide a benefit for employees	91
For the tax advantages	74
For anticipated effects on labour force:	
Improve productivity	70
Decrease turnover	36
Decrease absenteeism	14
Avoid unionization	8
Exchange for wage concessions	3
For financial reasons:	
Buy stock of a major owner	38
Transfer majority ownership to employees	32
Raise capital for investment	24
Less vulnerability to hostile take-overs	5
Save company from going out of business	4
Turn company private	1

Source: US General Accounting Office (1986*b*: 20).

Some degree of caution is necessary in interpreting the responses shown in Table 4.1. Although the GAO promised its respondents that their answers would remain confidential, the plan administrators who filled out its questionnaires may, nevertheless, have been reluctant to give responses that could prove embarrassing to a company or might cause it to run foul of federal law. The most popular response, 'to provide a benefit for employees', is partly relevant in this light as federal law explicitly requires that ESOPs, like all other employee retirement plans, must be established for the benefit of employees. In any case this response is uninformative because we already knew that, by setting up their ESOPs, these employers were providing a benefit to their employees. The more important question is why they wanted to give their employees this particular benefit, and that question is more effectively answered by the next three categories of response.

The second most popular avowed motive for forming an ESOP is perhaps the best-known attraction of the ESOPs, namely, their tax advantages. Nearly three-quarters of the ESOPs (74 per cent) indicated that the desire to utilize the tax advantages associated with the ESOPs was one of their major reasons for forming their plans.

Beyond their tax advantages, the ESOPs have a variety of more specific uses and attractions that have already been surveyed in a number of previous works (e.g. Rothschild-Whitt, 1983; Klein and Rosen, 1986; Rosen *et al.*, 1986). The major contribution of the GAO data in this regard is in giving us our first reliable estimates of how common each of these previously identified uses actually is. As noted in Russell (1984, 1985), these additional uses of ESOPs can be sorted into two major groups. First, many employers are attracted to the ESOPs by the effects they hope the ESOPs will have on the labour force of their firms. These employers see the ESOPs specifically as a means either to raise the quality or quantity of their employees' labour or to lower its cost. Secondly, employers are attracted to the ESOPs by a number of financial uses of the ESOPs, such as those that are listed at the bottom of Table 4.1.

In so far as employers do turn to ESOPs for their potential effects on their firm's labour force, GAO data indicate that the most common expectation is that employees' new financial stakes in the success of their companies will inspire them to become more productive. Fully 70 per cent of ESOP adminstrators gave this response. Smaller but still substantial numbers of plan sponsors expect the ESOPs to make their employees less likely to seek jobs in other firms (36 per cent) or to be absent from work (14 per cent). A still smaller but not insignificant 8 per cent of firms with ESOPs acknowledge that they created their ESOPs at least partly in the expectation that owning stock in their company would make workers less likely to want to join a union in the future. In only 3 per cent of ESOPs, however, were the employer's ESOP contributions explicitly granted in exchange for wage concessions from employees. This is a mechanism that has received a good deal of publicity for its use in many airline, road transport, and steel-making firms, but apparently it has had little impact on the ESOP population as a whole.

Finally, the GAO data document the frequency of several financial uses of ESOPs that were not anticipated in the initial ESOP legislation, but that have risen to prominence in the years since. Most importantly, it has become increasingly apparent that an ESOP is a very attractive way to divest a firm. The sale of a firm to an ESOP provides a retiring owner with a mechanism for divesting himself of the business at a low rate of tax in a way that ensures the continuity of the firm and allows the owner to depart from the firm at a time and on terms of his own choosing. The power of these inducements is evident from the high frequency with which ESOPs are established to buy the stock of a major owner (38 per cent) and to transfer majority ownership to employees (32 per cent).

It is important to note that these companies being sold to their employees are generally healthy firms, not declining companies being bought by their workers in a last-ditch effort to save the firm. ESOPs have occasionally been used for this purpose, some of the most prominent instances having been described in *The International Yearbook of Organizational Democracy* (e.g. Rothschild-Whitt, 1983: 393–6; Blasi *et al.*, 1983: 641–2, 646–7, and 1984: 309; Klein and Rosen, 1986: 392). While these worker buy-outs of failing firms have captured the largest share of the headlines about the ESOPs and have also figured prominently in the ESOPs' politics, the GAO data indicate that they account for only 4 per cent of the ESOP population as a whole.

The GAO data also document the frequency of a number of other prominent financial uses of the ESOPs. Both the ESOPs' intellectual father Louis Kelso and their chief legislative sponsor Russell Long have often expressed the hope that the ESOPs would become important mechanisms for raising capital for their firms. About a quarter (24 per cent) of the GAO's respondents report that they do view their plans in this light. Another unanticipated and currently quite controversial financial use of the ESOPs is to make a firm less vulnerable to hostile take-over attempts. This is acknowledged to be a major reason for forming an ESOP by 5 per cent of the GAO's respondents—a remarkably high number, when one considers that only 25 per cent of ESOPs are in publicly traded corporations, the corporations that are most likely to become targets of attempts of this type (US General Accounting Office, 1986*a*: 19). In only 1 per cent of the GAO's cases, however, has an ESOP been used to turn a publicly traded corporation into a privately traded one.

Employee participation within ESOP firms

As we have just seen, ESOPs are employee benefit plans that employers establish at their own initiative to suit their own ends. Once created, the plans are governed by trustees whom the employer appoints. Employees are rarely consulted about the design of the plans, and their permission is not required to put the plans into effect, even if the plan is intended to buy out the entire company, or is being offered as a substitute for a more conventional diversified pension plan. So why should anyone expect the ESOPs to have any impact on decision making in their firms?

Expectations that ESOPs will have such an impact usually focus on the voting rights that go along with the employees' ESOP stock. Federal law requires that stock in ESOPs in publicly traded firms must carry full voting rights, and that those rights must be 'passed through' to individual employees, rather than being exercised by plan trustees. For closely held corporations, federal law requires pass-through of voting rights only on major corporate issues like mergers and acquisitions, but plan designers are permitted to provide fuller voting rights if they wish. Closely held ESOPs that in the past have provided full voting rights to employees have included ESOPs created for union-led buy-outs of ailing firms, plus some ESOPs in companies whose owners are philosophically committed to a concept of employee ownership that includes full voting rights (for examples, see Quarrey *et al.*, 1986; Rosen *et al.*, 1986).

Thus, for a subset of ESOPs, at least, one can anticipate a day when the ESOPs will have acquired a controlling interest in their firms and that controlling interest will be exercised by the firms' employees. But how many ESOPs is this, and how far off is that controlling interest today? The GAO study has unearthed a number of pieces of information that are relevant to these issues. First, the GAO found that, while only 25 per cent of ESOPs are in publicly traded firms, 39 per cent pass through full voting rights to employees (calculated from US General Accounting Office, 1986*a*: 9, and 1986*b*: 39). Secondly, the GAO found that while the median ESOP owned only 5 per cent of its firm's voting stock in 1985, 19 per cent of ESOPs had acquired 25 per cent or more of their firms' voting stock by that time (US General Accounting Office, 1986*b*: 40). The GAO did not report what proportion of ESOPs own 50 per cent or more of their firms' voting stock, and has also not released data on what proportion of ESOPs with substantial voting strength pass through full voting rights.

Other data that the GAO has released, however, make it clear that very few ESOPs have to date exerted any substantial impact on the governance of their firms. One sign of this comes from the GAO's data on the composition of company boards. The GAO found that in only 4 per cent of ESOP firms do representatives of unions or non-managerial employees serve on the company's board of directors, and in no case did a sampled firm report that such representatives constituted a majority on its board.

Thus the GAO survey did not unearth one single instance of the voting strength in ESOPs being used to allow rank and file employees to take control of their company. The GAO survey also included questions designed to find out whether the ESOPs had increased employees' participation in decision making in more modest ways as well. One such question asked respondents to compare the involvement of non-managerial employees now to what it was before the ESOP was introduced. In response to this question, 27 per cent of ESOPs reported that the involvement of non-managerial employees was greater now than it had been before the ESOP was introduced; 68 per cent said that employee involvement had remained unchanged; and 1 per cent indicated that employee involvement had actually declined (another 4 per cent of ESOPs did not respond to this question).

For the 27 per cent of ESOPs that indicated that the involvement of non-managerial employees had increased after the introduction of the ESOP, the GAO included a follow-up question that asked whether this increase in involvement had occurred 'mostly through informal means such as casual meetings or conversations' or 'mostly through formal means such as new committees or task forces'. In response, 76 per cent of ESOPs that answered this question reported that the increase in employee involvement had occurred through informal means. Only 23 per cent of that 27 per cent, or 6 per cent of all ESOPs, indicated that an increase in employee involvement had occurred through formal means or through a combination of formal and informal means (US General Accounting Office, 1986*b*: 41).

The GAO also asked a number of other questions that add further detail to this generally modest assessment of the extent of employee involvement in decision making in ESOP firms. One question, for example, asked respondents to identify the specific issues, if any, that are addressed by work groups or committees involving non-managerial employees in their company. The issues most frequently mentioned were generally shop-floor issues like safety (42 per cent), working conditions, job design, and quality of working life (34 per cent), maintaining good relations between management and employees (33 per cent), and reducing production costs (30 per cent). The use of Quality Circles was indicated by 19 per cent of responding firms. Only rarely, however, did non-managerial employees become involved in developing new products or services (14 per cent), strategic or long range planning (13 per cent), or budgeting and financial control (11 per cent).

The GAO data thus make it clear that the ESOPs have so far had nothing like the revolutionary impact on decision making in their firms that has occasionally been anticipated for them. They do, however, appear to have contributed to slight and largely informal increases in employee involvement in decision making in about a quarter of all ESOP firms. This gain, though modest, should not be taken lightly as, depending on how one defines and estimates the population of ESOPs, it may have affected as many as a million or more American employees. But do the minor gains that have come out of the federal ESOP programme justify the often enormous expenses that the federal government has had to pay for them? On this question, too, the GAO has had a good deal of valuable light to shed.

Do the benefits of the ESOPs outweigh their costs?

Perhaps the most challenging task that Senator Long assigned to the GAO was his request that the GAO assess what the net effect of the ESOPs on the federal treasury had been. Long knew that the ESOPs had incurred heavy expenses in the form of both tax deductions and tax credits, but he also hoped that these costs might to some extent be mitigated by what he referred to as 'feedback' effects. The potential feedback effects of the ESOPs include the future increases in federal tax revenues that might occur when retiring employees receive and pay taxes on the stock in their ESOP accounts, plus possible increases in corporate income taxes if corporations that establish ESOPs become more profitable as a result. When these favourable feedback effects are added to the various intangible social benefits of the ESOPs, Long hoped that the ESOPs might be shown by the GAO study to be well worth their costs.

The questions asked by Senator Long raise many technical issues, some of which the GAO is still grappling with as this article is finalized. GAO estimates of the impact of the ESOPs on corporate profits, in particular, were not yet available when this chapter was written. Some data already released by the GAO, however, suggest that the effects of the ESOPs on company productivity have been less than their sponsors had hoped. In the GAO's second-wave survey, respondents were asked to indicate not only which factors had been major reasons behind the formation of their plans, but also which of a list of potential consequences were among the 'important advantages' they had actually derived from having an ESOP. In response to this question 66 per cent of ESOPs cited 'improved employee morale', but only 36 per cent ticked 'higher productivity', and only 23 per cent thought that the presence of an ESOP had caused company profits to improve (US General Accounting Office, 1986*b*: 22).

While the economic benefits from the ESOPs wait to be determined, the GAO has made more rapid progress in assessing their costs. The tax benefits that the US government has offered to corporations for forming ESOPs come in two major types: tax deductions and tax credits. GAO figures indicate that the tax credits for ESOPs are by far the more costly of the two. The GAO estimates that the total cost of the corporate tax credits for ESOPs and the personal income tax deductions associated with them amounted to $11.8 billion for 1977 to 1983 (US General Accounting Office, 1986*b*: 29). This was by far the biggest expense associated with the federal ESOP programme, and it was being used to subsidize the most superficial of ESOPs. The GAO found that only 26 per cent of ESOPs had ever claimed the ESOP credit, and these were generally large companies that were contributing relatively small amounts of stock to each employee. Thus while the typical ESOP owned 10 per cent of its company's stock and held $5,226 in the account of each employee, the typical tax credit ESOP owned only 2 per cent of its company's stock and had only $2,952 in the account of each employee (US General Accounting Office, 1986*b*: 23, 39).

The remaining 74 per cent of ESOPs, which relied only on tax deductions, had involved the federal government in much lower costs; depending on the assumptions one makes about these plans, in fact, they may not have cost it anything at all. The GAO calculates that, if the money contributed to these three types of ESOPs between 1977 and 1983 had been added to corporate profits instead, an additional $417 million in corporate income taxes would have been paid; or, if these same funds had been paid out to workers as wages, an additional $589 million in personal income taxes would have been paid by these employees. But if one assumes that the amounts contributed to these ESOPs would merely have been contributed to some alternative benefit plan, then these contributions did not cost the federal government anything at all.

Even before the GAO's cost estimates were released in December 1986, the ESOP programme had come under close scrutiny on Capitol Hill. Congress in 1986 was once again rewriting the federal tax code, and its plans this time called for reductions in personal income taxes to be compensated for by tax increases at the corporate level. Federal cost cutters quickly seized upon the ESOP tax credit as an obvious target, as it clearly amounted to a quite enormous expense, and even its past beneficiaries did not seem to care much whether it was eliminated or retained. The ESOP tax credit was therefore abolished as from 31 December 1986. But as the costs of the ESOP tax deductions were smaller and more ambiguous and were ably defended by the ESOPs' many allies in Congress, these preferences were retained, and in some cases even enhanced.

The future of the ESOPs

In losing the ESOP tax credit, the ESOPs have lost an incentive that in 1983 accounted for 79 per cent of all ESOP assets and 90 per cent of all ESOP participants. Nevertheless, with the help of the new tax deductions added in 1984 (see Klein and Rosen, 1986: 393–5) and others heaped on in 1986, the ESOP population appears well poised for further growth (for current summaries of the federal laws and tax incentives available to the ESOPs, see Rosen *et al.*, 1986: 13–32, 251–3, and US General Accounting Office, 1986*b*: 56–9).

It now appears in the USA, however, that Congressional redrafts of the tax code are becoming an annual or at most biennial event. As pressures to reduce the federal budget deficit continue to mount, it becomes legitimate to ask how much longer the ESOP tax deductions will succeed in avoiding the budget-cutter's knife.

This question is made even more appropriate by the retirement of Senator Russell Long from the Congress in January 1987. Senator Long had always served as the ESOPs' most powerful advocate in the Congress, so it is quite legitimate to ask who will continue to protect them after he is gone. Judging by the number of members of both Houses of Congress who spoke out on behalf of the ESOPs during the debates over the new tax law of 1986, it appears that the ESOPs will have many new champions to step into Long's place.

The politics of employee ownership legislation in the United States have already been discussed in *The International Yearbook of Organizational Democracy* (see, especially Blasi *et al.*, 1983). Accounts of this legislation often emphasize the absence of a conventional political constituency that lobbies on behalf of the ESOPs, and instead attribute the ESOPs' legislative successes to enthusiasm for employee ownership on the part of the legislators' themselves. This situation has changed somewhat in recent years, as the growth of the ESOPs has made the ESOP companies themselves a major source of lobbying on behalf of their tax benefits. Thus the ESOPs' staunchest allies in the Congress now include legislators who have prominent ESOPs in their constituencies. One generalization made in the past that remains true today is that ESOPs created to help save failing firms from closing their doors have a political significance that is far out of proportion to their actual numbers.

Even if the ESOPs' tax allowances were eventually to be curtailed, they would already have given rise to a new population of firms that was hitherto unknown in the American economy—firms that are owned by their employees, but not controlled by them. In an article published in *The International Yearbook of Organizational Democracy*, Rothschild-Whitt (1983) classified the ESOPs as the major American example of 'worker ownership without control'. The GAO data document the extent to which that classification was appropriate, as they indicate that the employees of as many as two thousand or more American firms are in the process of becoming the majority owners of their companies without gaining anything more than a minor and largely informal voice in the governance of their firms.

While piecemeal increases in workers' power have been taking place in many conventionally owned firms throughout the world for decades, it has long been argued that substantial changes in ownership are necessary before workers can take a leading role in governing their firms. But, as we have already learned from examples such as the Russian Revolution, the experience with trade union ownership in Israel, and the more recent experimentation with 'social ownership' in Yugoslavia, ownership by workers on paper is not easily translated into the reality of workers' control. There has been much talk in Sweden and elsewhere in the West in recent years about whether the employee-owned assets in wage-earners' investment funds might one day serve as a basis for further increases in workers' influence over corporate affairs. The American Employee Stock Ownership Plans are a form of pension plan that appears to be well suited to bringing about increases in this type of influence for employees, as they invest all their assets in a single company and can rapidly acquire a controlling portion of that company's stock. But, as we have just seen, the American ESOPs have so far done little more than demonstrate once again that employee ownership in itself is no guarantee of workers' control.

References

Blasi, J., Mehrling, P., and Whyte, W. F. (1983), 'The Politics of Worker Ownership in the United States', in C. Crouch and F. Heller (eds.), *International Yearbook of Organizational Democracy*, i (Chichester: Wiley).

—— —— —— (1984), 'Environmental Influences on the Growth of Worker Ownership and Control', in B. Wilpert and A. Sorge (eds.), *International Yearbook of Organizational Democracy*, ii (Chichester: Wiley).

Klein, K. and Rosen, C. (1986), 'Employee Stock Ownership in the United States', in R. Stern and S. McCarthy (eds.), *International Yearbook of Organizational Democracy*, iii (Chichester: Wiley).

Quarrey, M., Blasi, J., and Rosen, C. (1986), *Taking Stock: Employee Ownership at Work* (Cambridge, Mass.: Ballinger).

Rosen, C., Klein, K., and Young, K. (1986), *Employee Ownership in America* (Lexington, Mass.: Lexington Books).

Rothschild-Whitt, J. (1983), 'Worker-Ownership in Relation to Control: A Typology of Work Reform', in C. Crouch and F. Heller (eds.), *International Yearbook of Organizational Democracy*, i (Chichester: Wiley).

Russell, R. (1984), 'Using Ownership to Control: Making Workers Owners in the Contemporary United States', *Politics and Society*, 13; 253–94.

—— (1985), *Sharing Ownership in the Workplace* (Albany, NY: State University of New York Press).

United States General Accounting Office (1985), *Initial Results of a Survey on Employee Stock Ownership Plans and Information on Related Economic Trends* (GAO/PEMD-85-11, Sept.).

—— (1986a), *Employee Stock Ownership Plans: Interim Report on a Survey and Related Economic Trends* (GAO/PEMD-86-4BR, Feb.).

—— (1986b), *Employee Stock Ownership Plans: Benefits and Costs of ESOP Tax Incentives for Broadening Stock Ownership* (GAO/PEMD-87-8, Dec.).

PART II

LANDMARKS REVISITED

Outline of Part II

A 'landmark' can be a trail-blazing study that leaves its mark on subsequent theories, investigations, and efforts to practise organizational democracy. Pateman's 'Participation and Democratic Theory' in volume i of the predecessor to this series, the *International Yearbook of Organizational Democracy* and Robert Guest's 'The Man on the Assembly Line' (in the same volume) are cases in point. There is also another kind of 'landmark', to wit: the development of models of organizational democracy which have become known as ideal examples of work organizations in accordance with democratic values. One can refer, for example, to the Yugoslav self-management schemes, the Israeli kibbutzim, or the British Glacier Metal Company.

The German system of *Mitbestimmung* (co-determination) belongs to this latter type of landmark and is still one of the most vital. As Leo Kissler writes in his contribution, it 'is enjoying a "silent" boom'.

The chapter by Ian Turner makes short work of the myth that the German system of *Mitbestimmung* was wholly or partly the result of British rule in Germany after the Second World War. The author shows that the characteristics of the typically German design of co-determination came into being not thanks to, but rather in spite of, the military government in the British zone. Turner analyses the genesis of the German *Mitbestimmungs*-arrangements as the outcome of a conflict between two models of organizational democracy, the British and the German, within British-occupied Germany from 1945 to 1949. The paper is not only of historical interest, but also demonstrates why it is so difficult even, for example, within the European Trade Union Federation to arrive at a common perspective on economic democracy.

Leo Kissler presents the evolution of co-determination research in West Germany over the last decades from its very beginnings. He follows fifty-three studies and shows the changing role of co-determination within society and the economy. In his view the model of co-determination has by now been widely accepted by nearly all social partners and nearly all politicians. Does this mean that economic democracy is also possible for other nations?

Edward E. Lawler III revisits three classics of participative management: *McGregor*, *Argyris*, and *Likert*. The writings of these Americans represent landmark studies that have made an important impact on the field. If we apply the Dachler–Wilpert and Greenberg schemes (for more details of these schemes, see the contribution by Sharon McCarthy in Part III of this volume) to the three authors whose work Lawler 'revisits', they clearly belong to the 'human growth and development' or 'humanistic psychology' school.

The main reasons for a delay of nearly twenty years in the implementation of participative management are, according to Lawler, the vested interests and the faith in their traditional 'top-down' style of leadership on the part of ruling managerial élites, and the underdevelopment of a new technology to make the change-over from customary to the participative system of management.

However, the political and economic crisis of the 1970s created a situation where new styles of leadership appeared to be attractive, necessary, and perhaps even unavoidable.

Two writers contribute reflections on the last landmark in Part II. Firstly, Thoralf Ulrik Qvale, Research Director of the Work Research Institute in Oslo, suggests that Norway may now be entering a new era in the development of industrial democracy in Norway. Secondly, and in support of this assertion, we are glad to include a document of a very unusual nature: the speech of the Norwegian Prime Minister, Gro Harlem Brundtland, delivered at the Einar Thorsrud Memorial Symposium and Workshop in June 1987 in Oslo. Without any doubt the Scandinavian socio-technical approach derived from the work of the Tavistock Institute in London has deeply influenced the development of organizational democracy over the last two decades, and it therefore seems appropriate that we should take this opportunity to present the assessment of this Norwegian landmark by a prominent and active politician. In the form of these two accounts we also pay tribute to Einar Thorsrud, a most resourceful scholar, who spent a lifetime vigorously applying his social scientific insights and knowledge to further the cause of democratization in society.

5

Co-determination in British-Occupied Germany 1945–1949

IAN TURNER

Introduction

In his review of West German co-determination in its fourth decade Wolfgang Streeck outlined the benefits to West German industry which accrued from improved management of manpower and the participation of the work-force (Streeck, 1984). He also, however, pointed to the structural rigidities which co-determination introduced into the enterprise and the costs to the management of lost managerial discretion and prerogatives. Moreover, he drew attention to the dangers which such 'mutual incorporation of capital and labour' poses for the trade unions, as increased identification with the aims and fortunes of the company by the work-force and its representatives can reduce class solidarity and undermine the political power of the unions.

The risks of 'excessive consensus' in the enterprise were also uppermost in the minds of the British occupation authorities in the immediate post-war period. This contribution looks at how the British military government, imbued with the traditions of British industrial relations—the separation of management and work-force interests, the emphasis on collective bargaining, and the commitment to voluntarism—responded to German demands for co-determination. It sets British fears within their proper historical context: the desire to break the social patterns which were thought to have produced National Socialism and the need to create a strong but independent labour movement capable of resisting political extremism either of the right or the left.

The clash of traditions

It is one of the most abiding myths of recent history that the British promoted co-determination in German industry. British labour policy in occupied Germany was implemented by the Manpower Division of the Control Commission for Germany (CCG). The staff of the Manpower Division was recruited mainly from the British Ministry of Labour and took with them the outlook and biases imbued in them by their departmental culture. Their 'world-view' was coloured by a deep commitment to the British pattern of industrial relations. The 'conflict tradition', as it is sometimes known, saw the main task of the labour movement as representing the work-force in collective bargaining with employers. Management and work-force interests were quite distinct. Grass-roots involvement in plant management threatened to usurp the authority of the trade unions, and legislation to implement worker participation went against the principles of voluntarism with its abhorrence of State control. It was a perspective, of course, which was widely shared by the British Labour movement and determined the generally unfavourable attitude towards worker participation which historically has characterized British trade unions.

Contrast this British view of industrial relations with the German tradition. In Germany, where *laissez-faire* capitalism had never truly existed and liberalism was in practice modified by the existing traditions of paternalism and State socialism, trade unions developed organizationally and functionally on a different pattern. The trade unionists of the Weimar era accepted the organic, conflict-free view of society as readily as any other group in German society. This meant that the German labour movement shared with many German employers a commitment to worker participation in the governance of enterprises. Admittedly, the trade unions differed from paternalist employers in that they saw a key role for the unions in the works councils, in management of the companies, and in the formulation of economic policy. This also distinguished them from a more radical tradition of workers' control which re-emerged for a short time at the end of the First World War in the form of the *Arbeiter- und Soldatenräte* (Workers' and Soldiers Councils) of 1918–19. Although workers' control of industry did not survive the post-war revolutionary period, Article 165 of the Weimar Constitution did provide for worker representation on bodies at works, enterprise, and national level (Thim, 1980: 6). A Works Council Law was passed in February 1920 making works councils obligatory for all firms with over twenty employees. It gave works councils the power to administer company welfare schemes, to co-operate in increasing efficiency and promoting health and safety at work, and to bargain on wages and conditions within the framework of overall agreements concluded by unions. It also permitted the works council to appeal to a conciliation board in the event of an intractable dispute with management. Whilst the Works Council Law failed to meet in full the aspirations of German trade unions, the attainment of *Wirtschaftsdemokratie* (economic democracy) remained an objective of the labour movement in the 1920s and 1930s and re-emerged after the defeat of National Socialism in 1945 (Clegg, 1963; 16–17).

The lesson the labour movement drew from the collapse of Weimar was that political democracy must, of necessity, be buttressed by economic democracy. To prevent a repetition of the alleged support by German industrialists of the National Socialist seizure of power, labour believed that an equal voice in industrial decision making, as a prelude to eventual nationalization of the basic industries, was essential (IG Metall, 1979: 137–41).

Such views were anathema to the British, of course. The attachment of the German labour movement to co-determination was viewed as fundamentally unsound, a traditional feature of German industrial relations which had weakened the unions and encouraged an identification of labour interests with those of the company and the State in a way which had led ultimately to National Socialism and the Deutsche Arbeitsfront (DAF). The task of British policy, as officials in the Manpower Division saw it, was to break the mould of German industrial relations and recast it on democratic lines (Turner, 1984).

Early developments in German works councils and the British reaction

Soon after the collapse of the Third Reich, workers' representative bodies sprang into existence in factories throughout the British Zone (Klessmann, 1979: 47–60). In some cases the Weimar works councils simply reconstituted themselves, in other factories new men came to the fore. The first reaction of military government officers was often to suppress these manifestations of grass-roots spontaneity (Steininger, 1978: 77–98). At that point, however, trade unions had yet to be sanctioned, as the military government was determined that the development of unions would proceed slowly, from the bottom upwards, under close supervision of the occupying authorities. This was to ensure their democratic nature and prevent any re-emergence of the Nazi Arbeitsfront (Hartmann, 1972: 29–33, 37–9, 54–5; Steininger, 1978: 68, 92–4). In the absence of officially authorized trade unions, therefore, the Control Commission perceived the need for some sort of makeshift system of joint consultation to promote factory production, 'but only as an interim measure to operate until such time as trade unions would be able to take over the job'. Once unions were functioning properly it was hoped they would be capable of providing all the worker representation necessary at plant level.

The tradition of works councils was firmly ingrained in the German labour movement, however, and the British came under pressure from the unions to legislate on the subject. This demand for legislation was also supported by the Soviet Union and France. Germany at that time was nominally governed on a Four-Power basis and the Allied Control Council in Berlin was the machinery by which quadripartite policy was supposed to be made. The British opposed Control Council legislation on worker participation from the outset. When the French and Soviet representatives proposed in January 1946 that representatives from works councils should be permitted on the *Aufsichtsrat* or supervisory board of companies, the British dug their heels in (Fichter, 1982: 195). General Robertson, the leading figure in the Control Commission, said the proposal would 'constitute an unwarranted interference on the part of the works council in the management of an enterprise'.

A compromise was reached. The final version of the law was passed on 10 April 1946 as Control Council Law 22—without the clause on works council representation on the *Aufsichtsrat*. Under Article 5 of the Law, the functions of a works council could include: negotiating collective agreements with management, submitting proposals for increasing production, negotiating health and safety regulations, assisting in grievance procedures, co-operation in demilitarization and denazification of the enterprise, and participation in the provision of welfare facilities for the work-force. Article 6 gave the works council access to the employer and to information on the enterprise whilst further clauses required works councils to operate in close co-operation with the trade unions and prohibited obstruction or discrimination by management.

The law was, however, in accordance with British thinking, *permissive* in nature: it circumscribed broad areas of responsibility for works councils without making them obligatory in law (IG Metall, 1979: 36–8). It was this feature of the legislation, together with the realization that, for the unions, Law 22 represented a step backwards from the degree of worker participation provided for by the Weimar Works Council Law of 1920, which led to the generally unfavourable reaction from the German labour movement (Thim, 1980: 8; Fichter, 1982: 188–9). The response of the German trade unions was to launch a campaign in the British Zone at plant level to conclude works agreements with the managements of industrial undertakings in order that worker participation would become a reality. The main trade union federation, the DGB, produced a model works agreement providing for full parity of decision making between management and labour at factory level, and strike action, most notably at the Bode-Panzer Works in Hanover, was used to support union demands. This was a development which caused great concern to the British, particularly when it affected the subsidiaries of British and American multinationals. In Hamburg, for instance, a military government report of May 1947 noted that several subsidiaries of foreign oil companies had signed works agreements under pressure from the trade unions— much to the consternation of head offices back home.

The British became convinced that works councils were not only a threat to management, however, but were also undermining the position of the trade unions themselves. Economic controls had distorted the relative importance of works councils and unions. Unions were prevented from engaging in collective bargaining with employers because wage rates were fixed by Allied agreement. Works councils, on the other hand, were widely involved in the distribution of goods at plant level in part-payment of wages. The prestige of the works councils was therefore high amongst the working population and this strengthened their independence *vis-à-vis* the unions. The strength of Communist influence on works councils, especially in the coal-mines of the Ruhr (Klessman, 1983), added to this danger and gave the military government great cause for concern. In response, the CCG's Manpower Division reasserted British opposition to co-determination and attempted to discourage trade union demands for legislation.

British policy towards co-determination in the iron and steel industry

It is necessary at this point to make a brief digression to deal with the question of co-determination in the German iron and steel industry. Because the far-reaching reforms carried out under the auspices of the British agency, the North German Iron and Steel Control (NGISC) undoubtedly set a precedent for the *Montan-Mitbestimmungsgesetz* of 1951, some observers have taken this as being indicative of British policy as a whole (Hartwich, 1970; Rudzio, 1981). In fact, as the Head of the NGISC and inspiration of the reform, W. Harris-Burland, described it, the motives behind the granting of co-determination in the iron and steel industry were largely pragmatic. Prior to the institution of British control, left wing works councils were said to be making far-reaching demands 'of an anarchical and impracticable nature'. These activities were threatening the authority both of the trade unions and of management. The resultant chaos was also having a detrimental effect on the production of steel (Spiro, 1958: 20–1, 32–5). Co-determination was designed to remedy this chaotic situation.

There was a further reason for embarking on this course of action: the Allies had decided as a precautionary measure against a resurgence of German military might that German heavy industry was to be deconcentrated. As the German employers could be expected to resist, the British looked to German labour for support. To secure union backing, the British were prepared to grant labour a substantial role in the management of deconcentrated enterprises, including equal representation on the *Aufsichtsrat* (supervisory board) and a labour nominee as *Arbeitsdirektor* (labour manager) on the management board or *Vorstand*. The co-determination granted in the steel industry was therefore atypical of British policy and was motivated by practical economic and political considerations. In other controlled sectors it was noticeable that the British attitude was much less favourable to worker participation. In the coal industry, for example, the British authorities explicitly rejected the possibility of worker parity on the *Aufsichtsrat* of mining companies. Perhaps most interesting of all is the case of the Volkswagen works (Turner, 1984). The VW car factory at Wolfsburg was taken into control by the British in 1945 as an ex-DAF enterprise. As in other factories, a *Betriebsvertretung* (works representation) had been created on the lines of the Whitley Councils common in wartime Britain in order to encourage consultation between management and work-force and increase productivity (see Clegg, 1963: 14–15). In the ensuing period a works agreement was negotiated between the works council and the German management at VW. This formalized the role of the works council, but stopped a good way short of co-determination. As soon as it became apparent that co-determination was to be granted in the iron and steel industry, the works council at VW approached the British Senior Resident Officer with a demand for an *Arbeitsdirektor* on the management, to be chosen by the work-force. A Manpower Division official was hastily dispatched to persuade the works council that 'no man could adequately represent workers and management together—as such an appointment would undermine the whole structure of labour/management relationships, in which T.U. and Works Council play important parts' (Turner, 1984: 403).

The British reaction to Länder works council laws

Despite the vigour of the trade union campaign for co-determination through works agreements at plant level, the employers proved more resistant than had been anticipated. The objective of co-determination, however, remained high on the agenda of the German trade unions. The establishment of elected parliaments with legislative powers at *Land* or state level now provided them with another means of realizing this aim. Many of the *Länder* had constitutional provisions for works councils' rights and these were now to be fleshed out with legislation (Conze, 1980: 716).

The first of these laws was the Hesse *Betriebsrätegesetz*, passed at the end of May 1948. Although Hesse lay in the US Zone of Germany, the promulgation of the Law was viewed by the Control Commission and the Foreign Office as a definite set-back for British policy. The problem was not the Law itself, which was far from radical. It was the realization that the Germans were set on institutionalizing the position of the works council in law as an organ of co-determination. What was more, there was evidence of a whole battery of laws in the pipeline of other state legislatures which would, the British authorities felt, be sure to undermine the principles of freedom of association, collective bargaining, and trade union independence from State control. How were the British now to react? 'We cannot *compel* the parties in industry to reach voluntary agreements', the head of the Manpower Division wrote, nicely catching the irony of the situation. The Control Commission and the Foreign Office debated the situation at some length. In the end the British and American military governors issued a joint statement in August 1948 which suspended any legislation on co-determination passed at *Land* level until after a Federal government had been formed (Müller-List, 1983: 133). For the German labour movement it meant that the last avenue to achieving full co-determination in the occupation period was closed. The decisive struggle would now be fought out with a West German government, under circumstances which were on the face of it less than favourable to radical reforms. In the event, the DGB leadership was able to secure a commitment from the Federal government in the form of a law to maintain full parity co-determination on the supervisory boards of the key coal and steel companies, in return for supporting Adenauer's policy of West European integration (Thum, 1983). For the rest of industry, a Works Constitution Act was passed in 1952, which covered the rights and obligations of works councils and provided for limited representation of the work-force on supervisory boards (Streeck, 1984: 392–3). Whilst the delays caused by the reluctance of the occupying authorities to approve co-determination laws were therefore detrimental to the German labour movement's chances of securing its aims in the short term, it did nothing to dampen enthusiasm for the principle of co-determination. For the British, on the other hand, it was the last shot in a rearguard action against the restoration of the traditions of German industrial relations: the appeal of *Mitbestimmung* was to prove more enduring than the British alternative of 'collectivist *laissez-faire*'.

Conclusion

This study has shown how the British occupation authorities in post-war Germany steadfastly opposed the demands of labour for co-determination in industry. As a result, legislation implementing greater worker participation was delayed until the early 1950s when Konrad Adenauer's Government passed two Acts of Parliament. The delay meant the outcome was less than favourable to the trade unions, but it failed to divert them from pursuing the aim of full co-determination into the 1970s. This highlights the strength of traditional patterns of industrial relations in Germany and the commitment to them by élites in the trade union movement and even in industry. Of course, many of the fears harboured by the British authorities during the occupation seem exaggerated now, and the assumptions underlying the policies appear rather arrogant in retrospect. In the light of subsequent economic performance, most Germans would probably not be sorry that the British authorities were unsuccessful in instilling a British pattern of 'adversarial' industrial relations in their country. At the time, of course, it was far from clear that the Federal Republic would develop into a mature and stable liberal democracy.

Paradoxically, the study also highlights the problems involved in transplanting a phenomenon like co-determination to an Anglo-Saxon society where liberal traditions are deep-seated. For all the apparent success of the West German experience with co-determination, it is probable, as observers have long noted (Spiro, 1958: 138–47; Clegg, 1963: 53), that it is not the institutions and processes which are crucial to achieving a stable and harmonious pattern of industrial relations, so much as the attitudes of the people who operate them. 'Enterprise patriotism', with all its positive and negative connotations, is commonly regarded as a typical characteristic of German workers, whilst British work-forces have traditionally been more noted for an adversarial approach to management. This is

72   *Ian Turner*

not to argue that traditional attitudes and prejudices cannot be modified and new models of participation adopted. Japanese companies with subsidiaries in Britain have recently shown how this can be done, at least when dealing with new workforces. With existing workplaces, however, the process of change is likely to prove more difficult.

References

Clegg, H. A. (1963), *A New Approach to Industrial Democracy* (Oxford. Oxford University Press).

Conze, W. (1980), 'Die Geschichte der Mitbestimmung in der Bundesrepublik Deutschland', in *Rapports II Chronologie* (Bucharest: Comité International des Sciences Historiques).

Fichter, M. (1982), *Besatzungsmacht und Gewerkschaft* (Opladen: Westdeutscher Verlag).

Hartmann, F. (1972), *Geschichte der Gewerkschaftsbewegung nach 1945 in Niedersachsen* (Hanover: Niedersächsische Landeszentrale für Politische Bildung).

Hartwich, H. H. (1970), *Sozialstaatspostulat und gesellschaftlicher Status quo* (Cologne: Bundverlag).

IG Metall (1979), *IG Metall: 30 Jahre soziale Gegenmacht* (Frankfurt-on-Main: IG Metall).

Klessman, C. (1979), 'Betriebsräte und Gewerkschaften in Deutschland 1945–1952', in H. Winkler (ed.), *Politische Weichenstellungen in Nachkriegs-Deutschland 1945–1952, Geschichte und Gesellschaft Sonderheft*, 44–73.

—— (1983), 'Betriebsparteigruppen und Einheitsgewerkschaft', *Vierteljahrshefte für Zeitgeschichte*, 31(2): 272–307.

Müller-List, G. (1983), 'Die Entstehung der Montanmitbestimmung', in W. Först (ed.), *Zwischen Ruhrkontrolle und Mitbestimmung* (Cologne: Bundverlag).

Public Record Office, Kew PRO/FO371/55651/C2372, CORC/P(46)74, 20 Feb. 1946.

PRO/FO371/64693/C11874, Chaput de Saintonge to Mark, 15 Aug. 1947.

PRO/FO371/64703/C8024, Extract from Mil. Gov. *Hamburg Monthly Report*, May 1947.

PRO/FO371/70840/CG3140, R. W. Luce, 'Works Councils, Mitbestimmungsrecht and German Legislation', 4 Aug. 1948.

PRO/FO945/798, Manpower Division, 'Works Councils and Workers' Participation in the Control of Individual Undertakings', Feb. 1947.

Rudzio, W. (1981), 'Großbritannien als sozialistische Besatzungsmacht in Deutschland: Aspekte des deutsch–britischen Verhältnisses 1945–1948', in L. Kettenacker *et al.* (eds.), *Studien zur Geschichte Englands und der deutsch–britischen Beziehungen: Festschrift für Paul Kluke* (Munich: Fink).

Spiro, H. (1958), *The Politics of German Co-determination* (Cambridge, Mass.: Harvard University Press).

Steininger, R. (1978), 'England und die deutsche Gewerkschaftsbewegung', *Archiv für Sozialgeschichte*, 18: 41–118.

Streeck, W. (1984), 'Co-determination: The Fourth Decade', in B. Wilpert and A. Sorge (eds.), *International Yearbook of Organizational Democracy*, ii (Chichester: Wiley).

Thim, A. L. (1980), *The False Promise of Co-determination* (Lexington, Mass. and Toronto: D. C. Heath/Lexington).

Thum, H. (1983), *Mitbestimmung in der Montanindustrie* (Stuttgart: Klett).

Turner, I. D. (1984), 'British Occupation Policy and its Effects on the Town of Wolfsburg and the Volkswagenwerk 1945–1949', Ph.D thesis (Manchester).

6

Co-determination Research in the Federal Republic of Germany: A Review

LEO KISSLER

Fluctuations in the incidence of research

In the period covered by this account, 1952 to 1985, a total of fifty-three empirical investigations into co-determination were carried out and completed.[1]

In the 1950s, the results of eight studies were published. Then, during the 1960s, material from twelve investigations was published. It was in the 1970s, however, that a notable increase in co-determination publications first came about with eighteen project publications. Today, research into co-determination is enjoying a boom—without there being political follow-up or spectacular legislative initiatives for the reform of the governing system of co-determination in the FRG.

In the last five years almost as many projects have been completed and published as in the preceding decade. There are many reasons for this. For one thing, the personnel and material resources available in federal German institutes for higher education and research have been substantially increased and improved during the last fifteen years. These increased resources have resulted from increased demands for advice and justification from the political and legislative spheres and, thus, from co-determination legislation itself. To this extent, the current boom in publications on co-determination represents a scientific response to legislative Acts dating from 1972 (amendment of the law governing works constitutions) and from 1976 (the introduction of co-determination law for enterprises with more than 2,000 employees).

The subjects of economic policies and of social policies do not pursue parallel courses within the realms of practical politics and research, yet they are synchronized, albeit with a certain delay. This also applies to empirical research into co-determination. It stands in close relationship to the processes of political

---

[1] See my evaluation of these in tabular form in Diefenbacher and Nutzinger (eds.) (1986: 291–304), including projects based on primary source investigations or empirical procedures which have left their mark on scientific discussions on co-determination in the FRG. Theoretical studies, programmatic texts, and those studies which are available only in the 'grey market' of non-public co-determination publications are not taken into account here.

decision making and legislation. These processes explain when, why, and with what form of approach to the questions, research into co-determination has been pursued up to the present.

Research objectives

Co-determination research in the FRG is, almost without exception, connected with legislative acts. The law on co-determination in the coal, iron, and steel industries dating from 1951[2] represented the legal basis of reference for more than half (thirty) of the total projects studied, either exclusively (in eight projects), or in combination with other co-determination regulations (in twenty-two). Only one project is related to the *Betriebsverfassungsordnung* (regulatory guide-lines on works constitutions) of 1948,[3] and two to the *Personalvertretungsgesetz* (the law governing personnel representation) of 1955.[4] In contrast, the *Betriebsverfassungs-gesetz* (the law governing works constitutions) of 1952 with thirteen projects, the 1972 amended version of this law with fourteen, and the *Mitbestimmungsgesetz* (the co-determination law) of 1976[5] with thirteen completed projects, enjoy about equal shares on the horizon of scientific interest. Five investigations deal with the theme of special regulations.[6]

Even if one takes into account the fact that research into the co-determination regulations of the 1970s is not yet complete—indeed, is in part only now getting under way—there is still one conclusion to be drawn: namely, that the inventory of completed empirical co-determination research is, for the most part, still research into co-determination in the coal, iron, and steel industries. (This does not apply, however, to current research.) The last publication on co-determination in these industries appeared in 1981, thirty years after the passage of the law. This shows the powerful impulse for research which this law engendered and, further, with what stamina co-determination research is pursued in the FRG. It was, however, the extension in 1956 of co-determination in the coal, iron, and steel industries to

---

[2] The so-called *Montan-Mitbestimmungsgesetz*—the law governing co-determination in the coal, iron, and steel industries—applies solely to mining companies and to the iron- and steel-producing industries. It provides for the composition of an *Aufsichtsrat* (supervisory board) based on parity. Such far-reaching co-determination within enterprises has not since been introduced by law in the FRG.

[3] These regulations were the forerunner of the *Betriebsverfassungsgesetz*—the law governing works constitutions—which, in its amended version of 1972, is still in force today. The law on works constitutions governs co-determination in the supervisory boards of enterprises with less than 2,000 employees and co-determination for works councils. The *Betriebsrat*—works council—is the central organ for the representation of the employee's interests within his company.

[4] The law on personnel representation governs the representation of employee's interests in the civil and public services.

[5] This law governs co-determination on the supervisory boards of large enterprises with more than 2,000 employees, which are not part of the coal, iron, and steel industries.

[6] At present, these special regulations, e.g. those at the Porst company, go far beyond the legal prescriptions on co-determination, in that they provide contractual assurance of more extensive rights of participation for the employee.

Table 6.1 Empirical co-determination research (1950–1985) in review

Period	Number of projects (53)	Legal bases of reference (i.e. laws on co-determination)	Research themes	Research fields	Research results	Financing
1950–1960	8 6 1 1	MontanmbG 1951 BetrVG 1952 PersonalvertrG 1955	Attitude of employees to their representatives; working climate; employees formative wishes, their expectations regarding co-determination and trade unions, their picture of society; management strategies	Iron and steel industries; population of the FRG; enterprises in the Ruhr valley	Dependence of the election and practices of works councils on the size of the business; works councils torn between management and staff	Scientific institute of the trade unions; management board of Mannesmann AG; Rockefeller Foundation
1960–1970	12 5 7 3	MontanmbG 1951 BetrVG 1952 None	General economic effects of co-determination; co-determination as the basis of a new social order; public reception of co-determination; the integrative power of co-determination in the works and in society as a whole	Iron and steel industries; enterprises in North Rhine and Westphalia; population of the FRG	Co-determination for works councils functions in social matters, and in direct employee concerns (dismissal) has an ameliorating effect; co-determination in practice within companies depends on the qualifications of employees' representatives	Sociological research centre in Dortmund; German Research Society; Co-determination Foundation; Federal German Federation of Employers; trade union of the chemical, paper, and ceramic industries

Table 6.1—*continued*

Period		Laws		Topics studied	Industries/sectors	Findings	Sources
1970–1980	18	MontanmbG 1951 BetrVG 1952 BetrVG 1972 MbG 1976 Others	9 6 7 4 3	Social consciousness of industrial employees; co-determination in the context of social and political interests; the supervisory board as an organ of co-determination; employees attitudes to co-determination; employee representation in the civil services; co-determination at the workplace; the effect of co-determination on corporate policies	Iron and steel industries; the population of the FRG; companies in a number of varying branches; public administrations in the FRG and France	The effects of co-determination on supervisory boards: (1) co-operation, (2) informal communication between capital and labour representatives; supervisory board co-determination without formative functions regarding corporate policies	Institute for Sociological Research and Social Policies; commercial demographic research; individual universities; German Research Society
1980–1985	15	MontanmbG 1951 BetrVG 1972 MitbG 1976 Others	8 6 10 3	Influence of the supervisory board on corporate policies; disclosure policies of companies with co-determination; co-determination choices in practice; practices of works councils; co-determination and workers' consciousness	Medium-sized industry; the automotive industry; various European and Israeli companies; foundries	Varying kinds of works council determine the practical aspects of co-determination; works councils' practical application of co-determination depends upon the engagement of employees and the degree to which they are organized in trade unions	German Research Society; Hans Böckler Foundation; Federal Ministry of Labour and Social Affairs; various universities

Notes:
Montanmbg = Co-determination law for the iron, steel, and mining industries
BetrVG = Laws governing works constitutions
PersonalvertrG = Law governing the representation of employees in the civil services
MitbG = Law governing co-determination in enterprises having more than 2,000 employees

cover holding companies, and the exemplary role which parity co-determination in these industries has come to assume for trade unions generally, as well as attempts by the employers (such as, for example, the Mannesmann Group) to get round co-determination regulations by restructuring their group concerns, which have, ultimately, contributed to the continuation of this form of co-determination in political and scientific discussions.

Legislative Acts trigger processes of co-determination, but what interests researchers in co-determination laws? The answer is, their effectiveness: how and to what extent do co-determination regulations take hold in practice? Almost all of the fifty-three studies set themselves this research objective. Only four projects apply themselves to different aspects of the law, namely, by questioning the conditions and prerequisites of co-determination regulations, for example, in the minds of employees.

One must conclude, then, that co-determination research generally investigates not the origins of the laws but the laws in practice.

Research themes

The effectiveness of the law demonstrates itself on two levels: in the area of the organized, objective reality of those to whom the law is addressed, and in their subjective capabilities for social action. Thus, the practice of co-determination laws takes its form both in the organization of the enterprise and its operations and in the attitude of those who are so organized. It follows that co-determination research will be undertaken as research into attitudes and/or organization. Both positions are clearly found in co-determination research, but with different emphases. On the global level, the main emphasis in co-determination research lies in *research into attitudes*. The majority of empirical projects concentrate their choice of theme on the anchoring of co-determination within the attitudinal and interest ranges of labour representatives, employees, and the total population. Only one-sixth of the projects concentrate their attention on decision structures, production organization, styles of leadership, and, thus, on the organizational dimensions of co-determination.

Upon closer examination, however, a notable development reveals itself: the proportion of organizational research is growing. While in the 1950s and 1960s the attitudinal dimension occupied, almost without exception, the centre of research interest, a third of the latest investigations are devoted chiefly to the organizational aspect.

This remarkable shift in direction in co-determination research results from an alteration in the perceptions in which co-determination researchers are interested. The earlier co-determination studies were *sociological* investigations. Moreover, they were the cradle of the speciality of industrial and organizational sociology which was reborn after the Second World War. By then, sociological co-determination research was suffering. An attempt to revitalize it with the creation of an appropriate range of topics at the Eighteenth Conference of German Sociologists in 1976 in Bielefeld met with no success (Pirker, 1978: 20 ff.). At meetings of sociologists in the 1980s, co-determination no longer plays a role as an object of research. Likewise, it is still kept outside the working contexts of industrial and organizational sociology.

With the removal of co-determination research from the sphere of industrial sociology, the central point for the reception of its results has also been transferred. In the 1950s and 1960s the evidence of co-determination research served the ends of labour consciousness and of trade union influence on corporate policies. In contrast, it was primarily the socio-political discussions surrounding neo-corporatism which profited most from empirical co-determination research in the 1970s. The results of this research served as evidence for the integrational and neo-corporate character of the governing system of co-determination.

If sociology as a profession in the FRG no longer devotes its attention to co-determination, this does not yet mean that co-determination as an object of research has completely disappeared over the horizon of sociologists' interests. But when sociologists concern themselves with co-determination these days, it is not with the practical interest of the co-determination researcher of the 1960s, but, rather, marginally and in connection with other research topics, such as the introduction of new technologies.

These days, the recruits to co-determination research in the FRG are, for the most part, lawyers who are interested in the social sciences and, above all, economists.[7] Furthermore, women are hardly to be found among co-determination researchers. Their underrepresentation is also a result of the transfer of co-determination research into scientific disciplines where still fewer women are active than in sociology itself. These shifts of co-determination research across the disciplines and in terms of personnel explain its evolution from a topic of sociological research into attitudes into a topic of business economics research into organization.

Fields and methods of research

By far the greatest proportion of these co-determination investigations (forty-two) were carried out in commerce and industry. This also applies to most of the current projects. One-seventh of the investigations were concerned with opinion polls on co-determination made by commercial establishments and using representative

---

[7] At a large symposium on research into participation and co-determination in the FRG and the rest of Europe, from a total of 37 speakers, more than half (19) came from the economic sciences. Besides 2 lawyers, 16 social scientists presented papers, of which 9 were sociologists. These papers offer a representative impression of the current situation in co-determination research in the FRG (Diefenbacher and Nutzinger (eds.), 1984).

samples related to the total population. Only one project chose the civil and public services for its field of research. The service industries hardly played a role in the completed studies (two projects). Co-determination up to now has barely taken into account the growing 'tertiarization' of the economy.

By contrast, the growth of case-studies has become evident in the publications of the last few years. Case-studies of co-determination were rare until the end of the 1960s. Up to 1970 there were only two; since then, however, seven have been completed and three are still running. This development indicates an opportunity for co-determination research to gain in depth through detailed analysis and to complement both the representative studies of the past and those studies which were more suitable for strategic political advice.

With the evolution of research interests, a change in the choice of methods is inevitably indicated. In the arsenal of methods available to co-determination research, the instruments of traditional social research (e.g. written questioning, semi-standardized interviews, and documentary analysis) are differentiated from action-oriented methods (e.g. group discussions) and active research procedures (Kissler, 1985: 22 ff.). In investigations of attitudes, with regard to the depth of focus of the methods and to the range of the statements which they produce, the standardized interview bears the relationship to group discussion which a bread-knife does to a scalpel. Nevertheless, co-determination researchers continue, for the most part, to turn to the methods of traditional social research. Only eight of the completed investigations make use of action-oriented methods such as group discussion. Active research also plays only a marginal role in co-determination research. Only three projects pursue this approach to research, and this is also one of the results described above of the removal of co-determination research from the field of sociology.

During the period under review one notes a remarkable concentration of investigations which carried out group discussions in the early phase of co-determination research during the 1950s (e.g. Pirker *et al.*, 1955) and again in the last decade (e.g. Hoppmann and Stötzel, 1981). Obviously, there is under way a reconsideration of methods which appear to have been forgotten during the long interim phase of representative studies. Social scientific research into the humanization of work[8] and its interweaving with participation research has had a decisive share in the rediscovery of the group discussion and of other action-based

[8] The government programme *Forschung Humanisierung des Arbeitslebens (HdA)*—research into the humanization of working life—has been running in the FRG since 1974 and is financed by the *Bundesministerium für Arbeit und Sozialordnung*—Federal Ministry of Labour and Social Organization— and by the *Bundesministerium für Forschung und Technologie*—Federal Ministry of Research and Technology (see the presentation and criticism of the HdA programme in Kissler and Sattel, 1982: 221 ff.). Within the context of this programme to promote research, a series of projects for the improvement of working conditions have been carried out during the last twelve years, with the active participation of researchers and, above all, of the employees concerned. These action-oriented projects (e.g. Fricke *et al.*, 1981) have been extremely fruitful in terms of producing ideas for themes and methods in co-determination research.

methods of co-determination research. All the same, the total picture suggests that co-determination research, in contrast with the social sciences, has in general remained basically resistant to Anglo-Saxon action-oriented and active approaches to research. The group discussion serves extensively as a method of reconnaissance preparatory to entry into traditional ways of research.

Research results

Dimensions of results

Co-determination research is, essentially, research into legal realities, that is to say, it looks into the effects of co-determination laws in practice. Therefore, its results may be ordered on the basis of three dimensions of this practice:[9]

1. in the *subjective–social dimension*, co-determination research provides data on employees' perceptions of co-determination rights and on their individual and collective reactions to co-determination rights as seen against the backgrounds of their work situation, the hierarchy within the enterprise, the qualifications structure, their individual life histories, and many other things.

2. in the *societal–economic dimension*, empirical co-determination research supplies answers to questions about the effects of co-determination on industrial relations, on the economic and social order, on the capital and labour markets, and on international co-operation and competitive capabilities. Both of these dimensions remain, to a large degree, unaddressed in the evaluation which follows.[10] I have limited myself much more to

3. the *institutional–organizational dimension*, since this is the focus of co-determination research up to the present.

Research which analyses the institutional–organizational realities of co-determination examines the interconnections of an enterprise's structure, the social structure within the plant, and the decision-making and problem-solving procedures in the enterprise, as these are dependent upon legal co-determination prescriptions. It looks into the possibilities and limitations of institutionalized co-determination at the workplace, within the plant, and in the business as a whole; that is to say, it looks into the relationship of the system of representation of interests to the practice of this representation at each respective level of participation.

---

[9] See also the similar structuring of research levels in Fürstenberg (1981).

[10] Results in the subjective–social dimension have been documented in Diefenbacher and Nutzinger (eds.) (1984). The societal–economic dimension of co-determination has, since the end of the 1960s, no longer been taken as a topic of empirical investigations. Spiro (1978) is representative of the earlier studies of this field of investigation and the 1970 commission report (Mitbestimmungskommission, 1970) provides a summary.

How does co-determination function at workplace level? Results regarding the co-determination practices of works councils

From the point of view of the employee, the most important legal form of co-determination is the representation of interests through the *Betriebsrat* (works council), since this level of participation is closest to the day-to-day work routine.

Whether a works council is ever elected and whether its rights of participation are ever applied depend to a large extent—as the earlier co-determination studies had already demonstrated (Mausolff, 1952)—upon the size of the enterprise: In small and medium-sized businesses entrepreneurial power relationships are still mostly marked by paternalism; furthermore, their inability to organize (e.g. to release sufficient works council members from duty) plays a major role in this.

Research work into the activities of works councils now indicates that their participation, in *social matters*, especially, is effective (Blume, 1964). However, the effectiveness of the works council in *personnel affairs* is less unequivocal. Various investigations reached the conclusion that the works council is most often drawn into involvement by the management when it comes to dismissals (Rumpf, 1965). In co-determination research, this phenomenon is interpreted as a strategy of social appeasement on the part of employers. A blessing given by the works council to a dismissal tends to check conflict. As an investigation into the effects of the 1972 law on works constitutions proves, such examples of the involvement of the works council in personnel matters lie, in part, outside the legal framework (Rummel, 1978). Rummel traces this development back to the positive effects of the law, since it is caused, on the one hand, by legally created pressures towards institutional co-operation (procedures of settlement and conciliation) and, on the other hand, by the acceptance of the law among trade unions and individual labour representatives in the companies. However, this area of co-determination also reveals weak points in the practice of the works constitution. These are related to, among other things, personnel planning, in which the works council is too little involved; this diminishes its opportunities to exert influence in the personnel field in the medium and long terms.

As already mentioned, the size of the enterprise is of great importance with regard to the works council's real potential for influence and its full exploitation of participation rights. A new study has pushed into the foreground a further aspect: that of the relationship between the structure of the enterprise and the opportunities for participation. Rancke (1982) points out that the law on works constitutions does not take the evolution of various forms of large enterprises enough into account, since, in reality, there is no uniform type of large enterprise. This analysis of the in-plant system for the representation of employees' interests and of the organizational and management structures in single-plant enterprises, in enterprises with various plants producing individual items, in affiliated enterprise structures, and in enterprises organized into activity divisions, arrives at the following summarized conclusions:

- that the decentralization and breaking down into affiliates of a unified enterprise means that it no longer fits, without contradictions, into the old legal catalogue of terms applied to works constitutions;
- that new forms of enterprise have led to substructures under the works constitution laws, into which co-determination authority has certainly shifted, but within which it is no longer institutionally secured;
- that, on these grounds, a possible diminution of the co-determination rights guaranteed under works constitution law could arise, or indeed, has arisen.

The way in which co-determination functions and the extent to which the legally determined possibilities for participation within the company are made use of depend, however, not only on the quality of the legal standards; they depend especially upon the specific power relationships within the enterprise, upon the social structure of the representation of interests, and, therefore, upon their own situation within the *social structure of the enterprise.*

Industrial sociological research into co-determination draws particular attention to this state of affairs. Its analysis of operational work and of the social position of works councils in relation to the management and organizational contexts of enterprises shows how strongly the realities of co-determination are affected by the social relationships within a company, and that the opportunities for employees' participation are not just a problem of the legal formulation of co-determination laws.

Thus, the works council is caught in a state of tension between the expectations of the employees and those of the enterprise's management. Already in the 1950s, Pirker pointed out that the weak point in the co-determination system was the works council (Pirker *et al.*, 1955). Pirker and his colleagues were able to demonstrate empirically:

- that works councils identify themselves particularly with the company and with the internal order of the enterprise;
- that cadres possess exclusivity in contrast with the rest of the work-force; and
- that it is typical of works council co-determination that conflicts of loyalty to the company and the work-force arise.

Other studies have taken up this point and conducted various further investigations. It was demonstrated that the standing of the works councils in small companies is often particularly unfavourable, because of the entrepreneur's proximity to operational events. In a study of the typology of participation patterns in the varying relationships of power within enterprises, Kotthoff (1981) has attempted to describe the relations of works council and management.

On the basis of this study, one may differentiate between various types of works council in the light of their co-determination practices: the 'ignored works council' in small, patriarchally organized companies, the 'isolated works council', and the 'works council as an organ of the management', which, as an executive power, takes over control, execution, disciplinary, administrative, and informational tasks from the employer. In practice, within the enterprises there are also to be found the 'respected ambivalent works council', which wishes to be equally useful to all sides, and the 'respected rigid works council', which in the pattern of intracompany relations sees itself as a consistent employee representative and openly pursues conflict with the management.

Of particular importance for the co-determination authority of the works council is the participatory behaviour of the work-force, that is the mobilization of the work-force, or its ability to mobilize, both of which are dependent on various factors. One important, if not unequivocal, factor is the degree of unionization of the work-force. In industrial sociological research into co-determination nobody questions that a higher degree of unionization of the work-force has a positive effect on the work of the works council. The IMSF, in its study published in 1972, points out that the ability of the works council to exploit co-determination rights depends upon the willingness of the work-force to enter into open conflict, as well as upon the support which the works council finds in the work-force factors which are promoted by trade union links.

The real chances for the participation of the works council are further influenced by the degree of liaison between internal labour representatives and the trade union. In response to the questions of research groups, works councils, especially in small companies, express the wish for stronger support from the trade unions. Ultimately, this also points up how important the specific power relationships within an enterprise are, and how they are a determining factor in the chance for participation of the work-force. The central results of industrial sociological research into co-determination prove time and again that the legal reality of co-determination can only be understood within this context of the social structure of an enterprise.

How does co-determination function in a company? Results regarding the co-determination practices of supervisory boards

A second central field of investigation for co-determination research is the analysis of the legal and organizational realities of co-determination at company management level. In the earlier studies, the topic of investigation given the highest priority in this area was co-determination in the coal, iron, and steel industries, particularly the effects of co-determination on industrial relations, the working climate, and so on.

At first, the *qualifications* of labour representatives stood in the forefront of research into the way in which co-determination functioned at company management level. Scientific interest in the competence of labour representatives originated during the phase of the implementation of co-determination and during the ensuing consolidation phase. In these early phases of co-determination in practice, the recruitment of suitable labour representatives was not always a simple matter, while the qualifications of these representatives were crucial in gaining recognition for employees' interests (Blumenthal, 1960).

The lack of qualified people with sufficient economic, socio-political, commercial, and technical knowledge on the supervisory boards influenced, at the outset, the development of co-determination competence (Potthoff *et al.*, 1962). It was hardly surprising, therefore, that the members of the supervisory boards showed a great interest in further education and training. Trade union training of their officials and years of experience with co-determination mitigated noticeably the qualifications problem in the course of the history of co-determination.

How does co-determination function nowadays on the *Aufsichtsrat* (supervisory board) and on the *Vorstand* (board of management)? This question occupies much of the scene in the history of co-determination research. Highly significant answers are provided by the 1970 report of the Biedenkopf Commission on co-determination in the coal, iron, and steel industries[11] and in the study by Brinkmann-Herz (1972) of co-determination at company management level in the FRG.

In summary, the following common conclusions can be found in the results of the relevant studies:

Generally speaking a good level of co-operation developed between the representatives of shareholders and labour on the supervisory boards of large enterprises in the coal, iron, and steel industries. The experiences of these branches with co-determination on a parity basis were positive throughout. The supervisory board evolved, in practice, into an organ for the institutional integration of the employee. The collaboration of employer and employee representatives was relatively free of conflict: controversy and direct confrontation seldom occurred. As both of the studies mentioned above make clear, the reason for this was to be sought in the informal mechanisms for the settlement of conflicts which had developed between the supervisory and management boards of the companies. As Brinkmann-Herz emphasizes, the informal channels of communication between these boards achieved particular importance as the chief means by which the contributions to decision making of the supervisory board and, in particular, of the labour representatives on it became company policy. In contrast, the formal channels of communication (board of management reports to the supervisory board) were mostly too superficial. As a rule, the supervisory board was first informed of policy discussions during the phase when resolutions were formulated. Thus, the importance of supervisory board co-determination lay in their co-operative supervision of the management of the company by advising the

[11] On this report by the Mitbestimmungskommission from 1970, see Streeck (1984).

board of management early in the policy-making process. The disadvantage of this informality was that the individual member of the supervisory board could bring into play only those means of influence which were available to him personally; as a result, the overall view and control of problem-solving processes were lost.

Empirical co-determination research has been able to demonstrate that the influence of co-determination on company policies is stronger in social aspects, since policies on capital investment, efforts towards concentration, plant closures, etcetera are only rejected by the representatives of labour when they are socially unacceptable. The supervisory board—and with it, its labour representatives—has little formative role in the area of business management policies. This applies, in comparison with the coal, iron, and steel industries, much more to the area covered by the co-determination law of 1976. A recent study has shown that labour representatives on the supervisory boards of most of the enterprises which are subject to the 1976 co-determination law can exercise only a very narrow influence on their company's business policies (Bamberg *et al.*, 1984).

Research financing and the application of research results

Co-determination research is not conducted in a social vacuum. Social and political interests have always influenced it. These interests determine not only the themes and methods of this research, but, above all, the way in which the research results are evaluated.

Who, in the past, has been using co-determination research for political reasons, and who has been using its results for argumentation which supports their own interests? In other words, for whom has co-determination research been really useful? The answers to these questions are relatively simple in that area of research which is financed by third parties. This concerns projects which were financed by social-interest groups or political parties and whose application was directly related to the practical political concerns of these groups or parties.

However, only a minority of co-determination projects fall into this category. The political parties and their related foundations do not participate in financial support for co-determination research, with one exception: the Konrad Adenauer Foundation, which is closely related to the CDU, has financed one project. The employers' associations and the trade unions present a different picture. Three research projects were promoted by institutions with close ties to business, while, in the trade unions and the Hans Böckler Foundation, we find the largest non-public promoter of co-determination research. About one-sixth of completed research projects were financed by the trade unions.

It is no wonder, therefore, that, in the past, when it has come to the question of expanding trade union influence on the co-determination system of the Federal Republic, it has been above all the trade unions which have based their arguments on the results of co-determination research. Thus, for example, during the discussions surrounding the co-determination law of 1976, the DGB, in order to promote the application in all large concerns of the model of parity representation on supervisory boards as it was established in the coal, iron, and steel industries, argued that co-determination in these industries was functioning well, that it did not affect the owners' profit concerns, and that it tended to take the edge off conflicts.

The majority of co-determination research projects in the Federal Republic, however, have not been financed by third parties. Co-determination research is, for the most part, institutionally anchored in the universities. A large number of these projects are devoted to increasing qualifications, especially the furtherance of postgraduate studies. A quarter of the projects were carried out by demographic and other research institutions outside the universities. For the most part, the university projects were initiated by the researchers themselves and financed with university funds. In contrast, research financing by the Federal government or Federal ministries (two projects) and state ministries (one project) remains marginal.

Even though the majority of these co-determination projects have not been directly related to the practical concerns of social and political interest groups, this does not mean that their results are without practical influence. Co-determination projects which are not designed for practical application share the basic problems of all 'neutral' sociological research, that is, their results are available to those who have the power to use them. In this way, co-determination research resembles a quarry, from which employers, trade unions, and politicians each remove those stones which are most useful for building the foundations of their own arguments and policies.

While in the case of research designed for application the relationship of theory to practice is clearly accessible to researcher and sponsor and easily reproduced, in the fields of research which are not designed for application this relationship is obscure. The result is that the practical relevance of co-determination research in the latter form eludes precise accounting and remains in the realm of pure speculation.

Future research prospects

Co-determination in the FRG is enjoying a 'silent' boom. This research is a response to legislative Acts; it has reacted, up to now, largely to the law governing co-determination in the coal, iron, and steel industries dating from 1951. Co-determination research is research into legal realities. It investigates the practical power of the normative, or, more precisely, the effectiveness of co-determination laws. Co-determination research has been increasingly shifting from sociological research into attitudes towards business economics research into organization. These days, its recruits are largely lawyers and economists. The research field of

Leo Kissler

co-determination research is commerce and industry. However, case-studies and interest in researching the tertiary sector are on the increase. In terms of method, a re-establishment of action-based procedures is taking place. Co-determination research is the domain of researchers from universities and research institutes. It is, for the most part, financed by the public purse.

The prospects for, and future tasks of, co-determination research lie in its current deficiencies in regard to method and topics. Further co-determination research must pursue more energetically the expansion of the research field into tertiary sector enterprises, and the reconsideration of methods beyond those of traditional social research. Other ways of analysing details in depth in accordance with the standards of the social sciences are not possible.

The real task for the future, however, has grown up in the area of research themes. Here, two deficiences are particularly evident: the exclusion of co-determination at the workplace from research topics and a reluctance to look across national borders. Only two of the completed projects concentrated their research on co-determination at the workplace (Schulze-Scharnhorst, 1985; Hoppmann and Stötzel, 1981). Clearly, co-determination research has not responded to the research done in the 1970s into the humanization of work and its results regarding participation in the enterprise.

The comparative perspective remains virtually unaddressed. Only one project concerned itself with a multinational study (IDE International Research Group, 1981).

The small and still diminishing relevance of co-determination in the coal, iron, and steel industries to the practice of co-determination in the FRG generally[12] is in striking contrast to its extraordinary importance in co-determination research. For this reason, the impression of 'phantom research' emerges, research which fails to cover the current practical problems in a co-determined economy, or, at least, whose topics are not up to date.

If social research and co-determination research also have the task of providing political advice in the broader sense, or, at least, of providing a scientifically controlled 'early warning system' for recognizing system failures, then a new direction is required for the latter. It must concentrate its interests more strongly on those areas where questions arise over the legitimization and survival of the prevailing system of co-determination, namely, at its foundations. The topic of co-determination for workers themselves, which has lately and not without good reason been pushed more strongly by trade unions,[13] and reports of experiences

[12] At present, only 31 companies are subject to the co-determination legally imposed on the coal, iron, and steel industries (Kronenberg, 1987: 438). Since further rationalization in the coal and steel branches are in sight, coal, iron, and steel co-determination will finally become an extinct dinosaur from the beginning of the Federal Republic, even if, now as previously, it is the only form of co-determination at company management level which deserves the name.

[13] See Leminsky (1985) and especially the concept of the German trade union congress for co-determination at the workplace in DGB-Bundesvorstand (ed.) (1985).

with direct participation at the workplace abroad[14] both point the way into the future for a vigorous co-determination research.

References

Bamberg, U., Dzielak, S., Hindrichs, W., Martens, H., and Peter, G. (1984), *Praxis der Unternehmensmitbestimmung nach dem Mitbestimmungsgesetz 76: Eine Problemstudie*, (Düsseldorf: Hans-Böckler-Stiftung).

Blume, O. (1964), *Normen und Wirklichkeit einer Betriebsverfassung* (Tübingen: J. C. B. Mohr).

Blumenthal, W. M. (1960), *Die Mitbestimmung in der deutschen Stahlindustrie*, (Bad Homburg: Gehlen).

Brinkmann-Herz, D. (1972), *Entscheidungsprozesse in den Aufsichtsräten der Montanindustrie: Eine empirische Untersuchung über die Eignung des Aufsichtsrates als Instrument der Arbeitermitbestimmung* (Berlin: Duncker & Humblot).

DGB-Bundesvorstand (ed.) (1985), *Konzeption zur Mitbestimmung am Arbeitsplatz* (Düsseldorf: Union).

Diefenbacher, H. (1983), *Empirische Mitbestimmungsforschung: Eine kritische Auseinandersetzung mit Methoden und Resultaten* (Frankfurt-on-Main: Haag & Herchen).

—— and Nutzinger, H. G. (eds.) (1984), *Mitbestimmung: Theorie, Geschichte, Praxis, Konzepte und Formen der Arbeitnehmerpartizipation*, (Heidelberg: FEST).

—— —— (eds.) (1986), *Mitbestimmung in Betrieb und Verwaltung* (Heidelberg: FEST).

Fricke, E., Fricke, W., Schönwälder, M., and Stiegler, B. (1981), *Qualifikation und Beteiligung: Das 'Peiner Modell'* (Frankfurt-on-Main and New York: Campus).

Fürstenberg, F. (1981), *Zur Methodologie der Mitbestimmungsforschung*, in H. Diefenbacher and H. G. Nutzinger (eds.), *Mitbestimmung: Probleme und Perspektiven der empirischen Forschung* (Frankfurt-on-Main and New York: Campus).

Hoppmann, K. and Stötzel, B. (1981), *Demokratie am Arbeitsplatz* (Frankfurt-on-Main and New York: Campus).

IMSF (ed.) (1972), *Mitbestimmung als Kampfaufgabe* (Cologne: Pahl-Rugenstein).

IDE International Research Group (1981), *Industrial Democracy in Europe* (Oxford: Clarendon Press).

Jansen, P. and Kissler, L. (1987), 'Organization of Work by Participation? A French–German Comparison' *Economic and Industrial Democracy*, 8: 379–409.

Javillier, J.-C. (1984), *Les Reformes du droit du travail depuis le 10 mai 1981*, (Paris: LGDJ).

Kissler, L. (1985), 'Arbeitswissenschaft für wen? Die Antwort der arbeitsorientierten Wissenschaft von der Arbeit', in W. Georg, L. Kissler, and U. Sattel (eds.), *Arbeit und Wissenschaft: Arbeitswissenschaft?* (Bonn: Neue Gesellschaft).

—— (ed.) (1985), *Industrielle Demokratie in Frankreich: Die neuen Arbeitnehmer- und Gewerkschaftsrechte in Theorie und Praxis* (Frankfurt-on-Main and New York: Campus).

---

[14] The great social experiment of right of say for the workers in an enterprise which began in France with the creation of *groupes d'expression*—workers' expression groups—on the basis of the reform of enterprises contained in the Auroux laws of 1982 should be followed with particular attention. See Javillier (1984), the contributions of Borzeix and Gautrat containing new research results on the practice of these *groupes d'expression* in Kissler (ed.) (1985), and Jansen and Kissler (1987).

—— and Sattel, U. (1982), 'Humanization of Work and Social Interests: Description and Critical Assessment of the State-Sponsored Program of Humanization in the Federal Republic of Germany', *Economic and Industrial Democracy*, 3: 221–61.

Kotthoff, H. (1981), *Betriebsräte und Betriebliche Herrschaft* (Frankfurt-on-Main and New York: Campus).

Kronenberg, B. (1987), 'Mitbestimmungsunternehmen nach dem Stand vom 31. Dezember 1986', *WSI-Mitteilungen*, 7: 433–8.

Leminsky, G. (1985), 'Mitbestimmung am Arbeitsplatz: Erfahrungen und Perspektiven' *Gewerkschaftliche Monatshefte*, 3: 151–60.

Mausolff, A. (1952), *Gewerkschaft und Betriebsrat im Urteil der Arbeitnehmer* (Darmstadt: Eduard Roether).

Mitbestimmung, Die (1983), 5 (Düsseldorf: Hans-Böckler-Stiftung).

Mitbestimmungskommission (1970), *Mitbestimmung im Unternehmen: Bericht der Sachverständigenkommission zur Auswertung der bisherigen Erfahrungen bei der Mitbestimmung* (Stuttgart: Kohlhammer).

Pirker, T. (1978), 'Einleitung: Von der Mitbestimmungsforschung zur Partizipationsforschung', in *Materialien aus der soziologischen Forschung: Verhandlungen des 18. Deutschen Soziologentages vom 28.9. bis 1.10.1976 in Bielefeld* (Darmstadt: Luchterhand).

—— Braun, S., Lutz, B., and Hammelrath, F. (1955), *Arbeiter–Management—Mitbestimmung* (Stuttgart and Düsseldorf: Ring).

Potthoff, E., Blume, O., and Duvernell, H. (1962), *Zwischenbilanz der Mitbestimmung* (Tübingen: J. C. B. Mohr).

Ranke, F. (1982), *Betriebsverfassung und Unternehmenswirklichkeit* (Opladen: Westdeutscher Verlag).

Rummel, C. (1978), *Die Beteiligung des Betriebsrats an der Personalplanung und an personellen Einzelmaßnahmen* (Cologne: Bund).

Rumpf, P. (1965), *Die Auswirkungen des Betriebsverfassungsgesetzes in der Sicht der Betriebsratsvorsitzenden aus dem Organisationsbereich der Industriegewerkschaft Metall für die Bundesrepublik Deutschland* Ph.D. thesis (Cologne: University of Cologne).

Schulze-Scharnhorst, E. (1985), *Partizipationspotential am Arbeitsplatz* (Frankfurt-on-Main and New York: Peter Lang).

Spiro, H. (1958), *The Politics of German Codetermination* (Cambridge, Mass.: Harvard University Press).

Streeck, W. (1984), 'Co-determination: The Fourth Decade', in B. Wilpert and A. Sorge (eds.), *International Yearbook of Organizational Democracy*, ii (Chichester: Wiley).

7

Participative Management in the United States: Three Classics Revisited

EDWARD E. LAWLER III

TODAY there is an unmistakable and important change taking place in the way many major US corporations are being managed. They are changing a number of their management practices and systems to encourage employees to become more involved in the management of their organizations. Recent surveys of management practice show that Quality Circles, work teams, profit-sharing plans, and skill-based pay systems are being adopted by a significant number of organizations (see e.g. New York Stock Exchange, 1982; Conference Board, 1984; O'Dell, 1987). A list of companies publicly committed to adopting participative management includes such major US corporations as Motorola, TRW, Ford, Honeywell, Digital Equipment Corporation, and Xerox.

Employee involvement has gone from being seen as an academic research and theory area to a potential competitive advantage in the world market-place. Organization after organization in the United States is concluding that, unless they utilize their people more fully, they cannot compete in world markets. Participative management is being recognized as a way to do this and to offset the higher labour cost which exists in the United States (Lawler, 1986). It offsets them because it utilizes people more fully in non-management positions by asking them to think, problem solve, and control their own work (Walton, 1985). This has the cost-effective impact of reducing the amount of management overhead needed to run an organization and tends to motivate individuals to do higher-quality work.

Adoption of participative management by American companies has a long and interesting history. One critical event in the history of participative management in the United States was the publication of three books: *Personality and Organization* by Chris Argyris (1957), *The Human Side of Enterprise* by Douglas McGregor (1960), and *New Patterns of Management* by Rensis Likert (1961). These three books established the philosophical basis for the current practice of participative management. They were the first to define a participative management paradigm for managing US organizations. Almost thirty years have passed since they were first published, and thus it is appropriate to ask two questions about them. What did they contribute to current practice, and why did it take so long for them to make an impact on practice?

The change from a top-down traditional management style to an involvement-orientated one can best be viewed as a paradigm shift (Mohrman and Lawler, 1985). In paradigm shifts one fundamental approach to organizing and thinking about an issue is replaced by another. Paradigm shifts are not easy to accomplish because they require the abandonment of an old, well-understood, and often effective approach to thinking and the adoption of a new, often underdeveloped approach.

Basic to a paradigm shift is the outlining of a new attractive paradigm. Without a clear vision of the new model or paradigm and the ability to articulate it in a way that makes it attractive, there can never be a paradigm shift. The major contribution of the work of Argyris, McGregor, and Likert was the outlining of a new attractive paradigm. In particular, McGregor's statement of Theory Y caught the imagination of a number of academics and managers. It reflected a value system that was more attractive than the value system underlying traditional management or, as McGregor called it, Theory X. In a paradigm shift, an appeal to values is often a powerful way to mobilize energy for change. As we will discuss in more detail later, it is rarely enough by itself to produce a paradigm shift but it is a necessary condition for a paradigm shift.

A second feature that is needed for a paradigm shift to occur is supporting evidence of the superiority of the new paradigm. Likert's book provided some supporting evidence. It discussed some classic research done by the Institute for Social Research at the University of Michigan. More than McGregor's book, it gave the idea of participative management a research base. Argyris also reviewed a considerable amount of research and helped provide a research base for the switch from traditional to participative management. Argyris and Likert also appealed to value issues, and clearly stated a much more positive view of human nature than the one underlying the traditional approach to management. Argyris was particularly effective in pointing out that the way organizations are traditionally designed assumes a kind of work-force that certainly did not exist at the time of his writing. His reference to work being designed for employees with low levels of intelligence and little self-control help highlight the differences between the participative management paradigm and the more traditional control paradigm.

Finally, all three books hint at the kind of technology that is needed for a participative management approach to work effectively. A big emphasis is placed on leadership and the skills that managers need in order to elicit participation in decision making. Indeed, more than any other feature of participative management these books stress the advantages of participative decision making led by the supervisor. Discussions are not limited just to consideration of leadership skills. Argyris talks about work redesign, as does Likert. McGregor suggests that new pay systems can be very useful in supporting participative management. Finally, Likert gives considerable attention to the information system and how information is handled in an organization. Overall, the three books taken together go a long way towards defining the participative management paradigm. They touch upon a number of the changes that need to occur in organizations, and they provide some initial evidence about the effectiveness of the new paradigm. In the case of Argyris's book they go one step further and talk about the dysfunctions and problems with the existing paradigm. More than any of the three, he talks about the kind of counter-productive behaviour that occurs when people are treated as if they are not capable of exercising self-control and are given meaningless, repetitive tasks to perform.

Impact on organizational practice

The initial impact of the Argyris, McGregor, and Likert books was limited. They immediately became required reading for Ph.D. students like myself and were used in some business school courses. The concepts of Theory X and Theory Y management became a shorthand way of referring to different management styles. Their immediate impact on practice, however, was minimal. Several surveys in the early 1970s confirmed that little change was occurring and called once again for the adoption of new management approaches (see e.g. Sheppard and Herrick, 1972; *Work in America*, 1973).

The books and their ideas about participative management did contribute to the development of a number of management training programmes that emphasized participative leadership skills. The T-group movement of the 1960s seemed to gain some of its energy from these books and the concepts in them. A number of managers in corporations like TRW and Exxon did go through one or two interpersonal training sessions that were intended to help them become more effective participative managers and relate better to individuals. The evidence on the effects of this training is mixed: most researchers have concluded that it did little fundamentally to change the management styles of organizations (Campbell *et al.*, 1970).

In retrospect, T-groups and leadership training may, if anything, have slowed the adoption of participative management more than it helped it. It slowed it because it created the perception that all participative management really involved was 'being nice to people', having leaders who ask subordinates' opinions, and having group meetings. It also contributed to the view that participative management is a nice thing to do and a good thing to do, but not necessarily the most effective way to manage. Indeed, much of the debate during the 1960s and early 1970s on the application of participative management revolved around the issue of doing good versus doing what is effective. All too often, critics of participative management won the day by arguing that, although it was a good thing to do, it was not necessarily an affordable thing to do. As a result of this and the other forces that worked against the adoption of participative management, adoption did not take place in most organizations until the late 1970s and 1980s.

Forces against adoption

In many respects, it is understandable that the writing of three seminal books on participative management did not produce a rapid adoption of the participative management paradigm. The adoption of a new paradigm takes much more than simply the statement of it; evidence that it can be effective and criticisms of the old paradigm are also needed (Mohrman and Lawler, 1985). Most important is widespread acceptance that the old paradigm is a failure. In the absence of widespread dissatisfaction with the existing paradigm, few organizations are willing to adopt a new one, no matter how attractive it is, because it means abandoning something which has proved successful. In the case of a management paradigm, adoption is aided when the technology to implement it is available. There is something of a chicken-and-egg problem because, without people being willing to try the new paradigm, it is hard to develop the supportive technology, just as it is hard to develop evidence to support it. It is hard to test and develop participative management in the laboratory. Indeed, even the adoption of it in a limited area of an organization may not be enough, because this is both qualitatively and quantitatively different from practising it on an organization-wide basis (Lawler, 1984).

One other major obstacle to the adoption of participative management practices needs to be mentioned. When old paradigms are abandoned and new ones adopted, there is often a tendency for one group to feel that they are the losers and another group to feel that they are the winners. Adoption of a new paradigm is particularly difficult when the people who must adopt it see themselves as potential losers as a result of its adoption. To a substantial degree, participative management creates a situation where many of the people that need to champion the adoption of it fear that they will lose as a result of its adoption.

In most cases upper-level managers have reached the top of organizations because they are good at traditional top-down management and they are very handsomely rewarded for their success in obtaining the top positions in their organizations. Movement to a more participative style can threaten them in two ways. First, in spite of the arguments of Likert and others that they will not lose power, they inevitably feel that they will. Secondly, there is the question of whether they can successfully practise the new management style. Obtaining a senior management position in a traditionally managed organization is based on a particular set of skills. Different management skills are appropriate in participatively managed organizations, as is emphasized in the Argyris, Likert, and McGregor books.

Adoption of a new paradigm of management does not require a fully developed technology to support it, nor conclusive evidence that it is a superior paradigm. If it did there would never be a change in management style since these can only be developed after adoption. Adoption is helped, however, by at least some significant supporting evidence and the existence of appropriate technologies. The Argyris, Likert, and McGregor books perhaps are most lacking in the area of evidence and specification of technology. Just a few experiments in participative leadership are cited as evidence that it is time for a major change in the way organizations are managed (e.g. Coch and French, 1948). None of these experiments involve changes in major corporations. Instead, they talk about either small organizations, changes in particular work groups, or the effectiveness of particular participative supervisors or managers. Obviously, the individual who is not inclined toward employee involvement can easily dismiss these as poor evidence that participation is a superior management style.

In the area of technology, although there is some discussion of the use of attitude surveys, changes in performance appraisal method, Scanlon plans, and job enlargement, the fact of the matter is that little technology existed in the 1960s to support the implementation of participative management. Indeed, even though a great deal of attention was paid to leadership, there were few good leadership training programmes available at the time and little evidence that any programme would change leadership behaviour. In the area of compensation practices, little was known about how to structure profit-sharing plans, and such ideas as skill-based pay, flexible benefit programmes, and all-salary work-forces were not discussed in any detail and in some cases were not even invented.

Finally, it was not at all clear what kinds of strategy could be used to change a major corporation's management from a traditional to a participative one. All too often the only answer to questions about how to change an organization was training. Training by itself has little ability to change the multiple systems which need to be changed if an organization is to be managed in a participative manner (Lawler, 1986). Indeed, the very point that organizations need to be restructured in almost every feature in order to adopt a new paradigm effectively is largely missing in the early writings on participative management. This is hardly surprising because the early writers had little chance to see participative organizations in operation and, therefore, little chance to develop their ideas about what is involved in operating an organization in a participative manner. The lack of a complete participative model probably did not hinder adoption in some respects. If managers had been fully aware what the change process involved it is quite possible that more rather than less resistance would have occurred, because they would have become even more overwhelmed by the enormity of the change process that was required.

In retrospect, it is painfully obvious why there was not immediate adoption of the participative paradigm. Once again, the luxury of hindsight makes things clear. Although attractive, participation was not a well-developed technology, the evidence favouring it was sparse, and it threatened the very individuals who needed to adopt it. Finally, dissatisfaction with the existing paradigm was relatively low. Most US organizations were quite successful, and the individuals who were running them were being handsomely rewarded for managing them in a traditional way. This points once again to the most important missing element for the adoption of the new paradigm proposed by Argyris, Likert, and McGregor: dissatisfaction with the existing paradigm. Because American businesses were admired for their managerial effectiveness and the country was dominating the world in the area of manufacturing, it was hard to argue that the traditional paradigm was causing major problems. Thus adoption of any new paradigm was virtually impossible.

The current situation

The environment for many US businesses changed significantly in the 1970s. Foreign competition became a major factor and many US corporations found themselves at a competitive disadvantage. Suddenly, many US products became high cost and low quality, and began to lose market share both in the United States and on a world-wide basis. This fundamental change in the US business equation provided the dissatisfaction with the existing paradigm which had been largely absent. Initially, this dissatisfaction was concentrated in such traditional manufacturing industries as steel, cars, glass, and rubber. More recently it has spread to a wider range of industries including paper, electronics, and even financial services. This change more than any other seems to have produced the increased adoption of participative management that is now apparent in the United States.

A number of other changes have also taken place since the early 1960s. There is clearly more evidence on the impact of participative management, and the technology of participative management is much better developed. The advent of computers has helped tremendously with the kind of information movement that is required to manage in a participative way. A great deal more is known about work restructuring and the relative effectiveness of teams, individual job enrichment strategies and how to develop them. Pay systems have been developed to encourage employee ownership, give employees a share of operating improvements, and pay them according to their skills, rather than traditional job structures.

In short, technology has advanced, but this probably is not the key reason why adoption has increased dramatically. The reason, to repeat, is increased dissatisfaction with the traditional style of management because of the loss of world-wide competitiveness by many US businesses. Among other things, this has changed the situation of senior management dramatically. Instead of being successful, highly paid leaders of growing businesses, they have come under attack as overpaid, poor managers of stagnant, overpriced, inefficient businesses. As a result, they have a reason to change, something which was historically lacking. The result in some cases has been to try to improve their use of traditional management practices. Salaries have been cut, controls tightened, budgets reduced, and in some cases this has helped to improve the profitability of corporations. However, a significant number of corporations have decided that changes of this type are not enough to produce the dramatic performance improvements that are needed to compete internationally. As a result, many organizations have adopted employee involvement as a way of staying competitive in a world-wide market. Those that have are implementing the basic ideas and philosophies that were stated by Argyris, Likert, and McGregor three decades ago.

In some respects, it has taken a surprisingly short time for the idea of participative management to go from paradigm definition to implementation, particularly when the ideas call for the kind of basic change that is represented in participative management. It is a tribute to the writings of Argyris, Likert, and McGregor that so much of what they wrote about has in fact proved to be correct and useful. Had the world economic scene changed earlier, it is quite possible that their ideas would have been implemented earlier. In any case, their time appears to have come, and the future will undoubtedly involve a period of further development of the paradigm which they initially proposed.

References

Argyris, C. (1957), *Personality and Organization* (New York: Harper).

Campbell, J. P., Dunnette, M. D., Lawler, E. E., and Weick, K. (1970), *Managerial Behavior, Performances and Effectiveness* (New York: McGraw-Hill).

Coch, L. and French, J. R. P. (1948), 'Overcoming Resistance to Change', *Human Relations*, 1(4): 512–33.

Conference Board (1984), *Innovations in Managing Human Resources* (New York: Conference Board).

Lawler, E. E. (1984), 'Leadership in Participative Organizations' in J. Hunt, D. Hosking, C. Schriesheim, and R. Stewart (eds.), *Leaders and Managers* (New York: Pergamon Press).

—— (1986), *High Involvement Management* (San Francisco, Calif.: Jossey-Bass).

Likert, R. (1961), *New Patterns of Management* (New York: McGraw-Hill).

McGregor, D. (1960), *The Human Side of Enterprise* (New York: McGraw-Hill).

Mohrman, A. M. and Lawler, E. E. (1985), 'The diffusion of QWL as a Paradigm Shift' in W. G. Bennis, K. D. Benne, and R. Chin (eds.), *The Planning of Change* (New York: Holt).

New York Stock Exchange (1982), *People and Productivity* (New York: NYSE).

O'Dell, C. (1987), *People, Performance and Pay* (Houston, Tex.: American Productivity Center).

Sheppard, H. and Herrick, N. (1972), *Where have All the Robots Gone* (New York: Free Press).

Walton, R. E. (1985), 'From Control to Commitment in the Workplace', *Harvard Business Review* 63(2): 76–84.

Work in America (1973) (Cambridge, Mass.: MIT Press).

8

A New Milestone in the Development of Industrial Democracy in Norway?

THORALF ULRIK QVALE

Introduction

At the Einar Thorsrud Memorial Symposium organized by the Work Research Institute in Oslo in June 1987 the Norwegian Prime Minister Mrs Gro Harlem Brundtland announced a new phase in the democratization of Norwegian working life.

Building on unanimous recommendations from a broadly composed tripartite commission on industrial democracy, she announced the start of a new programme aimed primarily at improving conditions for direct participation in decision making at work. The programme will be linked to a centre, which will be organized as a foundation created jointly by the Government, the employers, and the various union federations across the public and the private sectors.

The new programme symbolizes the political penetration of the ideas and experience from the field experiments and projects within the Norwegian Industrial Democracy Programme (IDP) started by Einar Thorsrud in the 1960s. While the issue of employee participation at board level in companies (employees have held one-third of the seats since 1974) has moved somewhat into the background, the interest in better utilization of human resources through participative forms of work organization and leadership has become intense and, in reality, close to uncontentious. This reflects the experience gained through both the Industrial Democracy Programme and a number of legal reforms in working life aimed at improving the work environment, participation, introduction of new technology, and collective agreements.

The new programme also indicates a shift in thinking about industrial democracy away from concentration on rights and the distribution of power towards developing strategies for learning and the utilization of external resources to improve the performance of work organizations. Of course, the economic crisis in both the public and private sectors is an important factor behind this shift. But the common experience from joint research and development activities in working life through the last twenty years in Norway has probably contributed substantially to the common view. The labour-market organizations, supported by the Confederation of Industry, are actually agreeing that the common experience and the high degree of consensus in working life should give Norway an advantage in international competition.

Professor Einar Thorsrud, who died very suddenly in 1985, played a major role in the development of industrial democracy and employee participation in Norway and elsewhere. He also contributed substantially to the preparatory committee work, which led to the programme announced by our Prime Minister on the symposium organized to commemorate his name. I shall try to elaborate a little on the background of this announcement and also on Einar Thorsrud's role in this.

The phases of research and action

When Einar Thorsrud and Fred Emery of the Tavistock Institute in London started Phase A of the Industrial Democracy Programme in Norway in 1960, with co-sponsorship from the Federation of Trade Unions (LO) and the Confederation of Industry (NAF), they had a clear vision of a long-term strategy in several phases:

- Phase A: looking into the possibilities of democratization of industry through representation of workers at board level (Emery and Thorsrud, 1969).
- Phase B: improving the conditions for direct participation in decision making in an individual's own job through concrete socio-technical changes. The idea was to start experiments in selected manufacturing industries to trigger off a more general process of change in industry, and through this to prepare the ground for later changes of a similar nature in other sectors—services, public administration, the school system, etc. (Emery and Thorsrud, 1976).
- Phase C: this third phase was foreseen as a more general democratization of society. Effects in terms of democratization of the family were expected to follow from the democratization of work. Changes in political institutions—a development towards a participative society in general—were, however, seen as the long-term goal.

Results from Phase A and the first stages of Phase B have been widely published. By 1970 the feasibility of the socio-technical approach to enhanced direct participation in industry had been well demonstrated. The challenge to the labour-market organization leaders, researchers, and consultants was to develop better strategies to promote such changes. The model of successful demonstrations in selected typical industries did not work well in Norway. Further, neither unions, managers, and schools, nor researchers alone seemed able to promote a general diffusion of such ideas and experience in working life.

Einar Thorsrud, together with colleagues at the Work Research Institute and abroad, therefore, devoted their energies to developing more efficient strategies (Elden, 1979; Gustavsen, 1985). The main national partners were still the LO and the NAF. A special collective agreement between these two organizations on company development represents the latest innovation in this process (Engelstad, 1986; NAF/LO, 1986). Participation by employees in the process of change towards more participative forms of work organization is the core of this agreement. The new programme announced by the Prime Minister incorporates the experience with this agreement, and aims among other things at widening the coverage of this approach.

In 1970, however, the ideas and experience from the IDP had not penetrated to national political level. Here, the rather conventional political models for industrial democracy still dominated. Reforms like employee participation at board level, therefore, were introduced in the private sector, and to some degree also in the public one. These reforms may be well justified in a number of ways (Qvale, 1979), but they certainly also drew attention away from more basic issues linked to the rank and file employees' possibilities for participation.

The emphasis on improving the working environment in the 1970s, however, contributed strongly to maintaining momentum also in the development of participation in organizations. Psycho-social factors were added to the more conventional physical, chemical, and ergonomic ones at the outset. Thorsrud's field experiments provided the civil servants drafting the legislation with the necessary economic arguments; productivity always seemed to increase when employee participation increased through socio-technical changes. In addition, new legislation (from 1976) allowed for much wider local union and employee participation in assessing and developing the work environment (see e.g. Gustavsen and Hunnius, 1981). The general problem encountered when trying to implement the law, however, was threefold, with a need for trigger mechanisms to mobilize the rank and file organization members, a need for expertise and capacity in the companies or elsewhere once a problem was identified, and a need for support from general company and union strategy to sustain long-term development. In short, the problems were very much the same as the ones identified by Einar Thorsrud through the IDP fifteen years earlier.

What happened in the 1980s was an emerging understanding of such links, together with a belated fear for the future, within both industry and public services. The first sign of acceptance of Thorsrud's main ideas at the political level came through the nomination of members to the new Commission on Industrial Democracy and its terms of reference in 1981. The Confederation of Industry was invited to join together with independent union federations covering white-collar workers, academics, the public sector, etc. The terms stated that enhanced employee participation could become an important part of a strategy for improving the utilization of human resources and hence securing future employment, in addition to having its own value in terms of employee rights, satisfaction, etc. (Qvale, 1984).

The programme proposed unanimously by the Commission (NOU, 1985) and formally endorsed by the Government is now starting up. Its purpose is initiation of and support for local (workplace and community) development. A new centre linked to a foundation created jointly by the Government and invited organizations which cover most of the Norwegian labour market was set up in June.

At the workplace level, the emerging economic crisis in both private and public enterprises tends to bring forth new leadership in both management and unions. Here we can probably see some fruits of the extensive management and union training and joint activities following the IDP in the early 1970s, and the introduction of board-level representation and the work environment programmes in the last half of that decade. Signs of regression to the managerial methods and tactics of the past have been very few. Similarly, unions generally have been willing to support (sometimes very drastic) programmes of change. There has been a slow but quite steady move towards more flexibility in industrial relations, together with a higher degree of employee participation (Gustavsen, 1986).

Further, LO centrally has renewed its interest in working with the employers on the programme. Otherwise, one would undoubtedly see employers running such programmes unilaterally or with only local employee support. One might expect that this could create a very heavy strain on the national union system in the long run. LO also welcomes the involvement of other professions through their (independent) unions, which can give the broader basis needed. Finally, LO and other union federations are accepting more flexibility in some laws and agreements—like making the Corporate Assembly voluntary, decentralizing some decisions about working hours, etc.

In this respect one may assume that the success of the new programme for democratization will depend on professional skills, competence, and the resources made available. Personally, I think the programme's ability to mobilize (and change) the education system to support the development of working life in time will be crucial. As may be known, Einar Thorsrud devoted considerable efforts from the 1970s to preparing the educational institutions for this, first at the level of vocational training, then throughout the system for the education of seamen, and, in his last years, at university level, using his Chair at Oslo University as a means of entry into this difficult field.

It seems that one can be fairly optimistic about the political conditions for future democratization of working life in Norway. A national programme of the kind starting now may be seen either as top-level sanctioning of what goes on locally, or as an initiative which can have direct effects locally.

In Thorsrud's terminology (1981), one may assume there has also been a learning process at national level. So when the industrial democracy issue appears again on the agenda, it is *not* in the form of 'back to square one', following a shift in political regime, for example. It is more a question of building upon earlier, largely common experience. The biggest weakness of this approach, where changes in national institutions take place to support local development, is probably the slowness of progress. One can easily foresee a development where national institutions break up because of local pressure for swift change. In the centralized and generally non-pluralistic Norwegian society (see e.g. IDE, 1981) this could be very threatening. On the other hand, the limited size of the society and the working population, and its relative homogeneity, may be assets in this connection and give the possibility of a balance between change and stability. Stressing this optimistic perspective certainly is in tune with Einar Thorsrud's way of thinking.

References

Elden, M. (1979), 'Three Generations of Work Democracy Experiments in Norway', in C. Cooper and E. Mumford (eds.), *The Quality of Working Life in Eastern and Western Europe* (London: Associated Business Press).

Emery, F. E. and Thorsrud, E. (1969), *Form and Content in Industrial Democracy* (London: Tavistock).

—— —— (1976), *Democracy at Work* (Leiden: Nijhoff).

Engelstad, P. H. (1986), 'Humanisation of Work in Norway in the Private and Public Sectors', paper presented at the *International Conference on Productivity and the Future of Work*, German Productivity Center, Munich, Oct.

Gustavsen, B. (1985), 'Workplace Reform and Democratic Dialogue', *Economic and Industrial Democracy*, 6: 461–79.

—— (1986), 'Evolving Patterns of Enterprise Organisation: The Move towards Greater Flexibility', *International Labour Review*, 125(4) (July–Aug.).

—— and Hunnius, G. (1981), *New Patterns of Work Reform: The Case of Norway* (Oslo: Oslo University Press).

IDE International Research Group (1981), *European Industrial Relations* (Oxford: Clarendon Press).

NAF/LO (1986), *Company Development Agreement* (Oslo: The Norwegian Employers' Federation).

NOU (1985), *Videreutviklingen av Bedriftsdemokratiet (The Further Development of Industrial Democracy)* (Oslo: NOU).

Qvale, T. U. (1979), 'Industrial Democracy in Norway: Experience from the Boardroom Approach', *Journal of General Management*, 6(7) (Autumn).

—— (1984), *Industrial Democracy: Current Overseas Trends and Developments* (Canberra: Department of Employment).

Thorsrud, E. (1981), 'Policy Making as a Learning Process', in A. G. Cherns, R. Sinclair, and W. I. Jenkins (eds.), *Social Science and Government* (London: Tavistock).

9

The Scandinavian Challenge: Strategies for Work and Learning

GRO HARLEM BRUNDTLAND

INDUSTRIAL democracy and worker participation have been and will continue to be central concerns of the labour movement in Norway. Today they are national concerns largely shared by all involved parties.

The content of the concept of industrial democracy, however, has been changing as a consequence of the experience we gain and the historical development of society. The underlying values are still the same. We want to create democracy in the workplace so that employees can have security of employment and a healthy working environment so that they can exert influence over their work situation, learn as they work, have equal opportunities irrespective of sex or ethnic group, take part in company decision making, have a fair share of the wealth created, and find a good balance between their working and private lives.

In general, we see progress in industrial democracy as a very important part of the overall strengthening of democracy in our society.

We believe that the social and cultural structures in Norway have given us favourable conditions for developing industrial democracy. Our Federation of Trade Unions, the LO, and the Employers' Confederation, the NAF, negotiated the first nation-wide collective agreement on participation and joint information procedures as early as in 1935. The need to join forces in the reconstruction of the country after the Second World War intensified the feeling of mutual interest between employers and unions. By this stage a system for the peaceful settlement of conflictual issues by means of annual or biannual collective bargaining had been well established in most sectors of working life. In the post-war period these agreements were then extended to cover participation in productivity improvement schemes, and more generally participation in joint consultation and information bodies at the company level.

Around 1960, however, unrest was felt in the labour movement, caused by the growing discrepancy between the democratic values in society and the visible lack of democracy within industry. The rationalization drive of the post-war period had provided the economic basis for the welfare state, but the opportunities for employees to participate in decision making at their workplaces actually had been reduced for large groups. At the same time the level of general education in the work-force had been considerably raised.

The known models for industrial democracy at that time were in the sphere of union rights, bargaining, and workers' representation on the board of directors. Industrial democracy had its strong advocates in the Norwegian trade union movement of the time, and their efforts led to the Company Act of 1973, which secured employees one-third of the seats on company boards.

However important this reform, Einar Thorsrud had a vision that pointed in a somewhat different direction. He saw clearly that changes in property rights and formal authority, though necessary, would by no means be sufficient to secure industrial democracy in the full sense of the word. Around 1960, Thorsrud appeared on the national labour scene suggesting to the employers' and employees' organizations, the LO and the NAF, that they should start a joint action research programme on the issue of industrial democracy. Referring to theories developed at the Tavistock Institute in London, he proposed a new model for industrial democracy. Thorsrud insisted that industrial democracy should mean something concrete for the individual employee. If jobs could be designed and work organized to allow for more decision making and learning *on the job*, employees could better make full use of the possibilities inherent in representative democracy in the workplace, Thorsrud claimed. He suggested that the two main organizations, the LO and the NAF, should try to utilize their relatively high degree of mutual trust to explore the opportunities for improving the conditions for direct participation in the work situation, for shared decision making and greater individual responsibility. Thus for the first time the Tavistock researchers' ideas of adapting technology and work organization to human needs were set into the context of industrial democracy.

The resulting research and development programme was organized under the joint auspices of the LO and the NAF. For the first time in their history these two organizations were using social science to explore new possibilities for the workplace. Thorsrud, together with his Tavistock colleague Fred Emery, designed a research project that could secure both freedom for local experimentation *and* centralized learning in the two labour-market organizations. Internationally the initiative was met with great interest.

From this start in the 1960s, many lines of development, both nationally and internationally, can be drawn. The first four field experiments showed that the ideas were fruitful. The idea of technological determinisms, which had been guiding the thinking in the post-war period, was gradually losing its hold. Plant-level changes in job design, work organization, and production technology showed dramatic increases in the degree of employee involvement, in employees' ability to handle demanding tasks, and in productivity. Workers who participated in these new developments and who discovered that the scope of their jobs had increased reacted very positively.

The publishing of the results of the research by Emery and Thorsrud and their colleagues at the Work Research Institute generated an immediate and widespread interest both in Norway and abroad.

With support from the main employers' and employees organizations a strategy for implementing the suggested changes in Norwegian industry was developed. Throughout the 1970s the strategy was modified several times, as we saw the methods used did not give us the speed of change we wanted, and which we thought was needed.

It was also with a touch of envy that we saw the Swedish Employers' Confederation promote a very rapid diffusion of 'our' new work organization concepts in Sweden. Volvo, SAAB–Scania, and others demonstrated to the rest of the world the viability of Thorsrud and Emery's ideas in large-scale manufacturing industries.

In spite of the relatively great efforts devoted in Norway to demonstration projects, information, training of shop stewards and managers, seminars, workshops, etc., the ideas did not penetrate beyond a relatively small group of enterprises.

In land-based Norwegian industry the focus in the 1970s shifted more towards the quality of the working environment and the issue of worker representation at board level. One of the reasons was undoubtedly the fact that the 1970s was a period of radical social and political reform, perhaps the most radical in modern Norwegian history. In 1973 employees were granted access to company boards. Again we found that the level of agreement on basic issues and of trust was high enough to enable us to institute this reform without serious problems and conflicts. Having the employees represented on the board of directors is today seen by both sides as a positive way of improving communication in the enterprise and removing undue suspicion.

When the old Workers Protection Act came up for review, following serious concern over occupational health problems, the Government also chose to advance the industrial democracy issue. Based on the research initiated by Einar Thorsrud on organizational and technological choice and participation, and Swedish research on stress at work, we could create a completely new Work Environment Act which included several innovations. Section 12 on psycho-social factors and the general idea of worker participation in assessing, planning, and improving the work environment, stem from these sources.

Following the passing of the Act the Government also contributed substantial sums to financing a general upgrading of the quality of the working environment in industry, to the Factory Inspectorate, and to research and development in this sphere.

In the 1970s also our large, new offshore-oil industry developed. This dynamic industry presented major challenges in terms of securing safety, pollution control, and the social rights of employees.

On this basis, the largest industry-oriented social research and development programme in the country's history was launched. Oil companies were invited to participate and to contribute with economic resources and expertise. Steering committees, in which unions were also represented, were set up. Altogether this greatly increased technological and organizational competence and capacity. Thus in a period of fifteen years this industry developed from a rather problematic position in terms of safety, working environment, and conditions, to become a leader in these fields.

In 1980 the issue of the further promotion of industrial democracy again was placed on the political agenda by a joint Labour Party–Trade Union committee of which I was a member. We observed that, in spite of all the efforts during the previous two decades, there still was a long way to go. Companies' organizational structure had become more complex and frequently more bureaucratic, the environment had become more dynamic, and the workers felt their opportunities to participate in decision making and company strategy matters were too limited. They also felt their resources were not being fully utilized.

A new clause in the national collective agreement between the LO and the NAF had, however, just been negotiated. It set up the framework for joint company development and also established a number of support functions for the central organizations. Thus a completely new approach had been launched.

Later, after becoming Prime Minister, I appointed a new commission to look into the further democratization of working life. The commission was given broad terms of reference: to review all avenues and make recommendations that could promote both participation and productivity.

At this stage—1981—it had also become clear that the future prospects of a number of our traditional industries were rather gloomy. The oil revenues and the oil industry would not be able to replace the jobs that were likely to be lost here. Thus large groups of employees were under the threat of unemployment.

The growth in the service sector on the other hand had made the industrial relations of the country more complex. The LO and the NAF no longer dominated them completely. Moreover, the Government felt that the active support of the new occupations and their federations was needed in order to achieve our national objectives.

The new commission, named after its chairman, Olav Brubakken, therefore was composed of representatives from two white-collar union federations in addition to the LO and the NAF. The Confederation of Industry and the Association for Smaller Enterprises (Norges Håndverkerforbund) were also invited, demonstrating the shift in political thinking. Industrial democracy was leaving the more narrow domain of rights and welfare and entering the broader domain of industrial policy.

It was an important aspect that industrial democracy should lead to the development and better utilization of human resources. We also knew that bureaucratic aspects of company organization and unprofessional, undemocratic management styles were often major obstacles to real participation for employees, and in fact prevented them from using their competence and abilities. Formal representation of employees at board level and collective agreements cannot fully compensate for such frustrations. Therefore, we also included in the commission experts in personnel management and organization design.

Einar Thorsrud's idea of building industrial democracy into the organization of the enterprise, rather than having two parallel systems, was incorporated from the outset.

A change of Government shortly after did not affect the terms of work of the commission, again demonstrating the high degree of consensus in this sphere within this country.

Early in 1985 the commission presented its unanimous recommendations. Looking to the future, it observed that the degree of change in technology and in the environments of enterprises would increase dramatically. Accordingly, the commission proposed an increased emphasis on changes to improve the competence and performance of the organizations and at the same time promote employee participation. It pointed to the need for professional management and for better utilization of external resources to improve internal competence.

The commission found that further changes in the proportion of employees on the boards of directors was not strategically the most important point. The main breakthrough in this respect came when the workers first took their seats on the boards in 1973. However, the commission proposed greater flexibility in how to organize board-level representation. These proposals will be presented to Parliament later this year [i.e. 1987].

The subtitle of this conference, the Scandinavian Challenge, has a double meaning for us. As a result of the experience we have gained and, from what we have learnt abroad, I think we are in a fortunate position in several respects here in Scandinavia.

A number of aspects that we take for granted—like a stable industrial relations system, a high degree of mutual trust, a long tradition of peaceful resolution of conflicts and problem solving—cannot always be taken for granted in other countries.

The sources of this social stability and the conditions for industrial democracy that it fosters, lie in a fruitful interplay between economic and political life. The ideals of economic and industrial democracy will more easily spread and grow in a stable democratic system where common welfare is seen as the ultimate goal of politics. Trade unions in Scandinavia do not act only as representatives of the work-force *vis-à-vis* employers, but as spokesmen in the political sphere as well. Thus they further and strengthen democratic ideals in economic life.

The Scandinavian challenge may also be regarded from a different angle. There is also a challenge *to* the Scandinavian countries *from* the rest of the world. We are aware that we are fairly slow in making changes in our working lives and hence in adjusting to new situations. We have seen how in other countries unilateral management initiatives and sometimes quite ruthless actions altered a single company in a very short time. We have also been able to benefit from the experience of special cases abroad where strategies and ways of working similar to those we favour have been applied more thoroughly and faster than in Norway so far.

For the Norwegian labour movement, and the Government, it is therefore now a major challenge to capitalize effectively on this country's consensus and proven industrial relations structure. We need a rapid national mobilization of resources without endangering basic human and political values. Our idea is that the employees' and employers' organizations shall play a key role in this, with support from the Government. We feel we have the attitudes, the experience, and most of the infrastructure to manage a large programme at the national level. We need, however, to engage the support of other institutions in society too: the education system, the research community, and other public services.

Today we also see that the whole public sector is in need of change. Rigidity caused by bureaucratization has made this sector expensive. Also, it has too limited opportunities for participation for large groups of employees.

We also find, however, that the competence and capacity we have built into our research institutions tend to be used mainly by the enterprises and local unions that have a tradition for such co-operation. The smaller enterprises, which provide the bulk of employment outside the public sector, do not yet seem to be in a position to benefit. In the future, however, we expect all sectors of the economy to need the ability to utilize research results. Therefore, a major effort should be directed towards smaller enterprises.

This challenge requires initiatives on two fronts. We must deepen our understanding of social processes in a changing world, and we must enhance our ability to take action to promote organizational change and development. 1987 is the year when we launch the most ambitious social science research programme in Norway to this day: the 'LOS' programme focusing on leadership, organization, and co-ordination problems in modern society. The main objective of this programme is the investigation of the complex interdependence of the public and private sector; the discussion of the bargaining processes in the labour market; and a deeper understanding of work life participation.

In addition, I can announce today that the Government this autumn will propose a programme for the further democratization of our working life on the basis of the Brubakken Commission. We will invite the employees' and employers' organizations to participate together with the Government in the creation of a centre to carry out this programme. Its main functions will be

- general information and networking
- initiation of local development

- organization of support to work life
- financing support activities.

The idea is that the programme should provide key personnel to support local activities. It should strengthen more direct co-operation between working life and the educational system, and create new links between industry and research and between industry and local community administration. We have the resources needed for the programme available in the country today. The main task lies in organizing these resources into more co-ordinated efforts.

The details of the new programme have yet to be worked out, and will largely be left to those appointed on the board of the resource centre that will be established in a few months.

The Government is happy to make the announcement at this international conference. It also gives us an occasion to confirm our indebtedness to Einar Thorsrud, who took a leading role in the development of industrial democracy and the quality of working life in Norway. We know Einar Thorsrud had an extensive international network, he contributed to positive development in other countries, including the Third World, and he brought home inspiration, insight, and competence from numerous other countries. I hope the conference this week will contribute again to strengthening international research and collaboration, and hope we can meet in a few years and observe that our joint efforts to promote human values in working life are indeed meeting with success.

PART III

RECENT THEORETICAL
DEVELOPMENTS

Outline of Part III

THIS section will at first sight appeal more to the scholar than to the practitioner, for it contains chapters in which various authors 'take stock' of recent advances or trends in social science thinking on a variety of manifestations of organizational democracy. Nevertheless, some of the following reflections on theory may be quite helpful to those who, either as managers or management advisers, or as works councillors or unionists, try to further or maintain certain forms of participation, co-determination, or self-management. After all, is not one of the main contributions which scholars provide for practitioners the supply of concepts, theories, or frames of reference, to be used as tools to organize their thinking about the intricacies and complexities of the social life they encounter in the course of their work?

Sharon McCarthy puts the intriguing question: what about the causes or reasons for *non*-participation rather than participation? She is surprised that, in spite of all the theories on participative management which postulate more productivity and/or a higher morale through more participation, so little is actually practised. It is remarkable that there is not more research on this question. One might answer that, if you are treating the problem of participation, you are implicitly dealing also with *non*-participation. But this is certainly only true to some extent, because different conditions may be operative at the 'positive' and the 'negative' ends of the participation continuum.

Annie Borzeix and Danièle Linhart question some of the unspoken presuppositions in discussions about participation in organizations. The French debate is very rich in this respect, but the existing models do not fit the historical reality of recent developments. The authors propose a more concrete approach and, in doing so, offer insights linked to those of other French contributions in this volume (Tixier, Bernoux).

Gerd Schienstock is taking stock of various theoretical approaches to issues of participation, co-determination, etc. He points out that the main focus should be on *organizational change*. He distinguishes three perspectives: systems theory, the Marxist approach, and the actor-oriented theory. He opts for the third type, which is able to explain the new coalition between capital and labour. It is worth while in this connection to refer the reader to Chapter 1 by Bolle de Bal, who prefers a twin-pronged approach using both functionalism (which can be seen as a special kind of systems theory) and the action perspective. In fact, many other authors in this book similarly combine elements of various models of analysis to deal with the many-sided problems they set out to study.

Silvia Gherardi, Antonio Strati, and Brian A. Turner enable the reader to get the feel of a relatively new brand of organization theory known as 'organizational symbolism', and sketch what industrial or organizational democracy looks like in the light of this perspective. They stress the role of culture(s), but, unlike the conventional treatment of this concept in anthropology and sociology, 'culture' in their view is differentiated and volatile.

10

The Dilemma of Non-participation

SHARON MCCARTHY

THERE is continuing awareness that programmes for employee participation are difficult to instigate and maintain (e.g. Rosenstein, 1970; Witte, 1980; IDE, 1981; Gamson and Levin, 1984; Russell, 1984). Programmes are developed which demand a wide range of participation levels and meet with various problems. A major problem is that many employees, when offered the responsibility of participation, choose not to become involved. As Leitko et al., (1985) note, 'Nonparticipation is the modal response of workers to worker participation schemes' (p. 285).

An exact definition of non-participation is important in clarifying the issues surrounding it. Non-participation can result because people do not want to participate and because they are not given opportunities to participate. In this chapter, it will refer to an employee's conscious choice not to become involved in workplace participation.

It should be emphasized that such a choice can occur for many reasons. Sometimes these reasons are individual, personal opinions about participation, such that the person just does not want to participate. Sometimes they may be more structural reasons, as participation may have costs to the employee. For example, being away from the work site for participation may cause the employee problems with co-workers or supervisors. In this chapter, the choice not to participate will be considered non-participation regardless of the underlying reasons for the choice.

The issue of non-participation is a serious one for theorists and practitioners. Practically, many intervention schemes rely on voluntary participation, and non-participation can threaten a programme's viability. Organizational change efforts provide a good example of this type of intervention. Lack of participation can hamper efforts to carry out an organizational change programme when basic aspects of the programme rely on voluntary involvement. Programmes may also be evaluated on the basis of how many people are involved. Practitioners who are called in to set up a programme often find that participation rate is an important component of success.

Theoretically, the question of non-participation has received little attention. There are some theories about why people do participate, many of which support the implicit suggestion that non-participation is the inverse of participation. This linear assumption about participation would suggest that the opposite of conditions that foster participation would lead to non-participation. To date, research has not focused on non-linear aspects of non-participation. This chapter, as a review of the current literature, will reflect the assumption of the linear form between participation and non-participation. Evidence for linearity or non-linearity remains on the agenda for future research.

With little specific research on non-participation, it is important to look at participation theory and research for theoretical clues about non-participation. This research has limitations. It does very little to explain non-participation directly, and instead must be used to set a context for it. Many of the studies discussed are correlational, and do not 'explain' participation, but instead show relationships between participation and other factors. A great deal of correlational research has been done on participation, and the results are important. However, these results were never intended to explain non-participation and are discussed here because almost no research exists on non-participation *per se*. Participation research does describe situations where non-participation might be more likely to occur, and factors that might influence non-participation.

The purpose of this chapter is to discuss non-participation from the perspective of the four major schools of participative thought described by Greenberg (1975) and Dachler and Wilpert (1978). Some of the schools of thought are more explicit than others on the question of non-participation, and some researchers fit more clearly into one school than another. The research findings described here have been grouped by school, reflecting the philosophical perspective of the research. There is a great deal of overlap between the schools, and some research is relevant to questions raised by more than one school of thought. Throughout the chapter, research is generally presented under one school, based on the perspective of the research and researcher involved.

The first of these divergent perspectives is called 'the management school' by Greenberg and 'productivity and efficiency' by Dachler and Wilpert. These programmes do not challenge basic management prerogatives, and simply seek to relieve worker dissatisfaction and morale problems through participation. The programmes are typically lower level (often shop floor) and have a narrowly defined scope of issues.

The second major school of thought is called 'humanistic psychology' by Greenberg and 'human growth and development' by Dachler and Wilpert. These programmes are motivated by a desire to enhance the well-being of the individual, by promoting the creativity, self-esteem, and ego strength which are assumed to accompany participation. Although one goal of these programmes is to foster industrial efficiency and productivity, an underlying assumption is that this will occur because the worker has become a more mature, self-actualized individual.

The third major school of thought is called 'democratic theory' by both

Greenberg and Dachler and Wilpert. These theorists see participation not only as a means to an end, but also as an end in itself. They advocate a change in the level of participation at work because it will transfer to a generalized greater participation in social institutions and society. The goal of programmes designed in this spirit is to create a strongly democratic society, characterized by active, participative citizens.

The final major school of thought is called 'participatory left' by Greenberg and 'socialist theory' by Dachler and Wilpert. These theorists see participatory programmes as a means to an end, with the goal being to change the overall structure of ownership to a collective base. From this perspective, the role of participatory programmes is primarily to educate workers to class consciousness.

Obviously, some participative programmes are a mix or hybrid of these schools of thought. What is important to recognize is that each school 'uses the term participation in . . . fundamentally different ways . . .' (Greenberg, 1975: 205). Dachler and Wilpert stress the fact that each of the schools arises out of different ideologies and value systems. Each school hopes for different consequences for the worker and the organization, and thus evaluates the 'success' of the programme differently.

There are limitations to using any framework, and the framework provided by Greenberg and Dachler and Wilpert is no exception. As mentioned, there is considerable overlap between the schools of thought described, making it difficult to assign research to one school or another. Further, the schools of thought do reflect levels of participation. At a gross level of analysis, management and humanistic perspectives deal primarily with individual and group-level participation, while democratic theory and the participatory left perspectives deal with system-wide issues of participation. No single school of thought deals with all the issues of participation; to do this, an integration of the schools is crucial. Dachler and Wilpert (1978) deal with this issue, and future research on non-participation will also need to confront the multitude of levels of non-participation. The fact that Greenberg and Dachler and Wilpert's schools of thought are not independent may be seen as a limitation, but the framework is a powerful one, and useful as an initial organizing tool for ideas about non-participation.

The management school perspective

The managerial school of participation research suggests two main reasons why people don't participate. First, there are expected to be individual differences among people, leading some to desire participation more than others. Secondly, certain features of participation make it inefficient, perhaps causing both managers and workers to be reluctant to get involved. Much of the research done in the United States on participation falls into the managerial school. This review will first cover individual differences, and then inefficient features of participation.

Individual differences

A variety of individual differences have been used to explain participation level. Vroom's work (1960) is perhaps the most well known. Vroom studied first-, second-, and third-line supervisors in a delivery service company. He found that level of participation and satisfaction were positively correlated, and that those with high needs for independence showed a stronger correlation between satisfaction and participation than those with low needs for independence. In supervisors with low independence needs, participation had little effect on job satisfaction. Those with highly authoritarian personalities showed a weaker relationship between job satisfaction and participation. Vroom's data has been interpreted to show that participation should 'increase job satisfaction substantially among those with high independence needs and "non-authoritarian" personalities' (Blumberg, 1968: 108). Although studies have not always replicated Vroom's findings (Tosi, 1970), Vroom's results would suggest that non-participation might occur more frequently in individuals with low needs for independence and highly authoritarian personalities.

Runyon (1973) studied locus of control, to determine whether internals and externals would differ in their reactions to management styles. He concludes that internals will be happier and more job involved with participative management. Externals were found to be happier with directive supervisors, and to have low job involvement regardless of supervisory style.

Efforts to determine the effect of IQ on participation have been scarce. Calvin *et al.* (1957) looked at supervisory style and group problem-solving behaviour. Their results generally supported the notion that groups made up of bright individuals would perform better under a 'permissive democratic social climate' (participative) and 'dull' groups would perform better under an authoritarian climate. Note the emphasis on performance, common to studies done from a managerial perspective. Few of the reported differences in this study were significant, and it is doubtful whether generalizations can be made from it, since workers are seldom grouped on the basis of IQ.

Another individual difference is suggested by Alutto and Belasco (1972), who hypothesize that individuals have a specific level of decision involvement which is most satisfying. By asking workers about their current level of decision making and their desired level of involvement, they arrive at three categories of workers: those in decisional deprivation, those in decisional equilibrium, and those in decisional saturation. Thus, careless implementation of a participation programme may simply result in many more people in the 'decisional saturation' category. Alutto and Belasco warn that adding participation when employees are already decisionally saturated may prove 'highly disfunctional' (1972: 124). The decision not to participate may occur in situations where employees are already faced with more decision making than they find comfortable.

The inefficiencies of participation

The actual process of participation is not always easy, efficient, and enjoyable. At best, participation is associated with a sense of self-efficacy and power. At worst, it can be a long, tedious, inefficient, and frustrating process. Several theorists have identified aspects of the process of participation which might actually discourage participation from occurring. For example, many management school researchers have hypothesized that participation would lead to unnecessary and uncomfortable levels of conflict. Derber (1970) comments on reluctance to participate, and mentions 'getting into arguments' (p. 133) as a negative factor for participants. Disagreements are seen as both an asset and a liability by Maier (1967). He suggests that another variable, the leader's perception of disagreement, can make the difference between disagreements resulting in hard feelings or innovative solutions.

A systematic study of conflict in participative decision making was undertaken by the Decisions in Organizations (DIO) group (1983). In a review of fifty-six decisions, results show conflict to be highest in the developmental stages of the decision, when alternatives are generated and screened. This finding is confounded with the fact that this is also usually the longest phase of decision making.

Another efficiency factor is the issue of supervision—the way in which the group leader manages the process. Maier believes that leadership is a determining factor in the success of group problem solving. The nature of the leader can determine whether the process is satisfying or frustrating to members. A good leader can prevent a group from becoming 'solution minded' too early, a bad leader can allow the group to drift towards conflicting interests and the resulting inability to make a co-operative decision.

Falcione (1974) found that subordinate satisfaction was a function of participation in decision making, but that the credibility of the supervisor mediated this relationship. Those workers who perceived their supervisor to be credible (trustworthy, expert, and have good intentions) were more satisfied with their supervisor. For these workers there was a strong correlation between satisfaction with supervisor and participation opportunities. For workers who felt their supervisor had low credibility, there was no relationship between participative opportunities and satisfaction with the supervisor. Non-participation may thus be more likely to occur in situations where the supervisor is perceived with little trust or respect.

Another efficiency factor is time. It seems possible that workers are frustrated by the time participation takes, and are thus reluctant to become involved. Strauss (1963), Maier (1967), and Derber (1970) state that time is a problem, although Derber admits that he has uncovered no systematic research on this issue. Marchington and Loveridge (1979) discuss managers' concern with time and their reluctance to use participation because of the need for quick decisions. The one study that does measure time as a factor in participative decision making is the DIO (1983) study, which traces fifty-six actual decisions in European companies. Their results showed no 'systematic relationship between method of decision making and the length of the decision making process, . . . apparently, participation does not automatically entail great delays' (1983: 15). In spite of these findings, it is clear that managers perceive participation to take longer, and workers may choose not to get involved because of either perception or 'reality'.

In summary, some non-participation is seen as inevitable by researchers from the management school. Levels of participation are determined by individual differences, and there will always be some individuals who are not interested in participation. Further, since some features of participation make it inefficient, non-participation is expected as a logical response in some circumstances.

The humanistic psychology school perspective

Theories by humanistic psychologists rely on the assumption that people are growing, striving, achieving individuals. The authors in question do not typically address the specific issue of non-participation. They feel it is a temporary condition, which will disappear once early resistance to change is over, and if the programme provides a genuine participation experience.

Argyris (1957) describes resistance to change which occurs when employees have become thoroughly indoctrinated by the traditional authoritarian, hierarchical system of organization. Changing over to a new, less autocratic style of management may be difficult in this situation. Argyris says, 'If the employees have learned to become dependent and submissive, a transition period is needed for the change to a different leadership pattern' (p. 204). He continues, noting that Reimer (1954) and others 'confirm the conclusion that employees and managers may resist employee-centered leadership because of the existing human relations climate' (p. 205).

The ability to cope with change is a variable extensively studied by Lewin (1947, 1952), who felt that processes of change needed to give great attention to the readiness of individuals to accept the new ideas. For example, Blum (1968) describes how early members of the Scott Bader Commonwealth actually went on strike to protest against the introduction of self-government. Trist *et al.* (1977), looking at the acceptance of semi-autonomous work groups in an American coal-mine, mention resistance to change as a factor influencing who participates. They note: 'the members within each area of the mine must come to terms in their own way with this process of minewide transformation . . . unquestionably, many, often older workers . . . cannot or do not wish to take advantage of the opportunities to learn' (1977: 232). Likert (1961), discussing the introduction of participation, notes that short-range reactions of hostility, resentment, and apathy may result when change occurs too quickly.

The second humanist explanation for reluctance to participate is that the programmes offered do not provide a genuine experience of participation. Verba (1961) calls this pseudo-participation, which may lead employees to distrust the programme, or see it as a sham. Workers may feel manipulated by participative schemes, or feel that the schemes are merely a gimmick. Falcione (1974) hypothesizes that workers who have supervisors who are not 'credible' would be most likely to come to these conclusions, although he does not systematically evaluate the question. Derber (1970) also mentions the possibility of manipulation and co-optation as a problem with participation. He says, 'Participation implicates workers in management decisions before they are applied and therefore makes it more difficult for the workers later to criticize managers if they are unhappy with the outcome' (p. 132). Pateman (1983) wonders whether participation schemes are likely to lead to democratization, or whether 'they merely prove to be a more sophisticated means of controlling the labour force? (p. 111).

Strauss (1963) suggests that increased expectations and subsequent disillusionment with participation may occur, and this process may result in less participation. As workers gain experience with participation, they may begin to desire a greater influence than management wants to allow. This may cause management to ignore participation or refuse requests which seem reasonable to workers. As this happens, workers begin to see participation as a fraud. Such pseudo-participation can prove more damaging than not allowing participation at all (Likert, 1961: 119 ff.; Walker, 1975; Lammers *et al.*, 1987).

From a humanistic psychology perspective, these questions are critical. For true gains in development to be made, employees must be confident that the participation scheme is not simply a management tool.

Humanist researchers, then, take two perspectives on non-participation. First, it may be seen as temporary, initial resistance. Secondly, it may be seen as a reasonable response to participation which is not genuine.

A third possibility also exists, based on the belief that participation provides an opportunity for self-actualization. Maslow (1965) presents a hierarchical system of needs. These needs range from primary, basic needs for love, affection, and belonging, to higher-level needs for self-esteem and self-actualization. He argues that in industrial society, basic needs are satisfied, and 'blocking the full development of mental health is the organization of worklife, and organization of work that prevents, in particular, the satisfaction of self-esteem and self-actualization' (Greenberg, 1975: 196). The introduction of participation programmes is seen as an important way of providing challenging and self-actualizing opportunities for employees.

As Greenberg points out, Maslow 'somewhat naively, assumes relative affluence satisfies physiological and security needs for most . . .' (p. 196). It is possible that individuals who decline to participate have not yet satisfied their basic needs. According to Maslow, employees who still have resolved needs for love and a sense of belonging would not be open to participation as a self-actualizing experience, since the fulfilment of needs proceeds hierarchically.

The democratic theory perspective

Democratic theorists feel participation is a learned behaviour. Non-participation occurs when individuals have had little experience with participation. The learning process, fundamental to maintaining the dynamic of participation, has not occurred (Pateman, 1970). Prominent theories of democracy in the 1960s argued that some people were just more naturally suited to participation, and suggested that it might not even be a good idea for everyone to participate. Pateman counters by noting, 'The empirical evidence showed that those least likely to participate are also least likely to have an opportunity to learn how to do so in the workplace or elsewhere . . . the social pattern of participation reflected not nature, but the structure of authority in liberal democratic institutions' (Pateman, 1983: 109). Democratic theorists feel all individuals can and should have an active part in their own self-governance, and non-participation occurs only when individuals have not had opportunities to learn how to participate.

Witte (1980) also contributes research on participation in the spirit of democratic theory. His study of a US high-fidelity equipment manufacturer supports Pateman's notion that many individuals have had little experience with participation. Talking to people about participation, he found that many had never considered the idea of participating in the hiring of supervisors or firing of fellow workers. He says, 'it was apparent to me and to the other interviewers that this was the first time most of those interviewed had ever thought of the idea of decisions being made outside the traditional hierarchical chain' (1980: 40).

Witte's research also supports the democratic theorists' idea that participation leads to greater participation. He found that activists in the participation programme were significantly more likely to have previous participation experiences in the political realm. Witte notes, 'Activists are much more politicized than the typical worker' (p. 49). Witte's research would suggest that non-participation would be greater with employees who are less active in politics or other aspects of self-governance.

Mansbridge (1973, 1982) emerges as a helpful critic of democratic theory, by studying some of the problems which occur as individuals try to learn to participate. One such problematic aspect of participation is emotion. As Mansbridge notes, participation requires face-to-face interaction, and the ability of individuals to 'get along with people' (1973: 358). Mansbridge argues that 'participatory groups often crack under the strain of emotional confrontations' (p. 359). Participants become strongly attached to their contributions, and it is often hard to separate criticism for an idea from criticism for an individual. Mansbridge (1982) studied participants in New England town meetings and in a democratically run counselling centre. Her research shows people become very tense and anxious before participative meetings, which she suggests is partially due to their desire to avoid conflict. Over time, anxiety and fear of conflict caused non-participation as members chose to remain silent or not to attend meetings.

In summary, democratic theorists view participation in work as an important component of developing a more democratic society overall. Where non-participation exists, it should be managed by teaching employees the skills and techniques of democracy. Democratic theorists would expect that employees who have few opportunities for participation outside work will also be more likely to decline the responsibility of participation at their workplace.

The perspective from the participatory left

It is important to recall that the participatory left views participation as a means of creating a more equal society. The participatory left is concerned with political change and sees participation as a way to achieve it. For many, the key issue is control of ownership, and a large literature exists on self-management.

The participatory left perspective allows several hypotheses to be inferred about why people choose not to participate. The most obvious is that most participative programmes do not provide substantial changes in the structure of ownership. If being separated from ownership and the means of control results in alienation (by definition), then participatory left theorists would argue that workers in traditional firms would be too alienated to realize the need for participation. This objective definition of alienation acknowledges that people may think they are satisfied with their work. Workers feel that they are happy and see no need to become more involved in decisions at work.

Programmes like job enrichment, autonomous work groups, and greater participation are seen by many from the participatory left as strategies by management to co-opt and manipulate employees. Workers who fail to participate may be those who recognize this manipulation and feel participation will only benefit management.

Hunnius comments on this issue, noting that many unions are opposed to increased worker involvement in decision making. He points out that job satisfaction research shows that workers evaluate their jobs partially 'by comparing their jobs to other jobs they have had or to jobs their friends now have . . . If that is true, it would seem to follow that . . . elimination of differences within groups can be expected to become a priority for employers' (1979: 297–8).

The participatory left feel that social and political constraints function to strongly deter self-management. Dachler and Wilpert comment that recent writers have described 'the prevailing capitalistic conditions and value frameworks which serve as obstacles to socialist revolutionary change in Western industrialized nations' (1978: 6). Those from the participatory left would argue that people are reluctant to participate because the social system does not value or reward participation. Greenberg discusses the work of Gramsci, who was troubled by the failure of socialist revolutions in Europe in the 1920s. 'Gramsci rightly saw that given objective conditions for change, change would not take place as long as and to the extent that the world-view and perspectives of workers were locked into capitalist frameworks, where capitalist values and goals seemed common-sensical' (1975: 202).

A few examples exist of worker participation that has been integrated into the political and economic system of a country. Yugoslav self-management provides a good example, where, as Rus notes, 'the goals of the Yugoslav self-management are explicitly political. They are directed towards such a distribution of political power as will make possible the establishment of the long-term interests of the working class' (1979: 223).

Yet Yugoslav programmes have not been overwhelmingly embraced by workers. Research has shown that management still tends to dominate decision making (Kolaja, 1965; Obradović, 1975, Bertsch and Obradović, 1979), and that worker influence has been limited (Rus, 1979). Recent results show management to be four times as influential as the nearest contender, the superintendents. Management is 'over 200 times more influential than the least powerful group (shopfloor workers)' (Bertsch and Obradović, 1979: 325).

In Israel, political and ethical beliefs support the kibbutz system, an egalitarian work setting. Research by Tannenbaum *et al.* (1974) shows that workers in kibbutz plants show a discrepancy between how much influence they want and how much they actually have, 'but the discrepancy is relatively small in kibbutz plants compared to elsewhere' (Tannenbaum, 1976: 83). Tannenbaum also notes that 'Labor–management conflict in kibbutz is virtually non-existent' (p. 84). These findings would support the belief of the participatory left that ownership and ideological structure are critical to genuine participation.

Other attempts to introduce participation in Israel have been less successful, as reported by Rosenstein (1970). He describes a continuing effort to involve workers in the management of the employee-owned Histadrut industries. Although a partial goal of these industries was 'a social mission of creating a just and egalitarian society' (p. 170), the system has repeatedly resisted attempts at greater worker involvement in management. Managers have been reluctant to accept worker participation, and workers have not expressed much interest in greater participation.

Theorists from the participatory left are aiming at a complete realignment of capitalist values and a redefinition of social relationships. The fact that workers may currently seem reluctant to participate is not critical, because the participatory left believes in the strength of the political and economic system to influence individual behaviour. From their perspective, when the system changes, people will become less alienated and more likely to participate. The system can change, because there are some people actively interested in greater participation, and these individuals can serve as the ideological core for increasing participation.

Discussion

Two questions will be addressed in this discussion. First, why has non-participation received so little research attention? Secondly, what kinds of question are raised by each of these schools of thought, which might lead to research on non-participation?

The lack of research on non-participation can be explained pragmatically and ideologically. Pragmatically, it is important to realize that many participation programmes are designed and researched by strong advocates of participation. Such researchers are reluctant to provide evidence which might diminish enthusiasm for participation, or even material which might be used as evidence.

Another pragmatic problem is methodological. It is very hard to define and measure non-participation. What constitutes non-participation? Is an individual who says less participating less? Measurement issues represent a serious hurdle for the study of non-participation. Measuring the absence of something often brings its absence to the attention of the individuals involved, confounding the measurement itself. Further, it seems likely that some social desirability effects may be linked to participation, and individuals may be reluctant to admit that they are unwilling to participate.

In the past, much research on participation has focused on group-level participation, and the actual contributions of individual members have been little studied. This is changing, as current approaches to research attempt to see what is 'really happening' rather than what is supposed to be happening. For example, the IDE study (1981) looks at *de jure* (legal) participation (what should be) and *de facto* participation (what actually is occurring). Trist *et al.* (1977) also discuss the practical, realistic factors in implementing participation schemes. Current studies which emphasize observation and in-depth understanding of participation schemes are more likely to provide information on what actually is happening, as well as suggestions about the causes of non-participation.

While pragmatic issues such as research methods help to explain the absence of research on non-participation, there are also ideological reasons. Ideologically, researchers from each school have different reasons for glossing over non-participation. It is contrary to a well-established model of human behaviour espoused by humanists, which contends that people strive for opportunities to be more involved. Researchers from the managerial school are minimally concerned with people who do not participate, since they view participation programmes as simply outlets for those who do want more involvement. Democratic theorists have given some thought to why people do not participate, but the global nature of their concerns makes specific hypotheses hard to identify. Researchers from the participatory left see participation as one way to change society as a whole. They have not focused on non-participation because they feel it is only a symptom of more serious problems.

In spite of these factors, each of the schools of thought provides valuable ideas for beginning to research and understand the question of non-participation. From a management school standpoint, questions of individual differences and the efficiencies of participation are highlighted. This perspective leads to hypotheses about how participants differ from non-participants, and how employees evaluate the effectiveness and efficiency of participation. For example, do personality traits differ between those who decide to participate and those who decide not to participate? How do employees perceive participation, and how does this influence their decisions about joining?

The humanistic psychology perspective focuses attention on the outcomes of participation for the individuals involved. Do people who are involved in participation actually desire greater self-actualization? Do people in fact 'grow and develop' as a result of participation experiences? And further, do employees evaluate participation as 'genuine' or 'not genuine' and is this important in their decisions about joining?

From a democratic theory perspective, questions about the dynamics of participation are evident. Are people who are already 'active' more likely to join in participation programmes? Do experiences with participation generalize into other life situations? Do people who participate at work actually emerge with skills to participate in other aspects of their lives?

Finally, the participative left accentuates questions of alienation and the relationship between alienation and participation. Does participation increase or decrease employee alienation? What circumstances influence the effect of participation on alienation, or the effect of alienation on participation? Does alienation help to determine who decides to participate? Certainly ideas about participation and alienation depend to some extent on the way alienation is defined, but still little is known about these issues.

All these questions deserve attention. The little research that has been done on non-participation suggests that the dynamics of it are more complicated than any one school would suggest. For example, research by McCarthy (1987) shows that joining behaviour in Quality Circles is not linked to previous participation levels (as democratic theory would suggest) and not linked to growth and development levels (as the humanistic psychology perspective would suggest). Research by Dean (1985) shows that the decision to join a Quality Circle is best modelled by a complex regression equation, including such intangible elements as whether one's friends decide to join. Leitko *et al.* (1985) described non-participation as flying in the face 'of sociological assumptions about behavior in the workplace' (1985: 286).

In spite of this, they suggest that non-participation is the modal response to labour management committees and that employees realize early on that these committees are ineffective and participation is not rewarded.

A great deal of research has been done about participation, and still essential questions remain unanswered. Research into non-participation and the questions of why employees reject the responsibility and opportunity of participation may shed new light on participation in general and suggest ways of making participation more effective and viable.

References

Alutto, J. A. and Belasco, J. A. (1972), 'A Typology for Participation in Organizational Decision Making', *Administrative Science Quarterly*, 17: 117–25.

Argyris, C. (1957), *Personality and Organization* (New York: Harper).

Bertsch, G. K. and Obradović, J. (1979), 'Participation and Influence in Yugoslav Self-Management', *Industrial Relations*, 18: 322–9.

Blum, F. H. (1968), *Work and Community* (London: Routledge & Kegan Paul).

Blumberg, P. (1968), *Industrial Democracy: The Sociology of Participation* (New York: Schocken Books).

Calvin, A. D., Hoffman, F. K., and Harder, E. L. (1957), 'The Effects of Intelligence and Social Atmosphere on Group Problem Solving Behavior', *Journal of Social Psychology*, 45: 61–74.

Dachler, H. P. and Wilpert, B. (1978), 'Conceptual Dimensions and Boundaries of Participation in Organizations: A Critical Evaluation', *Administrative Science Quarterly*, 23: 1–39.

Dean, J. (1985), 'The Decision to Participate in Quality Circles', *Journal of Applied Behavioral Science*, 21: 317–21.

Derber, M. (1970), 'Cross-Currents in Workers' Participation', *Industrial Relations*, 9: 126–36.

DIO International Research Team (1983), 'A Contingency Model of Participative Decision Making: An Analysis of 56 Decisions in Three Dutch Organizations', *Journal of Occupational Psychology*, 56: 1–18.

Falcione, R. L. (1974), 'Credibility: Qualifier of Subordinate Participation', *Journal of Business Communication*, 11: 43–54.

Gamson, Z. and Levin, H. (1984), 'Obstacles to the Survival of Democratic Workplaces' in R. Jackall and H. Levin, *Worker Co-operatives in America* (Berkeley: University of California Press).

Greenberg, E. S. (1975), 'The Consequences of Worker Participation: A Clarification of the Theoretical Literature' *Social Science Quarterly*, 5: 191–206.

Hunnius, G. (1979), 'On the Nature of Capitalist-Initiated Innovations in the Workplace', in T. Burns, L. E. Karlsson, and V. Rus (eds.), *Work and Power* (Beverly Hills, Calif.: Sage Publications).

IDE International Research Group (1981), *Industrial Democracy in Europe* (Oxford: Clarendon Press).

Kolaja, J. (1965), *Workers' Councils* (London: Tavistock).

Lammers, C. J., Meurs, P., and Mijs, T. (1987), 'Direct and Indirect Participation in Dutch Firms and Hospitals', *Organization Studies*, 8: 25–38.

Leitko, G., Greil, A., and Peterson, S. A. (1985), 'Lessons at the Bottom: Worker Nonparticipation in Labor Management Committees as Situational Adjustment', *Work and Occupations*, 12: 285–306.

Lewin, K. (1947), 'Frontiers in Group Dynamics', *Human Relations*, 1: 5–41.

—— (1952), 'Group Decisions and Social Change', in G. Swanson, T. Newcomb, and E. Hartley (eds.), *Readings in Social Psychology* (New York: Henry Holt).

Likert, R. (1961), *New Patterns of Management* (New York: McGraw-Hill).

Maier, N. R. F. (1967), 'Assets and Liabilities in Group Problem Solving', *Psychology Review*, 74: 239–49.

Mansbridge, J. J. (1973), 'Time, Emotion and Inequality: Three Problems of Participatory Groups', *Journal of Applied Behavioral Science*, 9: 351–68.

—— (1982), 'Fears of Conflict in Face-to-Face Democracies', in F. Lindenfeld and J. Rothschild-Whitt (eds.), *Workplace Democracy and Social Change* (Boston: Porter Sargent).

Marchington, M. and Loveridge, R. (1979), 'Non-participation: The Management's View?', *Journal of Management Studies*, 16: 171–84.

Maslow, A. H. (1965), *Eupsychian Management* (Homewood, Ill.: R. D. Irwin).

McCarthy, S. A. (1987), 'Some Theoretical and Empirical Perspectives on Nonparticipation at Work: Levels of Nonparticipation in a Company Quality Circle Program', Ph.D. thesis (Cornell).

Obradović, J. (1975), 'Workers' Participation: Who Participates?', *Industrial Relations*, 14: 32–44.

Pateman, C. (1970), 'Participation and Democratic Theory' (London: Cambridge University Press).

—— (1983), 'Some Reflections on Participation and Democratic Theory', in C. Crouch and F. Heller (eds.), *International Yearbook of Organizational Democracy*, i (Chichester: Wiley).

Reimer, E. (1954), 'Creating Experimental Social Change in an Ongoing Organization', *American Psychological Association Symposium on Change in Control Processes in Social Organizations* (New York), 7–12.

Rosenstein, E. (1970), 'Histadruit's Search for a Participation Program', *Industrial Relations*, 9: 170–86.

Runyon, K. E. (1973), 'Some Interactions between Personality Variables and Management Styles', *Journal of Applied Psychology*, 57: 288–94.

Rus, V. (1979), 'Limited Effects of Workers' Participation and Political Counter-Power', in T. Burns, L. E. Karlsson, and V. Rus (eds.), *Work and Power* (Beverly Hills, Calif.: Sage Publications).

Russell, R. (1984), 'The Role of Culture and Ethnicity in the Degeneration of Democratic Firms', *Economic and Industrial Democracy*, 5: 73–96.

Strauss, G. (1963), 'Some Notes on Power-Equalization', in H. Leavitt (ed.), *The Social Science of Organizations: Four Perspectives* (Englewood Cliffs, NJ: Prentice-Hall).

Tannenbaum, A. S. (1974), 'Systems of Formal Participation' in G. Strauss, R. Miles, and A. S. Tannenbaum (eds.), *Organizational Behavior: Research and Issues* (Madison, Wis.: Industrial Relations Research Association).

—— Kavčić, B., Rosner, M., Vianello, M., and Wieser, G. (1974), *Hierarchy in Organizations* (San Francisco, Calif.: Jossey-Bass).

Tosi, H. (1970), 'A reexamination of Personality as a Determinant of the Effects of Participation', *Personnel Psychology*, 23: 91–3.

Trist, E. L., Susman, G. I., and Brown, G. R. (1977), 'An Experiment in Autonomous Working in an American Underground Coal Mine', *Human Relations*, 30: 201–36.

Verba, S. (1961), *Small Groups and Political Behavior* (Princeton, NJ: Princeton University Press).

Vroom, V. H. (1960), *Some Personality Determinants of the Effects of Participation* (New York: Prentice-Hall).

Walker, K. F. (1975), 'Workers' Participation in Management: Concepts and Reality', in B. Barrett, L. Rhodes, and J. Beishon, *Industrial Relations and the Wider Society* (London: Collier Macmillan and The Open University Press).

Witte, J. F. (1980), *Democracy, Authority and Alienation in Work* (Chicago, Ill.: University of Chicago Press).

11

Participation: A French Perspective[1]

ANNI BORZEIX AND DANIÈLE LINHART

THE firm[2] is changing, it is said. The convergence of various currents of opinion in France on this point is striking. Employers and unionists of all persuasions, politicians and planners, men of action and men of theory seem, for once, to agree; and sociologists agree with the opinion-makers who have voiced such a surprising consensus about the obviousness of the change—which, despite contradictory appearances, is inevitable—toward a model of the firm founded on industrial democracy and so-called participative management.

This is in contrast with the disillusion of France's social democratic neighbours (Goetschy, 1985) who, after fifteen years of serious experimentation in, and legislation on, joint management, now seem to be much more sceptical about the promises of industrial democracy, even though more direct forms of participation at the workplace are now becoming key issues in the social debate. After some delay France is discovering, at least officially since 1981 (Auroux, 1982),[3] the virtues of industrial democracy both at institutional and at shop-floor level. This time-lag can be attributed to specifically French socio-economic and political factors, which will be examined here and should be kept in mind throughout the following pages.

The liveliness of current debate in France about 'participation' is almost more revealing of the revision of the various actors' strategic positions—a revision essentially at the level of discourse, but we know how important words are—than of the contents of participative management programmes. Rather than comment on the present state of organizational democracy in French firms we would like

- to comment upon the conditions under which sociological discourse about 'the firm' is being produced;
- to examine critically the epistemological foundations (which is seldom done) of the writings of French sociologists so as to inquire into the theories of social change implicit in their interpretations and thus 'shed light upon what is left unsaid in sociological discourse, what is subsociological—the set of

---

[1] This article has been translated from the French by Noal Mellott, CNRS, Paris.

[2] The term 'firm' is used here to refer to production-oriented organizations. For the purpose of this article a firm is defined as the place where labour and capital meet; where working conditions, wages, job content, and work organization are located; where social relations in work are structured; and where the interests of the work-force and management are negotiated.

[3] For more details see the Appendix to Ch. 19 by Bernoux in this volume.

implicit, ontological presuppositions that condition the explicit discourse of postulates and hypotheses' (Paradeise and Tripier, 1982);

- to plead, by using observations from our empirical research on the application of employees' right to direct expression (Borzeix *et al.*, 1985), for a 'principle of reality' so as to formulate propositions that are more modest and proceed from the recollection that social order is never either fully given or imposed from the outside but that it is the constantly negotiated result of regulated adjustments.

The production of a sociological discourse

To begin, let us look first at the context in which the theme of participative management has emerged so triumphantly. Might French sociologists' positions on, and attitudes about, the firm not have changed as much as firms themselves?

Until the late 1970s, following the Friedmann tradition labour sociology in France focused mainly on the workshop, job qualifications, workers' activities, and labour disputes (Groupe de Sociologie du Travail (ed.), 1985). Most sociologists entered the field through unofficial channels (via the unions). Many were restricted to observing and analysing experiments in work organization—pilot projects of limited scope that were confined to a part of a firm. They considered the company as a mere setting, a piece of scenery used to locate their analyses. Their position was critical: the firm was, most of all, the place where class struggle could be heard and seen, or, to use Perroux's evocative phrase, 'the cardinal institution of capitalism'. These surveys within—but not on or about—companies did, none the less, stimulate interest in, and research on, problems having to do with Taylorism, the work performed by wage-earners in all its complexity, employers' policies for reorganizing it, and the forms of action launched by unions. Tripier (1984) describes the situation quite accurately by saying that 'The most fertile approach used the rules of classical tragedy and organized its analyses in terms of the unity of place, of time and of action.' Unity of place, in that analyses were restricted to the workshop; unity of time, in that the work situation was photographed instantaneously; unity of action, in that only acts of production came under study. The firm itself, as such, existed only as a backdrop for scenes of social antagonism.

A long road has been travelled since. A milestone along the way was the publication of a special issue devoted to 'the firm' by the classical review, *Sociologie du travail* (1986). Another milestone was the conference attended by most (French) sociologists organized in 1987 by the National Centre for Scientific Research (CNRS) on the theme 'Is the firm a pertinent category for analysis?' In the 1980s, a number of sociologists have, just like other opinion-makers, fallen under the spell of 'the enterprise' and many have taken an interest in 'the participative enterprise'.

The conjunction of several factors—the economic recession, the massive diffusion of new technology, the left coming to power, and the decline of the labour movement—apparently created the conditions for a 'New Deal' between labour sociologists and the subject of their research. Following the election of a socialist president and government in 1981, these factors all pointed to the firm as a legitimate subject of inquiry.

First of all, the recession challenged firms with the crucial problems of jobs, and the need either to become or to remain competitive entailed mobilizing employees. The problem of unemployment, which had previously been analysed in terms of the labour market, was converted into the question of saving or creating jobs in firms, thus leading labour sociologists toward the firm as an object.

Secondly, new technology, by opening up new possibilities, has justified, at least symbolically, the belief (by sociologists) that the firm has been potentially cleansed of the original sin committed by Taylorism. Changing the model of the productive system should eventually make it possible to reconcile automation and job qualifications.

Thirdly, the fact that the left came to power was a virtual guarantee that good choices would be made among the many possibilities opened by the new technology. For many sociologists this political change-over took the moral sting out of becoming involved in social experimentation and innovation. After all, many firms had been nationalized, and a new 'citizenship' could be imagined for workers within them. Sociologists found inside companies a place from which they could be the observers of, even participants in, the many changes being wrought as the socialist government passed laws that, for the first time, shifted issues from nation- or industry-wide regulations and negotiations to company-level arrangements. Firms were deliberately turned towards participative democracy as measures were passed under the Auroux Laws that placed each company under the obligation to hold yearly negotiations with local union branches about wages and working hours, granted wage-earners the right to direct and collective expression so that their voices be heard on working conditions and how work is organized, increased the powers of labour–management company committees in matters of economics and technology, and set up in firms labour–management committees for handling problems of working conditions as well as occupational hazards and risks.

Fourthly, the crisis of the labour movement has forced French unions to reconsider their strategies (Krasucki, 1987; Maire, 1987). These strategies had, during the period of economic growth, centred on the employment contract; accordingly, continual pressure had been brought to bear to win regular increases in wages and to stabilize the conditions of employment. Since then, unions have had to tackle directly, for the first time, problems related to productivity, efficiency, and quality—managerial problems. The time has come to make concrete proposals and mobilize the work-force around issues of the choice of new technologies and their application at company level. This 'recentring' of the unions around the firm has also affected French labour sociologists, who have always been very receptive to union priorities.

In the early 1980s everyone suddenly became much more interested in 'the enterprise'. Whether this combination of factors—what we might call a back-to-business cycle—might also be structural remains an open question. The result has been the rehabilitation of 'the firm' in French society (Monthé-Gautrat, 1986).

Rehabilitated and forgiven, the firm has become a place where a possible—perhaps even necessary—consensus can be worked out, where social relations are to be transformed, where current economic, technological, and societal challenges have to be met (Sainsaulieu and Segrestin, 1986). Social amnesty has been declared, an amnesty with an ideological middle term—participation—of indeterminate extension. This word suits everyone, or almost. For some, it refers to a more realistic form of self-management, a union issue during the 1970s. For others, participation might mean that a new actor—lay workers—will be taking the stage and playing a third role alongside management and unions. For still others participation could be the coming of a form of industrial democracy, French-fashion, to be generalized at all bargaining levels.

The various sensibilities running through the French group of labour sociologists all seem to have nested somewhere under the generic term—both vague and operational—of participation. The word has a flavour that, by whetting all appetites, gives a good excuse, conscious or not, to accept the invitation to enter—should we say 'join'?—the company. Besides, workers are invited too. In fact, they are the staple—the salt of the earth—the work-force that is to be 'mobilized', 'associated', 'motivated', 'involved', 'implicated' . . . so that the firm becomes more 'democratic', 'competitive', 'modern', 'efficient', 'flexible' . . . Of course, for the alibi to remain effective the academic who ventures into a firm must be greeted by a reality that suits his reason for accepting the invitation: the firm's progress toward participative democracy.

Sociological postures

Labour sociology has, fortunately, corrected its short-sighted belief in technological determinism (Maurice, 1980). But it must avoid blind faith in the discourse of the most convinced, or convincing, social actors and shun the inner conviction of the academic who 'knows' where history is heading. It must be wary of what we shall call 'ordinary teleologism' (Linhart, 1987), as attractive as this is when it pulls a complex, multifarious reality into a purposive, intelligible order.

The conference mentioned earlier organized by the CNRS is noteworthy because so many labour sociologists were gathered there to discuss conceptions of the firm. From the twenty-four papers submitted (CLERSE-CNRS, 1987), it can be clearly seen that, with respect to participation, three major positions are adopted by sociologists. They will now be summarized so as to bring out their salient points. As over-simplifications, we will carefully avoid personalizing their postures and proceed in an abstract manner: no names will be cited here.

The first posture: when the sociologist unobtrusively listens to and accepts what social actors say, in particular, about the meaning or direction of change. Without seeking to deepen his own understanding of the underlying factors—seen as both internal (the crisis of social relations in firms) and external (the changing environment)—this kind of sociologist begins by 'observing' a consensus about the need to manage firms differently. This turning toward the very dynamics of change and away from its origins, or even from the social processes underlying it, focuses so sharply on what the actors involved in change have to say that all else is blurred and this discourse becomes the only reference point of the empirical studies that have questioned only these actors. In most cases these are managers, the very persons who, given their social position, hold the limelight. As a consequence, the issues raised, the hypotheses formulated, and the concepts elaborated by the sociologist merely reproduce those of the social actors who are the most articulate about the change under way. The sociologist then resorts to nearly empty, though sometimes crucial, concepts such as identity, culture, 'company project', or autonomy, that, left vague, are reduced to an almost commonsensical meaning. Usually in the hope of contributing to social reforms, such a sociologist embraces the idea that his activities as a researcher will react upon his subject. This explains why 'research-intervention' will often be his methodology.

The second posture: when the sociologist hides behind the presumed course of history. Two main trends occur in this second posture. The first one is classical. It goes back to the origins, to the basic concepts of the founding fathers of sociology. The second one is of Marxist inspiration. Paradoxically, these perspectives have more in common than one would imagine.

In the first case, the factors underlying change are ignored; for, whatever these may be, history is marching towards something we already know, namely, the new firm in which participation is regenerating an authentic community of producers. The firm is no longer the field of inevitable conflict characterized by 'sociation' (a social order founded on a contract) but is becoming a place of 'communalization' in Weber's terms (Weber, 1971). Nothing is put forward to explain why this did not happen sooner, nor why it is happening now. This new firm in which the human community is at last restored seems (if we keep in mind the contradictions that, according to many recent studies, plague companies from the inside) to have appeared by magic. Anyway, history is heading forward; and its direction is so well staked out, its culmination so well known, that the sociologist, blinded as he is by its future spirit, ignores its actual flesh and bones.

In the second case, attempts to keep in step with a Marxist analysis do lead the sociologist to review the factors underlying change. He notes the technological upheaval caused by computerization, which has torn up the boundaries between manual and non-manual labour, transformed job qualifications, and freed time during the working day. He also points to the crisis of managerial culture, which entails redefining job qualifications and adopting participative measures as, in a shift from labour to capital intensiveness, priority passes from economizing on wage costs to using the capacities of plant and equipment more efficiently. Of course, everyone's favourite factor is the crisis of Taylorism, the discovery that young wage-earners' truly' aspire to have a role in management. The sociologist who has adopted this second possibility does, at least, discuss the factors determining change. However, the new model of the firm follows mechanistically, automatically, from the selected determinants, as if identifying the possible reasons for change suffices to deduce the exact nature of the change and its outcome. This model is at work, we are assured, and will necessarily be used generally because, for its advocates and for this sociologist, it is the best model. Since this change is progressive, the sociologist refuses any evidence which does not point to progress. Does all evidence not clearly indicate, for example, that direct-expression groups, which embody the advance of democracy in the firm, are running out of breath? 'That's true', the sociologist says, as he points to signs foretelling a second incarnation, a new generation of such groups that will fulfil the promises he has made for them. Referring to one or two experiments here and there, he thinks he can prophesy changes and a new model of the firm. As long as his only certain evidence comes from what is possible or, at best, experimental, he is surely right.

The third posture means taking into account the 'principle of reality'. What must be inquired into are the causes or conditions that in fact advance or impede the change from one model of the firm to another. To do this, it is necessary to start with an adequate description of the model that is changing—what exists—and, therefore, to clarify concepts. It is senseless to talk about change or modernization by simply referring to what will be changed without inquiring into how the thing that is to be changed already works. We would like to propose now such an approach addressing the question of participation.

From the principle of reality back to participation

In the guise of more democracy, what is really happening is that the boundaries within firms between what is formally made known and what is informally kept under cover are being redefined. Empirical evidence leads us to discern between visible and invisible, revealed and concealed forms of workers' participation.

Participation, a long-concealed reality

Let us set aside all aspects of institutional participation—the greater access of personnel representatives to various decision-making committees, etc.—whether this be called joint management or not. This indirect representative participation, which has been developed especially in countries with strong social democratic traditions, is not what we have in mind, nor, for that matter, the participation of employees in firms' economic results through profit-sharing schemes. What we would now like to discuss is the direct participation at shop-floor level of wage earners representing only themselves.

Direct participation as such has been introduced in many ways in most industrial countries and under various names during the last fifteen years: expression groups, production islands, Quality Circles, autonomous work groups, project groups, etc. Whenever employees are asked to discuss, in the presence of someone from the supervisory or executive staff, how to improve product quality, how to change working procedures, how to rearrange space at the workplace, or how to improve working conditions, one begins to see the participative spirit. But is it certain that such groups, apart from their evident institutionalization, embody a radically new phenomenon? Might direct workers' participation not have existed prior to the specific forms that it has now taken?

To get a better idea of what is going on today, of what is new and what is not, one should bear in mind the findings of sociological and psychological research since the 1970s, that is to say, the positive involvement in production of workers acting beyond hierarchical orders and technical directions, an involvement proceeding from the store of knowledge and know-how they have acquired through practical experience (Duraffourg *et al.*, 1972; Bernoux *et al.*, 1973; Desbrousses and Peloille, 1975; Lescot *et al.*, 1978 Linhart, R., 1978; Bernoux, 1981; Linhart, D., 1981; Oddone *et al.*, 1981). This involvement, which refers to the jobs actually performed as distinct from the jobs prescribed by and inscribed in Tayloristic rules, is necessary for production to run smoothly; it may be undertaken individually or managed collectively as a function of the norms and values that workers in a shop adopt. Even though it takes place out of the sight of industrial engineers and top executives, is this involvement not a concrete form of direct participation? Here, participation simply means taking part, a full part, in the microdecisions of the day-to-day management of the production process.

Formulated in this way (knowing what we do today), this seems obvious. None the less, it took time to be recognized. It was not until the 1980s that management discourse on human resources, on the unexplored wells of know-how, on the forgotten capacities and intelligence of employees, spread from a narrow circle of enlightened humanists to management at large (Serieyx, 1982; Archier and Serieyx, 1983). This informal contribution of employees to production, once revealed to and recognized by managers, could not but change status. To be fully productive this concealed involvement had to be controlled and formalized.

The main reason for this lies in the recent technological revolution which has transformed the conditions of productivity and profitability. The mechanistic models following from the principles of scientific management have been replaced by models that, based upon automation and computerization, necessitate the use of human resources of understanding, communication, responsibility, intervention, learning, training, and adaptation (Delpierre, 1984, D'Iribarne, 1984).

French labour unions have also shifted recently from denouncing—and justly so—the deskilling and alienation caused by scientific management, to defending and re-evaluating the hidden treasures embedded in productive activity. The actual complexity of so-called routine tasks (in contrast to the job slots prescribed) and the store of collective qualifications (even of unskilled workers) that enable groups or teams to regulate their activities despite or beyond the bounds set by official procedures have only recently become subjects of debate (Borzeix and Linhart, 1986). Motivated by the class struggle against the capitalist system, the industrial labour movement in France has always resisted the idea that workers on the production line could be positively involved in doing their work. After all, might not this form of active participation, once recognized, undermine a position based upon concepts of exploitation, oppression, and alienation? Until recently, the unions did not admit the very term 'participation' in their discourses because they resolutely refused anything resembling 'class collaboration'. To talk about participation when referring to the intervention of wage-earners in the daily management of their activities is still unsettling, even though opinions are changing rapidly (CGT, 1986, 1987a and b; CFDT, 1987). Thus, in the early 1980s, a combination of factors shed light upon what had been in the shadows: workers' involvement in production. But is this involvement, by being exposed in broad daylight, by being made official and recognized as 'participation', not threatened?

Overt and covert participation

Side-stepping through history as we have done helps us see beyond the effects and meanings of the various participative schemes in vogue today. The new, revealed forms of participation must be understood in relation to the concealed forms referred to earlier.

Informal participation, or involvement, comes out of transactions within work groups. It results from a compromise which is always provisional and which employees seek to arrange among themselves and make with their immediate superiors. The rules of this game, namely, the norms drawn up through negotiations and interactions within the work group, both ensure that production runs smoothly and make life at the workplace bearable. This compromise deals with problems such as assigning (good and bad) jobs, setting the speed of work, inventing and using the 'tricks' that, by compensating for the shortcomings of machines and the inadequacies of materials, mitigate the consequences of ineffective operational instructions, breakdowns, and unforeseen circumstances. These norms and rules—which are often called 'workshop culture'—maintain an equilibrium, a *modus vivendi*, within the work group. They also reflect a balance of power between production line and staff. They give shape to precarious working compromises between contradictory production rationales. These norms also determine a negotiable social order for managing working life that, adjusted only informally, must remain concealed, hinted at but not officially proclaimed, if it is to continue.

The new, formal participation deviates from this natural, private order. It is initiated, organized, and supervised from the outside by management. It is artificial—conducted round a table away from the shop floor. It is alien to work practices on the production line—for, normally, only technicians, engineers, and office staff sit round a table talking about work. It is exceptional in that such meetings are held weekly or quarterly.

What all new forms of participation have in common is to centralize and formalize arrangements made by work groups, who are confronted with alien rationales, and with new intermediaries or partners. They face new actors around the discussion—we dare not say 'bargaining'—table, actors from other shops, from offices, from operational and administrative services, from the 'staff' in the broadest sense. The work group is asked to forgo its internal solidarity, to come out of its 'hole', to realize that it belongs to a 'whole', that it has a place in an organization chart, that it is an integrated part of the firm. The rules of behaviour that had been made for the workshop or for a section of the assembly line or office must now be scrutinized: are they efficient? are they compatible with the general principles that govern the company?.

Private arrangements must now become publicly accountable. What has been concealed must be revealed; what has been closed, open; what has been hinted at, stated plainly; what has been formulated orally, formalized, often in writing. During the participative meeting, informal arrangements and compromises which make the work situation bearable while ensuring production are brought out into the open. Such meetings force the group or its members to make public the divisions inside the group, to expose illicit compromises with immediate supervisors.

This exposure, this public accountability, means that what has been clandestine should now become licit. What has been felt to be a way of deviating from or getting round the rules, a way of winning some autonomy against official prescriptions—all this should now be emptied of its subversive content, not voided but legalized (Linhart and Linhart, 1985). Organizing work so as to be effective in spite of the shortcomings of official instructions is a kind of protest; this rationale, motivated though it is by the intention to ensure production, is paradoxically part of a counter-culture created in opposition to what is imposed from higher up. This social order that workers create from the mosaic of their on-the-job experiences has neither the same meaning nor feeling as an order openly negotiated on an explicitly contractual basis: for what has held the tacit arrangement together is its transgressive nature (and the silence of workers).

The foregoing remarks lead us to be somewhat sceptical about the declared intentions of the persons who are promoting various forms of participation that aim at more closely 'associating' workers in decision making, at advancing democracy and 'citizenship' within the firm. Beyond ideological discourse, this trend towards participation seems to aim at something else: at shifting the boundaries between formal and informal activities, at reorganizing through joint discussion and action the interface between two central rationales—prescription and protest—at work within companies (Chabaud and de Terssac, 1987; Reynaud, 1988). The characteristics (automation and computerization) of the new systems of production entail recuperating transgressive action and legalizing what has been held secret; otherwise, the system will not work efficiently. The new forms of participation attempt to break down the compartments within which these two rationales have been operating. To do this, new centres of decision making are set up in order to expose tacit forms of participation concealed in the workshop. More than democracy at the workplace the new forms of participation mean inventing places where the hidden forms of involvement in work can be brought out into the open.

The reluctance of wage-earners to become actively involved in this process—most studies on this subject provide clear evidence of this reluctance (Ministère du Travail, 1985)—is understandable. Why should they leave the shadows to take so dangerous a spot in the limelight if all they are offered in return is the assurance that they will have thus corroborated the predictions of participative theories formulated by other social actors? This assurance does not, perhaps, suffice to make them move towards the front of the stage.

Towards a conclusion

With regard to the general pattern most Western industrial nations have followed in the last ten or fifteen years, France seems to be out of step. In a way, the French situation can best be described as counter-cyclical in terms of the cycle analysis suggested by Ramsay (1983) and further discussed by Poole (1984). This is not only because of the time-lag, industrial democracy and participation having waited until the early 1980s—the middle of a full-blown economic crisis—to become major and legitimate topics for the main institutional actors involved (management, unions, and State). It is also because of the reversed socio-historical circumstances in which participation has developed in our country: as a solution to the organizational constraints imposed on firms, for economic and technological reasons, and not as a result of any labour challenge to management, nor of any threat to its control. Participation management is being diffused in France through both legal arrangements (the Auroux Laws) and managerial initiatives (Quality Circles, firm projects, and the like). And the weakness of the labour movement since 1975 is patent, whether this be measured by union membership or by militancy.

The French experience could therefore be considered rather exceptional, local features having managed to confuse the cyclical model. But it may also carry a wider significance as an opportunity to question the very notion of cycle as well as that of participation.

Is participation in France today not more of a mode of management (Midler *et al.*, 1983), supported, although for different reasons, by union, officials, and the State, than a credible issue for workers and militants?

Such a question leads to a more fundamental one. Can the idea of participation be used as a transhistorical and transcultural concept, as both the cyclical and the evolutionist models implicitly suggest?

Having had the 'privilege' of studying participative schemes in an atypical country such as France, we are convinced of the need to look for the meaning of participation in relation to the concrete conditions under which productive activities are actually managed in firms, and to consider the specific set of labour relations in which they are located historically. This means trying to take into full account the complexity, the contradictions, and the ambivalences social reality is bound to be made of.

References

Archier, G. and Serieyx, H. (1983), *L'Entreprise du troisième type* (Paris: Seuil).

Auroux, J. (1982), *Les Droits des Travailleurs* (Paris: La Documentation Française).

Bernoux, P. (1981), *Un travail à soi* (Toulouse: Privat).

—— Motte, D. and Saglio, J. (1973), *Trois ateliers d'OS* (Paris: Éditions Ouvrières).

Borzeix, A. and Linhart, D (1986), 'Droit d'expression: La Boule de cristal', *Temps modernes* (Jan.).

—— —— and Segrestin, D. (1985), *Sur les traces du droit d'expression*, 2 vols. (Paris: CNAM).

CFDT (1987), 'L'Expression des salariés', *CFDT Aujourd'hui*, 84.

CGT (1986), 'La Participation', *Analyses et documents économiques*, 23 (Dec.).

—— (1987a), 'Entreprise et interventions des travailleurs', *Analyses et documents économiques*, 24 (Feb.).

—— (1987b), 'Cercles de qualité, groupes d'expression, culture d'entreprise et syndicats', *Analyses et documents économiques*, 25 (May).

Chabaud, C. and Terssac, G. de (1987), 'Du marbre à l'écran: Rigidité des prescriptions et régulations de l'allure de travail', *Sociologie du travail*, 3.

CLERSE-CNRS (1987), *L'Entreprise, catégorie pertinente pour la sociologie?* (Oct.).

Delpierre, M. (1984), *Automatisation: État des débats et enjeux sociaux* (Paris: LAST-CLERSE).

Desbrousses, H. and Peloille, G. (1975), *Pratiques et connaissance ouvrières dans l'industrie capitaliste* (Lyons: Centre de Sociologie Historique).

Duraffourg, J., Laville, A. and Teigger, C. (1972), 'Conséquences du travail répétitif sous cadence sur la santé des travailleurs et les accidents', *CNAM*, 29 (Mar.).

Goetschy, J. (1985), 'La Démocratie industrielle à l'épreuve de la crise: Grande-Bretagne, Suède, Allemagne', *Économie et humanisme*, 283 (May–June).

Groupe de Sociologie du Travail (ed.) (1985), *Le Travail et sa sociologie* (Paris: L'Harmattan).

Iribarne, A. d' (1984), *Textes sur les nouvelles technologies, les politiques d'entreprise et les qualifications* (Aix-en-Provence: Rapport LEST).

Krasucki, H. (1987), *Un syndicat moderne? Oui* (Paris: Messidor).

Lescot, Y., Menahem, G. and Pharo, P. (1978), *Savoirs ouvriers, normes de production et représentations*, Rapport CORDES (Paris: Entreprise et Personnel).

Linhart, D. (1981) *L'Appel de la sirène* (Paris: Le Sycomore).

—— (1987), 'A propos de la modernisation des entreprises, quelques réflexions sur le téleologisme ordinaire', *Cahiers CLERSE* (Oct.).

—— and Linhart, R. (1985), 'La Participation des salariés: Les Termes d'un consensus', in *Décider et agir dans le travail* (Paris: CESTA).

Linhart, R. (1978), *L'Établi* (Paris: Seuil).

Maire, E. (1987), *Nouvelles frontières pour le syndicalisme* (Paris: Syros).

Maurice, M. (1980), 'Le Déterminisme technologique dans la sociologie du travail', *Sociologie du travail*, 'Sociologie du travail a vingt ans', special edition.

Midler, C., Moire, C., and Sardas, J. C. (1983), *Les Méthodes de gestion innovatrices* (Paris: CRG, École Polytechnique).

Ministère du Travail, de l'Emploi et de la Formation Professionnelle (1985), *L'Expression des salariés, deux ans d'application dans les enterprises* (June).

Mothé-Gautrat, D. (1986), *Pour une nouvelle culture d'entreprise* (Paris: La Découverte).

Oddone, I., Ré, A. and Briante, G. (1981), *Redécouvrir l'expérience ouvrière* (Paris: Éditions Sociales).

Paradeise, C. and Tripier, P. (1982), 'Sociologie génétique et utilisation de données longitudinales', in *L'Emploi, enjeux économiques et sociaux*, Colloque de Dourdan (Paris: Maspero).

Poole, M. (1984), 'Comparative Approaches to Industrial Conflict', in B. Wilpert and A. Sorge (eds.), *International Yearbook of Organizational Democracy*, ii (Chichester: Wiley).

Ramsay, H. (1983), 'Evolution or Cycle? Worker Participation in the 1970s and 1980s', in C. Crouch and F. Heller (eds.), *International Yearbook of Organizational Democracy*, i (Chichester: Wiley).

Reynaud, J. D. (1988), 'Les Régulations dans les organisations: Régulation de contrôle et régulation autonome', *Revue française de sociologie*, 1.

Sainsaulieu, R. and Segrestin, D. (1986), 'Vers une théorie sociologique de l'entreprise', *Sociologie du travail*, 3.

Serieyx, H. (1982), *Mobiliser l'intelligence de l'entreprise* (Paris: Entreprise Moderne d'Édition).

Sociologie du travail (1986), 'Retour sur l'entreprise', 3.

Tripier, P. (1984), *Rapport sur le développement de la sociologie du travail*, report prepared for the PIRTTEM (Paris: CNRS).

Weber, M. (1971), *Économie et société* (Paris: Plon).

12

Industrial Relations Theory and Employee Participation

GERD SCHIENSTOCK

Introduction

The discussion of new trends in the shaping of the labour process and business decision-making structures was initially dominated by psychologists, group theoreticians, supporters of the human relations school, and management consultants. Organizational models, management concepts, and strategies of organizational change were developed with a view to contributing to the humanization and democratization of work. On the one hand job satisfaction and on the other productivity and product quality were selected as indicators of the success in the practical evaluation of concepts such as job enrichment, job enlargement, job rotation, autonomous work groups, Quality Circles, and shop-floor committees. Regardless of the fact that not only the social, but also the economic efficacy of such experiments have repeatedly been called into doubt (Ramsay, 1985: 57 ff.), the prescriptive orientation of a scientific preoccupation with business restructuring processes has been subjected to a variety of criticisms (Silverman, 1970). This is associated with two further deficiencies:

1. Industrial organization is largely regarded as a closed system; environmental factors such as market conditions or technological development that necessitate or favour organizational change are not taken into consideration.

2. Allowance is not made for the fact that business structures are the result of social processes, of at least limited co-operation and conflict-laden confrontations. The result of such processes cannot be expected from the outset to be an increased degree of democracy and humanity, even if they are labelled as such experiments (Knights and Collinson, 1985).

In contrast to other disciplines, industrial relations research only recently took up the discussion of new forms of participation and job organization. This is all the more surprising in view of the fact that even the definition of the object of investigation indicates a thematic similarity: 'The rules of the work place and work community become the general focus of inquiry to be explained by theoretical analysis' (Dunlop, 1958: 380). What this means, to quote Dunlop again, is the following' 'to explain why particular rules are established in particular industrial relations systems and how and why they change in response to changes affecting the system' (Dunlop, 1958: ix).

This programme contains a clear rejection of a prescriptively oriented science; at the same time, the humanization debate is placed on the broader basis of organizational design and redesign. Although there is, largely, agreement on the specific focus of interest, there is still controversy in industrial relations research as to which factors initiate processes of reorganization of industrial work and determine the specific form of the new regulation in each case. Above all, it is disputed whether actor or structure variables have a greater explanatory value, and to which factors the greatest importance should be attached in a structural explanation (Giddens, 1979). This controversy is reflected in the existence of three theoretical approaches (Schienstock, 1981: 171):

- Systems theory
- Marxist approach
- Actor-centred approach.

The system model

The frame of reference of Dunlop's approach results from his definition of a system of industrial relations which, in his view, can be 'regarded [as comprised] of certain actors, certain contexts, an ideology which binds the industrial relations system together, and a body of rules created to govern the actors at the work place and work community' (Dunlop, 1958: 7).

Dunlop takes his focus of interest from the central question of Parsons' structural functionalism as to the conditions for the stability of social systems (Parsons, 1951). He regards industrial stability as being provided by the introduction of collective rules for the labour process, the industrial organization, and the course of the decision-making processes. The interest of the actors in such rules is attributed to the existence of a paramount ideology. In a sort of vicious circle, Dunlop introduces the existence of a common ideology as a precondition for co-operation and thus simultaneously strikes it off the list of problems requiring explanation. His systems analysis can therefore be confined to the question of why certain industrial relations systems produce specific forms of rules. Dunlop's explanation of this amounts to asserting that market changes, technological developments, or changes in the balance of social power exert a pressure which virtually forces a reregulation of industrial relations. It is in the actors' own interests to submit to these largely independent dynamics.

Dunlop's structural determinism is encountered in one form or another in various approaches to the explanation of the development of industrial organization. It is often claimed that an evolutionary process takes place in the direction of humanization and democratization. A central line of argument links such a development with the transition from the industrial to the post-industrial society. An important feature of the post-industrial society is regarded as the dissemination of immaterial values (Inglehart, 1977). This development also has its effect on the economic sphere; it is expressed in the demand for more interesting and better-qualified work, for increased autonomy in the labour process, and greater involvement of the employees in the industrial decision-making process (Block and Hirschorn, 1979).

The potential for humanization and democratization of post-industrial societies is frequently attributed to the growing percentage of service work. This is substantiated by referring to its specific character, which finds its expression particularly in two features:

- it involves an interactive relationship between people;
- the moment when the service is provided is often undetermined.

Both features are closed to a restrictive, strongly formalized, and centralized work organization: on the contrary, they necessitate an extensive autonomy and a decentralization of the decision-making process (Berger, 1984: 22 ff.).

For Sabel, who like Dunlop puts considerable emphasis on institutional aspects, it is above all the increasingly complex and unstable market conditions that are conducive to the establishment of new forms of work organization (Sabel, 1982; Piore and Sabel, 1984). Such dynamic markets pose almost insoluble problems for traditional mass production and the rigid system of Fordist organization or production based on it. They force enterprises to adopt a new production strategy of specialization which is characterized by the continuous generation of problem solutions, frequent production changes, and continuous improvement of production quality. The flexibility of the production process necessary for such a strategy is achieved by the use of electronic data processing and microelectronics-based technologies and by adapting work organization in the direction of largely autonomous work groups. Furthermore, increasingly complicated labour processes place increasing demands on the employees, requiring a kind of multi-skilled craftsman. Basically, Sabel concedes, although even a neo-Fordist organization of production is reconcilable with the concept of flexible specialization, in his estimation this is more of a transitional period in the organizational evolution process.

Kern and Schumann, although on the whole certainly not adherents of the system model, describe a similar evolutionary process in the development of industrial work organization. For them the introduction of 'new production concepts' means the end of a previously uninterrupted trend which sought to channel and control animated work as far as possible by restrictive job organization. The new production concepts, on the other hand, are characterized by two diametrically opposite features:

(a) Autonomisation of the production process of animated work by mechanisation is of no value in itself. The extensive compaction of animated work does not of itself bring about the economic optimum.

(b) The restrictive access to a labour force gives vital productivity potential. There are no dangers in complex design, but opportunities, qualifications and professional sovereignty even of the workers are the productive forces that must be harnessed. (Kern and Schumann, 1984*a*: 19)

Although the authors do not expressly adopt the position of technological determinism in their study, they at least implicitly attribute the role of a leading evolutionary mechanism to the new production technologies (Malsch, 1987: 62 ff.). The abandonment of the long-established principle of strict division of labour and the reprofessionalization of production work are due in the final analysis to technical development. Like Sabel, Kern and Schumann also confirm an almost irreversible development trend towards such new forms of work organization, as they anticipate that in the longer term a restructuring of the labour process on the basis of integral concepts of job implementation even in less mechanized fields of production of repetitive unskilled work will come about. This would correspond, the authors state, to an all-prevading reason if the new production concepts could be turned into a modernization policy supported by all the actors (Kern and Schumann, 1984*a*: 320 ff.).

The Marxist approach

A differentiation between real and formal subsumption is of corresponding importance in a Marxist analysis of industrial restructuring processes. Formal subsumption means that the capitalist attains the power of disposal over the labour potential of a worker by conclusion of a work contract, and can then use this to produce added value in the production process. Private ownership of the means of production and the superior power of the capitalist on the labour market are important preconditions for formal subsumption. One problem is that the capitalist does not buy 'an agreed amount of labour, but the power to labour over an agreed period of time' (Braverman, 1974: 54). This has certain advantages for him in that, due to the vagueness of the labour capacity and the incompleteness of the labour contract, he can make very flexible use of the labour potential thus purchased. However, the capitalist is obliged to share his right of disposal over this labour capacity with the labour force itself, as labour capacity as a commodity cannot be separated from the people who sell it. Thus the labour contract leads to the 'institutionalisation of a conflict over labour capacity . . . thus creating a sphere in which concrete claims are made on one and the same thing, the labour capacity, and similar rights must be effectively counterbalanced' (Offe and Hinrichs, 1977: 21).

Under the conditions of formal subsumption, control over the use of labour capacity and over the labour process remain largely in the hands of the employees. Thus they also have the possibility of withholding their labour capacity. In order to be able to survive, faced with the growing rivalry of individual capital, the capitalist, argues Braverman, must eliminate the threat to the production of added value posed by the autonomy of the employees. Consequently, he is also obliged to seize direct control of the labour process and the work behaviour of the employees. Thus he not only has to decide what is produced, but also the means to be employed.

According to Braverman, the application of Taylor's organizational principles represents the conventional form of capitalist control over the labour process and industrial operation. The most significant features are as follows: the separation of planning and implementing activities, the extensive fragmentation of work tasks, and the minimization of qualification requirements. This also includes in the broadest sense the assembly line as an integrative mechanism characteristic of Fordist work organization. At the same time, Taylorism represents a decisive step towards real subsumption: the worker is subjected to new technical and organizational systems. Behavioural sovereignty as a possible disruptive factor in the achievement of added value is eliminated in this manner.

If, like Braverman, industrial humanization and democratization concepts are evaluated from such a control perspective, a negative evaluation is bound to result. If the Taylorization of work organization is simply equated with the capitalist mode of production, different strategies of organization and labour capacity use can at best be classified as a management style which alters nothing in the basic trend to restrictive work roles and increased control of work behaviour.

Braverman expresses himself as follows on such concepts:

They are characterised by a studied pretense of worker 'participation', a gracious liberality in allowing the worker to adjust a machine, replace a light bulb, move from one fractional job to another, and to have the illusion of making decisions by choosing among fixed and limited alternatives designed by a management which deliberately leaves insignificant matters open to choice. (Braverman, 1974: 39)

The development logic of capitalist work forms described by Braverman did not remain unrefuted by Marxist-oriented social scientists. They raise the objection that the resistance of the employees, the cumbersome nature of the production process, and above all the changes in the markets at least partly prevent the application of Taylorist and Fordist forms of work organization. Accordingly, the function of humanization concepts and participation models consists mainly of resolving the contradiction between market requirements and profit-oriented production by organizational means (Benz-Overhage *et al.*, 1982). In many instances the concept of partially autonomous group work is regarded as a transitional form on the way to a flexibility of the labour process provided by the production technology itself in the course of automation. At the end of this, development production is carried out virtually without human intervention (Mendner, 1976). By way of contrast, other authors emphasize that it is precisely the use of flexible technologies that favours the development of the new forms of work organization described as neo-Fordism.

> ... there is a change in the general principle of work organisation whenever there is a change in the modulations of capitalist management of the labour process. Automation brings with it the possibility of such major transformation because it replaces the rigid integration of the mechanical principle with an integration that is both more flexible and more far-reaching. ... The workers are no longer subjected to a constraint of personal obedience, but rather to the collective constraint of the production process. ... (Aglietta, 1979: 128 ff.)

Thus, from the viewpoint of the worker, the establishment of partially autonomous groups does not lead to the elimination of control, it means merely a displacement of the object of control from the work activities of the individual to the co-operative structure of the group.

The Marxist camp also points out the ideological function of humanization and democratization models. An integration of the employees in the labour process enforced by the technical organizational structure involves the danger of increasing job alienation. Resistance of the employees, whether in an active or passive form, is frequently a consequence of such conditions of work. This results in the necessity of an integration of the worker as a person, of the motivation of the employees, and of their ideological involvement (Malsch, 1987: 67). Participative programmes and humanization models are not aimed at work integration in the sense of a reversal of the division of labour, but are designed rather to facilitate the implementation of intensification of labour linked to neo-Fordist organizational forms. For this reason they are not therefore conceived as a replacement for Taylorist job organization, but rather to supplement it. They act as elements of real subsumption and fulfil the same function at the level of social integration as the Taylorist organizational principles at the level of system integration (Düll, 1985: 144).

At the same time, the ideological function of the job-redesign philosophy also consists of denying the existence of a fundamental economic conflict (Kelley, 1985: 49). It is intended to demonstrate that the apparent shortcomings of Taylorist work organization coming to light in the resistance of the employees can be solved within capitalist enterprises. Thus any attempt to consolidate the entrepreneurial position of power and reject the demands of trade unions for more extensive co-determination is also linked with the acceptance of a humanization and democratization of work as a central task of management (Schienstock *et al.*, 1987: 312).

Actor-centred concepts

Such theoretical approaches are based on the assumption that, although structural factors are always latently effective through their presence, in more complex social relationships their value is largely strategic. The reorganization of industrial structures and the reproduction and reinterpretation of existing rules are interpreted as the result of intentional action. The assumption of strategic choice is also linked with this (Child, 1973). The actors have various possibilities at their disposal for the organization of the labour process, and are able to choose between them on the basis of established criteria. Thus their decision is not clearly determined by any environmental factors. On the contrary, in the selection of its structural concept it is oriented towards specific interests, objectives, and the problem and situation definitions.

Generally speaking, it is assumed that at least two actors with different objectives are involved in the organizational design of industrial activity. However, a unilateral implementation of rules for the labour process cannot be precluded. Walton and McKersie define the investigation of an actor-centred concept as the 'deliberate interaction of two or more complex social units which are attempting to define or redefine the terms of their interdependence' (Walton and McKersie, 1965: 3). In contrast to the system model, conflict in the setting of an action-centred analysis is not regarded either as a superficial phenomenon or as exclusively destructive. The actor relationships are more typically represented as being conflict-laden. However, the assumption of a Marxist approach that the relationship of the two central actors, capital and labour, is characterized by an irremovable class conflict is also refuted. The different objectives and interests of the actors are regarded rather as basically reconcilable, and conflicts as being resolvable through negotiation.

Several authors assume that the introduction of industrial humanization and democratization concepts is principally in the interests of management, and is deliberately encouraged by the latter. Such concepts are the expression of a new control strategy of industrial management which Herman characterizes as hegemonic (Herman, 1982). It is based on a new management philosophy which no longer regards the worker as the principal opponent and objector, but as an upholder of interests open to compromise (Kern and Schumann, 1984*b*: 152). This is based on the expectation that the employees do indeed realize that their interests are linked with those of the enterprise, and that they are therefore able to identify not only with their work, but over and above this with the enterprise as a whole, with its objectives and structures, and that their moral involvement is expressed in conscientious work and innovative achievement. For this reason, it is also possible to dispense with direct supervision of work activities and give the workers more responsibility in the production process.

The hegemonic form of control, as defined by Herman, 'is characterized by relations of consent and legitimation between labour and management rather than coercion. The essence of the hegemonic model is . . . that commitment and participation replace alienation and domination as the *modus vivendi* of labour process control' (Herman, 1982: 15). However, it is not possible to establish a general trend towards increasingly autonomous decision making and integral work roles on the basis of hegemonic control. Large enterprises in key economic sectors are most likely to be in a position to experiment with humanization and democratization models.

The view that the introduction of new organizational models and participatory concepts represents above all a changed control strategy on the part of industrial management is not shared by several authors. Thus Burawoy states that 'concessions in advance' are possible with enlightened management, but that more frequently the antagonistic behaviour of the employees causes a reorganization of the labour process and industrial structure (Burawoy, 1979: 180–3). Specialized knowledge and professional experience represent power which the employees can use in order to prevent Taylorist restructuring of the work organization or to implement more humane work structures and extended participative models. This is why Edwards also talks about work organization as a 'contested terrain' (Edwards, 1979). The increased involvement of the employees in the industrial organization process and the transfer of greater responsibility and autonomous decision making are therefore interpreted by these authors primarily as reactions of management at the executive level to the struggle on the shop floor.

Occasionally the expectation is expressed that a process of democratization once instituted, regardless of which side it received its impulse from, develops a certain dynamic energy of its own, as the employees exert an ever-increasing pressure in the direction of greater participation (Herman, 1982: 19).

In the approaches described above it is at least implicitly assumed that industrial management on the one side and the employees on the other represent a homogeneous actor with uniform interests, who in the organizational development process will accordingly pursue only a certain strategy based on consensus. However, in no case does industrial management form a uniform collective; often decision-making processes in industrial management do not evolve rationally, but rather in the form of trench warfare, so that one can talk about the absence of a strategy (Chandler, 1962: 11). Thus not only with regard to the relationship between management and employees, but also with respect to the processes in management itself, the processes of designing work organization are a struggle for power between different groups pursuing completely different interests (Crozier and Friedberg, 1979). Weltz writes that 'An understanding of the evolution, of the course and also of the results of the rationalisation processes of the individual enterprise ... can no longer be obtained with respect to the interests of the enterprise as a whole. It would appear to be necessary to refer to a further level of explanation: that of the internal behavioural constellation' (Weltz, 1986: 157).

The behavioural constellation of individual social actors is constituted by the interplay of various influences such as: task, field of responsibility, granting of authority, personal abilities, and interests. According to the concept, differences in the management of organizational design measures are based primarily on personality traits, and these are also decisive in the struggle for power between the protagonists of different organizational concepts. On the other hand, Hyman refers to contradictions in the system of objectives of capitalist enterprises that are opposed to decisions on organizational concepts in the sense of the selection of a clear-cut optimal solution (Hyman, 1987).[1] He demonstrates this in the light of the following decision-making complexes (pp. 36–48):

- the technology of capitalist production;
- the social organization of labour;
- direction and delegation in the labour process;
- discussing the commodity status of labour;
- the mediation of representative organizations of labour;
- the reproduction of social relations of production.

The contradictions occurring here will be illustrated in the light of several examples. Thus the decision on the production technology to be used could turn out differently depending on whether product quality, price, or the need for control over the labour process is taken as the main criterion for selection. In the choice of social organization of labour, though a rigid division of labour can produce savings on staff costs, this is frequently at the expense of internal flexibility. The decision between direct control and delegation in the labour process is not an easy one to take either. Although direct control makes it possible to enforce a certain attitude to work and performance, it has a demoralizing effect and prevents strong emotional involvement. Delegation of the authority to make decisions, on the other hand, involves the danger of employees pursuing egoistical interests. Measures for the humanization of work are a suitable strategy to conceal the commodity character of work, but they often represent a considerable cost factor. The argument against the early involvement of the elected representatives of the employees in the organizational evolution process is that this may considerably complicate and delay the process of finding a compromise. On the other hand, this generally greatly facilitates the process of implementing collectively agreed rules for the organization of work. Above the level of the enterprise, the involvement of capital and labour in the corporative arrangements can produce social stability as a precondition for the production and acquisition of added value, but this is frequently at the cost of the growing influence of the selected employee representatives and government authorities on industrial work and hierarchical structures.

As a result of the decision-making dilemma illustrated here in several aspects, the conflicts in industrial management over the strategies for restructuring the labour process are pre-programmed. These structural conflicts are aggravated by

---

[1] It is difficult to associate Hyman unequivocally with a specific theoretical position. The quotation brings him nearer to the actor perspective but in general Hyman has to be considered as representative of neo-Marxism.

departmental egoism and the personal ambition of individual managers. It must be assumed that organizational change is accompanied by conflicts in management, so that it is scarcely possible to predict a general development trend for industrial organizational form, especially as controversies between the various groups in management give the employees the possibility of intervening in the design process and having an influence on their own interests.

However, in the context of organizational change even the interests of the employees are characterized by contradictions. From the limited perspective of work capacity the employees evaluate new organizational and participative models according to whether they may facilitate the sale of this commodity as a result of better opportunities for co-determination, for instance, or complicate it as a result of the reduction of jobs. On the other hand, from an expanded subject perspective it is aspects such as qualification, prestige, career prospects, relief, and reduction of stress that are of central importance in the limitation of industrial structures (Schumann *et al.*, 1982).

Although this double reference to work already indicates problems which the employees are faced with in the development of a conflict-free strategy for industrial restructuring processes, further difficulties emerge when one takes into consideration the fact that social classification and differentiation processes among the employees also create different interests with regard to the design of the labour process and industrial structures. Older and younger employees, qualified and unskilled, men and women, employees in large enterprises in key economic sectors and those in peripheral enterprises, foreign and indigenous workers, all these social groups act differently in industrial organizational processes according to their own specific interests, becoming protagonists, sufferers, or opponents of one or the other structural concept.

Summary

The above remarks have shown that any theory that assumes a linear trend for the development of the labour processes and of industrial organization, regardless of whether increased democratization or greater Taylorization is expected, cannot deal with the complexity of the organizational processes of innovation. There can be no question that individual structural factors such as market conditions, competitive situations, training system, prevalent system of values, and even production technology have an influence on the design of work organization. However, they open up only opportunities for the implementation of certain industrial structures and define the limits to freedom of organizational design which are taken into consideration by the social actors in the decision-making process. An example to illustrate this point: a stretched labour market offers better conditions for active and passive resistance by employees, to which industrial management in many cases reacts with an improvement of working conditions and an extension of the leeway for decision making. On the other hand, in the case of high unemployment industrial management is scarcely under any pressure to improve the quality of working life.

Occasionally environmental conditions also open up contradictory perspectives. This can be clearly demonstrated using the example of 'new technologies'. Their introduction frequently necessitates the involvement of workers with specialized knowledge. They also open up work organizational measures in the direction of integral work roles and the use of qualified workers, but there can be no doubt that they also favour an increasing segmentation of the labour force and as an information medium they can provide the basis for extensive industrial control systems. When one considers that decisions on the design of industrial structures are influenced by a variety of material and institutional background conditions, it is to be expected that the pressure which they produce and the various opportunities associated with them do not always indicate the same direction of organizational design.

It should also be taken into account that, in describing the interests involved in designing labour processes and industrial structures, referring to an insoluble contradiction between capital and labour will scarcely be sufficient. On the one hand, the assumption of homogeneous interests within the two classes is not necessarily correct, and, on the other, organizational design measures do not necessarily involve a zero sum play in the relationship between capital and labour (Burawoy, 1978: 256 ff.). This situation leads us to expect that new coalitions will form over and above the borders of class in the process of organizational restructuring. Under these conditions, the questions of the opportunities for a wider application of a humanization and democratization model and whether or not a computer-aided neo-Taylorism will become the predominant organizational concept cannot be answered without further ado. They must be preceded by investigations to find out which internal coalitions form under which constellations and with which overlapping of interests, and which executive powers the latter have at their disposal in order to implement their interests. Thus it is to be expected that the broad spectrum of organizational alternatives will find application between the extremes of Taylorism and 'responsible autonomy' not just at the level of individual enterprises. The process of structural differentiation is more likely to be continued at the level of industrial departments.

References

Aglietta, M. (1979), *The Theory of Capitalist Regulation: The US Experience* (London: New Left Books).

Benz-Overhage, K., Brumlop, E., von Freyberg, T., and Papadimitriou, Z. (1982), *Neue Technologien und alternative Arbeitsgestaltung: Auswirkungen des Computereinsatzes in der industriellen Produktion* (Frankfurt-on-Main and New York: Campus).

Berger, U. (1984), *Wachstum und Rationalisierung der industriellen Dienstleistungsarbeit* (Frankfurt-on-Main and New York: Campus).

Block, F. and Hirschorn, L. (1979), 'New Productive Forces and Contradictions of Contemporary Capitalism: A Post-industrial Perspective', *Theory and Society*, 7: 363–95.

Braverman, H. (1974), *Labor and Monopoly Capital: The Degradation of Work in the Twentieth Century* (New York and London: Monthly Review Press).

Burawoy, M. (1978), 'Toward a Marxist Theory of the Labor Process: Braverman and Beyond', *Politics and Society*, 3(4): 247–312.

—— (1979), *Manufacturing Consent: Changes in the Labor Process under Monopoly Capitalism* (Chicago, Ill. and London: University of Chicago Press).

Chandler, A. D. (1962), *Strategy and Structure: Chapters in the History of the American Industrial Enterprise* (Cambridge, Mass.: MIT Press).

Child, J. (1973), 'Organisation: A Choice for Man', in J. Child (ed.), *Man and Organization* (London: George Allen & Unwin).

Crozier, M. and Friedberg, E. (1979), *Macht und Organisation: Die Zwänge kollektiven Handelns* (Königstein/Ts: Athenäum).

Düll, K. (1985), 'Gesellschaftliche Modernisierungspolitik durch neue "Produktionskonzepte"?' *WSI-Mitteilungen*, 3: 141–5.

Dunlop, J. T. (1958), *Industrial Relations Systems* (New York: Holt, Rinehart & Winston).

Edwards, R. (1979), *Contested Terrain* (London: Heinemann).

Giddens, A. (1979), *The Class Structure of the Advanced Societies* (London: Hutchinson).

Herman, A. (1982), 'Conceptualizing Control: Domination and Hegemony in the Capitalist Labor Process' *The Insurgent Sociologist*, 3: 7–21.

Hyman, R. (1987), 'Strategy and Structure: Capital, Labour and Control', *Work, Employment and Society*, 1: 25–55.

Inglehart, R. (1977), *The Silent Revolution, Changing Values and Political Styles among Western Publics* (Princeton, NJ: Princeton University Press).

Kelley, J. (1985), 'Management Redesign of Work: Labour Process, Labour Market and Product Markets', in D. Knights, H. Willmott, and D. Collinson (eds.), *Job Redesign: Critical Perspectives on the Labour Process* (Aldershot: Gower).

Kern, H. and Schumann, M. (1984*a*), *Das Ende der Arbeitsteilung? Rationalisierung in der industriellen Produktion* (Munich: C. H. Beck).

—— —— (1984*b*) 'Neue Produktionskonzepte haben Chancen', *Soziale Welt*, 1(2): 146–58.

Knights, D. and Collinson, D. (1985), 'Redesigning Work on the Shopfloor: A Question of Control or Consent?' in D. Knights, H. Willmott, and D. Collinson (eds.), *Job Redesign: Critical Perspectives on the Labour Process* (Aldershot: Gower).

Malsch, T. (1987), ' "Neue Produktionskonzepte" zwischen Rationalität und Rationalisierung: Mit Kern und Schumann auf Paradigmensuche', in T. Malsch and R. Seltz (eds.), *Die neuen Produktionskonzepte auf dem Prüfstand: Beiträge zue Entwicklung der Industriearbeit* (Berlin: Ed. Sigma Bohn).

Mendner, J. H. (1976), ' "Humanisierung" oder Automatisierung? Zur Zukunft der kapitalistischen Arbeit', *Kursbuch*, 43: 135–45.

Offe, C. and Hinrichs, K. (1977), 'Sozialökonomie des Arbeitsmarktes und die Lage "benachteiligter" Gruppen von Arbeitnehmern', in *Projektgruppe Arbeitsmarktpolitik*: C. Offe (ed.) *Opfer des Arbeitsmarktes* (Neuwied: Luchterhand).

Parsons, T. (1951), *The Social System* (New York: Glencoe).

Piore, M. J. and Sabel, C. F. (1984), *The Second Industrial Divide: Possibilities for Prosperity* (New York: Basic Books).

Ramsay, H. (1985), 'What is Participation for? A Critical Evaluation of "Labour Process" Analysis of Job Reform', in D. Knights, H. Willmott, D. Collinson (eds.), *Job Redesign: Critical Perspectives on the Labour Process* (Aldershot: Gower).

Sabel, C. F. (1982), *Work and Politics* (Cambridge: Cambridge University Press).

Schienstock, G. (1981), *Towards a Theory of Industrial Relations, British Journal of Industrial Relations*, 19: 170–89.

—— Flecker, J., and Rainer, G. (1987), 'Kontrolle, Konsens und Ideologie: Ein Beitrag zur Diskussion über einen Paradigmenwechsel in der Industriesoziologie', in T. Malsch and R. Seltz (eds.), *Die neuen Produktionskonzepte auf dem Prüfstand: Beiträge zur Entwicklung der Industriearbeit* (Berlin: Ed. Sigma Bohn).

Schumann, M., Einemann, E., Siebel-Rebell, C., Wittemann, K. P. (1982), *Rationalisierung, Krise, Arbeiter—Eine empirische Untersuchung der Industrialisierung auf der Werft* (Frankfurt-on-Main and New York: Campus).

Silverman, D. (1970), *The Theory of Organisation* (London: Heinemann).

Walton, R. E. and McKersie, R. B. (1965), *A Behavioural Theory of Labour Negotiations: An Analysis of a Social Interaction System* (New York: McGraw-Hill).

Weltz, F. (1986), 'Wer wird Herr der Systeme? Der Einsatz neuer Bürotechnologien und die innerbetriebliche Handlungskonstellation', in R. Seltz, U. Mill, and E. Hildebrandt (eds.), *Organisation als soziales System: Kontrolle and Kommunikationstechnologie in Arbeitsorganisationen* (Berlin: Ed. Sigma Bohn).

13

Industrial Democracy and Organizational Symbolism

SILVIA GHERARDI, ANTONIO STRATI,
AND BARRY A. TURNER

Culture and symbols

The growth of interest in the cultural features of industrial and administrative organizations over the past decade (Pondy *et al.*, 1983; Frost *et al.*, 1985; Gagliardi, 1986) has implications for those concerned with organizational democracy and industrial participation. The new emphasis broadens the range of human behaviour considered relevant to an understanding of organizations, so that topics, concepts, arguments, and techniques from a variety of disciplines are being brought into the organizational debate: from linguistics, history, psychoanalysis, folklore, and cultural anthropology.

To be concerned with symbolism and culture in organizations is to be sensitive to interpretative processes. Tacit understandings, complex social negotiations, and other intersubjective processes become as important as more evident physical and linguistic symbols (Louis, 1985). But while verbal and physical symbols are reasonably available to the skilled observer, access to the more deeply shared meaning systems and their significance is much less straightforward, especially given the accidental or conventional elements which grow around symbols and add to the meanings which they carry. For some the symbols and rituals of organizational activity can reasonably be seen as vehicles which carry ideologies, values, and beliefs (Morgan, 1986), but for others interpretation is much more problematic, requiring evidence to be scrutinized as a critic would assess a literary text, or as a theologian would decode a myth.

Approaches giving a central place to culture and to symbols pick up and intensify earlier symbolic interactionist and anthropological work which sees organizations as the outcome of continuous processes of social negotiation. A sense of community cannot be created by decree, and the full acceptance of a new industrial regime cannot be guaranteed in advance. Such outcomes only emerge out of rather complex, delicate, and often ambiguous patterns of social interplay, which give a sense of how one behaves as a member of a community or how one displays deference to authority. Cultural approaches seek to gain a sense of the shared realities through which organizations exist and function (Strati, 1986).

When, within culture, such topics as 'technology', planning', or 'budgets' are tackled, there is, therefore, less concentration upon technology, say, as a physical entity, and more upon technology as a socially determined process of task-related activities and social agreements (Berg, 1984; Barley, 1986). Plans and budgets are seen not as unchallengeable proofs of the rationality of behaviour in organizations, but as indicators of activities which also have social (Hofstede, 1967), symbolic, and even 'magical' components (Morgan, 1986). At a symbolic level it is not merely their rational content which needs to be noticed, but the imagery which they embody, the myths which they express (Westerlund and Sjostrand, 1979; Broms and Gahmberg, 1982) and the extent to which they function as channels of 'autocommunication' through which managers talk back to themselves about their organizational aspirations (Broms and Gahmberg, 1983).

Symbolic investigations have taken note of the form and significance of celebrations, ceremonies, and rituals, from the office party and the retirement presentation (Turner, 1971; Rosen, 1985*a*) to large corporate anniversaries. Such events may be intended to create a 'thread tying all employees together' (Dandridge, 1986) but they also exhibit organizational culture in less planned ways. The intended and unintended transformations which occur when an organization puts on its 'party dress' can help to illuminate the meaning of participation within that organization.

The tacit assumption that organizations are devoid of aesthetic or sensuous elements is also challenged. Skilful organization needs not only cognitive intelligence but also an 'intelligence of feeling' (Witkin, 1974). Clues about the sensuous life of the organization are provided by organizational style, rhetoric, and imagery, and by characteristic anecdotes, myths, and sagas used to explain or give coherence to the organization. Difficult to interpret though they may be, all of these elements therefore become important parts of the symbolic analysis of an organization which can help to uncover aspects of organizational life which would otherwise be unseen.

Since cultural studies mostly depend upon qualitative methods, they have focused new interest upon techniques for qualitative data analysis (Glaser and Strauss, 1967; Turner, 1981; Lincoln and Guba, 1985; Martin and Turner, 1986) and the communication between organizational actors and researcher is seen to have its own significance which must be taken into account in the analysis (Strati, 1986).

Individual and organization

The relationship of individual workers or managers to the organization can be considered in a variety of ways. We can see from some recent cultural studies that, in varying circumstances, products, modes of operation, or corporate achievements might all serve to influence employees' identification with their organization. Glamorous products, imaginative forms of participative planning, or enlightened employment policies can all induce strong commitments among employees (Blackhurst, 1986; Bolognini, 1986; Raspa, 1986).

The imagery which surrounds this relationship may be examined, as may the ceremonies and rituals through which it is defined, supported, and celebrated. Or the crux of interest might be the individual's involvement with the shared system of meanings within the organization (Fine, 1984). This last option is complicated by the likelihood of there being several systems of meaning competing for a member's allegiance.

Much recent managerial writing following Peters and Waterman's *In Search of Excellence* (1982) assumes that some organizations have a single, managerially inspired 'culture of excellence', which can be installed as though there had previously been a void. But any organization is a complex cluster of subcultures and 'systems of symbolic representation' (Aktouf, 1985: 104). Workers and managers are likely to have their own work cultures, in which characteristic attitudes, anecdotes, and jokes express their identity and their stereotyped relationships with other groups (Turner, 1971; Santino, 1979; Van Maanen and Barley, 1984).

Even when these separate traditions are not hostile, they still serve to communicate distinctly different sets of values (Gregory, 1983; Grafton-Small and Linstead, 1986). Police administrators, for example, have quite different perspectives on routine than do officers on the beat (Manning, 1977). In routine police work discretion is essential, but it poses a problem for administrators, forming a pivot around which cultural differences are organized (Lang, 1981; Peyrot, 1981; Lynxwiler *et al.*, 1983). In genetic engineering companies differences in perspectives arise between managers and accountants and the young, research-minded biological scientists. The accountants have much more limited time-horizons than the scientists and this cultural duality dominates the functioning of these companies (Dubinskas, 1987).

Thus to talk of culture is not necessarily to talk of harmony. Cultures in an organization may be negotiated cultures, but several groups will negotiate and those with different degrees of power will have a differential influence on negotiations (Riley, 1983).

This is not to say that a shared culture cannot at times provide a way of meeting problems repeatedly encountered by organization members. In an abortion clinic, for example, the ordered set of practical values, themes, and routines in the culture can offer solutions to the moral and emotional problems encountered in work. Those who repeatedly terminate life in their daily work find that the related sense of solidarity can help them to try to make some positive use of their own distress at their activities (Witkin and Poupart, 1986).

Participation in culture

In pursuit of 'excellence', many managerial enthusiasts seek to build 'corporate culture' into their organization, taking a view of culture which is regarded sceptically by most social scientists. But others find more of the appeal of culture in its recognition that organizations must rely on the capabilities of *all* of their members if they are to create, sustain, and recreate an adequate work culture. 'The workers . . . invent a microculture' (Reynaud, 1983: 254), and the workplace is still important for the generation of alternative forms of collective identity for those who spend their lives there. Much of the relevance of these new developments for industrial democracy hinges upon precisely this point: that the symbols and the culture of an organization must, in the last resort, be sustained by the members of the organization and careful study may suggest ways in which these potentially profoundly democratic features of organizational culture might be enhanced.

Symbolism and culture draw our attention anew to issues of spirit, morale, and co-operation within industrial organizations and provide serious reasons for considering collective life, in its many manifestations, as the nub of that which constitutes an organization. If we wish to grasp fully the way in which the relationship between organization and individual employee is to be defined in the remaining years of this century and beyond, we cannot neglect these symbolic and cultural dimensions of participation. In many contemporary settings employee involvement now requires the employee to give maximum performance to some notional 'team' in order to allow that team to survive and prosper. This performance is also expected to include a commitment to the sustenance of an appropriate corporate culture, even though the long-term interests of employees and their organization remain as divergent as ever. Even in some of the Japanese companies supposedly committed to an ideology of life-time employment, according to current reports core staff are being pressed to take 'voluntary retirement' (McGill, 1987).

The current corporate rhetoric of participation can lead, paradoxically, to *demands* for participation which are to be met on the company's terms. The success of such policies is likely to be inimical to the development of what is normally understood as industrial democracy, where everyone has not only recognized views and contributions but also rights. Discussions about industrial participation need, therefore, to take account of the changing nature of employment demands in the era of corporate culture, as attempts at control through social anthropology supersede earlier forms of control through social psychology.

Implications for industrial democracy

It may help to sharpen up questions of the implications of culture for industrial participation if we turn away from mainstream commercial and industrial organizations and look instead at some recent studies which have emphasized cultural themes within organizations in the co-operative sector—organizations, that is to say, which are centrally committed to participative and democratic modes of operation.

Organizations with this kind of commitment are atypical within Western societies so that they have to establish, justify, and legitimize themselves both internally and externally. They have to support their own members in their involvement with such an atypical organization, and they have to persuade those outside the organization that in running a co-operative they are acting in a reasonable, a permissible, or even a praiseworthy manner. Where, as in most countries, there is a national co-operative movement, this both offers support in dealing with these tasks and complicates relationships by adding another player to the game. When co-operative organizations are established, if we think of the generative idea behind their establishment as a form of 'co-operative pact', then it is possible to observe the various cultural forms taken by this pact under different initial circumstances. Running through all co-operative analyses we find reflections of the tension which has existed since the nineteenth-century British Rochdale initiative proposed a non-utopian way of establishing and promoting co-operative enterprises within the existing economic order, rather than attempting either to withdraw completely or to change everything by violent revolution. This tension underlies the problems of internal and external legitimization, and it also runs through diagnoses of the future prospects of the co-operative movement.

The problems of external legitimization have been dealt with instructively by Brown in a cultural–historical study of co-operatives in Nova Scotia, Canada (Brown, 1987). The legitimacy of the pursuit of private business for profit rests upon an acceptance of the ideas of wage labour, of private property, of exchange, of the market, and of profit itself. Co-operatives may express doubts about the rightness of any or all of these assumptions, and such doubts will pose problems for the legitimate acceptance of the co-operative within the wider culture. In consequence, a variety of strategies may be needed to defend the co-operative initiative. The impoverished farmers setting up co-operatives in Nova Scotia earlier this century had to take great pains to present their organizations as 'private' enterprises and not as some form of communism. An image frequently used in the rhetoric of the movement portrayed the Canadian economic order as a 'leaning tower': it represented an impressive achievement, but it might fall if building continued and it became too high; the remedy was to rebuild it on surer foundations. Another argument advanced was that democracy had a place in business in a democratic society. Also the experience of running their own co-operatives could offer a means of 'helping working men to appreciate the difficulties of the capitalist', this being an argument advanced in 1905 by the future Canadian federal Minister of Labour, MacKenzie King. On such bases it became possible for co-operatives to secure support and legitimization from the government, from the Catholic Church, and from regional universities.

Many of the protagonists of co-operation saw it as a 'great social religion' (Brown, 1987: 22). It was not only necessary to carry the message to those outside the movement, but also to persuade, cajole, and convert those within whose presence there might be merely pragmatic, or those whose original commitment might be wavering, to convince them of the rightness of their adherence. A recurrent dual theme in the history of the Nova Scotia movement, therefore, has centred, first, upon how the meaning and the effects of acts undertaken within a co-operative organization should be understood by those participating in them; and, secondly, upon how the interpretation of these acts can be symbolically transformed so as to demonstrate that they conform to the tenets and values of the 'social religion' of co-operation. When this transformation is successfully achieved, the identity of members of co-operatives is reinforced in such a way as to sustain their allegiance to their organization.

We suggested above that one of the pre-eminent questions which is emerging in cultural or symbolic studies of co-operative organizations relates to the nature of the co-operative 'social pact' formed when the organization is established. Following Norman's discussion (1977) of 'the business idea', it is helpful to define a 'co-operative idea' as the logic of action through which a co-operative organization defines its relationships with its environment and, at the same time, models its own structure. We can then ask how the social pact forming the basis of any new co-operative organization embodies the 'co-operative idea' (Gherardi and Masiero, 1987). And, extending this central idea to include cultural, ideational, and symbolic elements, it becomes possible to look at the patterns of meanings which develop within the organization concerned, and how these are expressed and transmitted both to members of the organization and to those outside it. The social pact may also be scrutinized for signs of the tension likely to be placed upon it by forces from inside and outside the co-operative organization.

A study of nine newly formed Italian producer co-operatives which followed this line of inquiry distinguished two typical forms of social pact within these organizations, the type emerging being dependent upon the characteristics of the founding groups and upon their internal dynamics (Gherardi and Masiero, 1987). When a small, socially homogeneous group had come together to establish a co-operative enterprise in order to 'work in a different way' or to 'establish egalitarian conditions' the social pact displayed a 'foundational' culture which emphasized the importance of maintaining a community within the organization and of creating conditions which made it possible to reform the rules of work, recognizing, at the same time, the need to survive economically. By contrast, a 'coalition' pact and its associated culture developed when diverse groups of, say, managers, white-collar, and manual workers formed a co-operative enterprise in order to protect or rescue jobs. Such groups, often getting together at the prompting of external bodies such as trade unions, placed employment in first place, so that for them economic success was not merely a minimum condition but an overriding objective. The success of their enterprise was to be assessed solely upon pragmatic criteria, with little or no sense of the establishment within the organization of a new ethical system, or of conversion to a 'great social religion'.

Within these nascent organizations distinctive patterns of action could also be seen to flow from the two basic types of culture (Gherardi and Masiero, 1987) as the new organizations passed through the perilous early stages of formation (Kanter, 1972) and started to address the problems of consolidation. In this phase, the two culture types dealt differently with issues such as the establishment of decision-making procedures and the assignment of the division of labour, and they also developed different ways of handling the central tension between the establishment and maintenance of meaning and the pressure towards rationalization and efficiency which we have already seen pervades the co-operative movement (Lodahl and Mitchell, 1980).

In a broader examination of the same set of tensions, Viviani (1987) has been concerned to try to account for the resistance to change which he encounters while working as a consultant with co-operative organizations, again in Italy. Since 1886, external legitimization has been provided for Italian co-operatives by the Lega Nazionale delle Cooperative, which establishes links with major national political parties, and also regulates reciprocal relationships between co-operatives. Again, Viviani notes the tensions which develop between the ideals of the co-operative pact in its various forms and the calculative, commercial constraints of the wider economy. These tensions develop in part from the growth of individual co-operative enterprises, and in part from the pressures upon the Lega and its constituent parts to accept a commercial language and a commercial paradigm into their cultures. Viviani notes the way in which individual co-operatives sustain their internal commitment by the adoption and reiteration of a left-wing rhetoric, style, and iconography within their offices and factories. He is concerned that the strong and reinforcing commitment generated by this embodiment of the original 'foundational' culture should not immobilize the movement in its attempts to deal with its contemporary problems. He sees the danger that the movement might eventually be impoverished by the loss of those co-operatives which become overly commercial, or that it might be weakened as key enterprises become 'bi-lingual', talking in one language to the outside world and reserving a co-operative style of discussion for relations within the movement. An alternative possibility is that the Lega might be pushed into effectively abandoning the co-operative paradigm completely by moving wholly into the commercial environment.

These examples of recent studies of cultural features of co-operative organizations offer some insights into concerns which might be of relevance not merely to the co-operative sector but also to broader symbolic examinations of industrial participation. Outside the immediate context of the co-operative movement, parallel cultural enquiries could be expected to portray equally clearly the ambiguities which recur in virtually every encounter between the values of industrial democracy and the values of commerce. Prior to the last decade, as the editors of this volume indicate, it was possible to see the onward march of industrial democracy as having an air of inevitability about it. However, we now find that the values of participation are being opposed to the values of entrepreneurship, not only in the West but also, in a muted form, within some areas of state socialism. In some situations, too, the meaning of participation is being modified as it is promoted in a mutated form which identifies participation with entrepreneurship and with the opportunity to become a player in an economic game of 'survival of the fittest'.

Cultural and symbolic analyses are thus likely to raise the question of whether participation is a progressive or a conservative ideology, and to ask what degree of social urgency lies behind contemporary requests for participation. Looking at the changing class background, it might be desirable to consider whether the idea of industrial participation itself is now a myth from the past, its imperative rooted in a particular historical moment in the class struggle, a moment which may now have passed. Such analyses could ask whether the rhetoric of participation is to be tied inevitably to the rhetoric of resistance, or whether other cultural possibilities can be developed.

The participative movements of the past were assisted ideologically by links with political parties and trade unions, which in turn offered connections with significant sectors of the working class. Now, by contrast, it might seem that participation is in danger of becoming depoliticized. Is its meaning and significance shifting so that participation becomes merely another mode of management (Jenkins, 1974) to be adopted or rejected upon pragmatic rather than value-based criteria? What cultural significance should we seek when large corporate structures themselves embrace forms of participation such as co-ownership or share distribution, or when they see participation in a new 'corporate culture' as essential for industrial excellence?

People assess work and the demands of work in the context of their times and against the background of their own upbringing. To what extent is participation still a value in Western culture? Recession generates different images of work and creates different attitudes to work, while the growth of new technology shifts many old issues into new forms which sometimes sit uneasily with traditional ideologies of industrial democracy (Daudi, 1985). Does society retain a value base which is coherent enough to offer a worthwhile resolution of such issues? Or will all future battles about participation be acted out in the media, as matters of style rather than as matters of political philosophy?

One final matter should be mentioned here which, although it has barely surfaced in the earlier discussions, is present throughout—the question of power.

With one or two notable exceptions (McGuire and Calas, 1984; Rosen, 1985*b*), there is little overt discussion of power in the new cultural literature, and the juxtaposition of this literature with the concerns of industrial democracy and industrial participation highlights this absence, for all of the debates about participation and democracy commence from considerations of access to power. For some writers, focusing upon culture rather than power suggests an 'idealistic' rather than a 'materialistic' approach, and a standard left-wing criticism of these writers would be that they concentrate upon the superficial rather than the essential. By looking at the 'superstructure' rather than at the 'relations of production' they are neglecting the *realpolitik* of industrial affairs.

We do not think that the relative silence about power in the literature on organizational culture and symbolism is readily defensible, and if this literature is to influence further work on democracy and industrial participation, this situation will have to be changed. And yet we would note that the standard criticisms are too simple, for considerations of power are not entirely absent from existing analyses. All power relationships draw upon predisposing resources, but they have to be expressed in practice through social relationships of obedience and command, of deference and authority, of followership and leadership. Domination must be related to an available cultural matrix.

Our discussion of the internal and external legitimacy of co-operative enterprises could be better understood against an analysis of the political and economic resources available to the co-operative as against the commercial sector. But legitimacy is concerned with the acceptable use of power and, without the cultural features which constitute legitimacy, power can only be exercised through coercion, by the use of brute force or the threat of the use of such force.

Attention to cultural and symbolic matters thus offers us the possibility of coming to a deeper understanding of the nature of power relationships in the industrial context, by illuminating, for example, those conditions which make it reasonable for individuals not to obey, not to defer, not to follow. The key issues of industrial democracy and participation need to be approached both through an examination of power and through an examination of culture so that we come to understand not only historical confrontations, political debates, and struggles for resources, but also the subtle ways in which it might be possible to promote the better integration of members into modern organizations and the dissemination of democratic values within the industrial community.

References

Aktouf, O. (1985), 'Business Internal Image: Conflictual Representation Systems', *Dragon*, 1(1): 104–18.

Barley, S. R. (1986), 'Technology as an Occasion for Structuring Evidence from

Observations of CT Scanners and the Social Order of Radiology Departments', *Administrative Science Quarterly*, 31(1): 78–108.

Berg, P.-O. (1984), 'Techno-culture', paper presented to the First International Conference on Organizational Symbolism and Corporate Culture, Lund, Sweden.

Blackhurst, M. (1986), 'The Role of Culture in Affirmative Action Strategy', *Dragon*, 1(5): 74–89.

Bolognini, B. (1986), 'Images as Identifying Objects and as Organisational Integrators in Two Firms', *Dragon*, 1(3): 61–75.

Broms, H. and Gahmberg, H. (1982), *Mythology in Management Culture* (Helsinki: School of Economics).

—— —— (1983), 'Communication to Self in Organizations and Cultures', *Administrative Science Quarterly*, 28(3): 482–95.

Brown, L. (1987), 'The Co-operative Way: Business not as Usual', paper presented to the Third International Conference on Organizational Symbolism and Corporate Culture, Milan, Italy.

Dandridge, T. C. (1986), Ceremony as an Integration of Work and Play, *Organization Studies*, 2: 159–68.

Daudi, P. (1985), 'The Discursive Legitimation of Managerial Practices', *Dragon*, 1(2): 73–93.

Dubinskas, F. A. (1987), *Making Time: Ethnographies of Culture, Time and Organization in High Technology* (Philadelphia, Pa.: Temple Press).

Fine, G. A. (1984), 'Negotiated Orders and Organizational Cultures', *Annual Review of Sociology*, 10: 239–62.

Frost, P. J., Moore, L. F., Louis, M. R., Lundberg, C. C., and Martin, J. (eds.) (1985), *Organizational Culture* (Beverly Hills, Calif.: Sage Publications).

Gagliardi, P. (ed.) (1986), *Le Imprese Come Culture* (Milan: ISEDI).

Gherardi, S. and Masiero, A. (1987), 'The Impact of Organizational Culture on Life-Cycle and Decision-Making Processes in Newborn Co-operatives', *Economic and Industrial Democracy*, 8: 323–47.

Glaser, B. and Strauss, A. (1967), *The Discovery of Grounded Theory* (Chicago, Ill.: Aldine).

Grafton-Small, R. and Linstead, S. (1986), 'The Everyday Professional: Skill in the Symbolic Management of Occupational Kinship', in Strati (ed.), *The Symbolics of Skill*.

Gregory, K. L. (1983), 'Native-View Paradigms: Multiple Cultures and Culture Conflicts in Organizations', *Administrative Science Quarterly*, 28: 359–76.

Hofstede, G. H. (1967), *The Game of Budget Control* (Assen: Van Gorcum).

Jenkins, D. (1974), *Job Power: Blue and White Collar Democracy* (London: Heinemann)

Kanter, R. M. (1972), *Commitment and Community: Communes and Utopias in Sociological Perspective* (Cambridge, Mass.: Harvard University Press).

Lang, C. L. (1981), 'Good Cases—Bad Cases: Client Selection and Professional Prerogative in a Community Mental Health Center', *Urban Life*, 10: 289–309.

Lincoln, Y. S. and Guba, E. G. (1985), *Naturalistic Inquiry* (Beverly Hills, Calif.: Sage Publications).

Lodahl, T. M. and Mitchell, S. M. (1980), 'Drift in the Development of Innovative

Organizations', in J. Kimberley *et al.*, *The Organizational Life Cycle* (San Francisco, Calif.: Jossey-Bass).

Louis, M. R. (1985), 'An Investigator's Guide to Workplace Culture', in P. J. Frost *et al.* (eds.), *Organizational Culture* (Beverly Hills, Calif.: Sage Publications).

Lynxwiler, J., Shaver, W., and Clelland, D. A. (1983), 'The Organization and Impact of Inspector Discretion in a Regulatory Bureaucracy', *Social Problems*, 30: 425–36.

Van Maanen, J. and Barley, S. (1984), 'Occupational Communities', in B. Staw, and L. Cummings (eds.), *Research in Organizational Behavior* (Greenwich, Conn.: JAI Press).

McGill, P. (1987), 'Sunset in the East', *Observer*, 2 Aug.

McGuire, J. B. and Calas, M. B. (1984), 'Organizations as Networks: A Study in Power and Symbolism', paper presented to the First International Conference on Organizational Symbolism and Corporate Culture, Lund, Sweden.

Manning, P. (1977), *Police Work* (Cambridge, Mass.: MIT Press).

Martin, P. Y. and Turner, B. A. (1986), 'Grounded Theory and Organizational Research', *Journal of Applied Behavioral Science*, 22(2): 141–58.

Morgan, G. (1986), *Images of Organization* (Beverly Hills, Calif., Sage Publications).

Norman, M. R. (1977), *Management for Growth* (Chichester: Wiley).

Peters, T. J. and Waterman, R. H. (1982), *In Search of Excellence* (New York: Harper & Row).

Peyrot, M. (1982), 'Caseload Management: Choosing Suitable Clients in a Community Health Clinic Agency', *Social Problems*, 30: 157–67.

Pondy, L. R., Frost, P. J., Morgan, G., and Dandridge, T. C. (eds.) (1983), Organizational Symbolism (Greenwich, Conn.: JAI Press).

Raspa, R. (1986), 'Creating Fiction in the Committee', *Dragon*, 1(4): 7–22.

Reynaud, E. M. (1983), 'Change in Collective Identities', in C. Crouch, and F. Heller (eds.), *International Yearbook of Organizational Democracy*, i (Chichester: Wiley).

Riley, P. (1983), 'A Structurationist Account of Political Culture', *Administrative Science Quarterly*, 28: 414–37.

Rosen, M. (1985*a*), 'Breakfast at Spiro's: Dramaturgy and Dominance', *Journal of Management*, 11(2): 31–48.

—— (1985*b*), 'The Reproduction of Hegemony: An Analysis of Bureaucratic Control', *Research in Political Economy*, 8, JAI Press Monograph Series (Greenwich, Conn.: JAI Press).

Santino, J. (1979), 'Characteristics of Occupational Narratives', see Abrahams, R. D. (1978), 'Toward A Sociological Theory of Folklore: Performing Services', in R. H. Byington (ed.), *Working Americans: Contemporary Approaches to Occupational Folklore* (Washington, DC: Smithsonian Folklore Studies).

Strati, A. (ed.) (1986), *The Symbolics of Skill* (Trento: Departimento di Politica Sociale).

Turner, B. A. (1971), *Exploring the Industrial Subculture* (London: Macmillan).

—— (1981), 'Some Practical Aspects of Qualitative Data Analysis: One Way of Organising the Cognitive Processes Associated with the Generation of Grounded Theory', *Quality and Quantity*, 15: 225–47.

Viviani, M. (1987), 'Partisans, Profit and Blank Walls: Crises and Culture Change in the Co-operative Company as Expressed in its Artefacts', paper presented to the Third International Conference on Corporate Culture and Organizational Symbolism, Milan, Italy.

Westerlund, G. and Sjostrand, S. (1979), *Organizational Myths* (New York: Harper & Row).

Witkin, R. W. (1974), *The Intelligence of Feeling* (London: Heinemann).

—— and Poupart, R. (1986), 'Shadows of a Culture in "Native" Reflections in Work in an Abortion Clinic', *Dragon*, 2(1): 56–73.

PART IV

RECENT RESEARCH FINDINGS

Outline of Part IV

IN this part of the Handbook we present a number of recent investigations of particular interest with respect to problems or aspects of organizational democracy that have not, or have seldom, hitherto been studied. We start with a report of historical research by Joop C. Visser on factory occupation as expressive of an aspect of industrial democracy. This radical form of social action has never been in the foreground of analyses of industrial relations, although when it happens it makes news headlines. The author distinguishes three phases of this kind of industrial action: 1917–21, 1935–7 and 1968–83. Such a historical perspective allows us a better understanding of similarities and differences between the three waves of factory occupation. It is astonishing that this form of action has little or no tradition, in the sense that there are practically no links between the periods mentioned and the different countries involved. The practice, it seems, has to be 'reappropriated' each time.

Eckhart Hildebrandt reports on an empirical study within the West German machine-building industry. The challenge to the system of co-determination presented by the introduction of new technologies is discussed on the basis of data concerning the involvement of works councils in the planning, introduction, and implementation of such innovations. The role of works councils in this respect is complicated mainly by two factors: over-information and lack of relevant competence on the side of worker representatives. Whether or not the German system of *Mitbestimmung* will be able to establish some control in this sphere in one form or another remains very much a moot point.

Artur Meier from the German Democratic Republic presents the first findings of a project similar to that of Hildebrandt but in a socialist country. Although the political conditions are completely different, the workers are confronted with similar problems in regard to work organization, work content, and autonomy. A long tradition of socio-technical research, which is mostly unknown in the West due to language and other barriers, exists in the countries of Eastern Europe. Officially the integration of new technologies in firms does not pose problems within a socialist society, where all means of production are supposedly owned by the working class. In practice, the existing legal rights of participation have still to be transformed into reality. The difference, compared with Western societies, is that the right to work (which eliminates the fear of unemployment) radically changes the possibilities of real participation.

A completely different theme is treated by Peter Abell. He reports results of his research in three developing countries: Tanzania, Sri Lanka, and Fiji. He supplies a link between the contributions of Chris Cornforth (Part I) and Hing Ai Yun (Part

V). In each of the articles concerning the co-operative movement, the central role of support organizations comes to the fore. Peter Abell deals principally with industrial or producer co-operatives, which have forms of horizontal and vertical integration completely different from those of consumer and agricultural co-operatives. Therefore, in his view, they require different and independent support organizations. This is without question also true for developed countries.

14

Factory Occupation and Industrial Democracy

JOOP C. VISSER

IN the action programme of the Red Union International of 1921 a separate paragraph was devoted to factory occupation. Great ideological value was attached to factory occupation in this paragraph. It could provide experience in industrial management and, at the same time, would reduce the aura of sanctity surrounding private property. The clearest expression of the importance ascribed to it is found in the words: 'Sie ist der klarste Ausdruck des Vorwärtsschreitens der Sozialen Revolution' ('It is the clearest expression of the progress of the social revolution') (*Aktionsprogramm*, 1921: 29–30). At that date, therefore, factory occupation as a means of action was linked directly with the phenomenon of industrial democracy.

The extensive use which has been made of factory occupation in industrial conflicts in most industrialized countries over the last fifteen years has received little attention, however, in the literature. One of the explanations for this is that most authors see scarcely any difference between this form of action and the classical weapon of the strike. Based on the assumption that it has always, or almost always, been used in an attempt to prevent the closing down of factories and mass redundancy, factory occupation is viewed as a tactical alternative to a strike. It is not considered to give a special meaning to industrial conflicts.

Some authors (e.g. Teulings and Leijnse, 1974: 187–8; Coates, 1981: 17–18; Hautsch and Semmler, 1983: 16–17) see a connection with the phenomenon of industrial democracy. These authors regard as an important characteristic of factory occupation the temporary, illegal violation of the employers' property rights, which makes it a more extreme means of action than a strike.

Both views are based on the use of factory occupation since 1970. A historical perspective is almost entirely lacking. At most, some reference is made to its earlier use. Whereas long-term analyses have been made of industrial conflicts in the form of strikes (Shorter and Tilly, 1974; Cronin, 1979; Edwards, 1981), no such analyses—with the exception of the research on which this article is based (Visser, 1986)—have been made of factory occupations.

The intention of this article is to demonstrate by means of a historical comparison, that the view that factory occupation is exclusively a tactical alternative to a strike (e.g. Greenwood, 1977: 40) is ill founded. This does not imply that the history of factory occupations should be seen as steps along the road to industrial democracy. It will, however, be argued that the relation between the phenomenon of factory occupation and that of industrial democracy can be made clear by looking less at the *instrumental* function of such actions and more at their *expressive* function.

Factory occupation is defined here as a form of action in industrial conflicts in which employees endeavour to compel the granting of certain demands by occupying the workplace during and outside normal working hours. If the employees occupying a factory refuse to work, the term 'sit-in' is used; a situation in which the workers continue production under their own management is referred to as a 'work-in'. As regards the meaning of the term 'industrial democracy', we agree with the general definition of Teulings (1981: 51)—the wielding of power by a dominated party within a mastery relationship—without going into the different forms, such as joint consultation, workers' self-management, and co-determination. Attention should, however, be drawn to the importance of the IDE researchers' assertion (1981: 169) that there must be a connection between the development of *de jure* and *de facto* participation.

As the above definition of factory occupation is restricted to industrial disputes, it excludes the taking over of enterprises by factory committees as happened in Russia in 1917, in Germany in 1919, and in Spain in 1936. These take-overs were not so much the result of industrial disputes as the by-product of a revolutionary movement, a by-product which in intent and execution unquestionably had to do with industrial democracy. What we are concerned with here, however, is factory occupations which take place within the framework of industrial relations and whose value as regards industrial democratization is disputed.

Whether they do have any such value will be judged on the basis not only of motives and objectives, but also of results and consequences. In addition, an indication of how radical a form of action it is can be provided by how the use of it is experienced. These various factors will, of course, be considered in a historical context.

If the demands put forward go beyond the customary negotiating points at the same time in question, we interpret the occupiers' motives and objectives as demands for a greater say. In such cases the employers' decision-making powers are challenged in an area in which they had hitherto been more or less undisputed.

Intentionally or otherwise, factory occupations can lead to industrial democratization, either at national or at company level. This effect can be seen in the inclusion in collective agreements of rules which make a greater control over the production process possible, in other words, in the institutionalization in organized negotiations of points disputed by means of occupations (Poole, 1984). The way in which property relations in the production process are viewed may also undergo change as a result of such actions. By way of comparison we can refer to squatting, which has fostered the introduction of legal restrictions on the exercising of property rights with respect to the home.

Finally, the fact that a form of action is related to industrial democracy can appear from the way its use is experienced, this being the case where those adopting a particular form of action regard it as more radical, more 'revolutionary'. A distinction needs to be made here between the leaders and the rank and file. Moreover, the radical nature of a form of action can also become apparent from the reactions of the employers.

Several authors (e.g. Tilly and Shorter, 1973; Cronin, 1979: 47–8; Ramsay, 1983) have noted that the changes which have taken place in the pattern of industrial disputes in the past have not occurred gradually but in waves. This view ties in closely with the cyclical perspective in which many authors look at changes, including in the field of industrial democracy. It would seem that a confirmation of this view can be found in the wave-like pattern exhibited by the use of the weapon of factory occupation in the past, with striking concentrations occurring in the periods 1917–21, 1935–7, and 1968–83.

1917–1921: Under the threat of a revolution

Companies were taken over by factory committees in Russia in 1917 during the political revolution. Factory committees also spread quickly in Germany and Hungary. In Britain, France, and Italy the workers' self-management movement developed in a different manner. In the case of Britain the shop stewards' movement grew up in the shipyards on the River Clyde in Scotland. Strike committees consisting of representatives of different occupations and working units developed into permanent bodies representing, in particular, the skilled machine operators on the shop floor. This occurred independently of the trade unions. At first they were concerned with wages and other conditions of employment. Gradually, however, workers' self-management became one of the objectives of the movement. In general the weapon used was the strike in its classical form; some unsuccessful stay-ins were also undertaken (Hinton, 1973: 103 ff.).

In France, representative bodies were set up in factories during the First World War. The initiative in this case came from the fairly radical trade unions themselves, and they operated within the framework of the unions. The occupations in the textile industry reported in this period were not occupations in the true sense of the word (Prouteau, 1937: 91 ff.). Rather, they were 'invasions' of factories by strikers and unemployed workers carried out to check whether there were people at work in them. Actions of the same kind occurred in Britain in 1921 in the struggle against compulsory overtime (Hannington, 1977: 45 ff.).

In Italy, the movement took two forms (Spriano, 1975). Firstly, there was the factory committee movement led by Antonio Gramsci and centred on Turin.

Secondly, there was the wave of factory occupations carried out by the metal-workers on the orders of their union, the FIOM. The latter saw the occupation of factories as the only effective action which could be taken against the lock-outs announced by the employers. In September 1920 over 400,000 workers occupied metal factories, mainly in three big northern cities, Milan, Genoa, and Turin. There was also some spread of the movement to other sectors. The massive proportions assumed by the occupation movement in the social struggle which was then taking place gave rise to hopes of radical changes among the occupiers themselves and the left wing of the Socialist Party (PSI). This was due, to a large extent, to the wide gap between the rank and file and the leaders of the labour movements, who were unable and unwilling to provide leadership for these changes, and to the absence of a reaction from the Government. The radicals wanted to give the struggle a political goal but failed

- for practical reasons: the occupations, which took an active form, encountered more difficulties than had been expected. Self-management was hampered by lack of money, raw materials, sales outlets, and technicians.
- for organizational reasons: the Socialist Party did not dare to lead a political revolution. That had already become clear in April 1920, when it had left the Turin movement in the cold.

In the period 1917–21, then, it was only in Italy that the weapon of factory occupation was used in an industrial conflict. The demands here were concerned initially with wages and working conditions, but shifted to the sphere of workers' self-management. The type of action, such as refusing to do overtime, go-slow actions, working to rule and sit-downs, had already been tried.

1935–1937: The position of the trade union in companies

Though the years 1936 and 1937 in particular saw waves of factory occupations, the workers in Eastern Europe had been ahead of their Western colleagues. In the first half of the 1930s extensive use had been made of this weapon in countries such as Romania, Yugoslavia, and, above all, Poland, with miners and textile workers as the most active groups.

In Britain it was also the miners who carried out the occupations in South Wales in 1935 in the form of stay-downs (Smith, 1973). Here they formed a part of the struggle which had been going on since 1926 between the managements of the mines and their workers, though it was actually more a struggle between a radical and a moderate miners' union for the right to represent the workers.

The best-known actions in this period, and the ones which appeal most to the imagination, took place in France: 9,000 occupations in addition to 3,000 strikes, involving a total of 1,800,000 workers in June 1936 alone (*Bulletin du Ministère du Travail*, Paris, 1936). This social explosion at the start of Blum's Popular Front

Government struck at the entire social and economic life of the country. Initially the actions were undertaken in support of wage demands and to prevent dismissals. Gradually, however, demands concerning the rights of workers and trade unions in companies came more to the fore: the right to be a member of a trade union, workers' representation, and workers' control. Finally, the most important role came to be played by the demand that the employers should sign a collective agreement which incorporated these rights.

A popular form of action in the United States in the years 1934–6 was the sit-down strike, particularly in the car industry. The 'quickies' (quick strikes) and the 'skippies' (skipping of certain actions in the course of work) were not factory occupations as defined by us but, rather, work interruptions on the shop floor (Bernstein, 1970: 498 ff.). What did fall under our definition was the occupation of General Motors, starting with the Flint plant at the end of December 1936 (Fine, 1969). The purpose of this action was to obtain recognition of the United Automobile Workers (UAW) as the sole representative of the workers in collective bargaining with the employers. The action spread to other General Motors plants and later to Chrysler and was successful.

The factory occupations which occurred in Belgium in 1936 under the influence of the events in France in June were immediately terminated by the police, sometimes with the help of the army.

As stated earlier, the events in Spain in 1936 were a special case. The collectivizations of companies sparked off by political changes in the country can not be regarded as occupations carried out as a means of action in an industrial dispute.

1968–83: In defence of jobs

In most West European countries a resurgence of the class conflict occurred in the second half of the 1960s. This found expression in a higher frequency of industrial disputes and in the use of different, more radical forms of action. One of these forms of action was the occupation of factories. The year 1968, with the events in Paris in May, marked the beginning of the renewed use of this weapon on a large scale.

The popularity of factory occupation among industrial workers was preceded by sit-downs and sit-ins by other groups: peace demonstrators, anti-discrimination campaigners, and students. It was not until three years later, however, that the third wave of factory occupations in Western Europe really gathered force. An important role in this process was played by three 'exemplary' occupations: that of the UCS shipyards on the Clyde in Scotland in 1971, that of Enka-Breda—part of the multinational corporation AKZO—in The Netherlands in 1972, and the spectacular work-in at the watch-making firm Lip in Besançon in France in 1973. Occupations to which much publicity has been given, such as the occupation of the

Süssmuth glass-works in Immenhausen (FRG) in 1970, were too small in size to be of much influence.

The third was the biggest of the three waves. Not only did occupations occur with greater frequency: they also extended over a wider area. The occupation of factories became an industrial weapon in countries in which hitherto it had been used rarely, if at all, such as West Germany and The Netherlands. Factory occupation developed from an exceptional means into an everyday phenomenon in industrial disputes in the 1970s.

In general the occupations seemed to have been aimed at preventing mass dismissals arising from factory closures and reorganizations. As we shall see, this general observation requires considerable qualification. A notable feature of this third wave was the participation in occupations of other employees aside from production workers. Another remarkable phenomenon in this third period was that large-scale occupations were also carried out in areas other than industry: universities were occupied by students, schools by pupils, houses by squatters, the offices of asociations by members, and embassies by national minorities and sympathizing protest groups.

In the midst of the flood of publicity caused by these actions the factory occupations, many of which were very peaceful, were less conspicuous. Consequently, the trade unions no longer seemed to be so concerned about their illegal nature. Can the (provisional) conclusion be drawn from this that factory occupation came to form part of the repertoire of means from which employees in most Western industrial countries and Japan could choose at will for use in industrial disputes, at least until the beginning of the 1980s? If the answer should be affirmative, it is at any rate certain that the path leading to this state of affairs was a long and difficult one.

What does this historical survey teach us about the use of factory occupation in relation to the phenomenon of industrial democracy? To answer this we shall look at the political and economic situation in which the large-scale use of factory occupation occurred, at the course, motives, and objectives, at the results, and at the way in which this form of action was experienced.

The political and economic situation

Each of the three periods of large-scale use which have been discussed coincided with a political situation which could be described as being more or less one of a crisis. In the period 1917–21 it was the First World War and its consequences which made the internal political situation in many countries unstable, while in the 1930s it was the Depression and the threat of fascism. There was also a political crisis in the years 1968–72. Established systems of political control no longer worked automatically. The authority of governments was no longer accepted unquestioningly. In contrast to the previous periods there was at first merely a question of slight recession. The real economic crisis did not occur until after 1973 and, to a greater extent, after 1979.

Consequently, the choice of factory occupation as a form of action cannot be fully explained by specific circumstances applying at the time which made it a logical alternative to a strike. Such a circumstance would be an economic recession. This view of factory occupations would appear to be incorrect. Firstly, a state of economic crisis did not exist in all cases. Secondly, where it did exist the possible tactical advantages of occupation over a strike were not always present. The fear that the effect of a strike would be nullified by blacklegs was not always realistic. For example, the massive scale of the actions in France in 1936 would have made it impossible to use them. Again, preventing machines from being removed can not always have been an important consideration in making the choice. Thirdly, the choice of work-ins argues against this view. The fact that the Italian workers in 1920 and, for example, the UCS workers in 1971 and those of Lip in 1973 took this course of action can not be explained by the aforementioned factors.

Moreover, only after a situation of economic crisis had already existed for some time did occupations take place in large numbers. This suggests that the occurrence of these actions can not be adequately explained by frustration and deprivation theories. The course taken by the large-scale actions does not point in that direction either.

The dynamics of the large-scale occupation movements

In each of the three periods there were forerunners and followers. The periods started with incidental, isolated actions. The frequency of occupations then greatly increased, concentrated at first in a particular region and later spreading over the entire country.

If we focus attention on the forerunners we find marked similarities between the three waves. In each case the first occupations took place in companies or industries which were not doing badly (the heavy metal sector, particularly the car and aircraft industries). In the 1920s and the 1930s the targets were frequently companies with an order book well filled by the government. In the 1970s, though the first occupations took place in industries which were not in very good condition, the companies concerned were doing relatively well. In the second place, the workers were therefore unable to accept that the employers failed to react positively to their demands. In their view, negative measures were not in accord with the company's present or expected future economic position. If the economic position of the company itself was poor, this was blamed on bad management. The workers frequently felt themselves to be the victims of arbitrary decisions by 'absentee owners' who had no heart for the business or, rather, for the employees. One also finds a third striking similarity as regards the local context of the companies concerned. Because of their size, they played an important role in the local labour market. Finally, a traditional bond existed between the companies and the local community. The latter could therefore be expected to provide the sympathy and support necessary for the success of factory occupations.

In our view, however, the rapid spread of the movements must be explained in a different manner, as a form of 'behavioural contagion'. The companies' economic position and local conditions played a much less important role in later factory occupations. The successes of the first occupations led to imitation. People became infected with an occupational urge, as it were.

The labour relations context

One is struck first of all by the similarity in government attitudes in the three waves. In each of them governments adopted a neutral wait-and-see attitude, sometimes even a sympathetic attitude, towards the occupations. In their attempts at mediation they put pressure on the employers to settle because they were seriously alarmed by the situation.

In Italy in 1920 the reason for the employers' fears lay in the revolutionary situation elsewhere, the type of actions (work-ins), and the fact that the occupations had been ordered by an official trade union. In France and the United States what alarmed the employers was not so much the type of action (sit-ins) as the rapid, large-scale spread of factory occupations. In the 1970s, on the other hand, in the case of the first occupations it was the type of action and the publicity it received through the media which troubled the employers.

In contrast to governments and employers, the trade unions exhibited wide differences in attitude. As mentioned earlier, the factory occupations in Italy were initiated by a trade union, the FIOM. When the movement began to display revolutionary tendencies, however, the union immediately distanced itself from it. In the 1930s the occupations in the United States and Britain formed part of the unions' fight for recognition, and to some extent also of the struggle between the unions. In France the trade unions adopted a wait-and-see attitude initially. Only after the first successes and the expansion of the movement did the CGT intervene with the object of bringing it under control. In the 1970s a clear distinction must be made between highly centralized unions and unions with a decentralized organization. In the case of the decentralized unions such as the French CFDT and the Dutch NKV, the original initiative for a factory occupation frequently came from local branches. The centralized unions openly backed occupations only at a later stage.

The attitude of the unions was partly determined by their desire to be seen by the two other actors involved in labour relations as a loyal fellow actor. It would seem that, viewed from a long-term standpoint, the change in the direction of greater caution in the matter of factory occupations supports the theory of the integration of the trade union movement into the established social order. If we accept that this is the case, the reverse tendency, which can be detected in the last years of the third wave, must be interpreted as a sign of social acceptance of factory occupation as a means of action. However, some remarks need to be made about this assumption.

In the first place, the unions' attitude to the weapon of factory occupation must be viewed in the light of the prevailing system of norms and values, in this case especially with respect to authority and people's attitude towards it. Increasing tolerance in this area enabled the trade union movement to accept the use of an illegal weapon without seriously endangering its position *vis-à-vis* its negotiating partner. Repeated overstepping of the limits in this area evidently caused the limits to be shifted.

Motives and objectives

Neither specific circumstances nor a specific labour relations context points unequivocally to the use of factory occupation purely as a tactical alternative to a strike. The demands of those who carried out factory occupations confirm this. Historical comparison reveals no conclusive logical connection between the form and purpose of the actions.

The actions carried out in Italy in 1920 were concerned with a wage dispute, though the first major factory occupation, that of the Romeo plants in Milan, was a response to a threatened lock-out. In the 1930s in Britain and the United States, as in France, trade union rights were at issue. In the 1970s the weapon was first used against closures and mass dismissals and later also in wage disputes.

It should be remarked that, even though the demands were not always directly translatable into wishes for industrial democracy, except in the 1930s, they often went further than had hitherto been customary. Compliance with them at any rate meant restricting the powers of the employers. Such radical demands were not, however, associated exclusively with factory occupations. They are sometimes found where the form of action chosen was the strike.

Results and consequences

Is a relationship with industrial democracy to be found in the consequences of factory occupations?

When the occupation movement in 1920 came to an end in Italy an agreement was drawn up which included a promise by the employers to realize a legal regulation of trade union control over companies. In practice, however, nothing came of this promise. In the United States in 1937 the UAW won a major victory by achieving recognition as the sole representative of the workers in collective bargaining. In France the Matignon agreement of 7 June 1936 constituted a great success for the workers: recognition of the collective contract, of the *droit syndical* (the right to be a member of a trade union) and of the system of *délégués ouvriers* (workers' representatives).

As regards the 1970s, one must look for legal changes at national level relating to industrial democracy. This last period can be seen to the same extent as the first two as a wave of closely connected actions. In the 1970s it was more a case of a very high frequency of isolated actions. However, the concrete results at company level should not be overestimated either, particularly if one looks at the longer term. In many cases, mass dismissals eventually did take place. Factory occupations have also given rise to relatively few production co-operatives: scarcely any in the 1970s, and none at all in the 1920s and 1930s as far as is known (Elliott, 1978: 190 ff.).

Finally, we must ask ourselves whether the results in the sphere of industrial democracy were the product of the choice of factory occupation as a means of action or, rather, attributable to the massive scale of the actions.

The expressive function of factory occupation

Does factory occupation have no significance at all in terms of the development of industrial democracy?

Thus far the discussion has been focused on objectives and concrete results and, hence, on the *instrumental* function of a means of action. From this viewpoint the assertion that factory occupation should be seen purely as a tactical alternative to a strike is understandable. In addition to an instrumental significance, however, actions have an *expressive* or demonstrative function for an actor (Parkin, 1968: 34). Whereas the instrumental function relates to the direct achievement of the goal, the expressive function has to do with the manifestation of the actor's values. In other words, the choice of the means of action is not only determined by its estimated effectiveness: it is also influenced by ideology. The means of action reflects the actors' view of what the desired situation is in the society with respect to the matter in question. This would mean that factory occupations—the sit-ins and, especially, work-ins—reflect the ideal of industrial democracy. In our opinion, sufficient arguments can be derived from the history of factory occupations to support this view.

In the reports, particularly on the first occupations in each wave, the atmosphere is described as *une fête de la révolution* (a celebration of the revolution). The Italian metal-workers celebrated the first Sunday of the occupations in September 1920 as 'Red Sunday'. The newspapers reported that the tension released itself in a celebration of liberation based on the belief in the possibility of a revolution. In the preceding days *Avanti* had spoken of a new era in the class struggle.

In what was to become a celebrated article in *La Révolution prolétarienne* Simone Weil gave an emotional description of the French occupations in 1936: joy emanating from a feeling of self-liberation. There was hope that the occupations would herald *contrôle-ouvrier* (workers' control). The picture was one of a utopian pastoral, with a happy and disciplined community of workers who hoped for a different society.

A similar atmosphere was also to be found in the first exemplary' occupations in the 1970s. When the Lip factory was occupied the slogan hung on the façade was 'Aujourd'hui on est en lutte pour défendre nos libertés, demain nous serons en fête dans une autre société' ('Today we are fighting to defend our freedom, tomorrow we will be celebrating in another society'). The occupiers of Enka in The Netherlands gave expression to their faith in the future in the words: 'After this week things will never be the same again.' The workers' feeling of impotence had made way for a regained faith in their own strength.

A difference can be detected between the three waves in this respect: whereas the first two were marked by a growing radicalization, the reverse was the case in the third wave.

The formulation of demands also argues in favour of emphasizing the expressive function of factory occupation as a means of action. Frequently, the demands as such were regarded by the occupiers as scarcely attainable. Sometimes, as in the second half of June 1936 in France, no demands whatsoever were made. The workers simply felt a need to take action. Factory occupiers were always aware of the illegal nature of what they were doing, though that awareness diminished in the course of time during the last wave. However, the employers had violated the customary procedures to such an extent that the workers had lost their belief in the justice and rightness of the employers' actions. Hence, radical resistance to those actions acquired a legitimate character in their eyes.

The occupation thus became a demonstrative 'no' to the capitalists, who—albeit temporarily—were prevented from freely exercising their property rights with respect to the means of production. This is also what the employers felt, which largely explains the emotional nature of their reactions. Moreover, the occupations recurrently sparked off fundamental debates among lawyers about property rights.

In this light it is understandable that official trade union organizations generally took no part in the factory occupations. The trade union movement has always seen as its primary task the direct promotion of the interests of its members, and, for this reason, adopts a posture which makes it an acceptable opponent (or partner) for the other parties concerned. Consequently, it must always impose restrictions on itself with respect to other objectives—in this case, making the workers aware of the need for a fundamental democratization of the labour system. In part, this aloofness arose from the powerlessness of the institutionalized trade union, which, in most West European countries, has only a week base in the companies themselves. The trade union organizations did, none the less, take the occupation movement under their wing after a time. This, however, sealed the fate of the radicalizing element originally present in the occupation movement.

The aloofness of the official unions and the workers' awareness of the impermissibility of the means have had an inhibitive effect as regards the decision to engage in factory occupation. Another inhibiting factor was ignorance of factory occupation as a form of action. The concentration of such actions in waves and the fact that they occurred only sporadically in the intervals between the waves meant that factory occupation had to be rediscovered each time. It was not without reason, therefore, that it was recurrently described as a new form of action. This brings us, finally, to an interesting phenomenon, which will be dealt with only briefly here, namely that of the collective memory of the working class.

Learning from experience

According to Charles Tilly, one of the most important factors explaining the repertoire of collective actions of a particular group is the relevant accumulated experience of a population with previous collective actions (Tilly, 1979). Leaving aside exceptions such as the Italian metal-workers in 1920 and the UCS workers in 1971, however, the history of the use of factory ocupation as a form of action does not point in that direction. In some cases the reverse would seem rather to apply. Inexperience appears to have a greater predictive value as regards the decision to occupy factories, at any rate at the start of the waves.

Did experiences in the more distant past play a role in the choice of the form of action? Must we look for the explanation in the experiences of a specific generation, as Phelps-Brown (1975: 17–20) does in the case of the mass movement of 1968–72? If so, the group must be a generation in the social sense, with common experiences and problems, rather than in the purely biological sense.

The spectacular nature of the waves of factory occupation might have caused them to be remembered longer. Traumatic experiences are considered to be more important in this respect than, for example, changes in the state of the economy. Defeats suffered by the workers could have left a more lasting mark. And the results achieved by the mass actions fell so far short of the workers' expectations that disillusionment was great. The experiences in earlier waves could thus have played an important role later. The workers could have learnt from factory occupations. A learning effect is present in any action. As far as the occupations are concerned, this could be the experience of a feeling of being the boss in the factory and, particularly in the case of work-ins, the feeling of being able to keep production going without managers and supervisors. This view, based on unilinear evolutionism, is not valid, however, in the case of the factory occupation movements. The cyclical nature of the history of factory occupations argues against it. In general, factory occupiers could not fall back on their own experiences in their immediate surroundings. The successive waves did not take place in the same countries, let alone the same regions.

Previous experiences do, however, seem to have played a role at international level. References by initiators to earlier actions abroad are numerous. Around 1910 the Polish workers pointed to similar actions previously undertaken by Italian railway workers and referred to their occupations as 'strikes in the Italian manner'. The factory occupations in France in the 1930s were frequently, as in *L'Humanité*, called *la grève polonaise* (the Polish strike). Again, references were sometimes made to almost simultaneous actions abroad in the same waves, examples being the sit-downs in the United States in 1936–7 and the French occupations.

Occupation actions in a rubber factory in Krakow in 1937 were considered to have begun under the influence of actions in Akron, a centre of the rubber industry in the United States. In the case of Enka in The Netherlands there were clear references to the UCS work-in in Scotland. One finds, however, that experiences were passed on only sparingly. For this reason, factory occupation remained a 'new' form of action. There was little, if any, awareness that it had a past.

References

Aktionsprogramm der Roten Gewerkschafts-Internationale, Das (1921) (Berlin: A. Losowski).

Bernstein, I. (1970), *The Turbulent Years 1933–1944: A History of the American Workers* (Boston: Houghton Mifflin).

Bulletin du Ministère du Travail (1936), Paris.

Coates, K. C. (1981), *Work-Ins, Sit-Ins and Industrial Democracy* (Nottingham: Spokesman).

Cronin, J. E. (1979), *Industrial Conflict in Modern Britain* (London: Croom Helm).

Edwards, P. (1981), *Strikes in the United States, 1881–1974* (Oxford: Blackwell).

Elliott, J. (1978), *Conflict or Co-operation: The Growth of Industrial Democracy* (London: Kogan Page).

Fine, S. (1969), *Sit-Down: The GM-Stike of '36/'37* (Ann Arbor: University of Michigan Press).

Greenwood, J. (1977), *Worker Sit-Ins and Job Protection* (Farnborough: Gower Press).

Hannington, W. (1977), *Unemployed Struggles 1919–1936* (first pub. 1936; London: Lawrence and Wishart).

Hautsch, G. and Semmler, B. (1983), 'Betriebsbesetzungen', *Soziale Bewegungen*, 13 (Frankfurt-on-Main: Institut für Marxistische Studien und Forschungen).

Hinton, J. (1973), *The First Shop Stewards' Movement* (London: Allen and Unwin).

I.D.E. International Research Group (1981), *Industrial Democracy in Europe* (Oxford: Clarendon Press).

Parkin, F. (1968), *Middle Class Radicalism* (Manchester: Manchester University Press).

Phelps-Brown, H. (1975), 'A Non-monetarist View of the Pay Explosion', *Three Banks Review*, 105 (Mar.), 19.

Poole, M. (1984), 'Comparative Approaches to Industrial Conflict', in B. Wilpert and A. Sorge (eds.), *International Yearbook of Organizational Democracy*, ii (Chichester: Wiley).

Prouteau, H. (1937), *Les Occupations d'usines en Italie et en France 1920–1936* (Paris: Libr. Technique et Économique).

Ramsay, H. (1983), 'Evolution or Cycle? Worker Participation in the 1970s and 1980s', in

C. Crouch and F. Heller (eds.), *International Yearbook of Organizational Democracy*, i (Chichester, Wiley).

Shorter, E. and Tilly, C. (1973), 'Les Vagues des grèves en France 1890–1968', *Annales: Economies, Sociétés, Civilisations*, 28 (1973), 857–87.

—— —— (1974), *Strikes in France 1830–1968* (Cambridge: Cambridge University Press).

Smith, D. (1973), 'The Struggle against Company Unionism', *Welsh Review*, 354–78.

Spriano, P. (1975), *The Occupation of the Factories: Italy 1920*, trans. Gwyn A. Williams (first pub. 1964; London: Pluto Press).

Teulings, A. (1981), *Ondernemingsraadpolitiek in Nederland* (Amsterdam: Van Gennep).

—— and Leijnse, F. (1974), *Nieuwe Vormen van Industriële Actie* (Nijmegen: SUN).

Tilly, C. (1979), 'Repertoires of Contention in America and Britain', in M. Zald and J. McCarthy (eds.), *The Dynamics of Social Movements* (Cambridge, Mass.: Winthrop).

Visser, J. C. (1986), *Bedrijfsbezetting, het Verleden van een Nieuw Actiemiddel* (Factory Occupation: The History of a New Form of Industrial Action) (Amsterdam: Stichting Beheer IISG).

15

From Co-determination to Co-management: The Dilemma Confronting Works Councils in the Introduction of New Technologies in the Machine-Building Industry

ECKART HILDEBRANDT

Introduction

This chapter is based on the results of a large empirical and theoretical research project which was carried out over three years in twelve companies by the Science Centre, Berlin under the title of 'Policy and Control in the Use of Computer-Aided Production Planning and Control Systems'. The point of departure of the project was the observation, now gaining acceptance in industrial sociology, that there are considerable variations in work organization design and structuring within the new and flexible information technologies.

Taking this as a basis, there are two further questions: first, the question of whether there are developments in or dimensions of the work situation which show that changes in work structuring do not necessarily result in more pleasant or humane jobs. In this regard we refer to the problems involved in management's control of employees' work performance and behaviour. For many, the introduction of information technologies in plants is associated with the vision of differentiated and comprehensive control access on the part of the management at every level of the plant.

Our second question involves a more precise determination of work-organization structuring. Once greater organizational latitude is determined, it is necessary to ask who does the organizing and how this process of organization takes place. Is it the employers who are implementing clearly defined rationalization strategies, or is it the employees who influence the interpretation of work structuring through their skills and direct involvement, or are works councils, which can put their mandate of a 'social organization' of new technologies into practice by implementing their own ideas, more influential? There is also the question of how the process of finding a concept and introducing it takes place, and what decisions are made in which phase of decision making.

The introduction and plant-specific application of new Computer-Integrated Manufacturing (CIM) systems raises the question of new conditions and needs for co-determination at plant level. International comparisons show a high level of regulated and institutional influence of works councils in the Federal Republic of Germany (FRG) given by a system of contracts like the Works Constitution Act, the Co-determination Law, collective agreements on protection against rationalization, and works agreements. But a more detailed investigation leads to the conclusion that their access to the reorganization of planning, steering, and control functions is slight. Similarly, one of the main results of our research shows that the most important rules of the Works Constitution Act (early and extensive information by management (Clauses 90 and 91) and prohibition of personal control (87.6)) open the introduction process to intervention, but real influence is hindered by a range of fundamental structures, as we shall see below.

We raised these questions in medium-sized plants (i.e. with some 500 to 1,000 employees) in the machine-building industry. As a rule these were machine builders producing one-off or small-series batches in a relatively stable economic situation. We chose this type of plant because in it there is a broad field of tension between traditional orientation to the skilled labourer and workshop on the one hand, and a relatively masssive wave of computer applications for control purposes on the other. We therefore expected to see confrontation between two different principles of work—structuring and manufacturing philosophy—as well as many different possible solutions.

The focus of our exploration was the rationalization by means of information technology, especially Computer-Aided Production Planning and Management (CAPPM) systems as a key element of Computer-Integrated Manufacturing. CIM describes the integrated application of electronic data processing in all departments connected with production. It comprises the co-operation between information technology systems. The interrelations of these technologies are explained in Fig. 15.1.

CAPPM systems are a central preliminary stage of CIM realization, because they increasingly integrate plant functions both horizontally and vertically. Vertically, the execution of orders from the sales department to the final installation is thoroughly planned and executed as scheduled, every department responsible for production being involved. Horizontally, all subfunctions of the plant involved in the organization of product manufacturing must be co-ordinated, based on the same data records, if possible, and performed in optimum fashion and time, if possible.

It is important to emphasize that the results reported are limited in principle to the type of plant studied. One of the main results of our study is that the nature of industrial relations, the management's handling of works council rights as well as

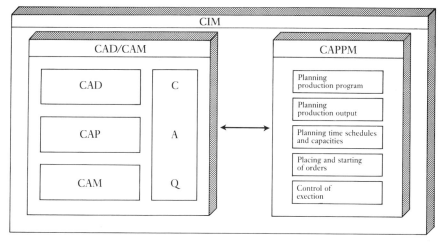

Fig. 15.1 Interrelations of Computer-Integrated Manufacturing (CIM)

CAD = Computer-Aided Design
CAP = Computer-Aided Planning
CAM = Computer-Aided Manufacturing
CAQ = Computer-Aided Quality Assurance
CAPPM = Computer-Aided Production Planning and Management

the scope and forms of works council engagement for structuring tasks, are closely linked to plant-specific conditions, which we call the 'plant social constitution' (Hildebrandt and Seltz, 1985; Hildebrandt, 1988). This plant social constitution clearly seems to vary, for example with the size of plant and type of production.

Information technology intervenes in this constitution and I refer to the four following characteristics of CIM systems:

1. CIM systems are systems that extend to overlapping areas, i.e. they integrate successive functions that are traditionally assigned to autonomous and relatively independent departments.
2. CIM systems are introduced step by step or in the form of partial systems, the final stage often being unclear and, accordingly, the status of the current configuration level as well.
3. The successive implementation of CIM concepts leads to an increase in centralized domination of the process, i.e. ever-greater control over job planning and production.
4. The so-called social effects of CIM systems on the employees are frequently indeterminate and/or ambivalent and vary significantly for different groups of employees.

I would like to explain the significance of these CIM characteristics for the activities of works councils:

Area integration

For the works council area integration means, in its first stage, that it must have information on what is happening and/or is supposed to happen in the various areas, and that it has the ability to control, rate, and influence these processes. The historically evolved state of affairs in which the works council has traditionally been a skilled workers' institution (the skilled-labour sector is the traditional field of recruitment for works councils) is clearly inconsistent with this. The question is: how can a works council meet the demands made on it by such systemic or integrated technology?

Surely the works council would receive the best information if it consisted of representatives from all departments in which the new information, organization, and production technologies were conceived, and from departments in which these technologies were employed and their social consequences occurred.

But there seems to be a limit to participation in works council activities by certain occupational and status groups. This is in part due to the traditional recruitment policy of the unions and the historical way in which skilled workers see themselves versus the way in which middle management (which has historically drawn a clear line between itself and the works council) sees itself. There is, so to speak, a rule to the effect that anyone who aspires to promotion in the plant must not become a shop steward. Being a shop steward in such plants gives no career prospects and is thus inconsistent with the upward orientation of engineers and computer specialists.

Another obstacle is the fact that works council policies hold little attraction for these groups, inasmuch as there is no specific approach to representation of middle and/or upper management's interest in the plants. To that extent, this plant group probably sees little value in becoming active in a trade union or on a works council.

A further issue relates to information. Where, in fact, does the works council obtain important information on new plant innovation projects, current readjustments, and so forth? One source, of course, is management. This will be dealt with in the next section. What we want to look at now is information obtained not only through members of the works council and their contacts in various departments, but also from employees who selectively convey this information to it. In addition to the fact that decisive strategic departments are generally not represented on the works council, our inquiries have shown that the daily flow of information to the works council from the employees and different departments is haphazard and coincidental.

But even if it is assumed that a situation exists within a plant in which the most important departments are represented on the works council and the works council has adequate information at its disposal on pending innovation and rationalization projects, there is still the question of how it is to understand frequently extensive reorganization based on information technology in the plant. There is no question that the list of modernization projects pursued simultaneously in a plant is becoming more extensive and complex; some of the plants already have project management departments that carry out long-term innovation planning and co-ordinate and implement individual projects. Every single one of these projects has, in the meantime, become so complex in its technical and social interpretation that it would be senseless even to consider that an individual shop steward could assimilate all these modernization measures entirely by way of plant information and advanced training. If one looks at the daily tasks to be performed by shop stewards, it is clear how poorly qualified they are to understand new technology. And even if a shop steward were constantly undergoing training, he would not be able to grasp the overall complexity of rationalization. Thus the need arises for a division of labour within the works council, implying specialization.

Although this specialization is a step the works council has to take in order to grasp these new subjects, it leads to serious subsequent problems. There is a widening gap between the technical competence of individual shop stewards and the way in which joint decisions on union policy are reached by the works council.

Such mechanisms not only weaken the collective formation of opinions on the works council, but also influence the position of works council experts on other bodies. Thus, cases were described to us in which representatives of the works council co-operated competently on project planning teams for CAPPM systems, but slowly removed themselves from the team because they were constantly forced to make their team votes dependent on discussion by the works council. They were never able to guarantee that they were bound by decisions of the project team and were therefore no longer recognized by the team.

Another way of acquiring the necessary qualifications is to use external experts for consultation with the works council.

In this respect we have observed the ambivalent development that, on the one hand, external consultants are quite prepared to operate with works councils, advising and informing them, and thus revealing to them possibilities for exerting influence. On the other hand, this collaboration does not usually lead to effective participation, but on the contrary to trivializing and falsifying the social components of organization.

The possibility provided for in the Works Constitution Act that the works council can enlist the services of scientific experts at the cost of the company has not been used by any of the plants we studied. On the other hand, there have been cases where consultation was provided by union experts. Apart from the fact that the number of these union consultants is much too small and that the time at their disposal is by no means adequate to adjust to the increasingly plant-specific problems of introduction, there is, in our opinion, another threshold to be crossed before unions can exert conceptual influence on plants. In the plants we investigated we discovered a very specific form of industrial relations which has traditionally been a sensitive process of co-ordination between the management, the various plant areas, and the works council. As far as possible plant innovations are regulated by consensus and the interests of individual plant groups are taken into consideration. This mutual process of co-ordination, which guarantees the works council its position in the plant and compliance with its main demands (for example, for job safety, the acquisition of qualifications, and maintenance of income), also aims at the survival of the plant among ever-keener competitors in the world market. Interpretations of the situation as a 'joint struggle of survival' predominate in this type of plant and, consequently, intervention by unions from outside is viewed as interference in this plant policy co-ordination process.

In the light of this analysis, it can therefore be stated that the ability of works councils to adjust to the integrating, overlapping nature of information technologies rests on a number of preconditions and that the first steps have been taken to meet this demand. These include a different way of nominating candidates for works council elections, the development of works council committees on new technologies or rationalization, the use of external experts, et cetera. All these steps are necessary to create at least the preconditions for works councils to continue to be accepted by the management as competent discussion partners.

Gradual introduction, partial realization

Problems might arise on how to inform the works council and establish with them an overall relationship regarding the introduction of a succession of technological changes. However, in our own field-work in the plants we canvassed we did not encounter any problem with management's not giving early and extensive information to the works council, nor was there any unwillingness to participate on the part of the works council. In the majority of plants the management had made concrete offers to the works councils, for example to participate in one or more CAPPM project teams, and in most of the plants there were a number of training programmes offered by the plant, and/or manufacturer, and/or consulting firm. There was, in fact, a problem of selective or over-information for the works councils and they were either unable to evaluate the available material and use the various possibilities of intervention open to them, or they saw no need to.

What is interesting, therefore, is the fact that, despite early and extensive information and an offer to participate, the works councils were unable to exert influence during the introduction of the technologies discussed here. We therefore deduce that, above and beyond the obstacle of information acquisition, there must be a number of other obstacles preventing effective organizational activity by the works council. This problem is closely related to the difficulty of conceptualizing the overall relationship between the different rationalization steps that often take place simultaneously.

Our experience shows that the management of these machine-building plants may define a few general objectives of a given project (in the case of CAPPM systems, for example, personnel cut-backs in job scheduling, reduction of intermediate stores in production, and reduction of processing time), but it cannot yet objectively estimate the exact outcome of these procedures and, in particular, the consequent precise interrelationship with other projects also under way (for example, the introduction of CAD in the design department parallel to modernization of the CAPPM system, the development of manufacturing islands in production, and the development of a central, automatic, intermediate store). A CAPPM system on its own is already highly complex. As a building block in a CIM system it is often impossible to calculate its individual effects. The thesis that these companies are in the grip of a highly risky technological maelstrom of indefinite duration and size is very plausible.

In plants, the effect is such that at the beginning of system planning there is at first only a rough concept which is then worked on in smaller parts by various project groups, departments, et cetera. Secondly, this also means that the effects on the employees have not been determined, since as a rule the only thoughts about them at management level are very general, and the individual consequences (for example, shifts in authority between the foreman, control room, and production control system, e.g. payments systems, control of work progress) are negotiated in the plant and between different groups of involved persons. Although the development from the targeting and implementation of a clear concept to the organization of a plant process can only be outlined in brief here, it is still of decisive importance for the works council because the works council is also unable to anticipate all the final results of this modernization project in the initial stage and thus react to them. To do so, it would also have to participate in this conceptualization and introduction process.

Another reason why the works council does not contribute more at the conceptual stage, despite considerable information provided in good time, is to be found in the identification of the works council with the objectives of such modernization projects. Technical innovations are discussed in technological, economic and organizational terms, and not in social terms. The social implications of technical terms are frequently unclear, and the information provided is in this respect rather one-sided. Thus, it is officially a matter of cutting processing times, lowering inventories, better adherence to deadlines, and so forth. These aims are also important and acceptable to the works councils. They appear to be conditions to assure the company's continuing existence, while the social implications are only considered to a very limited extent. For this reason there is little possibility of the works councils intervening on a massive scale.

Another situation to be analysed is our observation that many works councils do not want any say in the decision making and structuring associated with these processes. One reason for this is the fact that, in general, the works councils feel overtaxed by these tasks and do not see it as their role to become involved in work structuring. Another possibility is that in the past works councils have often been unable to get their way when they put forward an alternative plan based on the limited amounts of information at their disposal.

The gradual working out of the CAPPM process, which involves people in various departments responsible for planning and implementation, has two consequences. In the first place, it means that the complex task of systems design now rests with a number of employee groups who take part in the various project teams to which we have referred. However, these project teams are not the traditional union core groups. They are more like a new technological élite and unions do not have easy access to them. Secondly, when the system has been fully worked out and the works council or union consultants then propose changes or demand different conditions, they come up against the problem that these aspects have, in the normal course of events, already been negotiated within the project teams and settled by agreement with the relevant departments. In practical terms this means that the union strategy of attempting to implement model agreements in individual plants, which was the usual procedure in the past, is no longer possible in such cases. The works council's inputs arrive too late.

The increase in control

With the spread of information technologies the concept of control has come under increasing public discussion, particularly in relation to pre-control, which makes it easier to monitor human activity and behaviour in the plant. In this sense, it is possible to distinguish between a wide and a narrow control term.

Control in a wider sense could be defined by the extent to which management succeeds in planning and controlling the development of the various elements of the desired technology, thereby shutting out the influence of other interest groups. Conversely, it would be possible to speak of control by the works council to the extent to which it gains influence on central company decisions such as market strategies, product development, central innovations, and investments, as well as work structuring and the division of labour. However, these areas of policy are increasingly determined by the new information technologies with their overlapping, integrating nature. While works council policy used to be concerned with isolated topics like wage systems, job descriptions, further education programmes, et cetera, when one moves to systemically integrated technologies, the treatment of isolated topics is no longer feasible.

On the basis of our analysis of the plant design process, we see considerable potential for intervention by works councils, but this will not come about of its own accord. It will only be possible when estimates of an overall rationalization strategy exist, when current individual projects are incorporated and when the respective negotiating possibilities are recognized and used effectively.

Control in a narrower sense involves preliminary planning, control, and monitoring of work and behaviour. This requires a much wider availability of data relating to job processing, departmental performance, machine performance, group performance, and even individual performance. The control mechanisms have lost some of the more direct impact they used to have through personal control, and are tending to grow together in a combination of 'systemic control'. For instance, under the CAPPM system the vast quantity of data is difficult to calculate and understand when assessing relevant changes.

To elaborate on this issue: in the past, work design only came up in works council discussions when it was relevant to wage rates and levels. Thus, when changes in work or the composition of work have suggested an upgrading in accordance with the agreed job evaluation system, or when, in the reverse case, the company has threatened to downgrade jobs, works councils have demanded stronger measures for the amalgamation of jobs and formation of work systems in order to raise and stabilize the wage rates and levels. When wage issues were not relevant, works councils were usually not involved in work design. This is why works councils regard it as an imposition when, as a consequence of new technology initiatives, they are asked to contribute to the design of new jobs.

What is interesting about the type of plant we studied is the fact that the traditionally central topics of works council work, namely, job safety, income maintenance, and training opportunities, were generally conceded or accepted by management without major conflict. As a result, the impression was gained that traditional issues do not seriously infringe the prevailing situation of the employees and the works council. But we saw earlier that other control areas are also predetermined by these traditional works council topics, even if they are not directly concerned with the introduction of new technology. A typical example of this is the piece-rate payments system. We found a number of plants in which management abolished piece-work without reducing individual incomes and introduced monthly wages by arguing that, first of all, individual performance can no longer be calculated in the same way as it used to be, secondly, the employees' willingness to perform should not be disturbed by piecework conflicts, and thirdly, wage costs now account for only a small portion of machine-hour rates.

The new topics slowly developing as a result of the establishment of CIM systems include new forms of work and behaviour control. There are, for instance, information technologies that are quite clearly oriented to personal control, for example personnel information and data acquisition systems. The term *gläserner Mensch* (transparent person) has been coined to describe the situation where, with the help of new technologies, management is informed about every move or mistake an employee makes and in this way can obtain complete control over him. Here unions reacted early and called attention to the violation of personal rights in circumstances where new information systems led to the 'transparent person'. But this narrow understanding of control is not sufficient to assess the control potential, for example in the case of CAPPM systems. Here the predominant opinion is that job description is no longer relevant because of the separation of the work flow and personal data, and—as it set out in many plant agreements—there is no formal control of persons. Instead, control is now exercised more extensively and intensively by making all plant operations and situations in effect 'transparent' at the time they take place. In German this situation is called *die gläserne Fabrik* (the transparent factory) because so much information is now available about everything that goes on in a factory as to make it 'transparent'. So far there is still no adequate answer to these forms of indirect systemic control, which have a restrictive effect on behaviour in the plant. Furthermore, since these processes of systemic-control implementation are not very obvious or easy to grasp, they are not often the subject of strategic discussions by unions. The few shop stewards who have become aware of these dangers have great difficulty expressing their views in the plant and gaining the support of fellow employees. It is precisely on this topic that there is very little backing for shop stewards who want to attack the dangers of control in a more general way.

Final remarks

All in all, when the depth and breadth of changes brought about by the companies' information technologies and new rationalization strategies are observed, and when the demands of the implementation programme for social structuring by the works councils is included, the works councils have little to show for their activity, even in plants with a high degree of organization in an area where unions are strong. An attempt has been made to analyse the need for works councils and unions to develop new policies and new capabilities. The first attempts made to tackle this further development of union/works council policy were described case by case. Examples were changes in works council recruitment, the establishment of works council committees, the use of external experts, etc. All these steps are important and should be adopted generally, not only to preserve works councils as important negotiating partners and/or opponents of management, but also to enable them to intervene in the design of new production concepts.

The results of our enquiries indicate that the general conditions of works council activity will have to be decisively changed, e.g. the number of shop stewards freed for full-time works council activity, the training possibilities offered, the training and provision of internal and external experts, the development of concepts for rationalization strategies, structuring orientation, and so on.

This line of thinking cannot be pursued further here. It cannot go only in the direction of a qualitative and quantitative expansion of works council activity—which would only lead to an increase in the present overload of works council functions. Instead, it is necessary to look for either existing or new strategies to relieve the works councils, for example by new forms of standardization and generalization of regulations, by the provision of expert support, and so forth.

One form of relief is obtained by the slowing down process caused by the interventions of the works council. The demands for information, further negotiations, and skill training, etc. certainly delay the process of introducing new technologies and this can be seen as a positive step in relation to the role of the works council.

In conclusion, we want to emphasize the importance of plant policy. It has been shown that the introduction of information technology requires a considerable shift in the role played by employees at various levels. Shop stewards and foremen often lose influence. Powerful data processing and production control departments are formed. The traditional dominant role of the works council is being weakened by the participation of a new kind of technical élite and by changes in the topics which formerly came under works council consideration.

How unions and works councils deal with these changes will be of decisive importance. It seems that there are a number of obstacles to union understanding of the changes we have described. One can observe that a number of new plant developments are deliberately excluded from union discussion by management. As a consequence, unions develop no initiatives or conceptual alternatives in these new fields or organization. This would require a change in attitude from looking at the technological changes solely as the result of exploitation to recognizing instead that there are considerable areas of common interest and that there are plant negotiating processes which end in mutual compromise and consensus. A realistic analysis of existing balances of power and structures of influence in plants could provide such opportunities prior to the introduction of new technologies, and this must be uncovered and utilized. Some of these opportunities have in the past been used by works councils along with semi-open or concealed negotiations with the management, pragmatic compromises by mutual agreement, and so forth. It is precisely the contradiction between the ideological paid-labour–capital thesis decisive for plant policy, on the one hand, and the effectively very pragmatic negotiating policy of the works councils, on the other, which in our opinion makes a strategic, powerfully planned policy largely impossible. At most, there can be individual cases of especially clever shop stewards who achieve results with their specific plant policy, results that are considered quite specific and unique, thus not capable of becoming general union policy.

References

Hildebrandt, E. (1988), 'Work, Participation and Co-Determination in Computer-Based Manufacturing', in D. Knights and H. Willmott (eds.), *New Technology and the Labour Process* (Basingstoke and London: Macmillan).

—— and Seltz, R. (1985), 'Trade Union Technology Policy between the Protection of Status and Work Structuring', *Economic and Industrial Democracy*, 6: 481–99.

16

In Search of Workers' Participation: Implementation of New Technologies in GDR Firms

ARTUR MEIER

Economic relations in a society are expressed primarily as interests.

F. Engels

The quest for participation in new fields

The fast-moving scientific–technological revolution transforming social structures in the West as well as in the East raises the crucial problem of democratic control of new technologies. Information technology (IT), which represents the major trend of technological change, can be used for better or worse depending on the economic, political, and social interests it primarily serves. Thus, the search for opportunities for workers and other groups of employees to influence the choice of technology with its implications for working life and job security becomes highly important for the whole participation issue. The question as to whether employees will succeed in averting negative trends when new technologies are implemented or whether they will be able to use their potential for improving their working conditions is related to the consciousness, the facilities, and, in particular, the power they have to articulate and to realize their particular interests in relation to these processes.

In a socialist society, for instance in the German Democratic Republic (GDR), the implementation of information technology in State-owned firms has not only to contribute to economic efficiency, but also definitely to follow socio-cultural imperatives. The modernization paradigm propagated by the Party and the socialist State and widely accepted by the masses is threefold and aims at combining technological innovations and economic rationalization with social progress. As a consequence, the claim of workers and other groups of employees in GDR companies for significant improvements of their working and living conditions by way of introducing IT cannot be interpreted simply as unrealistic wishes or pressure from below, but clearly refers to daily official statements in which social advancement is regarded as equally important as the economic outcome of the application of new technologies. Moreover, the workers' interests and rights to participate in the planning and implementation processes of new technologies are sanctioned by legislation. It is explicitly formulated by law

(Labour Code 1977) that technological change in socialist enterprises should lead to higher productivity on the one hand and to a better working environment and greater opportunity for personality development for working people on the other. This is a fundamental legal basis on which control of technological and organizational change in firms may be exercised. Again, it depends on the strength and competence of employees' representatives whether, in practice, solutions will be found by which technological change, economic efficiency, and social progress in work organization are made compatible.

The introduction of IT (i.e. new technologies covering the whole field of computer-aided machinery, industrial robots, process control, and data technology ranging up to office automation) in the GDR has just reached a level where various consequences for the interests of more and more social groups become obvious. People begin to ask the simple question, 'What's in it for me?' While the majority accept technological change without hesitation, they are now beginning to feel the real consequences for the quality of their working lives.

Sociological investigations in the GDR have revealed a positive attitude amongst working people of all classes and strata of socialist society towards the wave of technological innovations. The acceptance of new technologies in the labour process is significantly higher amongst the younger generation and correlates, in general, with the level of education and vocational training. The avant-garde of the technological revolution are young professionals and highly skilled workers. Sociological research indicates, too, the high expectations of employees in socialist firms across the social strata. The introduction of IT is considered imperative for economic reasons and regarded as a promising instrument for more meaningful and effective work under improving social conditions (Hahn, 1986: 169–74).

Among social scientists, as well as in the wider public of the GDR, the prevailing view of the changes can be labelled, in general, as socio-technical.[1] Changes concerning technology and organization are not seen as following natural laws and, therefore, not treated as autonomous factors.[2] On the contrary, a core element of the widespread socio-technical view is to consider the development, implementation, and use of technology as influenced by a set of economic and social factors

[1] The socio-technical approach seems to have developed along parallel lines in East and West. Though the impressive Tavistock–Scandinavian tradition (see Kalleberg, 1986) remains almost unknown in the GDR, much of the research work and practical experimentation of the past 20 years is worth mentioning. It has been accomplished predominantly within a socio-technical perspective mainly by departments of GDR universities as well as by companies known as *Wissenschaftliche Arbeitsorganisation*. Focusing on workers' democratic control over new technologies, it seems inappropriate to enter the long debate on the merits of 'real' participation contrasted with 'socio-technical' participation.

[2] The view that technology is the most—if not the only—important factor for increasing productivity and that the new technologies are progressive in every respect is undisputed among social scientists and also in the wider public of the GDR. On the other hand, technological determinism is labelled as a 'bourgeois' idea and rigorously rejected. However, it still remains an open question how far technology can be treated as a dependent or an independent variable. My suggestion is to elaborate a theoretical framework which can be based on a 'soft' socio-technological–deterministic approach (to put it very briefly here).

capable of creating socially desirable work patterns. Often it is even proclaimed that, given socialist relations of production, the results in all cases tend to be 'positive', i.e. harmonious and 'progressive'—without profound discrepancies between economic requirements, technological rationality, and social compatibility. Such a promise of 'joint optimization' might, on the one hand, stimulate the search for solutions in the interests of working people; but, on the other hand, it seems also more likely that under socialist conditions the interplay between the three variables will be complex rather than straightforward. It can be foreseen, therefore, that the assumption that the use of technology will achieve more satisfying work patterns will lead to disillusion as soon as the researchers and/or the groups they investigate realize that quite a number of social decisions are already built into actual techniques, with the result that the possibilities for choice are limited (Meier, 1987: 7–8).

Perhaps it is still too early to draw general conclusions about the full range of technological and organizational choices which workers' representatives might have in relation to the implementation of IT in GDR firms. At present it is, for objective reasons, neither easy to predict the far-reaching social consequences of new technologies applied in a socialist economy, nor easy to make generalizations from features occurring in particular sectors or single companies, i.e. under very specific conditions. GDR industry is still at the initial stage of the information technology revolution, new technologies usually being implemented successively in isolation, CAD-CAM systems and robots in particular, so that at the present moment the impact on working conditions appears less dramatic. Furthermore, the process of innovation, though in its initial phase, is very fast, so that a considerable degree of uncertainty emerges, with the result that conceptions of its nature and impact constantly have to be updated.

Nevertheless, scanning the limited body of evidence from current sociological research, although it is mainly at an experimental stage and based only on case-studies,[3] it seems possible to formulate two assumptions concerning the future of employees' participation in the implementation of IT in GDR companies. Firstly, the growing number of social groups affected by the introduction of new technologies should be enabled to influence choice in this matter in order to improve their working and living conditions. Secondly, there are real new opportunities to move forward in this direction, since even within existing limits there is considerable potential for their greater influence.

Thus sociological studies still in progress are indicating ways in which employees can control technological change.[4]

[3] The empirical foundation of my argument consists of case-studies from a research project which I am conducting at the Institute of Sociology, Humboldt University, Berlin, entitled 'Social conditions and solutions in the implementation of high technologies in industry, the service sector, and administration'. The project is at the initial stages and will be completed with reports in 1989–90.

[4] Evidence comes from studies just carried out within my research project (see n. 3).

Opportunities for participation in IT implementation processes

Users' participation

Naturally, the companies' interest in introducing IT is to increase productivity and at the same time to secure adequate job performance from employees. All our investigations in socialist firms show that it is impossible for the management to achieve the intended economic benefits if it is unable to gain the commitment of employees to making the new technologies function effectively. As a result, co-operation between high-level experts and the main groups who have to apply IT in the production process—between top and bottom, so to speak—has become more common practice. This is the opportunity for the various groups to declare their specific interests and to try to influence changes in work patterns from the very beginning, sometimes with regard to complete job redesign, sometimes less—to the extent of only minor modifications within a given rationalization concept. In any case, users' interests usually amount to a reduction in the division of labour and/or the traditional work burden connected with heavy or dangerous tasks. In short, what they want, evidently, is more meaningful, creative work which is easier to perform. However, the implementation of IT all too often cannot fulfil these high expectations, since its social impact appears to be ambivalent—more than that: in a real sense, contradictory.

Sociological and psychological studies on industrial robots, for example, given clear evidence that, on the one hand, these modern 'industrial slaves' do, indeed, take over hard and dangerous labour, but, on the other hand, they inflict on operators new and monotonous tasks and force them to work at their speed (Merboth, 1986: 170–80). It seems appropriate, therefore, to overcome the new unsatisfying situation for particular groups within the automation process by giving them opportunities for job rotation and enlargement according to their abilities. Such arrangements were made in some firms after negotiation with 'users'. Since their skill in maintaining the machinery was necessary, management had to take their interests into account and come to an agreement with them.

Another case-study shows that turners at Computerized Numerical Control (CNC) machines were powerful enough to prevent further reduction of their work content. The management had at first projected a new work pattern by which groups of technicians developed the programs, while the skilled turners' work was to have been reduced to rather simple, repetitive operations. However, in the course of time these operators took over the function of programming and began to work at two or even three places. This happened with the full agreement of the technicians who, by the way, were generally paid less than the highly regarded turners. The management accepted the new scheme and conceded that the operators could decide for themselves whether they wanted to work at one place or more. This was also fixed by a written agreement (Aßmann and Nagel, 1985: 671–4).

A third case investigated was of user participation in project groups. This seems to have become the most common form of participation in system designing, especially in producing software packages. Standard software at present often does not fit into existing systems in GDR firms, in particular within their R. & D. units, so that the need is felt to adapt ready-made packages to the special purposes of the organization or to entrust their own experts with that task. In this context two observations should be made. In some firms a clear distinction can be made between those who design software and those who apply it. In such cases the latter complain of having to defer to the former, and they are afraid of losing their expertise and of being downgraded to the level of semi-skilled operators (Frentzel, 1986: 35; Lungwitz, 1986: 8). In other firms, following the advice of Party and trade union bodies within the company, project groups are formed consisting of experts as well as users, who try to manage the system jointly and to produce software which meets the demands of the latter groups for more creative work. In the beginning, however, the problem has been twofold: the users have experienced severe difficulties in formulating their requirements and the same has applied to the experts trying to find out what the real work situation of particular groups of users happens to be.

The number of examples based on actual case-studies could be extended. However, all these studies arrive at one major, though cautious, conclusion, namely, that in socialist firms, where personnel are needed to master the new technology and cannot be fired or easily replaced by other people ready and waiting at the firm's door for a good job, there seems to be room for compromise between management and employees' representative bodies. From the management's point of view users' participation in project groups might be seen as crucial for the functioning of the organization and for contact with further potential users, in other words, as a sort of organizational development. From the users' point of view project groups can serve as an instrument of economic democracy at company level where it is possible to discuss alternative job designs and to make technological–organizational choices.

Certainly, in many cases one might find the possibilities for choice rather limited, in some of them, indeed, no alternatives seem to exist or to be considered. Many groups of employees are far too weak to articulate their interests and to insist on their participation rights. Once system decisions have been made by the management, ignoring their duty to include employees' representatives and thus regarding the staff as a purely operational body, the organization often appears to be unalterable. Usually, technical reasons or economic arguments are used as justification in these cases and the hierarchical division of labour and power continues within the firm, sometimes accompanied by a neo-Tayloristic application of new technology. However, there is always a price to be paid. If the management ignores the 'go-in' mechanism, i.e. refuses to respect participation, it runs the risk of the 'go-out' mechanism, i.e. workers slow down production and/or the rate of absenteeism goes up. Among the staff of several firms we have also found severe 'fluctuation'; unthreatened by unemployment and with underemployment in the labour force of many sectors in the GDR economy, it is not difficult for them to get new jobs (Lungwitz, 1986: 2).

So, in fact, the general position of workers and other groups of employees in GDR socialist enterprises is very strong. They are able not only to counteract negative trends, but also to influence system design considerably, if they are conscious of how their interests will be affected by IT implementation and use their opportunities for democratic participation.

A new structuring of the overall division of labour within a company which is generally expected may well change some entrenched structures. However, even if there is no fundamental restructuring of the division of labour, which, for the time being, is true of the majority of companies and sectors, technological–organizational choice may be exercised under conditions in which the relevant social groups participate actively in concrete decision-making processes.

Participation through information and skilling

In order to formulate requirements and possible options for system design and work patterns it is necessary to have the relevant knowledge. Workers' participation and control essentially requires competence, whose central role in a successful democratization strategy is much debated and heavily emphasized (Széll, 1985, 1989).

For democratic control of new technologies two types of knowledge are indispensable: general job competence, including the necessary level of skills, experience, and education, that is, in general, the qualifications to manage new techniques in technological systems; and specialized information on prerequisites, strategy, and presumed consequences of the particular system design to be adopted and of its possible alternatives. The borderline between both—information that comes from existing knowledge and information needed in a specific situation when a certain technology is going to be applied—clearly fluctuates.

Information of the latter type normally comes from the management or from experts working with system development. By law (Labour Code 1977) the management has a duty to inform employees and their trade union committee about planned rationalization measures at the first opportunity and, at the same time, come to an agreement with them on qualifications and further training if there is felt to be a need to increase the level of skills.

Sociological research shows that information given early enough promotes workers' participation in the planning and implementation process and strengthens their positive attitude to technological change (Stollberg, 1985: 127–32). On the other hand, several studies indicate that workers received information too late or incomplete; the result of this has been a considerable degree of dissatisfaction with management information policy (Forschungsbericht, 1981; Schellenberger, 1987).

One of our recent studies on the involvement of engineers—since engineers were regarded as a key group of employees to influence system design—points also to lack of information. Two-thirds of them were insufficiently informed, one third were better informed but also without having the impression of a complete overview. Forty per cent demanded more information, whilst 36 per cent did not insist on it assuming managerial design concepts to be, as a rule, capable of being only marginally influenced. Only about 5 per cent of the respondents were generally uninterested in relevant information and participatory opportunities.[5]

Employees are confronted with structural difficulties in gathering information. This does not mean that in socialist enterprises the management can simply withhold relevant information. But all too often there may be no clear idea or sufficient experience of hardware and software appropriate to the system; or the planning of desired new technology is too vague, since it depends on decisions from above as to what the firm will acquire, and when (or even whether) it will acquire it. If the information is unavailable or incomplete the employees and their representatives are usually neither able to determine what their special interests are, nor to develop the competence for meaningful participation.

The second type of knowledge necessary to solve the problem of the socially advantageous use of IT in the firm relates to the general level of professional skills. Only if a high degree of competence exists among the personnel is there a chance of competing with specialized knowledge in the field of new technologies and of getting a working understanding of the information technology in order to evaluate it and to know what to expect from it.

In general, the qualifications of the GDR labour force are very high (they seem to be amongst the highest in the world): about 65 per cent are skilled blue- and white-collar workers, 20 per cent are professionals with diplomas from university or college (technical and engineering colleges and related institutions), and only 15 per cent are semi-skilled or have no formal vocational training. Of course, the level of qualifications varies with the branches of the economy. It still correlates significantly with age and sex but only with regard to the population over 40. If we now relate the macrostructure to the microstructure, it can be concluded that, as a rule, the staff of a firm is highly skilled and, in terms of general education as well as of vocational training and competence, prepared to master IT, especially if it is introduced by relatively small steps, which usually seems to be the case.

Beyond this universal level of education and qualifications, in many companies today a broad campaign for further training has been initiated. There is a widespread belief in the need for special knowledge for the successful introduction

[5] This result was also found in my research project (see n. 3).

of IT. The controversies about deskilling (Braverman, 1974, and his followers) versus enskilling (Fuchs, 1968; Touraine, 1969; Bell, 1973, and similar optimistic accounts) and the polarization thesis (Kern and Schumann, 1970), later replaced by the reprofessionalization approach (Kern and Schumann, 1984), neither contested the assumption among social scientists in the GDR that advanced technologies require an increasingly educated labour force, nor were known to the general public. Generally, since the 1960s there has been a permanent emphasis on manpower training in GDR firms, at present reinforced by the central argument that the competent and efficient use of IT has its prerequisites in further training measures and the emergence of a higher level of skills.

Further training to master new technology has become an area where the interests of the management and those of employees and their representatives tend to coincide. The strategies of both parties aim at greater utilization of abilities and development of skills to ensure good job performance. Companies, moreover, often use training courses to gain social acceptance of IT. And, indeed, sociological research confirms that in many cases new technologies, for example CAD/CAM, were more easily accepted and more satisfactorily applied by those groups who had been included in advance in special training programmes (Radtke, 1986: 408–15). Especially when female employees are involved, social acceptance and requisite job performance at new workplaces may be achieved through carefully constructed training programmes, an insight that comes from recent studies in banks, finance, and insurance (Barbarino, 1986: 206, and following studies; and at Humboldt University). Basically, a training course can be used as a forum for discussion on social solutions associated with the implementation process of IT. This could be an appropriate opportunity for participation.

The vast expansion of in-plant further training is in full accordance with the rights of the employees concerned. Everybody whose qualifications profile is in some way affected by technological change is entitled by law to receive further education during working hours at the expense of the firm. If he or she has to change his/her workplace, training programmes have to be provided by the company which should enable him/her to fulfil the new task or even a new job. This has to be fixed by formal agreements on a consensual basis and with the approval of the local trade union committee. If the management proves unable to establish early further training for groups or persons faced with new technological requirements, the employees cannot be forced to do jobs for which they are not qualified. Legislation as well as the representative bodies within the firms protect their skills and are powerful enough to secure guaranteed educational rights.

However, the generally accepted strategy of further education has important implications for the methods and extent of participation. If the scope of training programmes is too narrow, they usually result in a mere adaptation to new technological situations. The foundation of competent participation must be much broader. This implies access to information which allows employees to form their own impressions of the social effects which the new technologies will probably have in the near future and, beyond that, to gain an awareness of the long-term consequences for themselves.

In the GDR, at the moment, the training courses leave much to be desired. The main cause of their deficiencies can again be found in structural conditions. The present phase of technological change in the GDR appears to be generally compatible with the overall social situation in enterprise, so that nobody is really threatened or even challenged by dramatic consequences. Moreover, the innovations implemented step by step often seem to be managed best when technological concepts predominate and social objectives are regarded as only secondary variables. The technicist outlook of the management in many firms often seems to be supported by groups of engineers who traditionally think in terms of the autonomous development of technology. Moreover, we found in our case study R. & D. engineers so overloaded with work that they were able only to acquire the necessary technical knowledge to master complicated new technology, but not to become aware of the social implications and consequences of IT.

To counteract technocratic approaches to the participation-by-information issue, employees in GDR firms increasingly find allies from the field of social policy and the social sciences. There is a growing awareness that social policy today cannot only be devoted to social justice in socialist society as a whole, but has also to focus more on improvements of working conditions at company level, in particular in connection with the implementation of new technologies and the interests of groups involved. As a consequence, experts offer information services to employees' representative bodies and also to the managements of firms in order to make them more interested in, and better qualified to estimate, the social implications of IT and to find socio-technical strategies which can be pursued in the best interests of both sides. In future this may become a third source of relevant information for more competent participation.

It should be possible to establish participation as a learning process developing simultaneously the relevant knowledge, consciousness of interests, and social objectives interrelated with technical and economic progress. There are many ways to shape competence in the context of workers' and employees' social reality and experience (Széll, 1989). Without competence based on knowledge which can be used for specific purposes it seems impossible to turn potential opportunities for participation into real influence.

Participation in employment matters: collective agreements

The basis of employees' power in GDR socialist firms has become largely institutionalized through legal regulations and agreements which protect employees entirely against principles of rationalization which are not compatible with their interests.

Dismissals are absolutely impossible. Staff reductions or any significant change in job design and work practices can only be achieved through legally binding agreements with the groups or persons concerned and have to be fully approved by the trade unions. The paragraphs of the Labour Code are, in practice, carefully observed. If they are not (such cases cannot be excluded a priori), the workers, supported by trade union experts, usually initiate legal proceedings on the 'conflict committee' of the company or in court—with an 80–90 per cent probability that they will win.[6] The law includes clear regulations on what has to be done if economic rationalization comes into effect as a result of technological change. At first, the management has at least three months to negotiate with the persons involved to find new work appropriate to their level of skill and qualifications and offering the same income. Employees cannot be replaced if their income will be lowered or their qualifications wasted. However, employees may be asked to participate in further training to acquire new skills. Secondly, a formal agreement has to be signed by the management, the person(s) involved, and the trade union committee to guarantee a smooth transition from the old to the new workplace. The management may not just transfer the employee to vacancies in another firm or refer him/her to local employment opportunities in general. The employee has to be consulted and up to three offers made. A final agreement between the parties is regarded as binding. Thirdly, there are clauses which describe the reasonable demands to be considered in connection with the new employment regarding, for instance, not only retraining, but also possible changes in personal circumstances (relocation, housing problems, children's education, and, in particular, consequences for the partner's employment).[7] In general, agreements are accepted as being in accordance with the legal regulation of the work constitution only if rationalization measures initiated usually by the management can be made compatible with job aspirations and adequate employment opportunities for the employee(s) involved. Cases are known where managements have had to postpone economically profitable rationalization because they were unable to find attractive jobs for groups who would become redundant—for instance, female workers over 45. Job security has priority, although a certain degree of flexibility on the part of the labour force is expected too.

The same holds, in principle, when rationalization might lead to changes in work practices. Effective use of IT demands in more and more firms the introduction of shift-work, even for groups who were not traditionally confronted with this kind of work such as technicians and engineers. Furthermore, it offers greater possibilities for centralized supervision and evaluation of workers'

---

[6] It was recently reported in the press that nowadays 28,000 conflict committees operate in GDR firms with 255,000 employees participating in their work.

[7] The GDR has the highest rate of female employment in the world: about 80% of women (able to work until 60) are employed. Nearly 50% of the labour force is therefore female. If female students and apprentices are included in the figure the percentage goes up to 91%.

performance. Finally, to maintain the existing pattern of collective work in the form of established brigades and other workers' teams sometimes turns out to be a hindrance to optimal organization. These are possible areas of conflicting interests.

Again, these conditions can only be changed by means of consensus between the management and the relevant groups, sometimes resulting in compromise. Our study on the situation and attitude of engineers regarding the introduction of IT shows much reluctance to transfer to shift-work, though there was a widespread understanding of the economic demands for using the valuable new techniques at a higher rate of working hours. In the plant under investigation part of the staff threatened the management that they would leave the firm and take new jobs if they were forced to work in shifts without negotiation. But the tensions were overcome by reaching a compromise offering flexible working hours, avoiding rigid shifts.

However, the reverse can happen. We investigated a case where the management intended to reduce shift-work but the workers were opposed to any alteration because, as a rule, they received much higher pay when working at night or weekends. Electronic performance recorders were set up to prove that there was room for labour intensification instead of longer working hours. Yet the workers found ways of invalidating the recorded data, so that finally the organization remained the same, even though the demands and proposals of the management were economically rational and socially justified.

Other cases are interesting with regard to collectivity. Much sociological research in the past has revealed, by the way, that between two-thirds and four-fifths of employees have a sense of well-being within their work groups, associated with a positive attitude to solidarity and a spirit of collaboration among the colleagues. As a result, existing collectives cannot be altered easily, or only at the risk of resistance from personnel (Kretzschmar, 1985: 28–35). To make existing team structures more flexible, the management has to be cautious and try to maintain social networks wherever possible. Otherwise, productivity may decrease, since workers' collectives are strong units and are essential to maintaining continuous production in order to meet the planning targets which they agreed with the management at the beginning of the year.

Employees in socialist firms are far from being 'hostages to modern technology'. Social security, firmly based on legislation and taken for granted in everyday life in the GDR, gives working people the strength to reject rationalization measures which could harm their interests and safeguards, indeed, their right to be employed under conditions equal to those they have already achieved. If they have to defend their interests they can, in fact, make use of a wide range of collective sanctions and are able to refer to elaborate legal regulations protecting their extensive labour rights. It is mainly by company agreements negotiated annually between management representatives and the trade union committee of the firm that legal or collective framework regulations are put into practice. They are usually powerful instruments for employees to use in negotiations with management, in particular with regard to current rationalization concepts. As long as a worker is not threatened by unemployement but, on the contrary, can rely on job security, he/she is in a good position to negotiate on his/her working and living conditions, thereby protecting his/her interests. Since, in principle, the managements of GDR firms have learned to co-operate with employees, in most cases negotiation is likely to lead to agreements or compromises which serve, more or less, the interests of both parties.

Conclusions

It is necessary, now, to approach realistically the task of increasing the representation of workers and other groups of employees with regard to the implementation of IT in socialist enterprises. That is why, at least at the moment and in some countries, the importance of 'weaker' types of participation such as consulting, information, and other forms of temporary, limited involvement is increasing. However, participation at the workplace resulting in joint decisions on changes to working conditions caused by the introduction of new technology should be regarded as being as important as the influence of employees on decision-making processes which are directed more towards allocating income, or fair distribution of various social awards which tend to improve general living conditions. Since the implementation of IT will affect the interests of ever more social groups in a firm, democratic control should be established along three main lines: system design and working conditions, information and qualifications, and rearrangement of work practices and employment circumstances. Latent and manifest interests of employees in socialist firms have a good chance of being realized if organizational forms already established or in the planning stage are used to transform fundamental participatory rights into real influence.

Consciousness of interests and the ability to exploit existing or nascent possibilities for joint decision making will lead to processes which sometimes might appear rather time consuming. But the same holds for the lack of knowledge of the social implications of new technologies, in particular where long-term consequences are concerned. Here we must rely on the dynamic elements of participation.

Sociological research can promote these processes by giving advice from outside. Designed and carried out as action research, sociological investigation is able to identify the best interests of the parties and groups involved, to indicate opportunities for democratic participation and decision making, and, finally, to formulate socially acceptable or even preferable solutions connected with the introduction of IT. Even if targets at present have to be modest and in some fields only minor changes can be expected, the time is ripe for ambitious intervention by social scientists.

The focus on democratic control of new technologies requires thoroughgoing comparative research work. There is a need to compare different groups and their interests; different types of firm in various economic sectors; most importantly, the types of IT available; and—last but not least—the different kinds of organization and possibilities of participation in different—in their socio-economic basis or even divergent—societies (see also Grootings, 1986; Kalleberg, 1986). Clarity and consistency in the understanding of IT and its implications for work can be gained more easily through comparison. The conceptualization of democratic control of its implementation makes comparative sociological research especially opportune, surely bringing deeper insight into the whole societal context within which the changes are taking place and broadening our knowledge of the wide range of circumstances nationally.

References

Aßmann, G. and Nagel, D. (1985), 'Soziale Konsequenzen der Einführung neuer Technik für die sozialistische Lebensweise' *Wissenschaftliche Zeitschrift der Humboldt Universität zu Berlin: Gesellschaftswissenschaftliche Reihe*, 8: 671–4.

Barbarino, I. (1986), 'Informationsverarbeitende Technik im Dienstleistungs- und Verwaltungsbereich: Betrachtungen aus soziologischer Sicht', *Sozialistische Arbeitswissenschaft*, 6: 206–12.

Bell, D. (1973), *The Coming Post-industrial Society* (London: Basic Books).

Braverman, H. (1974), *Labor and Monopoly Capital: The Degradation of Work in the Twentieth Century* (New York and London: Monthly Review Press).

Forschungsbericht (1981), 'Die Rolle der Leiter bei der Einbeziehung der Werktätigen in die Gestaltung der Arbeitsbedingungen' (Humboldt University, Berlin: rotaprint).

Frentzel, R. (1986), 'Der subjektive Faktor bei der Entwicklung der rechnergestützten Ingenieurarbeit in Forschung und Entwicklung', *Wissenschaftliche Beiträge der Friedrich-Schiller-Universität Jena*, 28–38.

Fuchs, V. R. (1968), *The Service Economy* (New York: Basic Books).

Grootings, P. (ed.), (1986), *Technology and Work: East–West Comparison* (London, Sydney, and Dover: Croom Helm).

Hahn, T. (1985), 'Persönliche Interessen und Motivation', in *Soziale Triebkräfte ökonomischen Wachstums*, Materialien des 4. Kongresses der m.-l. Soziologie in der DDR (26–8 Mar.) (Berlin: Dietz), 169–74.

Kalleberg, R. (1986), 'Some Scandinavian Contributions to the Field of Organization of Work and Technology' paper presented to the International Workshop on New Technology and New Forms of Work Organization (Berlin: Vienna Centre and Nationalkomitee für Soziologische Forschung der DDR).

Kern, H. and Schumann, M. (1970), *Industriearbeit und Arbeiterbewußtsein*, 2 vols. (Frankfurt: EVA).

———— (1984), *Das Ende der Arbeitsteilung? Rationalisierung in der industriellen Produktion: Bestandsaufnahme, Trendbestimmung* (Munich: C. H. Beck).

Kreher, S. (1986), 'New Concepts for White Collar Work Automation: Trends in Socialist

Enterprises', paper presented to the Eleventh World Congress of Sociology in New Delhi.

Kretzschmar, A. (1985), 'Sozialistische Persönlichkeit und intensiv erweiterte Reproduktion', *Deutsche Zeitschrift für Philosophie*, 1.

Labour Code (1977), *Arbeitsgesetzbuch der Deutschen Demokratischen Republik vom 16.1.1977*. GBl.I. No. 18.

Lungwitz, R. (1986), 'Aspekte des Leistungsverhaltens von Ingenieuren unter den Bedingungen der Einführung arbeitsplatznaher Rechentechnik: Pilotstudie' (Humboldt University, Berlin).

Meier, A. (1988), 'Die Neuen Technologien: Ein offenes soziales Potential?', in *Soziologie und Sozialpolitik*, Symposien und Kolloquien IV, Akademie der Wissenschaften der DDR, Berlin, 170–81.

Merboth, H. (1986), 'Die gezielte Gestaltung der Arbeitsinhalte: Ein Erfordernis bei dem Einsatz moderner Technik', *Wissenschaftliche Beiträge der Friedrich-Schiller-Universität Jena*, 170–80.

Radtke, H. (1986), 'Soziale Prozesse und ideologische Probleme beim Einsatz von CAD/CAM', *Sozialistische Arbeitswissenschaft*, 6: 408–15.

Schellenberger, G. (1987), *Technisch rationell—ökonomisch effektiv* (Berlin: Dietz).

Stollberg, R. (1985), 'Kollektivität und wissenschaftlich-technischer Fortschritt', in *Soziale Triebkräfte ökonomischen Wachstums*, Materialen des 4. Kongresses der m.-1. Soziologie in der DDR (26–8 Mar.) (Berlin: Dietz), 127–32.

Széll, G. (1985), 'New Technology and the Role of Trade Unions in the Democratization Process', paper presented to the Conference on 'The Role of Trade Unions in the Coming Decade', Maastricht (20–2 Nov.).

—— (1989), 'The Role of Competence in Regard to Participation, Workers' Control and Self-Management', in G. Széll *et al.* (eds.), *The State, Trade Unions and Self-Management* (Berlin: de Gruyter).

Touraine, A. (1969), *La Société post-industrielle* (Paris: Édition Minuit).

17

Designing Support Organizations for Industrial Co-operatives in Developing Countries

PETER ABELL

Introduction

A number of authors, notably Vanek (1970), have advocated the creation of a promotion and support organization if an Industrial Producer Co-operative (IPC) sector is to be established and then to flourish.[1] Superficial empirical evidence also points in this direction. Few would wish to deny the importance, for instance, of the Caja Laboral Popular in accounting, at least in part, for the dramatic success of the group of Mondragon co-operatives in Northern Spain (Thomas and Logan, 1981). The 'Caja' is a bank, drawing upon a local savings effort which, at the time, plays a central role in supervising all aspects of a group of industrial co-operatives. It is a quasi-secondary co-operative, the membership being the primary co-operatives themselves and, in addition, elected employees from the bank. It is perhaps best described as providing supervised credit, its management consultancy section being particularly well developed.[2]

Defourney *et al.* (n.d.), in a detailed comparative statistical analysis of IPCs in the UK, France, and Italy, find 'a productivity enhancement from the clustering of co-ops in a region', and go on to advocate 'the creation of a system of regional co-operative banks to provide shorter term credit, to advise on longer term capital supply and to internalise the externalities of stimulating an inter-connected regional co-operative complex'. Lewis *et al.* (1985) have also shown that, in the UK, there is a correlation between the regional concentration of IPCs and the existence of a regional support organization. Systematic evidence from Third World countries is less forthcoming, but Abell and Mahoney (1988) find much

---

[1] By an IPC I shall mean throughout a co-operative managed and owned by the people (members) who work within it (sometimes called a workers' co-operative). Although variations around this basic concept are possible (e.g. external members and some employees) producer co-operatives should be sharply contrasted with consumer or buying and marketing co-operatives. In each of these the members enter into an employment contract with employees.

[2] Recent reports suggest that bank and management consultancy section have grown to such a size that they are to divide into two separate support organizations.

informal evidence which would suggest that appropriately structured sponsoring and support organizations can improve the prospects of IPCs. A great deal, however, revolves around the phrase 'appropriately structured', and the evidence from these authors suggests that the negative impact of inappropriately structured systems can be equally dramatic. The question, thus, naturally arises as to what form the structure should take.

Research

In an attempt to answer this question, research (sponsored by the Overseas Development Administration in London) has been carried out by the author in Tanzania, Sri Lanka, and Fiji. In this paper I will report some of the salient findings of this research and comment upon their implications. For further details, the reader is referred to Abell (1988). This paper is written so as to be easily accessible to those with little knowledge of co-operatives.

Some general conclusions from the case-studies in Tanzania, Sri Lanka, and Fiji

The established movement

In each of the three countries studied—and they are most probably not exceptional in this respect—attempts to establish an IPC sector took place within the framework of an established co-operative movement. Moreover, these movements were themselves, to a greater or lesser extent, under the tutelage of governments, although this varied in each country with the passage of time.

The most controversial and far-reaching conclusion which may be drawn from the case-studies suggests that there is a fundamental divergence of interest between, on the one side, *consumer* and *agricultural* (i.e. agricultural buying and marketing) co-operatives and, on the other side, *producer* co-operatives. If this conclusion is correct it carries very profound implications for the formulation of policies directed towards the promotion of an IPC sector, which run counter to current practice in most less developed countries (LDCs). It is useful to start by seeing why this divergence occurs; the essentials of the argument are depicted in Table 17.1.

An established consumer co-operative has an interest in extending its activities by either horizontal or vertical integration. Horizontally, it can increase its size by acquiring new consumers–members and, in so doing, it is likely to increase the size of its retail outlets (or multiply them, i.e. create new *branches*). In either case it will, in all probability, increase its number of *employees*. It is incidental whether they happen to be members (as consumers) of the co-operative or not. Vertically, a consumer co-operative can integrate backwards into wholesaling and ultimately, if

Table 17.1 Horizontal and vertical integration of different types of co-operative

Owner/controller	Primary co-op	Horizontal integration	Vertical integration
Consumer	Consumer co-op	Additional members Additional retail outlets	*Backwards:* retail → wholesale → production consumer goods → production producer goods
Private farmers	Agricultural/marketing	Additional members Additional products	*Backwards:* buying wholesale → Production or producer goods (e.g. fertilizer) *Forwards:* Selling wholesale → Retail → Agro-processing → Retail
Member producers	Producer co-op	Secondary co-ops marketing/buying Amalgamation	*Backwards:* production → production of inputs by enlarged co-op *Forwards:* production → retailing (if not already) enlarged co-ops

it wishes, into production also. Any established production branches will, of course, then employ individuals and production will *not* be organized according to producer co-operative principles—in so far as any employees may be members, their status will drive from their being consumers. Thus, the consumer movement has an interest in establishing *co-operative industries* and, presumably, in minimizing production costs (including remuneration to employees), *not* in establishing producer co-operatives.[3] Indeed, this pattern of extended interests of the consumer movement has long been recognized in co-operative theory (Knapp, 1936).

Turning now to 'agricultural co-operatives', by which is normally meant buying and marketing co-operative societies,[4] they are, by their very nature, constituted as a horizontal integration of specific functions (buying and marketing) and their members (i.e. private farmers) have an interest in expanding both forwards and backwards (see Table 17.1). Once again, any branches of agricultural co-operatives which are established—in various lines of agro-processing for instance—will not normally be based upon the principles of *producer* co-operation but will enter into an employment contract with employees.

In their respective patterns of vertical integration, consumer and agricultural interests can, of course, clash, and the proper role which should be assigned to each has been debated in co-operative theory (Abrahamson and Scroggs, 1957). At what point should the forward and backward processes inherent in the expansionary aspirations of the agricultural and consumer movement meet? There have been advocates of complete 'consumerism' (Lincoln, 1936) and 'agriculturalism' (Knapp, 1936), but international experience suggests that both movements have come to some practical compromise without going to either extreme. But where, we might ask, do producer co-operatives fit into the scheme of things?

Producer co-operation is, of course, based upon a principle whereby the control of societies is vested with the producers themselves. In the agricultural sector, such an arrangement only occurs with agricultural co-operation, where private farms are one-person or one-household enterprises, i.e. where they are not employing anyone. Otherwise, agricultural co-operation of this sort is at odds with producer co-operation. Agricultural *producer* co-operatives are rare and the established marketing–buying movement has little incentive to promote them either. The kibbutzim in Israel, which are producer co-operatives, were not, for example, the creation of a buying and marketing movement.

In the industrial sector the same issues arise. Household producers (e.g. in handicrafts) can organize themselves into *primary* marketing and buying co-operatives, but as soon as production expands beyond the household (unless employment relations are entered into) the focus of the primary co-operative must

---

[3] 'Co-operative industries' should be contrasted with 'industrial producer co-operatives'. Co-operative industries are employing organizations.

[4] Once again, *not* agricultural producer co-operatives.

switch to the production unit itself and, if collective buying and marketing are retained, these functions are now best assigned to a *secondary* co-operative.

The producer co-operative movement, if it is to remain faithful to the principle of control and ownership by producers, comes into headlong conflict with the agricultural and consumer movements.[5] Each of the latter has an interest in acquiring additional added value by vertically integrating away from its traditional concerns and, in so doing, placing producers in the role of employee.

It is for these reasons that an established consumer–agricultural movement does not provide fertile ground upon which to encourage the growth of an IPC sector. In practice, this has not been sufficiently recognized in developing countries, with the inevitable consequence that, when a nascent producer movement (industrial or agricultural) is placed within the ambit of the established co-operative movement, it is almost inevitably entirely marginalized. Evidence from the three countries studied clearly demonstrated this. Though token support for industrial producer co-operatives was present in each country, lucrative agro-processing opportunities were subsumed by the established movement.

In addition, the co-operative banking system (or thrift and credit societies) invariably reflects the interests of the strong and powerful sectors of the co-operative movement and, since these are without exception in less developed countries (LDCs) not industrial or producer sectors, it is also unlikely that a 'voluntary' co-operative banking sector will actively promote the interests of IPCs.

Registrar's Departments and the State

In each of the three countries studied the Registrar's Department was nominally charged with promoting the co-operative movement. Registration and audit, which are in fact perhaps best placed in a government department, require legal and accounting expertise. These are not the skills needed, however, to promote and sustain commercially viable co-operatives—particularly IPCs—which in practice need continuing managerial supervision (Abell and Mahoney, 1988). Registrar's Departments are inevitably dominated by a 'civil service mentality', which is not what is required to promote a flourishing IPC sector. Although it might at first sight appear rather tidy from an organizational point of view to link the functions of promotion with those of registration and audit, the expertise required for the two activities is so different that the amalgam appears not to work. The performance yardsticks motivating officers of a Registrar's Department, namely, to complete audits and to legally oversee the registration of new co-operatives, are not appropriately aligned for promotion activities.

The role of the State in promoting, maintaining, and supervising the co-operative movement has, of course, been much debated (Abrahamson and Scroggs, 1957). Broadly speaking, convinced co-operators (and here we mean the

---

[5] This conclusion applies equally to agricultural *producer* co-operatives.

advocates of any sort of co-operative) are antagonistic towards the intervention of government in the affairs of the co-operative movement. Certainly the evidence (Abell and Mahoney, 1988) is that the movement can easily become a political football, being used for narrow, political purposes, which may then shift abruptly with a change in administration. Nevertheless, the co-operative movement when left to itself is also often liable to varying sorts of corruption; government inquiries proved necessary in all the countries studied. Whether, though, corruption is worse in this sector than elsewhere in the same society is a moot point. Be this as it may, the movement often seeks governmental support and a variety of exemptions which make it difficult to envisage complete freedom from regulation.

When we turn specifically to the promotion of an industrial producer co-operative sector then things look even less clear. In the early stages of the growth of an IPC sector there is no realistic likelihood of resources being made available voluntarily by the already established societies in order to maintain a support and promotion organization. A specialized marketing and buying union (i.e. secondary co-operative) may be a possibility, but that is all.

It seems inevitable, then, that if a support system is necessary to generate systematic growth in the IPC sector, it must in some way be underwritten by the State. There seems no escaping this conclusion. We should, nevertheless, be clear why this is so for the IPC sector, whilst probably not necessarily so for other co-operative sectors. Although the wider co-operative movement has evolved in many countries under varying levels of State supervision and intervention, the motivation behind the establishment of co-operatives has arisen as a natural extension of the self-interest of private citizens engaged in various activities. Agricultural co-operatives are, for instance, strong in the highly individualistic and competitive agricultural sector in the USA. Agricultural marketing and buying co-operatives may well be almost a 'natural' development in a farming economy based upon the private tenure of land—economies of scale inherent within the horizontal integration of certain specific functions being the driving economic force. Indeed, as we have seen, the establishment of co-operative industries in agro-processing (as opposed to IPCs) springs from the very same motive. Similar reasoning applies to the consumer and the credit–banking sectors. Whether, and the degree to which, the state sees fit to get involved in these movements is essentially a cosmetic matter. The State may in practice facilitate, retard, or distort, but the basic dynamic is there, to be tampered with or not as the case may be.

With IPCs, however, the background is different, and this has not been sufficiently recognized by the members of the co-operative movement from the International Co-operative Alliance downwards. IPCs are the voluntary and spontaneous response to production–marketing possibilities only under rather unusual circumstances, and the case for their promotion must rest in part with a desire to activate as yet unmobilized management–entrepreneurial skills (Abell and Mahoney, 1988). This being true there is, except in isolated instances (e.g. the

Mondragon co-operatives), no spontaneous movement to channel or direct. IPCs need to be encouraged and sponsored in a way that other co-operatives do not. The responsibility for this cannot, for reasons already given, fall to the established co-operative movement—at least in the early phase of the establishment of the IPC sector.

Small-scale industries promotion organizations

Most developing countries seek to promote small-scale industries, often in rural areas, and there is a natural inclination to attach any governmental promotion of IPCs to a small-scale industries promotion organization. However, more often than not such organizations are staffed by personnel whose competence lies in promoting private enterprises. Their knowledge of the nature of and problems unique to IPCs is usually very limited indeed. It is probably wrong to assume that development officers trained in traditional commercial skills can easily switch these to the promotion of IPCs.

IPCs, particularly in their vulnerable first two years or so, are likely to fail because they almost inevitably lack adequate management.[6] Initial enthusiasm of members and willingness to make sacrifices for the sake of future success may initially offset this deficit, but without some success this enthusiasm will fast diminish. Loans or grants made without a recognition of these issues will turn stale. IPCs need some managerial input from the support system (Abell and Mahoney, 1988).

Provision of funds by the State for the specific purposes of promoting and supporting IPCs will, when placed in the unfettered hands of a promotion organization, usually be disbursed come what may. There must, therefore, be some commercial constraint on their disbursement—perhaps best provided by a link between the promotion organization and the commercially orientated banks. The constraint must, however, be monitored, for the enthusiasm in the banking sector for IPCs will not be high. On balance, IPCs are not best served by the State provision of concessionary or earmarked funds (e.g. tax breaks and soft loans); State subsidy is better provided by underwriting the cost of a promotion organization.

Co-operative education

The specialized skills needed to operate an IPC are not imparted by the standard co-operative education which is almost invariably directed towards other sorts of society. Specialized IPC sections will be needed in the co-operative training centres and colleges. Colleges, as presently constituted, have little incentive to move in this direction and any support organization for IPCs will need to be invested with powers to intervene in curriculum planning.

---

[6] Statistics seem to demonstrate an early vulnerability (Abell, 1988).

Co-operative law

Co-operative law also usually proves problematic for IPCs. It is almost invariably formulated with the structure of agricultural (marketing and buying) consumer and credit co-operatives in mind. In this respect the statutes are often not best designed to promote or sustain IPCs (Munkner, 1983).

In particular, the statutes must allow for the following, but rarely do:

1. the legal designation and registration of (industrial) *producer* co-operatives as such;
2. limitations upon *employment* in such co-operatives to specialized categories (e.g. temporary workers, probationary members);[7]
3. linking membership to provision of labour rather than capital;[8]
4. no restrictions upon the minimum number of members;[9]
5. restrictions upon the establishment of *co-operative industries* as branches of the consumer and/or agricultural (buying and marketing) societies;
6. flexibility in the financial structure of societies (e.g. allowance for personal capital accounts and no fixed specification about reserve funds)'[10]
7. the possibility of secondary and tertiary structures established independently of the parallel agricultural and consumer structures;[11]
8. the right of established members of an IPC to limit the number of new members (i.e. disallowance of open membership);[12]
9. explicit specification in the by-laws of the measures to be adopted if membership is to be reduced.

Voluntary support organizations

The conventional wisdom amongst members of the co-operative movement is that primary co-operatives should, in an ideal world, create their own secondary and tertiary support mechanisms, financially sustained by levies upon their primary members, and thus not dependent upon State subventions. It is, furthermore, assumed that this objective applies, without exception, to all types of society— agricultural, consumer, credit, and producer. This may not, however, be the case as the incentives for promoting secondary and tertiary societies are not always identical.

As we have had occasion to observe, the incentive for primary agriculturalists to

---

[7] Research (Estrin *et al.*, 1984) shows that permitting employment can lead to degeneration of IPCs.
[8] Nominal capital provision is possible.
[9] Most co-operative legal codes enjoin a minimum membership of ten.
[10] See Thomas and Logan (1981).
[11] Multi-purpose secondary and tertiary structures which are based upon the agricultural or consumer movement will marginalize the producer sector.
[12] Open membership is a principle of co-operation but, as many have argued, it is inappropriate to producer co-operation.

form a (buying and marketing) *primary* society rests with the economies of scale which reduce costs to each member. Presumably established members have an incentive to increase the membership of their co-operative to the point at which there are no additional net economies available. With a suitable regionalization of secondary co-operative societies and the establishment of an apex, this point may well allow for completely open membership whilst aligning the interests of all. It is, thus, reasonable to expect a voluntary growth of secondary and tertiary structures. The State may need to promote the early phases of growth, but eventually there is every reason to suppose the system will become self-generating and self-perpetuating.

This argument only applies, however, as long as the higher-order co-operatives are not used as instruments to increase economies of production (over and above marketing and supply). If they are, there is no necessary coincidence of interests; for instance, each member may well wish to expand operations at the expense of other members. It does appear that it is when agricultural co-operatives are used by governments as instruments for the allocation of resources to the point of production (e.g. soft loans, concessionary priced inputs) that the democratic nature of the co-operative begins to break down and, in the absence of appropriate regulations, corruption often occurs. There is always a tendency towards vertical differentiation in co-operative affairs whereby the effective democratic control by the primary societies is undermined. This tendency is exacerbated by unregulated government interventions.

Similar reasoning applies to primary consumer societies; established members have a common interest in increasing sales by signing up new members and benefiting from any inherent economies.

Historical evidence suggests that governments may often wish, nevertheless, to control the potentially spontaneous movement of consumer and agricultural co-operatives to varying degrees. The motives for this are often very mixed—ranging from a desire to subvert a focus of popular mobilization to a desire to control prices, especially those going to producers of primary foodstuffs. But, these adventitious factors aside, there is no problem in anticipating a voluntary phase in the development of consumer and agricultural societies at both primary and higher levels.

The argument does not, however, carry over easily to (industrial) producer co-operatives. If a *secondary* co-operative is established merely to market products and buy inputs, then the member *primary producer* societies are in a position which is, in most respects, similar to private agricultural producers and one can envisage a limited alignment of interests of societies which in other respects are competitively placed. But, as with agricultural co-operatives, once the co-operative (secondary in the case of producer co-operatives, primary in the case of agricultural–consumer co-operatives) is used as an instrument of promotion and expansion, competitive issues take precedence. It is perhaps significant in this respect that the Caja

Laboral Popular, in the Mondragon group of co-operatives, adopts a policy of not establishing directly competitive member societies and that the support organizations in France and Italy also draw the line at promoting new competitive societies (Defourney *et al.*, n.d.).

There is little incentive for an established primary industrial producer co-operative to provide funds to secondary and higher-order co-operatives, which will be used to promote and establish competitors. Of course positive sentiments may, and indeed often do, include primaries to promote the co-operative sector as an 'ideal' (educational promotion may, in part, ensure this) but, in the long run, and particularly when economic circumstances are not clement, this is a fragile disposition upon which to structure higher-order co-operatives with a promotion function. Insufficient recognition has been given to this point and the conclusion must be that an entirely 'voluntary phase' for the successful promotion of an IPC sector, comprising primary, secondary, and higher-order co-operatives, is not likely. This conclusion goes, however, very much against the grain of co-operative thinking.

The conclusion should, nevertheless, not be taken to imply that voluntary structures have no role to play in sustaining an IPC sector. Firstly, there is no reason why secondary co-operatives, which play a marketing and buying role parallel to that of primary agricultural co-operatives, should not be anticipated. Presumably only *multi-purpose* secondaries will be feasible initially, but, with the growth of the IPC sector, *special purpose* secondary and even a tertiary apex could also be encouraged. These may eventually generate a regional structure and the State-funded promotion and support organization may then gradually relinquish to them any responsibilities it has acquired for buying and marketing. Secondly, these higher-order co-operatives may take upon themselves additional activities where there is a common interest amongst their members for them so to do. In general, the promotion and support organizations should progressively relinquish functions to the secondary and tertiary co-operatives in this manner. It is, nevertheless, essential that the State-sponsored promotion and support organization is retained—albeit with a reduced range of activities. Its continued existence will prove necessary in order to vigorously promote new societies when opportunities arise and where it is not in the interests of the existing co-operatives to promote them.[13] The promotion and support organization should also maintain a competitive policy within the movement.

---

[13] It is probably essential in a labour-managed (co-operative) sector that entry of new competitors is permanently encouraged for two additional reasons. Firstly because, as is well known (Vanek, 1970), the 'income per member maximising enterprise' reacts to improved market conditions by restricting output (and membership). The entry of new co-operatives is thus essential. Secondly, if labour-managed enterprises are risk aversive (again, as some theories would suggest) new societies adopting new methods of production (i.e. risky methods) also need to be encouraged.

Conclusions

If the conclusions in the preceding section of this paper are correct, then it would be unrealistic to expect the established co-operative movement to promote an IPC sector effectively.[14] Furthermore, it is also highly improbable to suppose that a vestigial IPC sector could itself establish voluntary secondary or tertiary co-operatives, equipped with the resources to promote and maintain an enlarged sector.[15] Herein lies the dilemma; the tendency is to hand the promotion over to the established non-industrial co-operative sector or to the government-controlled Registrars' Departments. Unfortunately, however, the former has little incentive to promote IPCs and the latter have little ability to do so.

The inevitable conclusion must be that in the early stages, before the IPC sector is strong enough to create and maintain its own support system, the government itself must establish an organization sufficiently independent of both the established co-operative movement and the Registrar's Department. What is more, it is probably asking too much for such an organization to flourish under the direct and sole supervision of an established (small-scale) industries promotion organization. However, in order to avoid duplicating effort, and to husband scarce resources, the proposed organization will most likely have to be organizationally adjacent to the small-scale industries promotion organization (Ministry). The establishment of a governmentally sponsored and supervised promotion and support organization should be seen as a temporary state of affairs in its fully fledged form, the ultimate objective being to transfer much of its support, though not its promotion activities, to an independent, voluntary structure of secondary and perhaps tertiary co-operatives. These should, eventually, be no more closely supervised or regulated by governmental agencies than is the co-operative movement at large. No doubt such a transition would prove difficult. There will be a political reluctance—particularly in countries prone to one-party politics—to relinquish control, and the organizational and personnel problems of effecting such a transiton should not be underestimated. One would envisage a period of transition with progressively increased, though not sole, reliance being placed upon the voluntary support structures.

References

Abell, P. (1988), *Establishing Support Systems for Industrial Co-operatives: Case Studies from the Third World* (Aldershot: Gower).
—— and Mahoney, N. (1988), *Small-Scale Industrial Co-operatives in Developing Countries* (Oxford: Oxford University Press).

[14] This is probably equally true in developing and developed countries.
[15] A notable exception is, of course, the Caja Laboral Popular in the group of Mondragon co-operatives. It is generally accepted (Thomas and Logan, 1981) that the Mondragon co-operatives are very atypical.

Abrahamson, M. A. and Scroggs, C. L., eds., (1957), *Agricultural Co-operation* (Minneapolis, Minn.: University of Minnesota).

Defourney, J., Estrin, S., and Jones, D. C. (n.d.), 'The Effects of Workers' Participation on Enterprise Performance' (London School of Economics; mimeo).

Estrin, S., Jones, C., and Svejnar, J. (1984), 'The Varying Nature, Importance and Productivity Effects of Worker Participation: Evidence for Contemporary Producer Co-operatives in Industrialized Western Economies' (London School of Economics; mimeo).

Knapp, J. G. (1936), 'Some Misunderstandings, Misconceptions or Prejudices regarding Farm Co-operation', in Abrahamson and Scroggs, *Agricultural Co-operation*.

Lewis, J., Cornforth, C., and Thomas, A. (1985), *A Survey of Co-operative Organisations in the UK* (Milton Keynes: Open University Co-operative Research Unit).

Lincoln, M. D. (1936), 'Producer Consumer Co-operative Realtionships', in Abrahamson and Scroggs, *Agricultural Co-operation*.

Munkner, H. A. (1983), *Development of Industrial Co-operatives in Tanzania* (Marburg; mimeo).

Thomas, H. and Logan, C. (1981), *Mondragon: An Economic Analysis* (London: George Allen & Unwin).

Vanek, J. (1970), *The General Theory of Labour Managed Market Economies* (Ithaca, NY: Cornell University Press).

PART V

COUNTRY STUDIES

Outline of Part V

THE idea of a section on country studies is to stimulate the diffusion of insights, experiences, and research findings concerning specific developments which have to be understood in the context of a particular society during a certain period. The study of organizational democracy thrives not only on studies trying to generalize across times and places, but also on investigations focusing on the—in their eyes—unique features of concrete forms or processes of organizational democracy in a particular social setting. No doubt such case-studies will inspire others to see if something similar can be detected or developed in another time and/or another place.

George Strauss takes stock of the specific US industrial relations system which manifests itself in the collective bargaining structure. Over the past few years—with the progressive introduction of participative management (as Lawler has shown in Part II), ESOPs (Russell, Part I), buy-outs, and concession bargaining—the USA may seem to have been entering the participation era. Superficially the new forms of US participation resemble the German model (including its mix of collective bargaining and participation); however, it is still unclear whether in fact they involve any increase in workers' power. Participation has been introduced for a variety of reasons, including to take advantage of tax laws, as in the case of ESOPs, or just as window-dressing, to mask substantial wage concessions by the unions. Often workers have been co-opted more than they have been empowered.

Philippe Bernoux describes the development of management strategies in France over the last four decades. There have been three phases: directly after the Second World War the American Taylorist methods; then, in the 1960s, the British and Scandinavian socio-technical models; and finally, since the 1970s, the Japanese approach. There is no clear pointer for the future, but the Auroux Laws of 1982 have perhaps given birth to a new French model (see the Appendix in Bernoux's article).

In The Netherlands there is a growing trend towards formal participation as has happened in some other countries (France, West Germany, the USA), covered in this volume. Are they all atypical or are the cyclical and/or evolutionary models simply wrong? Jan C. Looise proposes the 'stairway theory', which overcomes the dilemma and the paradox that unions fear forms of participation for which they have always fought. Here we join the reflections and experiences of Marcel Bolle de Bal in the neighbouring country, Belgium. The explanation for this growth in participation is the decentralization process, which will itself lead to another form i.e. *direct* rather than *representative* participation. This is what trade union officials may fear, since it means less power for them. But, in Looise's eyes, unions will still be necessary for co-ordination and federation tasks in the process of organizational democracy.

Some German observers already speak of a historic compromise between capital and labour after the collective bargaining round of 1984, which opened the way to the 35-hour week after the longest and largest strikes and lock-outs in West German history. The price unions seem to be ready to pay is more flexibility at the workplace, longer duration of agreements (three years), and more centralization in collective bargaining.

Rudi Schmidt and Rainer Trinczek illustrate this situation on the basis of the first and only empirical research so far on this topic. It challenges the West German system of co-determination through the problems of implementation of union–management agreements, which means at the same time a trend towards decentralization. As we see in the Dutch, US, and French cases, and in the theoretical reflections by Schienstock, similarities appear on a large scale. The future of organizational democracy is at a crucial stage. It is the right moment to take stock.

A quite different case-study is given by Hing Ai Yun. It is not research within an industrial, administrative, or service organization, but within a huge co-operative established and to a great extent administered by the State. The conflicts within such an organization newly created from above seem to be similar in many Second and Third World countries in the twentieth century, though not necessarily for the West. However, since the majority of the world's population is not living in the West, it is worth while to study these experiences more closely, especially since the one presented here has a thirty-year history. What is interesting is that, under very tight political, economic, and social constraints, there is also a demand for more real participation. Our initial assessment of the set-backs to the cause of organizational democracy, therefore, appears to have been unduly pessimistic. However, let us resist the temptation to draw conclusions at this point. We will come to that in a final chapter reflecting on the general trends emerging from the contributors' efforts to take stock.

18

Workers' Participation and US Collective Bargaining

GEORGE STRAUSS

AT first glance the USA would seem to be making great strides toward organizational democracy. Jointly sponsored union–management Quality of Work Life (QWL) projects are spreading rapidly. By contrast with a few years ago, when collective bargaining was the only form of indirect participation felt to be legitimate by either labour or management, today union representatives sit on the boards of directors of a significant number of companies. A mosaic of union–management committees has developed, some with substantial budgets. Employee stock ownership has become more common. Some companies are now entirely employee owned.[1]

How significant have these changes been? Why have they occurred? How have they worked out in practice? Do they presage a fundamental shift toward organizational democracy—or do they merely disguise a shift towards greater management power? In particular, how do they affect American collective bargaining, which has always stressed the adversarial relationship and a strict distinction between labour and management?

The context of change

The nature of these changes can be understood best in the overall context of American economic and industrial relations developments and the immediate context of concession bargaining.[2]

Economic and organizational changes

Recent years have seen substantial changes in the American economy, especially in its manufacturing sector. US companies were badly hurt by a variety of problems: oil price increases in the 1970s, until recently an overvalued dollar, and largely

---

[1] My discussion is concerned with the unionized sector alone. Participation schemes have become increasingly common in the non-union sector as well, but that is another story (see also Chs. 4 and 7).

[2] To save space many references to events reported in the daily press or the *Daily Labor Report* have been deleted throughout the paper. For further information, contact the author.

obsolescent technologies or product design in such industries as steel, cars, tyres, and machine tools. Legal deregulation of transportation and the break-up of the former telephone monopoly led to fierce competition. The destabilization process was accentuated by financial 'take-over artists', who raided vulnerable companies, stripping them of their assets. Together, these factors forced many previously stable industrial giants to restructure and lay off many employees. Permanent shut-downs, involving millions of employees (including many managers) have been common in industries as diverse as banking, transportation, electronics, steel, and retail groceries.

Furthermore, the US economy is moving from manufacturing to services and from mass production to custom–craft and process–continuous flow technologies. Computers are greatly changing the way much work is done. On balance the new technologies probably increase the need for employee participation. Additionally, inspired in part by the presumed success of Japanese management, American managers have been giving greater priority to human resources policies designed to develop broadly trained, highly motivated employees who are prepared and trusted to exercise high orders of discretion. Many personnel and industrial relations departments were renamed human resources departments and given larger budgets, salaries, and status. Both top management and top staff people began encouraging shop-level participation.

Another development was a revised policy toward unions. In those situations which were already non-union, management fought hard and successfully (and sometimes illegally) to keep them that way. In unionized situations some companies (such as Greyhound) did their best to break the union. In others, such as Xerox and GM, management sought to enlist the union in a common struggle to regain competitiveness.

Meanwhile, the unionized sector of the economy has grown less fast than the non-union sector. Unionized firms have lost employment and unions have had great difficulty organizing new, non-union firms. As a consequence, union membership has fallen from one-third of non-agricultural employment to 18 per cent.

Concession bargaining

Most commonly in unionized situations, management demanded 'give-backs' or concessions. Faced with massive unemployment and the threatened (as well as actual) bankruptcy of key employers, a number of unions agreed to significant cutbacks in their economic benefits. During 1982 three of the country's largest unions, the Auto Workers, the Steelworkers, and the Teamsters gave up hard-won gains, especially cost-of-living adjustments (indexation). In 1983, 32 per cent of the workers covered by new contracts in manufacturing took pay cuts and another 24 per cent received no wage increase (*Daily Labor Report*, 30 Jan. 1984: B-3). Concessions have continued through to the present.

While early concessions were concentrated on wages and fringe benefits, more recent concessions have involved work rules, especially restrictions on management's ability to combine jobs or transfer workers from one job to another. In most instances, the union was able to negotiate at least some sort of token counter-concession in return for its own concessions. Often this counter-concession took the form of a modest increase (or apparent increase) in union influence over subjects previously strictly subject to management's sole control. For a while, too, the parties suspended their adversarial relationship and co-operated in making difficult personnel decisions. There were at least two reasons for these developments. First, both sides recognized that co-operation was essential for mutual survival. Faced with bankruptcy, managements anxiously sought greater worker involvement, while unions became convinced that co-operation might save their members' jobs. Secondly, it was politically difficult for union officers to ask their membership to give up wages and working conditions without getting *something* in return. From the point of view of companies who were in a poor position to make financial counter-concessions, concessions in power were cheap and the only quid pro quos available.

Growth of participation

Much of the early US experience with formal participation involved QWL activities in greenfield, non-union plants. Unions were generally sceptical. But by 1973 the national agreements negotiated by the United Auto Workers (UAW) and the major motor manufacturers contained provisions endorsing QWL programmes. To protect worker and union sensibilities, early programmes focused on job satisfaction, safety, absenteeism, and quality. At first, increased productivity was rarely mentioned as a possible outcome of participation. But, with concession bargaining, the emphasis shifted more openly to cost cutting and productivity. In some cases participation was introduced only after the union lost a strike.

Since 1980 formal participatory schemes have emerged from the experimental stage and have been increasingly adopted in both union and non-union sectors. Estimates based on fairly reliable samples suggest that up to 50 per cent of unionized manufacturing firms enjoy some sort of joint participative scheme, with the great bulk of these being established after 1980 (Cooke, 1987; Voos, 1987).

Forms of participation

According to Kochan, Katz, and McKersie (1986), industrial relations occur at three levels: the workplace, the collective bargaining–personnel, and the strategic. Forms of participation are discussed below under this headings, though some fit them imperfectly. Discussion of the relationship between these forms and unions or collective bargaining will be deferred till later.

The workplace level

A variety of forms of workplace participation have been adopted. Perhaps the most common are job enrichment, Quality Circles, autonomous work groups, and the Scanlon Plan.

Job enrichment is often associated with 'broad banding', the combining of separate job classifications. For example, at NUMMI (the joint General Motors–Toyota plant in Fremont, California), close to fifty unskilled job classifications were combined into one. At GM's Kokomo parts plant the union agreed that workers would assume greater responsibility, including some budget planning, thus eliminating several management positions.

In theory, job enrichment adds autonomy, new skills, and a sense of completion to the job, and so should increase job satisfaction. In practice, management's true motive for introducing this form of 'participation' was often to break down job demarcation lines, use its work-force more flexibly, and so eliminate workers. For this reason, as we shall see, workers often fiercely resist its introduction.

Autonomous work groups are spreading rapidly, especially in the motor industry where they are sometimes known as 'operating teams'. In at least ten General Motors plants, such teams have the responsibility for 'inspection, materials handling, housekeeping, and repairs'. They meet periodically 'to discuss production problems, review the pay system, and discuss impending business decisions such as the introduction of new machinery or prospective work schedules . . . the team regularly reviews the costs and revenues associated with the work area' (Kochan, Katz, and Mower, 1984: 92–3). In practice, teams differ considerably in their autonomy. In many cases, team structure means merely that management has greater flexibility to move workers from job to job, without regard to work rules or seniority (Katz, Kochan, and Keefe, 1987).[3]

Quality Circles (QCs) represent the latest American fad. The main difference between them and autonomous work groups is that in theory QCs can only recommend changes while autonomous groups can implement them. Further, QCs are voluntary; to have 30 per cent of the work-force to participate is considered good. Often such committees begin by considering quality but move on to working conditions and productivity. Although instructed not to do so, at times they tread on areas normally reserved for collective bargaining and the grievance procedure. Understandably, supervisors and union leaders sometimes view them as potential threats.

With a fifty-year-old history the Scanlon Plan represents an effort to harness

---

[3] Nevertheless, a study of major car firms finds a 0.7 correlation between two measures, the first 'concerning the formal use of team work systems' and the second 'concerning the extent information about costs and quality is received on a regular basis by the workforce and the extent of worker involvement in group decision making' (Katz and Keefe, 1987: 5).

workers' ideas for increasing productivity through combining participation with financial incentives. The typical plan provides for a series of workplace and plant-wide committees to evaluate workers' suggestions and to formulate plans for improving productivity. Savings due to increased productivity are shared by workers and the company.

The collective bargaining–personnel level

Joint plant- or company-wide representative committees were fairly common in American industry well before the concession-bargaining era, especially during wartime and recessions, periods when labour and management objectives appear most congruent (Jacoby, 1985). Traditionally such committees dealt with matters that were considered peripheral to collective bargaining—such subjects as safety, training, and scrap reduction—matters about which the interests of the parties were seen to be sufficiently congruent that they could be resolved in a co-operative, non-adversarial way. Like joint consultative committees in Britain (sometimes called 'tea and toilet committees'), these American committees played rather minor roles.

Recently, US joint committees have proliferated (particularly in the motor industry) and they have been given more important duties. Some of them deal primarily with personnel issues, such as child care, containment of medical cost increases, or developing special chairs for people working on video terminals. Other national and local representative committees monitor and facilitate the development of QCs and job redesign at the shop level. Still others have been charged generally with enlisting worker ideas and energies to reduce costs, improve productivity and quality, and facilitate team-work.

Recent car contracts have spawned a maze of committees. Special plant committees have been established to review job design, new plant layout, changes in manufacturing equipment, and major new processes. Plant-level committees (called 'mutual growth forums' at Ford) permit exchange of information and the discussion of investment and other issues which might affect employment or workers' welfare.

Another series of company-wide and plant-level committees administers the funds ($1 billion at GM) to provide training and new forms of employment for employees laid off due to technological change or outsourcing (subcontracting). A joint union–management study group (including sixty union representatives) helped plan GM's new Saturn project to build subcompact cars. At GM still other company-wide committees deal with subjects such as health and safety, attendance, and skill development and training. Many have local counterparts, for example, a hazardous material control committee at each plant. Finally, the GM contract provides a capstone, overall executive board–joint activities committee whose function is to co-ordinate the activities of other committees and to reassure union activists who fear these committees will insufficiently protect workers' interests.

In only a few cases do such committees, whether union or not, have independent powers or budgets (the joint GM–UAW training committee is very much the exception). For the most part these committees are advisory to management.

The strategic level

Information

Company financial records have traditionally been viewed as confidential in the USA, except in so far as they are required to be divulged by law or Stock Exchange rules. A common counter-concession was to permit the union to inspect the company's books. Indeed, under adverse conditions many companies became anxious to share financial information. As a cynical unionist put it, 'When companies are making a loss, they open the books; when they are making a profit they close them tight.'

Though few companies have formally agreed to share information beyond that now required by law, on an informal level information sharing has increased. Some managements appear convinced that frankness may facilitate co-operation. Kochan, Katz, and Mower (1984: 89) describe how, at a Ford plant, 'for the first time, the plant manager was forewarning union officials about upcoming layoffs and new machinery, and asking for advice on how they might best be implemented'. The better understanding so generated contributed to a new agreement on work rules.

Membership on company boards of directors

Union representatives have been placed on the boards of Chrysler and American Motors, Republic, Pan American, and Western Airlines, Wilson Foods, and several financially troubled steel and road transport firms. In addition, there are workers directors (not always selected by the union) in a considerable number of Employee Stock Ownership (ESOP) buy-out situations, as described below.

Union leaders are troubled by the apparent conflict of interest that union-selected board-member representation occasions. They are divided as to the extent that they should take responsibility for making difficult production and investment decisions, some of which may involve lay-offs. To date this dilemma has been resolved in three ways: (1) the worker representatives are eminent outsiders who presumably are sympathetic to workers' interests but receive no specific instructions as to how to vote (this is the approach followed by the Teamsters union); (2) a key union representative is selected, but he resigns his union role (as did Robert Gould, formerly chief negotiator for Pan American pilots); or (3) a key union representative is selected but he absents himself from the board when collective-bargaining strategy is discussed (as did Auto Workers President,

Douglas Fraser, while on Chrysler's board).[4] All three strategies are inconsistent with the view of some Europeans that the union selected director's main role is to influence industrial relations decisions.

US experience with union-selected directors is still too limited to generalize with confidence. As has been the experience in other countries (Strauss, 1982) union-selected directors in some cases have been handicapped by rules keeping board deliberations confidential, thus restricting themselves from communicating with constituents (Hammer and Stern, 1983). Directors from the shop floor lack the technical expertise to make contributions in areas such as finance; by contrast, outside experts lack knowledge as to conditions within the company. Further, regardless of the union-selected director's skill, management can usually keep issues key to workers off the board's agenda. In any case, boards, which meet as infrequently as once a quarter, may exert little real influence.

Nevertheless, Fraser reports that while on the Chrysler board he was able to stave off some plant shut-downs, and he vigorously (though largely unsuccessfully) opposed paying high salaries, bonuses, and substantial stock options for management while workers were still making concessions.

Although some observers view these developments as leading toward German-style co-determination, union representation on boards is unlikely to spread much beyond a few crisis situations. Union leaders are still reluctant to be held responsible to their membership for management's decisions. In none of the major co-operation cases other than Rath (to be discussed below) did unions select a majority of the board. Further, although union leaders no longer oppose board membership on principle,[5] neither is it high on their priority list.

Taking sides in struggles for control of management

Perhaps the unions' greatest opportunities for intrusion into management have involved struggles for company control. Four sets of activities may be involved: (1) unions may force a change in management by refusing to make concessions until present management is replaced (as at Wheeling Steel and Pan American); (2) they may agree to make concessions to one side in a take-over fight, but not to the other (TWA); (3) utilizing their stock ownership they may make take-over offers themselves (Eastern, Pan American and United Airlines, and the Southern Pacific Railroad); and (4) they may use their political power to favour one set of buyers, as

---

[4] When originally appointing Fraser to its board the company took the position tht he was being selected as an individual, not as union president. After Fraser retired from both positions the company eventually appointed his union successor to the board—but only after much delay.

[5] Thus, Steelworkers President Lynn Williams predicts that 'in the future, particularly with the growth of Employee Stock Ownership Plans, I expect workers' interests to be represented on many corporate boards' (*Daily Labor Report*, 3 Jan. 1986: D-3); but he warns against the election of union officers, which 'might give rise to conflict of interest accusations'. Instead, unions should seek board representation by 'outside professionals' (*Daily Labor Report*, 12 July 1985: 2).

the rail unions did when federal government was trying to sell Conrail (formerly the Pann–Central railroad) to private owners. Though the union stock ownership bids failed, in most of the cases listed above the unions' real objective—to win a more favourable management—succeeded. To assist in these efforts, unions are increasingly hiring the services of high-priced investment bankers (e.g. Lazard Freres, Rothschild, and Salomon) or Wall Street lawyers. Shades of Karl Marx!

ESOPs

An ESOP (Employee Stock Ownership Plan) is a trust established to receive stock from the employer (or cash to purchase stock from existing owners) for distribution to individual accounts of participating workers. In the majority of instances stock ownership has resulted from employers taking advantage of recently enacted tax laws designed to encourage widespread share ownership. In a smaller number of cases, stock ownership has been a quid pro quo arising from concession bargaining. In 1986 ESOPs and stock bonus plans covered an estimated 7.9 million workers (National Center for Employee Ownership, 1987*b*). Probably only about 15 per cent of ESOP companies are unionized (Blasi, 1987).[6]

Unionists have traditionally been antagonistic to worker stock ownership. They argued that stock ownership gave workers the illusion of ownership without any real control and that it was chiefly a management technique to make unions unnecessary or to cut wages. They have been particularly opposed to company plans to replace pension plans with ESOPs.

Faced with the prospect of substantial job losses, however, many unions changed their position (Rothschild-Whitt, 1985). Wage cuts combined with stock ownership are better than cuts with nothing at all. Today, when companies plead poverty, unions increasingly respond, 'If you can't give us money, give us stock.'

A rather more dramatic case involved Chrysler, which had to contribute $165 million worth of company stock to an ESOP as a condition for a government $1.5 billion loan guarantee. As from 1984 Chrysler employees owned 16 per cent of its stock, with the typical holding being worth $4,500 (*Daily Labor Report*, 10 July 1984: A-11).[7] ESOPs are also common in the financially troubled airline industry, where employees received 13 per cent of Pan American, 25 per cent of Eastern Airlines, and 33 per cent of Western. Similar stock-for-wages trades have also been common in smaller road transport and steel firms (Rosen *et al.*, 1986).

Stock ownership, some unions now argue, is a legitimate union objective, provided it is on top of decent wages and fringe benefits. In practice, stock

---

[6] On ESOPs, see also the contribution by Russell in this volume (Chapter 4).

[7] According to one calculation, the workers gained more from the increase in value of their stock than they gave up in wage concessions (Rothschild-Whitt, 1985). At Western, PSA, and Republic Airlines, each of which was bought up by larger airlines, workers made at least as much money by selling their stock as they had lost earlier through concessions (National Center for Employee Ownership: 1987*a*).

ownership has had little impact on day-to-day labour relations in the companies involved, nor does owning stock make union members significantly less loyal to their unions (Sockell, 1985). Studies of the impact of ESOPs on productivity, job satisfaction, and the like are rather inconclusive (e.g., Kruse, 1984; Rosen *et al.*, 1986).

Buy-outs

A new trend has been for workers to buy out their plants, rather than see them shut down altogether. The largest of these buy-outs involved the 8,000-employee Weirton Steel and the 3,000-employee Rath Packing Company (the latter unsuccessful). A number of buy-outs during the mid-1970s occurred when conglomerates sought to shake off relatively unprofitable plants or plants in the wrong line of business. The more recent wave of buy-outs involved more seriously troubled firms in which immediate infusions of capital were necessary to avoid complete closure. In these cases jobs were saved by a combination of worker equity contributions, bank loans, government loans and grants, benefit and wage cuts (as much as 30 per cent at GMs former Hyatt-Clark plant), and work rule changes.

The appeal of such rescues is obvious. Companies find buyers for their worst operations rather than incur the costs and public blame for closing them. Workers save their jobs, and unions get credit for helping them. But changes in ownership often meant no (or very little) change in control, even though individual workers received voting shares of stock in some cases, and were occasionally elected to boards of directors. In fact, buy-out arrangements were often put together under chaotic financial conditions and with such haste that little thought was given to internal governance. Workers' prime motivation was to save their jobs and radical new ideas might have scared off financial support. Indeed, bank loans and other financial assistance were often contingent on the presence of stable hierarchical management structures (Whyte *et al.*, 1983). Unions could offer little guidance in this strange new situation.

Worker buy-outs appear very successful at first: profits improve, productivity climbs, turnover declines, and a number of apparently hopeless plants have been restored to seeming prosperity (for summary articles see Long, 1980; Zwerdling, 1980; Strauss, 1982). At least three factors may be at work: (1) wages and manpower have been cut, thus increasing profits, (2) the newly independent plants are freed from the requirement to contribute toward corporate overheads, and finally, (3) once the often formidable barriers to worker ownership have been overcome, workers feel a sense of triumph; in turn this leads to an immediate burst of enthusiasm and co-operation as the parties enjoy the hope that, by pulling together, their previously threatened jobs can now be saved.

In many cases, after a year or so of worker ownership, disillusionment sets in. Workers move 'from euphoria to alienation' (Whyte *et al.*, 1983: 87). Once fear of job loss subsides, worker ownership, by itself, seems to have little impact on either productivity or satisfaction. For the average worker, the job and the boss are unchanged. On the other hand, Weirton Steel appears reasonably successful, at least financially. Its formal organization is quite traditional, but there is considerable shop-level participation as well as a good deal of informal union–management collaboration. The company has paid its employees fairly good profits, though not enough to make up for their wage cuts.

Combining ownership and control

By now many authorities believe that for worker ownership to have a lasting impact on production or satisfaction it must be combined with some form of workers' control (e.g. Whyte *et al.*, 1983: ch. 5). Doing this is not easy.

The problems are illustrated by the experience at Rath Packing. Here, in return for concessions, workers won worker ownership and the right to elect the board of directors. An elaborate structure of workplace productivity teams was established, but effective union–management collaboration never developed at higher levels. Despite gains in productivity the company was economically too weak to be saved. As top management was replaced several times, in the end by the union president, relationships fluctuated in a yo-yo fashion from adversarial to co-operative (Hammer, and Stern, 1986). Finally the plant expired, in bitterness. Many of the same problems affected Hyatt-Clark, another unsuccessful worker buy-out.

Impact on unions and union–management relations

As we have seen, recent US industrial relations have been marked by (1) an extension of the subjects regarding which unions and managements have developed co-operative, non-adversarial relations, and (2) union intrusion into areas which were previously exclusively management prerogatives (what some call an extension of the 'frontiers of union control'). Both developments, it should be stressed, occurred in the context of concession bargaining. *None* of the participative schemes discussed above, from job enlargement to worker buy-outs, occurred because unions really wanted them. They were either imposed by management on an unwilling union or accepted reluctantly by the union as second-best to maintaining previous wage levels. Certainly all these developments were foreign to the American collective bargaining tradition.

Traditional US collective bargaining

Foreign visitors, influenced by the widespread union support for industrial democracy in Europe, often used to ask why the American labour movement did not seek to share in management control. American unionists' standard answer, at least until recently was that American-style collective bargaining already provided an effective form of industrial democracy. To some extent American unionists were right. Once they win an election and are certified as bargaining representatives, American unions have the legal right to insist that management bargain over a broad range of issues: from wages and health benefits to discipline, technological change, and practically everything covered in Britain under the term 'custom and practice'. Beyond this, American industrial relations has developed an extensive quasi-bureaucratic grievance system which interprets and applies the contract as specific issues arise and often works out solutions to problems not covered by the master document.

From an American point of view the European demand for industrial democracy represented merely an attempt to strengthen plant-level bargaining and to extend its scope to cover the broad range of subjects already standard in the USA. Nevertheless, the similarity between US collective bargaining and, for example, German co-determination can be overdrawn. While US unions negotiate over the *impact* of plant shut-downs (e.g. they can negotiate redundancy payments, retraining allowances, and the like), they rarely negotiate over whether a plant should shut down in the first place. Neither do they normally negotiate over investment policy, the location of new plants, or the acquisition of new subsidiaries. At least in Germany, workers and unions have more influence over these subjects than they do in the USA. Further, German works councils have greater legal rights of access to information than do US unions.

In fact, American law draws a distinction between *mandatory* and *permissive* subjects of bargaining. Included among the permissive subjects are such strategic managerial issues as the decision whether to shut down a plant. About these the union has no right to strike. Indeed, the Supreme Court has ruled that 'Congress had no intention that the elected union representative would become an equal partner in the running of the business enterprise' (*First National Maintenance Corp* vs. *N.L.R.B.*, 452 US 666, 1981).

Nevertheless, recent recession and concession bargaining has done much to reduce union reluctance to become involved in management. The problems were too serious to be resolved on a traditional basis. Change did not come easily, however, and numerous problems occurred as attempts were made to accommodate co-operation to an adversarial tradition.

Clashes over strategy

In terms of their attitudes toward concession bargaining, union leaders may be spread along a continuum with the two extremes labelled the 'militant' and the 'co-operativist' (Katz, 1986) and with most leaders uncertain where they stand. These differences and uncertainties carry over to attitudes toward participation.

Noting that participative programmes have been introduced into many strongly anti-union companies, militant unionists view these as chiefly union-busting techniques. Some oppose the entire participative movement on almost ideological grounds. They see participation as a form of manipulation and speedup as well as an attempt to co-opt the unions and to deflect workers' attention from their economic problems. As one put it, 'The best way to enrich the job is to enrich the pay.'

'Co-operativists' view the militant position towards concession bargaining as almost suicidal. They see co-operation as helping the company survive and thus saving jobs. They argue that shop-floor participation may yield valuable non-economic benefits. However, by contrast with their European counterparts, few US unionists have developed an ideological interest in controlling management. Indeed, attitudes are determined less by ideology than by economic circumstances. Unions whose members' jobs are most severely threatened are more likely to support participation (Cappelli, 1985).

At the national level, the Auto, Steel, and Communications Workers have been generally supportive of participation (subject to appropriate controls). The Machinists have been somewhat hostile. In between are national unions which encourage local-level experimentation and provide staff support for such experiments, and those which adopt a position of neutrality, allowing local unions to make their own decisions (Kochan, Katz, and Mower, 1984). There are similar variations at the local level, and most unions grope their way through *terra incognita* without a firm policy. In general, economically strong unions have felt little need for participation while weak ones see it as means of preserving and even extending their influence (Wever, 1986).

Participation and concession bargaining have been central issues in union politics and union elections in many (most?) of the plants into which co-operation has been introduced, especially where, despite co-operation, lay-offs have occurred. A significant number of local union officials supporting participation have been defeated. There has been much opposition, for example, to the Auto Workers' agreement with General Motors with regards to the new Saturn plant, even though this agreement purportedly gives the union unprecedented managerial rights.[8]

Job redesign and the union contract

Historically the thrust of US collective bargaining has been to rigidify and codify personnel practices. In the typical unionized plant, decisions as to the allocation of work among workers are made on the basis of collectively bargained seniority and job description rules. Many workers believe strongly that these rules give them quasi-property rights in their jobs, rights they are willing to fight hard to preserve.

Among the major causes of resistance to 'concession contracts' is that they require giving up these long-enjoyed work rules. Broad banding (job enlargement)

---

[8] According to Victor Reuther (1986), brother of the famous Walter, 'The Saturn agreement makes a mockery of free collective bargaining and represents little bargaining and much surrender . . . [C]oncessions were exchanged for the illusion of a worker voice in management and a mythical partnership. Yes, a voice in raising productivity and profits, but no real voice in corporate investments, none in scandalously high executive salaries and stock options. No voice for workers or consumers in car prices.'

requires the combination of some jobs and the blurring of boundaries between others. Self-managing work teams tend to erase the sharp line between workers and managers, a distinction which American unions have long sought to maintain. New career patterns disturb established promotional ladders. In plants with the most advanced of the new forms of participation, decisions as to the allocation of work are made by the work teams on a flexible *ad hoc* basis. Autonomous work groups may even determine pay and discipline.

In short, collective bargaining leads to what the Webbs called the 'common rule'; by contrast, the whole participation movement promotes experimentation and diversity. It involves a trade-off of predetermined rules for greater participation in the management of work on a day-by-day basis. Transition from one system to another is difficult and divisive.

Often changes in work rules have been introduced only despite determined worker resistance. The company proposal to combine certain skill and craft jobs was one of the main causes of the six-month 1986–7 Steelworker–USX (US Steel's new name) strike. Not infrequently management has set unions in two plants competing against each other, offering to make investments in the plant agreeing to the greatest changes in work rules and threatening to close the other. Thus GM agreed to invest $80 million in its North Tarrytown plant rather than at Framingham when the Tarrytown local union branch agreed to slash the number of job classifications from over 100 to seven (*Wall Street Journal*, 2 Feb. 1987).

Unions often negotiate guarantees of 'shelter agreements', which provide that the participative agreement may not supersede the collective-bargaining agreement except by specific joint consent. At Xerox, for example, the parties initially distinguished between 'on-line' topics, which could be discussed by QWL teams, and 'off-line' subjects, which were covered by collective bargaining and therefore outside the team's purview (Kochan, Katz, and Mower, 1984: 19).

In practice, however, a rigid separation between participation and collective bargaining was difficult to maintain at Xerox (as it has been elsewhere). All is simple as long as the participative team confines itself to purely housekeeping issues. But, once the group begins exploring possible means of cutting costs or making changes in the socio-technical system (for example, through changing job assignments and pay), it inevitably impinges on matters which relate directly to the heart of US collective bargaining. In companies which have moved into more advanced forms of participation, such matters are typically referred to plant- or company-level representative committees—in Kochan, Katz, and McKersie's (1986) terms, to the bargaining or strategic levels.

Problems with the participative process

Representative joint participation (including joint committees) has enjoyed various degrees of success. Union optimists anticipated that it would give workers greater say in how plants were operated. Pessimists saw it merely as a forum in which further work rule concessions would be orchestrated. In practice, both optimists and pessimists have been proved partly right.

In the past, participative efforts were often launched with great fanfare but either stalemated because of the parties' continuing hostility or gradually atrophied because of lack of interest (Schuster, 1983). For example, the 1959 steel contract gave a high-level 'joint human relations committee' the mission to develop more co-operative relations in the steel industry. In 1964, with the election of a new national union president, this committee died. The 1971 steel contract established joint 'productivity and security of employment committees' in every plant. By 1978 these had practically disappeared, the victims of internal struggles and lack of priority on either side's agenda. In 1980 these committees were reintroduced with much the same charge, but this time called 'labour–management participation teams'. Understandably there was much cynicism as to whether these new committees would do any better than their predecessors. But economic conditions had changed since the 1970s, and some of these steel committees have begun to take root (Kochan, Katz, and Mower, 1984: 65–84).

There have been at least some successful cases where joint committees, having weathered strikes and lay-offs, seem to have acquired an institutional life of their own. A careful study of joint committees in the motor industry suggests that they have had at least intermittent success, particularly in improving quality, if not productivity (Katz, Kochan and Gobeille, 1983).

By now enough experience has been accumulated that we can specify some of the problems that need to be overcome if participative efforts are to take root.

Trust and expectations

Aside from the tangible agreement represented by concession bargaining, there was often an unspoken agreement that the parties would turn over a new leaf and start to trust each other. As Ford's director of industrial relations put it, attitudes began changing 'from *we* vs. *they* to *us*: from adversarial to converging; from rigidity to flexibility; and from partisan to common interest' (Slaughter, 1983: 54). Indeed for a while in some companies a spirit prevailed akin to that in Britain after the Dunkirk disaster of 1940. According to some reports, when Chrysler's fortunes were at their lowest, its president Lee Iacocca was cheered by workers as he toured the assembly line.

Unfortunately, a Dunkirk spirit is pretty fragile. Management frequently missed its chances. Too often management insensitivity to workers' feelings (and good public relations) did much to dissipate early goodwill. An implicit understanding in most concession bargaining was that there would be 'equality of sacrifice'. In numerous cases, however, management violated this expectation by such acts as raising managerial salaries shortly after workers accepted substantial pay cuts or by breaking implicit understandings not to shut down plants. Thus

GM damaged its relations with the UAW in 1987 when it awarded big bonuses to its officers at a time when its workers received no profit-sharing bonuses and Ford workers earned an annual bonus of $2,100 each. By contrast a steel company improved its relations when it agreed quickly to a union demand that its officers cease flying first class while workers still suffered pay cuts.

Another expectation was that the sharp lines between management's prerogatives and practices covered by the contract would be blurred. The expectation was that a broad range of strategic (not just workplace) decisions which had previously been made unilaterally by management would now be made only after mutual discussion. In particular, management would consult with the union before taking major actions that might jeopardize workers' interests. When management violated these expectations, as US Steel did in deciding to import steel rather than make it at its Fairless plant, co-operative efforts were set back at all levels. Similarly, AT&T violated these expectations when it announced substantial personnel cut-backs without giving its union leadership at least advance notice.

In short, for unions and management to make the fundamental changes necessary for effective participation, trust on both sides is required. Yet the participative model is so different from the parties' normal behaviour that it is easy for each side to suspect the other of hypocrisy. At NUMMI, the joint GM–Toyota plant, where union and management are trying to move to a more participative culture, one observer commented:

The workers have a pretty clear model of the wrong style of management—that's the old GM style. They also have a clear model of right management, that's what they are now convinced is the Japanese style. The trouble is that they are forever waiting for management to make a mistake—to act in the old GM way—and so prove what they inwardly suspect—that the whole thing is a sham. There is not much forgiveness yet, or a realization that the other side, however sincere, consists of human beings who can make mistakes.

Trust is particularly difficult to develop in situations where concession bargaining has engendered considerable bitterness.

Key individuals

Success of participation depends heavily on the support of key high-level leaders (sometimes called 'champions') on both sides. Despite a formal agreement participation never got off the ground at GM until strong supporters of it were appointed as vice president of the company's industrial relations department and as director of the union's General Motors department. Similar developments occurred at Ford, Chrysler, and elsewhere.

Distrust at the top can easily destroy a relationship. Despite early success, the co-operative relationship between Eastern Airlines and its union broke down, in large part because of personal hostility between union leader Charles Bryant and Charles Borman, Eastern's chairman. As Bryant put it, Borman has 'totally betrayed the confidence of employees . . . I could never trust [him] again' (*Wall Street Journal*, 2 Jan 1985). At the time of writing the same problem exists at Pan American.

Threats to power

Participation brings in a 'parallel organization' (Goldstein, 1985) of committees, ranging from autonomous work groups to company-wide committees, all of which to some extent compete with traditional union and management hierarchies.

Union leaders derive much of their power and satisfaction from the fact that they control the workers' main avenue of communication to management. If workers resolve their problems through discussion groups, there will be fewer grievances, thus giving shop stewards less to do. Further, participative committees often trespass on areas normally subject to collective bargaining. First-line supervisors may be threatened even more. They lose authority when workers make decisions on their own. Their status may also be threatened (loss of separate parking lots may be symbolic of much wider losses). In some cases their very jobs are threatened, since job redesign may lead to one or more levels of management being eliminated.

In many companies the QWL or organization development staff, who deal with participative relationships, are separate from the labour relations staff. Rivalries between the two groups are almost inevitable (Kochan, Katz, and Mower, 1984). Much the same problems exist on the union side. Some agreements call for union-selected but company-paid, part-time or full-time 'facilitators'. These people may develop interests and approaches which are quite different from those of the old-style, adversarially minded shop stewards. Having been trained in consensus-building skills, they often develop political constituencies of their own. As a dissident union magazine put it, commenting on the GM relationship:

> Already, many of these facilitators think of themselves as representing the 'joint QWL process' rather than the union . . . The program has expanded chiefly because the company and the union have 'institutionalized' it by rapidly increasing the number of full-time QWL jobs and QWL perks . . . These are especially attractive now that job losses have caused a cutback in the number of union positions. (Parker, 1984)

Often decisions which were previously made by middle managers acting on their own are now made by joint committees. Even if the line manager sits on the committee, his or her voice is just one among many. True, managers may be accustomed to their decisions regarding personnel matters being questioned via the grievance procedure, but joint committees permit union or worker representatives to 'interfere' with a much broader range of issues. Often, for example, these committees discover inefficiencies which managers should have discovered on their own.

At times the participative network represents an alternative route for advancement. Driscoll (1979) observes that sometimes members of Scanlon Plan participative committees may challenge incumbent union officers in elections. In other cases, committee members and union officers tend to stay in their own career paths, with the Scanlon path often leading to a job in management.

Participation also threatens top leadership on both sides. Under the adversarial system, decisions tend to be centralized. Every variation from the common rule is suspected as setting an undesirable precedent that might spread generally. By contrast, participation tends to substitute a new form of joint but decentralized decision making which reduces central union and even management power, even if it increases the power of individual workers and work groups (Katz and Sabel, 1985).

In short, participation makes the basis of power uncertain. Until new power relationships are firmly established and legitimized, all parties suffer from uncertainty.

A complex relationship

There is a complex relationship between participative activities, mutual trust, economic success, and the overall union–management relationship (Kochan, McKersie, and Katz, 1986).

1. Without generally good union–management relations, participative efforts are not likely to be successful; on the other hand, successful participation may improve labour relations (Wallace and Driscoll, 1981).

2. Both successful labour relations and participation develop trust. On the other hand, the mere introduction of a participative system may engender unrealistic expectations. If these expectations are violated, trust suffers, union–management relations may become embittered, and participation atrophies.

3. Without some economic pressures few recent participative efforts would have got started. Though moderate amounts of participation may promote joint activity, excess economic pressure may endanger labour relations and so poison trust and participative effort. If participation is associated with improved economic conditions, overall relations will improve, at least in the short run; on the other hand, if the company returns to prosperity, the urgency which led to the new co-operative relationship will eventually be dissipated. (And even if participation avoids these fates, it may suffer from and even succumb to plateauing.)

4. Job redesign and other forms of shop-floor participation almost inevitably raise problems which can be solved only through higher-level negotiations. For example, in return for changes in work rules, workers may demand greater job security. Unless such issues are resolved participatively through negotiations at higher levels, shop-level participation is likely to be confined to trivia. US

experience confirms the experience of other countries: for participation to be lastingly successful it must involve all levels.

Conclusion

As has been stressed above, participation's spread in the USA has been closely linked to concession bargaining. At first few unions and few workers had much interest in participation. Some forms, such as broad banding (job enrichment), were accepted by workers as defeats rather than victories. Others, such as stock ownership, were the best that could be salvaged in return for wage concessions (See also Ch. 4).

Given these inauspicious beginnings, the concept of participation has achieved a surprising amount of acceptance and legitimacy. A large number of shop-floor and joint union–management committees are functioning. The Teamsters and Steelworkers now make board membership and stock ownership a precondition for further concessions. Superficially the new forms of US participation resemble the German model (including its mix of collective bargaining and participation); however, it is still unclear whether they involve any substantial increase in workers' power. Participation has been introduced for a variety of reasons, including to take advantage of the tax laws, as in the case of ESOPs, or just as window dressing, to mask substantial wage concessions, or as part of an attempt to develop a 'high involvement' organisation in which workers feel a moral (as opposed to calculative) commitment to their employer (Etzioni, 1961).

Participation in the USA has meant two things: first, a more co-operative relationship between the parties, and secondly, a weakening of previously fairly rigid boundaries between management's prerogatives and the union's contrac-tually guaranteed rights. Neither change comes easily.

Participative structure alone does not guarantee true participation. The fact that committees exist does not mean that agreements will be reached or that attitudes or behaviours will change in any lasting way. It is still uncertain which aspects of current schemes will become institutionalized and which will wither away, as have others in the past. The half-life of participation schemes has always been short.

The new participative schemes are still quite fragile. At the moment they are highly dependent on both overall good labour–management relations and on good interpersonal relations among key participants. For participation to become institutionalized it needs pay-offs, both economic and psychological. Management needs to see it as leading to lower costs and greater flexibility. Workers need to believe that it is making their jobs not just more interesting but also more secure. (Indeed, how workers perceive participation may depend on their perception of the success of concession bargaining generally.)

Even where the parties are intellectually convinced that co-operation is essential for survival, there is still much ambivalence and vacillation between co-operation and conflict. The parties have learned to perceive each other in adversarial non-trusting terms. Neither side is comfortable giving up its traditional rights. Further, union leaders in particular have a vested interest in the continuance of the present system, which is the basis of their power and which permits them to exercise valued skills.

Even with trust, the existence of participative mechanisms will not eliminate differences of interest. For example, it is occasionally possible to redesign jobs so that workers are *both* more satisfied and more productive. But it does not always work out this way. Trade-offs are often required among such factors as productivity, satisfaction, and job security. The new participatory mechanisms may make it possible for the terms of trade to be bargained with less hostility than has been traditional. But differences of interest remain. To resolve these, goodwill may not be enough. Clout is required as well.

Nevertheless, I am moderately optimistic that the current wave of participation will end up being more than a fad. Having tried job enrichment and participative shop-floor management, a considerable number of workers (not all) find they like it. In some plants trained facilitators have developed a fairly strong political constituency for further co-operation. Some managers have found that in the long run participation makes it easier to manage. Participation has become better accepted in the USA than I thought likely a few years ago (Strauss, 1979).

References

Blasi, J. (1987), *Employee Ownership: Revolution or Ripoff?* (Cambridge, Mass.: Ballinger).
Cappelli, P. (1985), 'Competitive Pressures and Labor Relations in the Airline Industry', *Industrial Relations*, 24: 316–38.
Cooke, W. (1987), *Joint Labor–Management Relations and Company Performance: New Paths or Going in Circles?* (Kalamazoo, Mich.: Upjohn Institute).
Driscoll, J. (1979), 'Working Creatively with the Union: Lessons from the Scanlon Plan', *Organizational Dynamics*, 8: 61–80.
Etzioni, A. (1961), *A Comparative Analysis of Complex Organization* (New York: Free Press).
Goldstein, S. G. (1985), 'Organizational Dualism and Quality Circles', *Academy of Management Review*, 10: 504–17.
Hammer, T. and Stern, R. (1983), 'Worker Representation on Company Boards of Directors: Effective Worker Representation?', *Proceedings of the 43rd Annual Meeting of the Academy of Management*, 364–8.
————— (1986), 'A Yo-yo Model of Cooperation: Union Participation in Management of the Rath Packing Company', *Industrial and Labor Relations Review*, 39: 337–49.
Jacoby, S. (1985), 'Union–Management Cooperation during the Second World War', in M. Dubofsky (ed.), *Technological Change and Workers' Movements* (Beverly Hills, Calif.: Sage Publications).
Katz, H. (1986), 'The Debate over the Reorganization of Work and Industrial Relations

within the North American Labor Movement', paper presented to the Conference on Trade Unions, New Technology, and Industrial Democracy, University of Warwick.

—— and Keefe, J. (1987), 'The Relationships between Changes in Technology, Work Practices, and Plant Performance', *Proceedings of the Industrial Relations Research Association* (28 Dec.).

—— Kochan, T., and Gobeille, K. (1983), 'Industrial Relations Performance, Economic Performance, and QWL Programs: An Interplant Analysis', *Industrial and Labor Relations Review*, 37: 3–17.

—— —— and Keefe, J. (1987), 'The Impact of Industrial Relations on Productivity: Evidence from the Automobile Industry', paper presented to the Brookings Microeconomics Conference, Washington (3 Dec.).

—— and Sabel, C. F. (1985), 'Industrial Relations and Industrial Adjustment in the Car Industry', *Industrial Relations*, 24: 295–315.

Kochan, T., Katz, H., and McKersie, R. B. (1986), *The Transformation of American Industrial Relations* (New York: Basic Books).

—— —— and Mower, N. (1984), *Workers' Participation and American Unions* (Kalamazoo, Mich.: Upjohn Institute).

Kruse, D. (1984), *Employee Ownership and Employee Attitudes* (Norwood, Pa.: Norwood Press).

Long, R. (1980), 'Job Attitudes and Organizational Performance under Employee Ownership', *Academy of Management Journal*, 23: 726–37.

National Center for Employee Ownership (1987*a*), 'The Short Flight of Employee Ownership in the Airline Industry', *Employee Ownership Report*, 7(1), 6 (Jan.).

—— (1987*b*), 'Employee Ownership Plans Grow at a Steady Pace in 1986', *Employee Ownership Report*, 7(3) (May.).

Parker, M. (1984), 'Appoint QWL Facilitators from the Top, UAW Officials Urge', *Labor Notes*, 66: 2.

Reuther, V. (1986), 'Limited Discussion on Saturn at UAW Convention', *Union Democracy Review*, 55: 3.

Rosen, C., Klein, K., and Young, K. (1986), *Employee Ownership in America* (Lexington, Mass.: Lexington Books).

Rothschild-Whitt, J. (1985), 'Who will Benefit from ESOPs?' *Labor Research Review*, 1: 71–82.

Schuster, M. (1983), 'Forty Years of Scanlon Plan Research', in C. Crouch and F. Heller (eds.), *International Yearbook of Organizational Democracy*, i (Chichester: Wiley).

Slaughter, J. (1983), *Concessions and how to Beat them* (Detroit, Mich.: Labor Notes).

Sockell, D. (1985), 'Attitudes, Behavior, and Employee Ownership: Some Preliminary Data, *Industrial Relations*, 24. 130 8.

Strauss, G. (1979), 'Quality of Work Life and Participation as Bargaining Issues', in H. Juris and M. Roomkin (eds.), *The Shrinking Perimeter: Unionism and Labor Relations in the Manufacturing Sector* (Lexington, Mass.: Lexington Books).

—— (1982), 'Workers' Participation in Management: An International Perspective, *Research in Organizational Behavior*, 4: 173–265.

Voos, P. (1987), 'Managerial Perceptions of the Economic Impact of Labor Relations Programs', *Industrial and Labor Relations Review*, 40: 195–208.

Wallace, P. and Driscoll, J. (1981), 'Social Issues in Collective Bargaining', in J. Steiber, R. McKersie, and D. Q. Mills (eds.), *US Industrial Relations, 1950–1980* (Madison, Wis.: Industrial Relations Research Association).

Wever, K. (1986), 'Power, Weakness and Membership Support in Four U.S. Airline Unions', Ph.D. thesis (Massachusetts Institution of Technology).

Whyte, W. F., Hammer, T., Meek, C., Nelson, R., and Stern, R. (1983), *Worker Participation and Ownership* (Ithaca, NY: ILR Press).

Zwerdling, D. (1980), *Democracy at Work* (New York: Harper & Row).

19

Firms in Transition: Towards Industrial Democracy? The Case of Reforms in France since the End of the Second World War

PHILIPPE BERNOUX

DURING the last forty years, French firms,[1] like those in many other industrialized countries, have experienced numerous organizational changes. Since the end of the Second World War, the principles underlying the division of labour, the distribution of roles, the distinctions between staff and lines, etc. have been called into question, modified, and reassessed in different ways. It is thus evident that there has been a change. We shall describe these changes in the following pages.

Can a pattern be detected in all this? Are companies, for example, emerging out of Taylorism into a form of democracy via stages like autonomous groups or Quality Circles? If some of these stages can indeed be identified, it is not certain that they have all evolved in the same direction, or that it would be possible to delineate an overall course of evolution. The most recent analyses, even when they offer long-term readings, are not unanimous. We will, therefore, inquire into the possible existence of a long-term tendency and discuss the existing hypotheses.

Whether or not there has been a change—and we think that there has—is it possible to attribute it to certain variables rather than others? Is the change due to the technical revolution, to the economic situation and/or the logic of capital, to social conflicts and the struggles between employers and trade unions to increase their power, to the logic of industrialization, or to that of mass consumption, etc.?

The first part of this study will address economic, technical, and industrial events which have taken place over the last forty years. It is intended to answer the question: what has changed with reference to the firm? In the second part, a similar question will be posed, but this time with reference to the firm itself, and for different types of management. Finally, in the third part, we will attempt to see if it

---

[1] For the use of the term 'firm' see Ch. 11 n. 2.

is possible to discern a logic in these developments. What will happen to Taylorism, participatory management, and the democratization of organizations? Are these trends part of a historical evolution, or are they simply minor incidents along the way?

The context

The socio-economic context in France

From the 1950s up to 1987, France experienced a contrasting evolution. The reconstruction period after the Second World War lasted up to about the middle of the 1950s. It was followed by a period of high growth called 'The Thirty Glorious Years' (Fourastié, 1979), although in fact these two periods stretched from 1946 to 1969 only. Several factors are usually put forward by way of explanation. Firstly, a large increase in the total population under the triple influence of a sharp upturn in the birth-rate, large influxes of foreign workers, and the arrival of the repatriates from North Africa. The population of France experienced a much higher increase during this period than during the preceding hundred years.

The structure of the working population also changed. In the aftermath of the War, roughly a third of the population was in agriculture, a third in the secondary sector, a third in the tertiary. In 1975, the percentages were, respectively, 10, 39 and 51 per cent. The agricultural world shrank in favour of the service sector.

The standard of living in France (real average national per capita revenue) rose by a little more than three times. The number of hours per year of work termed full-time went down from 2,100 to 1,875, that is a fall of 11 per cent, the number of dwellings constructed was multiplied by ten, the number of private cars manufactured by fifteen.

Overall, the Gross National Product went up between 1948 and 1959 at a rate of about 5 per cent per year, then by 6 per cent between 1960 and 1973. This increase was probably due to the fact that the French maintained, even more so than other nations, a high level of production; that production units equipped and reorganized themselves; in particular, that investment was higher than in the past (an average rate of 20 per cent, compared to 15 per cent for the years from the beginning of the century); and, finally, that the economic administration showed great dynamism in the creation both of the Commissariat for the Plan, and of institutes for the analysis of the economic situation and for forecasting, etc.

At the beginning of the 1970s, France was basking in a euphoria of economic growth. She did not immediately understand, or did not want to understand, the turn-about which accompanied the first petrol crisis of 1973.

The reversal in the situation

At the time of the first petrol crisis, in 1973, a certain number of indices demonstrated that, in the case of France, the factors for growth were running out of steam, and that the tendency was already beginning to reverse. An in-depth study of the data proved that the slow-down had begun in 1969. The increase in the price of petrol in 1973, having set off a shock wave in the Western economies, hit France at a time when most of the growth factors were starting to decelerate.

From 1965 onwards, the birth-rate began to decline, and more sharply still at the start of the 1970s. It had stabilized by 1980, but at a level much lower than in the 1960s. The structure of the working population continued to change in the same direction as during those years, and the farming sector continued to decline slowly in favour of the tertiary sector.

The drop in the indices of industrial production in all the industrialized countries began in the autumn of 1973, a little before or after OPEC's tripling of prices. It hit France only in the autumn of 1974, after a period of stability that had lasted from 1969. In 1976, the drop by comparison with 1975 was of the order of 15 per cent, and, while the price of certain raw materials dropped sharply, domestic consumer prices continued to rise. In 1978–9, there was a slight upturn in industrial production, then another fall, which certain commentators went so far as to describe in terms of a collapse, from the end of 1970 to 1982. In France's case, this was not really followed by a new upturn (Jeanneney and Barbier-Jeanneney, 1985, ii. 86). The apparent increase in total productivity (combining the factors of production, work, and capital), was 5.8 per cent per year for the period from 1963 to 1969, 4 per cent from 1969 to 1973, and 2.6 per cent from 1973 to 1979.

At the beginning of the 1960s, unemployment in France was very low (160,000 unemployed in 1957, and 270,000 in 1963, the year following the return of the repatriates from Algeria). It was from 1965 onwards that there was a progressive rise in unemployment, a rise which was to continue regularly, reaching nearly 11 per cent of the working population then accounted for. But this long-term rise took place within a period of growth which was no higher than before. At most one may observe, on the slowly rising unemployment curve, a declivity superior to the mean for the years 1975, 1979, and 1981. The main thing to be borne in mind is the rise in unemployment, from 2.5 per cent in 1972 to 11 per cent in 1987.

Socio-political events

This review of the main elements of the socio-economic context would not be complete without a glance at political and international events. It is difficult to know how important these events were to the organizational evolution of the firm. We shall come back to this later. Let us note, however, two major events in internal politics.

On the one hand, there was the accession to power of General de Gaulle in 1958. What appears to be the most important thing here is the break with a republican political tradition going back almost a century (1871), a break whose consequence was the displacement of political life from Parliament to the Elysée Palace. This was followed by a reinforcement of political power, accentuated by the presence at the head of the State of a man endowed with charismatic power. The paradox of the presence of General de Gaulle in power was that it restored to the French a sense of national grandeur just as they were losing their last colonial possessions, which had for a long time been symbolic of that grandeur. By the time de Gaulle left office, France had the feeling of having become, once again, a major power.

The second important event in French domestic political life—more than twenty years after the first—was the arrival in power of a socialist team. The socialists had often been in power since the beginning of the century, but never in the context of political bipolarization, and never in such strength. The socialist members of Parliament had an absolute majority in the Chamber of Deputies, François Mitterrand having been elected with 51.75 per cent of the vote. The socialists governed in a manner described as 'realist', and one of the most surprising results of their presence in power was the rehabilitation of the firm, and the idea of economic rigour (for example, a prices and incomes policy), as their electors perceived it.

Technology and the work-force

One cannot, however, analyse the change in the organization of firms on the sole basis of the economic situation and of socio-political events. These circumstances certainly influenced the strategies of firms, but firms were playing a game that had its own logic, constructed according to a choice of policy on technical equipment, management of the work-force and, in general, systems of industrial relations.

From 1945 to the present day, technological evolution has been considerable. However, automation, the use of computers (modest at the beginning; the general application of real time—i.e. direct dialogue with the computer—began in 1980), the appearance of continuous-processing industries, the introduction of the first numerically controlled machines, all these technologies were introduced by degrees until 1980 and had little effect on the organization of work in the firm. Though such a statement might be difficult to prove, a certain number of indices demonstrate that the substitution of automation for human labour occurred gradually, especially during the 1970s. In 1974, data processing was considered a new science, and the best-known applications of automation were the integrated-process machine and auto-regulation. According to the director of a large car firm, the hiring of unskilled workers, mostly foreigners, seemed, up to the middle of the 1970s, to be as rational as their replacement by automation. The number of unskilled workers began to decrease in 1975, the trend accelerating in the 1980s. It was from 1979 onwards that companies began to equip themselves on a massive scale, and that it became possible to speak of a technical revolution.

The analysis of changes in the organization of companies brings out some periodicities. We shall now look at these, leaving the continuation of the theoretical debate until after an examination of the facts.

Managerial policies

We shall not draw up here a general history of the firm, not of its economic evolution. We are participating in a work dedicated to organizational democracy, and our aim is to look at the appearance, the existence, and the evolution of this theme in French firms. It is therefore from this particular point of view that we shall take up the study of companies during the period which extends, more or less, from the end of the War to the present day.

The period of rationalization and the American model

The period which extends from the Second World War to the end of the 1960s is characterized by high growth. This takes place within the already existing Taylorist–Fordist scheme: mass-production of standardized products for which demand is such that it is not necessary to have multiple models at a time when competition is less keen. In this scheme, the basic problem is to produce the same item in sufficient quantities to lower the costs of production. Production runs have to be large, and the replacement interval reasonably long.

In the USA, the wartime organization of industry promoted the development and diffusion of Taylorist techniques of work organization. These were largely used in the arsenals and the armament firms. The war material which was produced there fulfilled the criteria of the mass product: standardization and a 'stable' market (one does not frequently change types of gun or tank; they are consumed in very large numbers). This model of organization was encouraged in France, all the more so as the rapid conversion of American industry from peacetime production to that of wartime was the object of admiration among French industrialists after 1945. Thus the scene was set for the American model to develop in French industry without very many modifications.

And so the internal organization of French industry during this period followed the application of the well-known rules of Taylorist organization, with those of Fayol (1918), the whole being drawn from the American model. This also drew upon the 'American way of life', a style of life marked by comfort and typified, for example, by that of the American army. The victory of the American armies brought with it a desire to imitate the life-style which was theirs, and at the same time the attraction of a model which was rapidly to be baptized 'le management'. Directors of large and medium-sized French firms turned towards America and its management model. They were aided in this by the productivity missions of the Marshall Plan.

Around the 1950s, opinion leaders (journalists, advisers) and economic decision makers (directors of companies, heads of production organizations) went to the United States to look at the benefits of productivity, and the techniques which permitted them to obtain. Having visited many factories they learned how to organize the production line, and how to analyse a market. Once back in France, they invited Americans over, and advised other French people to make the trip to the United States. Thus, American practices gradually became the rule, the final answer, the incontrovertible argument that closed the debate . . . All management literature proceeds from this attitude: everyone will one day accept these methods or, in the face of competition, will disappear. Salvation by management or death. (Morin, 1974: 303–5).

The author of the cited text, who was well informed on the theories of modern management and French management practices, judged that 'the French are right to go to the United States to learn how to run an organization' (ibid.). He attributed the incontestable success of French economic growth during the 1960s to the systematic assimilation of this model.

One of the best-known applications was management by objectives. This method clearly illustrates what management was like at that time. It consisted of putting all the tools of management (planning, budgeting, control) into the hands of the executives, their directors having negotiated with them the objectives that they could and/or should set themselves. This was one way of allowing the subordinate, once his framework of action had been defined, a certain freedom and a measure of autonomy in its application.

Management by objectives sprang from the human relations trend. The rigorous application of the principles of Taylorism had indeed caused serious malfunctions in organizations. The excessive simplification which Taylorism brings to relations between individuals turns them into mere cogs in the machine, executing orders that they need not understand, and whose justification they have to rely on simply in terms of their supposed rationality. Only management, in its different echelons, knows what is good for the enterprise. It has a monopoly on rationality. The executants must obey, and admit, if management is assumed to be acting in good faith, that the orders are the best possible.

If this rigorous organizational logic advanced by F. W. Taylor and H. Fayol provoked at the time of its first applications vigorous protests, these later subsided. And it is remarkable that French trade unions, which were violently hostile at the time of the first applications of Taylorism to industry, finally admitted its advantages. The reaction against Taylorism came from another direction.

The reaction of labour and the Scandinavian model

As France entered the 1970s, the set of factors which had contributed to the great euphoria of growth began to regress. But no one was yet aware of it.

Events

At the same time, a number of reactions to this behaviour occurred in the industrial world. They led to a rethinking of the Taylorist model, with its admixture of the human relations model, which had been in vogue previously.

Did the shake-up in this new period begin with the movement around May 1968? It is true that the slogans of May 1968 indicted the society of work and even the consumption model. 'Metro, work, sleep'—this slogan pilloried an organization of life that left space neither for time outside work, nor for dreams of anything else. The constraints of professional life, deskilling labour, conditions of work, the authoritarianism of hierarchical relations in the factory ('little chiefs'), all these factors were to be violently denounced in the literature of the 'May movement', which, in this sense, was the result of changes in a society that had arrived at a certain stage of abundance and consumerism while retaining organizational structures from the previous period. However, one cannot say that May 1968 generated a movement: it was, rather, one of its first spectacular manifestations. Without doubt it stimulated a deeper and more rapid awareness of change; but the movement existed independently of May 1968.

It was exemplified, in concrete terms, by signs such as a lack of interest in work, absenteeism, turnover of staff, labour relations conflicts, and even sabotage. During this period, attention was drawn to lack of interest in work in the form of what was called 'work allergy' (Rousselet, 1974), that is to say, a growing disaffection with industrial employment (in certain branches the number of job offers not taken up was very close to the number of job seekers). A certain type of work was being turned down.

As to absenteeism, rates of 10 per cent to 15 per cent, and even 25 per cent, were recorded in many large and medium-sized industrial companies, in services, in shops and offices. For the years 1970–3, one study gave a figure of 425 million working days lost annually in France due to absenteeism alone, a figure to be compared with the 150 million days lost because of the strikes of May–June 1968, and to the average of 4 million during these years. The phenomenon became general in the industrialized countries. Absenteeism from work became a characteristic phenomenon of industrial society.

Staff turnover, too, rose regularly. Among the most frequently quoted cases were those of the foundries of certain car factories, chemical, textile and electro-metallurgical works, and the service departments of department stores, where staff turnover was as high as 100 per cent per year. (Bernoux, 1975: 21–2)

Conflicts at work in the early 1970s took on new aspects, becoming at once lengthier and more numerous. Most of them took the form of wildcat strikes, that is to say, the unions had no direct part in launching them and, in particular, they were led by unskilled workers without the support of their skilled colleagues. The first and best known was that of the Renault works in Le Mans. It mobilized a large proportion of the workers in the plant and blocked production for more than a month, which, for France at that time, appeared considerable. Other highly-publicized strikes occurred during this period, in particular strikes of women in the tertiary sector, and also of immigrant workers. The number of working days lost to strikes was high (for more details, see following section) and, most importantly, their level was very stable. There was the feeling of a 'conflictual consensus' (i.e. society was living in conflict without its foundation being questioned), while at the same time something else was brewing. This was seen in the swift turn-about in the incidence of industrial conflict, whose fall was as dramatic as had been its rise during the period that we are examining.

Experiments or change?

Faced with this double set of circumstances, that is to say, the end of economic growth and a set of deviant traits with regard to traditional norms, certain firms reacted. The dominant idea was that these actions represented a general feeling of 'enough is enough', which was attributed to the excesses of Taylorism and to the rigours of working conditions.

Two theories were fashionable during this period: on the one hand, those of the socio-technical school, resulting from research done at the Tavistock Institute in London and from theories of industrial democracy that had been tried out in Scandinavia, and, on the other hand, theories of motivation, which originated principally with the socio-psychologist A. H. Maslow (1954) and the business consultant F. Herzberg (1959, 1966).

The socio-technical school came to the attention of managers because of possibilities for practical application. Three of its general principles were accepted: the definition of the organization as the interaction between a social and a technical system, the importance accorded to the principle of self-regulation for small groups as much as for large ones, and, finally, depending on the situation, a new role of organization and technique within the company. The awareness of these principles spread with the popularization of experiments carried out by the researchers at the Tavistock.

These experiments became well known in France from the beginning of the 1970s. The dominant language was that of the humanization of work, of working conditions, of a 'more human organization of industrial work' (Delamotte, 1972). It even appeared on the political level in the theme of the 'upgrading of the worker's condition' (Bunel and Meunier, 1972: 285). And reforms in these areas, acceptable to the employers if they did not jeopardize the profitability of the firm, seemed to harmonize with the principles which had guided the socio-technical school and the researchers of the Tavistock.

In the theoretical perspective of the Tavistock's socio-technical analysis, the widespread type of experimentation was that of autonomous groups, which can be summed up by the trust placed in the workers' ability to organize themselves spontaneously in groups, proceeding to the self-regulation in their work. This stimulates the initiative of the workers, and allows them to be more flexible in the face of the variables of production, to take part in control and maintenance, and to work in an environment which they generally find much more pleasant. The setting up of autonomous groups involves a reduction in supervisory staff and ancillary production services. It generally leads to a rise in production, and thus in the work-load, and to a fall in absenteeism, though the duration of this has rarely been measured. Among its possible consequences are competition between and within groups, a fall in the influence of the unions, and a certain integration into the firm (Ruffier, 1976, and, for the detailed description of a French experiment, Bernoux and Ruffier, 1974).

Within the perspective of motivation theory, the main changes were in the rotation of work and the enlargement and enrichment of tasks. Rotation of work aims at making operatives equally competent at posts requiring equivalent qualifications. Rotation can develop by the extention of tasks and the grouping together of operations requiring similar qualifications but permitting operatives to carry out unified sets or subsets of tasks. The enrichment of the tasks consists of putting together more qualified tasks, so that operatives master most or all of the aspects of an operation (fitting, minor maintenance, control of their own production). It is difficult to measure the effect of this motivation theory in terms of concrete results. It contributes to a growing awareness of the changes that are possible in an organization where there is little technological change.

It is indeed an important characteristic of these currents of reform that they were not initiated for reasons of technological change. Most of the examples quoted, in France and elsewhere, were situated in a fundamentally unchanging technological context. Car assembly work, for example, is modified by passing from the production line to the module. Of course, technological innovation is necessary to this evolution, but technology is not the source of these initiatives. They are the result of the social context rather than of technical change. But things altered at the end of the 1970s.

The period of mobilization and the Japanese model

Several events marked the period between the late 1970s and the early 1980s.

The first of these, it seems to us, was the end of the illusion of facility, an illusion which characterized the 1970s. There was the beginning of a realization that world economic changes (the rise in oil prices, the increasing flow of economic exchanges between countries, the rise of Japan and the countries of South-East Asia) were felt in France in the form of a crisis. The euphoria of the beginning of the 1970s was transformed into anxiety about France's, and Europe's, capacity to maintain a role—if not an important one, at least an active one—on the international scene.

The second event, also in the area of attitudes, and an extension of the preceding one, concerned work and the firm. It has already been said that the previous period was marked by a certain disaffection with work and with hierarchical relations in the firm, which was resented, disliked, regarded solely as a place for making profit, and radically contested for that reason. It needed the whole period of the 1970s for the employers, the unions, and the State to become aware of this phenomenon, of the fact that 'the conduct of the workers called into question the industrial order, and weakened the instruments of the social regulation which ensured the economic performance of firms' (Bunel *et al.*, 1985: 6). It was only then that these three forces reacted. And, even when they opposed one another, a number of facts show that there was a tacit consensus among them to reassert the value of the firm. For example, the law on the right of expression (see the Appendix to this article), passed by the Socialist–Communist majority in 1982, reflected this anxiety on the Government side. However, the section of this law concerning expression retained much of the spirit of a report drawn up by experts brought together in 1974 at the request of Valéry Giscard d'Estaing. For example, one of the sections of the report drawn up by the committee was entitled 'Providing a channel of expression for every worker' (Sudreau, 1975: 56); and the Prime Minister of the time, Jacques Chirac, in the debate of 12 May 1976 in the National Assembly, proposed 'the institution of a real right of expression for the worker, as fundamental as the right to work itself'. Despite certain divergences of interpretation concerning its application, the 'political class' came to a broad consensus on this point. In the same way, directors of firms who were apparently unfavourable to the groups that sprang from the law passed by the Socialists did not really oppose the idea, despite a few verbal outbursts at the time of the vote. And in the end the majority of unions, which were split over the idea of 'groupes d'expression directe'[2] ('expression groups') as they were known (the CFDT and the CGT were in favour, the FO against them), while they were committed, to different degrees, to the introduction of laws intervening in the affairs of industrial and commercial organizations, signed the agreements on expression.

Other notable events were the development of the working class, the rise in unemployment, and the fall in unionization. The growth in the number of manual workers in France was smaller than that of other socio-professional categories after 1945 (the growth in the category 'manual workers' was on average half that of middle-range employees and executives), but it was still real up to 1975. From 1975 to 1982 (the date of the last population census for which the figures are known), the manual-worker category stagnated; its growth was zero. But this stagnation concealed a double movement: the number of skilled workers continued to rise, while that of unskilled workers (who were the main support of the social movement during the former period) experienced a sharp drop. The figures are, of course, to be taken relatively, as they may conceal changes in the classification of jobs. The movement was, however, too large not to correspond to a manifest reality. All the studies show that modernizing industrial firms experienced,

---

[2] See Appendix to this chapter.

between 1975 and 1980, a sharp reduction in unskilled workers and a slight increase in skilled workers.

Moreover, the sectors which lost a large proportion of their work-force were, in many cases, those which had forged the traditional worker, the bastions of the working class: mining, steel, shipbuilding, machine tools. A journalist on the very solemn *Monde de l'économie* could entitle an article on the change in salaried staff: 'France see-saws' (Lebaude, 1986: 2). He states: 'Between 1970 and 1973, the number of salaried workers (taking all sectors together) increased by 340,000 per year. Then, between 1974 and 1984, the tendency became clearly negative'. To this it must be added that the percentage of salaried workers in firms employing less than fifty people rose considerably. It had been 41.6 per cent in 1973; it was 49.9 per cent in 1984. In firms of more than 500 people, it fell from 21.8 per cent in 1974 to 16.1 per cent in 1984.

The decrease in unionization is another fact to be noted. If it is difficult to put a precise figure on it, all observers agree that there was a net decline in membership of unions and in their ability to mobilize their members, or even to be present everywhere that the works council asked them to be. The causes of this very real movement are difficult to analyse, nor is it our intention to do so here. Let us simply note the fact.

A final point, which we have already mentioned, was that technological evolution accelerated rapidly after the beginning of the 1980s. On the whole, the decade of the 1970s was a time of maturing: numerically controlled machines, robots, flexible workshops, integrated management systems, data banks, etc., appeared here and there. They were not integrated into the overall picture, and only began to be so in the 1980s, when it became necessary to learn how to operate an automated ensemble, or a number of digitally operated machines.

Have all these events produced, or accompanied, or been the pretext for changes in the organization of firms? The management style in France in 1989 is that of Quality Circles, which feature working meetings comprising only volunteers led by a member of the management whose aim is to analyse a particular problem in the operation of the firm which confronts them directly; they are trained to use a particular method of analysis. The aim of Quality Circles is to root out hidden malfunctions and poor product quality. The spirit of the Quality Circle is to de-Taylorize the firm, to make it into a 'firm of the third kind' (Archier and Serieyx, 1984). At the moment, Quality Circles are becoming very widespread in French firms. Launched around 1980, there were some 12,000 of them in 1984, and the number can only have increased since then.

The other formula attempted in France was launched on the initiative of the Government and through the agency of the law. (Is it thus a reform which is typically *à la française*? Perhaps, but let us beware of fashions.) The law of 4 August 1982 accorded the employee a right to direct and individual expression at the workplace during work time. This expression was to bear upon the conditions and organization of work. Agreements on the implementation of this right were to be negotiated between the unions and the management. Many agreements were signed, but the establishment of expression groups in firms has not really taken place. Although this right is related to a long-standing claim by the workers, that is to say, self-management, there was no strong demand on the part of the employees to come together. The CGT and CFDT, during the years 1978–9, had pressed to obtain this right, but its concrete application obviously bothered them. Workers who were active in the expression groups discussed working conditions, which embarrassed the unions as these problems had previously been discussed by the shop stewards; or, again, the workers talked about the organization of work, and the trade unionists suspected them of something that smacked of co-management, which is disliked by French unions. Management, typically, held one of two attitudes: either they were hostile to this law for political reasons (or because they feared a questioning of the hierarchy), or certain elements of management were favourable to it because they considered the right of expression to be a tool of management, a means of effecting change in the structure of the firm as a whole; but these managers were rarely approved of by the other executives or the supervisors who, in fact, blocked the movement. The very rare cases where expression groups had a positive effect were those where the management was able to impress upon the lower-level hierarchy as a whole the need to apply the right of expression and where this same management had an open attitude towards the unions. Expression groups were then an element of change in relations within the firm. But, on the whole, the current management looks to Japan and favours Quality Circles.

Is there a pattern to these changes?

Several managerial policies have succeeded one another in France since the end of the Second World War. Has this succession been haphazard or can one see an overall pattern in it? Several explanations have been suggested:

The explanation in terms of fashion

Some researchers (Midler, 1986) offer an explanation in terms of fashion. According to them, it is for the moment impossible to find an explanation for this succession of managerial models. It can only be analysed in terms of fashion determined by certain factors.

Firstly, there is the fact of succession. This is of a cyclical type, disaffection with one model coinciding with the arrival of another without there being any particular reason for this change-over; at least, no reason is given by those who put forward the replacement of one model by another. In the second place, what allows this replacement is the existence of a system of diffusion which has its own structures (consultants backed up by 'modernizing' executives in the firms). And in the end the new fashion appears self-evident in view of a threefold argument: an argument based on the industrial world in general and on its current evolution, an overall argument concerning the firm, its identity, and the factors which make it successful, and an argument that describes a practical management structure, the whole being accompanied by a project and a model based on a fashion that is exterior to the industrial world (the 'American way of life', the Scandinavian model of social harmony, and exoticism and the will to win, or the Japanese model).

Fashion sells itself as a new product in an highly volatile market. Its production has changed from the tailored to the ready-made. Firms of consultants now recruit young engineers (this designation being necessary in order to win over heads of firms who would be wary of social science diplomas), who, in a few months, learn to 'place' standardized products in more and more firms where smaller rivals come looking for 'miracle' products.

This explanation in terms of 'fashion' allows us to understand the phenomena of succession, diffusion, and markets. Even better, the value of the 'fashion' concept lies in the fact that it explains very well how, in order to change, a system of convictions and distribution which appeals to models must be used, and that these are not solely of a rational order, but are highly stimulating. One does not change an organization, any more than one creates or runs one, without a powerful vision. The attraction of an image, of a social model, or of a personality, is necessary to inspire the sense of identification of individuals with the group, and to legitimize change.

We do not, however, agree that changes in policy can be reduced to a phenomenon of fashion, since they appear randomly, without any link to a particular context. We believe that these policies correspond to the conjunction or the influence of particular events and that they have to be interpreted in relation to these changes.

The workers' movement, conflict, and social control

France is a country where the power of the unions is traditionally weak (it is estimated that less than 20 per cent of workers are members of a union). In addition, the social-conflict model in France is a model where movements are triggered by the grass roots alone, and where the unions jumping onto the bandwagon take charge of the outcome. It is true that the presence of a union, whether or not it is representative, facilitates the outbreak of conflicts; the unions play the role of protector to the workers, making recourse to the law easier; it also plays a catalysing role due to its network of communication and its capacity to carry conflict through to company level and even beyond.

During the period that we have identified as one of economic growth and rationalization and of American fashion, numerous industrial disputes centred upon the sharing out of the fruits of growth. The workers demanded a rise in purchasing power, shorter working hours, and equalization of income. It was a period of growth, during which the social consensus remained strong. It seems to us to be true to say that 'the sharing out of the dividends of progress smooths out conflicts', despite the excessive influence of the economic situation which this schema suggests (Reynaud, 1982: 30). It explains why, during this period, management did not attempt to modify the organization of work in the direction of de-Taylorization, nor the running of the firm, wherever a salary raise or some other material reward sufficed. Management remained, moreover, very influenced by the rationalizing American model. The influence of industrial conflict on organizational change was slight.

But from 1971 to 1979 the rate of industrial conflicts rose sharply, and remained high from one year to the next. From 1954 to 1970, the average working days lost annually due to strikes was high—3,110 million—but with a high dispersion index with regard to the average. (If one leaves aside the years of severe conflict, that is to say, 1950: 11,710 million, 1953: 9,772 million, 1963: 5,991 million, 1968: approximately 150 million, the average falls to 2,105 million). From 1971 to 1979, the average is high as well—3,757 million—but with a low dispersion index (1976: 5,010 million, and 1978: 2,195 million are the extremes). Finally, from 1980 to 1986 the average is very low—1,466 million—with a still lower dispersion index (own calculation).

A certain number of elements came together to account for this. The first, it seems to us, was a change in attitudes on the part of the workers, as mentioned above; after the period of fast economic expansion, they felt that henceforth anything was permissible. The slogans of May 1968 accurately expressed this feeling, in the value placed on dreams and on the realization of the impossible. One could thus demand a profound change in the form of work, and in the place of work in life. Can one go so far as to evoke the thesis of the lossening of social control, with its effect on the prosperity of the 1960s (Reynaud, 1982: 31)? According to this thesis, there was a weakening of the economic constraints that had traditionally shackled the workers, involving a weakening of other social constraints such as those of the family and the Church, but also in firms and unions. This thesis appears to us, however, to be too general. If the hierarchy, the forms, and the criteria of authority, the procedures of decision making and control, and traditional moral standards were indeed called into question, the link with a high level of industrial conflict appears to us to be tenuous if only because the effect of this evolution of social control is not easily observable in industrial conflicts (in the sense of Sabel, 1982: 5). This hypothesis of the loosening of social control is tainted with essentialism, and appears not to be easily verifiable.

What is more easily verifiable is the socio-professional origin of these conflicts, and the form that they took. They were the work of minorities which, up until then, had rarely been the ones to spark off conflict. From 1971 to 1979, unskilled workers, women, and immigrant workers started the most numerous and largest of strikes. These groups were often non-unionized. They were composed of workers belonging to both labour markets, the one which was protected and the one which was not. The one included workers protected by law or collective bargaining and the others were in a precarious position. We would put forward the hypothesis that these workers went on strike because, in a phase of economic expansion, with a form of Taylorist organization in the firm, at a time when anything seemed possible, when certain forms of social control (submission to the hierarchy of the firm and to the union's rallying calls) were losing their power, at that time their conditions of work, their low salary levels, and the absence of a professional future, appeared unsupportable. In a classic phase of economic expansion—and this was the pattern of the period before 1970—it is the strongest workers, in terms of qualifications, who start disputes and involve other workers. In a phase where expansion appears so assured that any change seems attainable (is it a loosening of social control? If this thesis is sustainable at all, it is demonstrated here), those whose work is hard, repetitive, without prospects and badly paid, take their turn in the challenge of the strike. Often of farming and/or immigrant origin, they had the hopes that have been held out to them of integration into industrial life dashed. Their 'world-view' has been cast into doubt by the reality that confronts them (Sabel, 1982: 14–20, 132–5). They often go on strike on their own, without union backing or the support of their colleagues, the skilled workers.

Faced with this, what does management do? Their financial resources begin to dwindle, and they are even more anxious than before to cut back on the wages bill. The wave of rationalization, in the form of the application of Taylorism, begins to show the limits of its efficacy. Taylorized factories become ungovernable. The brutality of the application of rationalization appears difficult to sustain in the context. And, indeed, the demands of the unskilled workers relate to their conditions of work, to Taylorism, and to the inhuman organization of work on the shop floor.

In these conditions, a revision of Taylorist rationalization allows a revision of the conditions and organization of work. To bring in autonomous groups and job enrichment at the same time is to modify simultaneously the organization and the conditions of work, without, however, letting go of the rein on salaries—or, at least, pay rises must correspond to a raised standard of qualifications. In many cases, this allows for a more efficient use of staff, or even a reduction in them (Bernoux and Ruffier, 1974).

For the period 1969–79, managerial reforms are thus explicable in terms of a combination of several factors: firstly, those were the world-views of salaried workers and of unskilled workers, which came out in disputes, demands, and negotiations; linked to this was the factor of economic recession, real enough materially but less so psychologically; and finally, the weakness of French trade unionism with its high proportion of skilled workers, which influenced management strategy so that it was mostly of the defensive type.

Return of the firm, control, and symbology

In the 1980s, a number of changes began to take place. The first was of the order of symbology. It was the end of dreams of the impossible. France was becoming dangerously weak, unemployment was continuing to grow, and realism in economic management was beginning to be acknowledged once again. There was a revived awareness that the firm is mortal, and it became a valued commodity, one to be safeguarded. It was the period of the rehabilitation of the firm, and of profit.

In June 1981, France came under the goverment of a Socialist–Communist coalition. After the economic upturn of the first two years, this coalition, which had so forcefully played an anti-capitalist line, and which had frequently condemned the idea of profit, rehabilitated this same idea. The Government encouraged firms to run at a profit. This attitude appeared natural to government, but it had not been expected to come from it so obviously. Linked to the aggravation of the economic crisis (1982 was a black year for the French economy) and to the unemployment that the Government of the left was unable to curb any better than those that had preceded it, public opinion became aware of the existence of severe economic and social constraints. The age of utopianism had ended.

The salaried workers' unions had been unhappy about the implications of earlier negotiations on conditions and organization of work. They were not really interested in discussing the problem of organization, fearing that they would be dragged into co-management, which most of them rejected; and they were ill-qualified to discuss working conditions, which they had negotiated in terms of quantifiable, collective guarantees. They had done so at national or professional branch level, but less so at the level of the firm, and very little at that of the shop floor. They knew how to handle the consequences of changing conditions and organization of work, but not real change itself.

Firms entered this period in a state of profound instability. With bankruptcies and buy-outs, take-over bids and splitting into smaller units, with early retirement and lay-offs, the traditions and the habits that gave the firm an identity tended to disappear. They could no longer appeal to the continuity of the past, because this past was no longer continuous and because its symbology had disappeared. There was a need for a common language, if not a shared faith (Pagès *et al.*, 1979). From this point of view, a model applicable to all firms, disseminating a common language, giving back to the hierarchy an explicit leadership function, sufficiently normative in its formulation and aiming at productivity gains while correcting organizational faults, had every chance of seeming like the long-awaited miracle model. We put forward the hypothesis that the current success of Quality Circles derives from the content of their objective, namely, the possibility of creating—or re-creating—a common language through a training process—a school—which delivers a common vision of the firm. Their success is also due to the fact that the idea came from Japan, the country of economic success during this period.

One last point, which concerns technology: it has been seen that the major period of transformation began at the end of the 1970s and the start of the 1980s. Automation, numerically controlled machines, robotics, and office machines then took on a real presence in trade union discussions and on the shop floor. These changes demanded very heavy investment. But, above all, their optimal utilization undoubtedly required an important change in organization. Indeed, many researchers now agree that the success of the new technologies sprang from the fact that they allowed greater flexibility of production, and therefore smoother adaptation to a market that was less and less ruled by Fordism. To be used with the maximum efficiency, they thus required more flexibility of organization and more integration of functions, even if it remained true that there was no technological determinism as such, in the sense that no technology determines an organization. This set of factors explains the success of the Japanese model in the 1980s.

Conclusion: the explanation in terms of symbology

An explanation of the succession of reforms in French firms since the end of the Second World War thus rules out a recourse to any one single explanation. On the contrary, it is a question of combining traditional factors with economic and technical ones, with those which have come out of industrial relations. But, above all, such combinations are illuminating only if they are understood in relation to what goes on in people's minds.

To explain the changes, we have used classic explanations in the context of economics, professional relations, and technology. But we think that their combination differs according to the period, and that, if one explanation is more appropriate than another to the changes during a particular period, it is as a function of its symbology within the different groups of actors. Very schematically, one may say that from 1945 to 1969—the period of reconstruction and growth—the perceived problem was that of rationalization and confrontation on the distribution of profits. Between 1970 and 1980, the problem was the inhumanity of work in the factory or the office for the marginal strata. From 1981 to the present day, the problem has been to save the firm. Each time, the actors who function as the agents of change are different: managing executives, then personnel directors, unionized skilled workers, then non-unionized unskilled workers and traditionally marginal groups, middle executives and supervisory staff. Changes can be explained only by reference to the interplay between these actors and explanations.

Can a pattern, nevertheless, be attributed to all this? Nothing is more difficult. There has been much talk of industrial democracy, then of the humanization of work, and today of product quality and competition. We express the hope that employees in general will be granted more responsibility and that their opinion will be sought more often. Is this hope becoming a reality? We are by no means sure, and it would require another article to examine in detail the kind of control that the worker in an automated factory exercises over his work. In the evolution of managerial fashions, we cannot say that we have yet discovered its logic.

APPENDIX

The Auroux laws[1]

On 8 October 1981, J. Auroux, the Minister of Employment, presented to the Cabinet a report on 'workers' rights', drawn up after a primary consultation with both sides of industry. The parliamentary debate began in May 1982, and the law on 'workers' freedoms in the firm' came into force on 4 August 1982. The three other laws, regarding 'representative staff institutions', 'collective bargaining and the settlement of industrial disputes', and 'the committee for hygiene, safety and working conditions' came into force on 28 October, 13 November, and 23 December 1982, respectively.

Furthermore, a bill concerning the democratization of the public sector was presented to the negotiating partners on 28–30 July 1982. The law was passed on 23 May 1983. It included, notably, reforms of the administrative council, where the workers, like the State and 'competent personalities', were, henceforth, to occupy a third of the seats. It also instituted, in firms with a staff of more than two hundred, *workshop* or *office committees*, which were to meet at least once every two months and for at least six hours during the course of a year, during working time. The workers, including executives were to express themselves during these meetings on all questions relating to their work including conditions, organization, investment, and technological innovation.

But it was more particularly the Auroux Law on 'workers' freedoms in the firm' that introduced one of the most innovative reforms, regarding the *workers' right of expression*. According to this law, in effect, workers today

enjoy the right to direct and collective expression on 'the content and organization of their work, as well as on the definition and implementation of actions designed to improve working conditions in the firm'; and any ideas put forward could not be used as a basis for sanctions or dismissal.

The forms of exercise of the workers' right of expression in firms with a staff of more than two hundred must be negotiated between the employer and the representative trade union organizations during the six months which follow the coming into force of the law:

The agreement must include three points:

1. the level, the form of organization, the frequency and the duration of meetings allowing the workers' expression;
2. measures designed to assure, on the one hand, the liberty of expression of all, and, on the other hand, the transmission of wishes and opinions to the employer;
3. the conditions in which the employer informs the workers concerned, the representative trade union organizations, the works committee, the committee for

---

[1] Olivier Corpet, 'The New Rights of Workers', *Le Monde*, June 1983.

hygiene, safety and working conditions, and any other competent body legally constituted in the firm or organization, of the action that he intends to take on these wishes and opinions.

In firms with a staff of less than two hundred, the head of the firm must consult the trade union organizations, or the works committee, or, in default of these, the representatives of the staff, about the forms of exercise of the workers' right of expression.

After two years, the head of the firm must draw up an analysis of the results obtained, seek the opinion of the shop stewards and of the works committee, or, in default of these, the representatives of the staff, and pass on the complete dossier to the Work Inspector.

The information thus gathered will permit the government . . . to draw up, before December 1985, a bill which will determine the forms of exercise of the workers' right of expression.

How has the law been applied? According to a report in *Le Monde* (5–6 June 1983):

Up to 1 May 1983, the Minister for Industrial Relations had listed 1,036 agreements, that is, 15% of the firms concerned. In 95% of cases, the negotiations, if not concluded, had already begun . . . The Minister has analysed three hundred of these agreements.

According to the Minister for Industrial Relations, the CGT, CFDT and CGC unions have signed, respectively, 57%, 45% and 50% of the 300 agreements, FO 37% and CFTC 16%.[2] The role of the executives in the leadership of the groups was confirmed (75% of cases). In one agreement out of five, a group leader other than the foreman was envisaged: it could, in such cases, be a worker from the group, a person from outside the group, or a rotating leadership among the participants in the group. The frequency of the meetings varied, and was indicated with precision in only four agreements. 50% of the agreements envisaged three or four meetings per year, 30% two, 15% one, 5% six or twelve. The duration of these meetings varied from one to two hours.

In the great majority of the agreements analysed, the object of the meetings is that which was defined in the ministerial texts: action for the improvement of working conditions, the characteristics of the work station and its environment, methods and organization of work. The expression groups have an average of fifteen to twenty members. Large firms opted for a progressive attitude to experimentation in the right of expression (steel, metallurgy, banks).

References

Archier, G. and Serieyx, H. (1984), *L'Entreprise du troisième type* (Paris: Seuil).
Bernoux, P. (1975), 'Changer le travail', *Lumière et vie*, 124.
—— and Ruffier, J. (1974), 'Les Groupes semi-autonomes de production', *Sociologie du travail*, 4.
Bunel, J. and Meunier, P. (1972), *Chaban Delmas* (Paris: Stock).
—— et al. (1985), '*Le Triangle de l'entreprise*' (Lyon: GLYSI).
Carré, J. J., Dubois, P., and Malinvaud, E. (1973), *Abrégé de la croissance française* (Paris: Seuil).

[2] See List of Abbreviations, pp. xxvii–xxix.

Corpet, O. (1983), 'The New Rights of Workers', *Le Monde* (June).

Delamotte, Y. (1972), *Recherche en vue d'une organisation plus humaine du travail industriel* (Paris: La Documentation Française).

Évolution de l'autorité dans l'entreprise industrielle (1971), Rapport CORDES, convention 40 (Paris: Entreprise et Personnel).

Fayol, H. (1979), *Administration industrielle et générale* (Paris: Dunod); first edn 1918.

Fourastié, J. (1979), *Les Trente Glorieuses ou La Révolution invisible: De 1946 à 1975* (Paris: coll. Pluriel, Fayard).

Friedmann, G. (1946), *Problèmes humains du machinisme industriel* (Paris: Gallimard).

Gelinier, O. (1968), *Direction participative par objectifs* (Paris: Éditions Hommes et Techniques).

Herzberg, F. (1959), *The Motivation to Work* (Cleveland, Ohio: World Publishing Co.).

—— (1966), *Work and the Nature of Man* (Cleveland, Ohio: World Publishing Co.).

Jeanneney, J. M. and Barbier-Jeanneney, E. (1975), *Les Économies occidentales du XIXe à nos jours*, 2 vols. (Paris: Presses de la Fondation Nationale des Sciences Politiques).

Lebaude, A. (1986), 'La France bascule', *Le Monde de l'économie* (16–17 Mar.).

Maslow, A. H. (1954), *Motivation and Personality* (New York: Harper & Row).

Maurice, M., Eyraud, F., d'Iribarne, A., and Rychener, F. (1986) *Des entreprises en mutation dans la crise* (Aix-en-Provence, LEST).

Midler, C. (1986), 'Logique de la mode manageriale', *Gérer et comprendre* (June).

Morin, P. (1974), 'La Philosophie du travail', in *Le Travail dans l'entreprise et la société moderne* (Les Dictionnaires du savoir moderne; Paris: Hachette).

Pagès, M. *et al.* (1979), *L'Emprise de l'organisation*, (Paris: PUF).

Reynaud, J. D. (1982), *Sociologie des conflits du travail* (coll. 'Que sais-je?'; Paris: PUF).

Rousselet, J. (1974), *Allergie au travail* (Paris: Seuil).

Ruffier, J. (1976), 'Les Nouvelles Formes d'organisation du travail dans l'industrie française', in *La Documentation française, L'Organisation du travail et ses formes nouvelles* (Paris: Bibliothéque du CEREQ).

Sabel, C. (1982), *Work and Politics: The Division of Labour in Industry* (Cambridge: Cambridge University Press).

Sudreau, P. (1975), *La Réforme de l'entreprise* Coll. 10/18; (Paris: UGE).

20

The Recent Growth in Employees' Representation in The Netherlands: Defying the Times?

JAN C. LOOISE

Introduction

In the introduction to this volume it is stated that since the mid-1970s—in particular as a result of the economic recession—there has been a retrogression in the development of participation in general and especially of the institutionalized and representative forms. It is questionable, though, to what extent such a statement accords with the actual development of participation in various countries. There are several indications of the growing importance of employees' representation in The Netherlands. Examples of these indications dating from the last ten years are:

- the establishment and implementation of new legislation on works councils in commercial and non-profit organizations, as well as similar regulations applying to the public sector;
- an explosive increase of the total number of representative bodies and, consequently, of the number of persons on these bodies, as well as of those represented by them;
- an improvement in the quality of the functioning of (a part of) employees' representation and, as a result, an increasing influence on decision making within organizations.

In this contribution we will deal with the following three questions:

1. Is it correct that in The Netherlands the position of employees' representation has been considerably strengthened during the last decade, formally as well as in terms of quantity and quality?
2. If so, what may be the causes of this development, which, on the face of it, is defying the times; or, in other words, how can this development be explained, given current economic, technical, and socio-cultural developments?
3. What will be the effects, in the first place for the employees' representation

system in The Netherlands itself, but also for other forms of participation, such as the position of the trade unions and forms of direct (group) participation?

In the following sections an attempt will be made to answer these questions. Where information on the quality of the functioning of the employees' representation is concerned, this will be done on the basis of the results of the present author's research into the functioning of works councils in companies with 100 or more employees conducted recently (Looise and Heijink, 1986; Looise and de Lange, 1987). In addition, the findings of other research in this field will be used where this is possible.

Employees' representation in The Netherlands in the 1980s

The formal regulations on participation

Since the late 1970s a number of major alterations have been made in the formal regulations (legislation and similar regulations) applying to employees' representation in our country. The most important of these are:

- the 1979 amendment of the Works Councils Act, applying to commercial and non-profit organizations with at least 100 employees;
- the 1982 extension of the scope of this Act—although in an adapted form—to include commercial and non-profit organizations with 35 to 100 employees;
- the adaptation in 1982 of the existing regulation applying to employees' representation in the public sector—similar to the 1979 amendment of the Works Councils Act;
- the introduction in 1982 of the Participation in Education Act for employees' representation in this sector—also similar to the 1979 amendment of the Works Councils Act.

In this contribution we will concentrate on the regulation mentioned first, the Works Councils Act of 1979. This regulation is by far the most important and the other regulations were modelled on it, though it should be noticed that there may be differences or restrictions in parts of these regulations.[1]

The principal differences between the Works Councils Act of 1979 and its forerunner (the Works Councils Act of 1971) are:

1. the so-called 'autonomy' of the works council, now consisting entirely of representatives elected by the employees; this means that, unlike before, the

---

[1] The works councils in companies with 35 to 100 employees, for example, do not on all points have the same rights and possibilities as the works councils in the large companies. There are, furthermore, specific regulations applying to the bodies representing employees in the public sector and in education, on balance working out slightly less favourably than the regulations applying to works councils in large companies.

employer (manager) is no longer represented in the works council; consultative meetings have been instituted to ensure communication between him and the works council;

2. the extension of the works council's right of advice to a great number of economic and organizational matters, such as: transfer of control over the company, co-operation with another company, closing down the company, major changes in the organization, major investments, obtaining major loans, etc.;

3. the introduction of the works council's right of appeal   to the Companies Division (ondernemingskamer) of the Amsterdam Court of Appeal (Gerechtshof)—in case the works council's advice on the aforementioned matters is either not asked for or ignored;

4. the extension of the works council's right of veto in social matters to include virtually all arrangements in the realm of personnel policy, such as working hours and holiday arrangements, remuneration or job evaluation schemes, working conditions, recruitment, dismissal, promotion, training, etc. (if these matters are not already settled in the collective agreement);

5. the introduction of the works council's right of initiative, obliging the manager to respond to any proposal put forward by the works council;

6. the extension of the works council's right to be regularly informed (in writing) by the manager of the economic position of the company as well as of present and future (economic and social) policies and other matters;

7. the extension of the facilities for works council members, such as the amount of time available for works council duties, the possibility of taking courses, consulting external experts, etc.[2]

All in all we notice a fairly fundamental strengthening of the formal position of employees' representation. This goes for large companies in the first place, but through subsequent regulations to a certain extent also for small companies and the other sectors.

Development in quantity

Fig. 20.1 shows that employees representation in The Netherlands in the 1980s is booming, in terms of quantity.[3] This is a result, in particular, of the establishment

[2] We are aware that this brief rendering of the Works Council Act of 1979, related to its forerunner, leaves unanswered many questions on its precise contents and the Dutch system of employees' representation in general. The scope of this article does not allow us to go more deeply into the matter; for more information on this subject see: Schuit *et al.*, (1983: ch. 11).

[3] Only limited data are available on the development in quantity of employees' representation, relating to the following years:
- works councils in large companies: 1972–4, 1977, 1983–4, 1986 (Min. of Social Affairs and Employment)
- works councils in small companies: 1983–4, 1986 (ibid.).
- employees' representation in the public sector: 1982, 1986 (Tolman *et al.*, 1986).
- employees' representation in education: 1982–5 (Smit and Pelkmans, 1985).

and implementation of the above-mentioned regulations. From this Figure it appears (among other things):

- that, comparatively, employees' representation in large companies, has, in terms of quantity, developed very gradually, and that since 1979 (when the law was amended) there has been only a limited increase; at that time already over 75 per cent of the companies concerned had a works council anyway—by now, that is over 84 per cent;
- that the number of works councils in smaller companies was very limited until 1982 (less than 10 per cent of these companies had a works council in that period), but that since then—i.e. after the extension of the legal requirements to this category—there has been a large increase: in 1986 already half of these companies had a works council and further growth is to be expected in the near future;
- that in the public sector (national, provincial, and municipal) employees' representation has also developed rather gradually, but that there, too, the introduction of the 1982 regulation induced a distinct increase;
- that, finally, the development of employees' representation is most spectacular in the educational sector; since the introduction of the Act in 1982 over 10,000 representative bodies have been constituted, as a result of which by now 80 per cent of the schools have a body representing the employees.

Altogether the number of bodies representing employees in The Netherlands has in the period 1977–85 multiplied by nearly five times from *c.* 4,700 to nearly 22,000. It should be noticed, though, that two-thirds of this growth is accounted for by the educational sector, while the other third can be attributed to private enterprises and the public sector. Assuming the average number of members of bodies representing employees to be eight in large companies and the public sector, six in the educational sector, and four in smaller companies, we arrive at a total of over 130,000 representatives.

Development in quality

Naturally, the development in quality of employees' representation can be outlined somewhat less easily than the development in quantity. As mentioned in the Introduction, for this purpose use will be made of the results of our own research into the functioning of works councils in large companies (at least 100 employees). Since the obligation to constitute works councils has been in force longest for this category of companies—and since this obligation is also the most far-reaching—the picture that will be given cannot be said to be representative of all bodies representing employees. Rather, the bodies involved in the research are, as regards quality, to be rated among the leaders, the other bodies, for the time

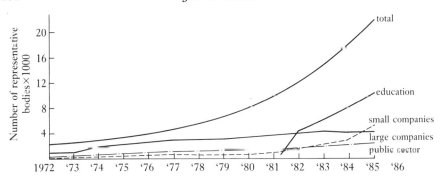

Fig. 20.1   Development in quantity of employees' representation

being, trailing behind.[4] All the same, on account of the existing regulations they, too, may possibly reach the level of the works councils in large companies.

Central to the functioning, in terms of quality, of employees' representation in the use of the various legal rights and the resulting influence on decision making in organizations. Our research shows that the average annual number of decisions covered by the law is about six per company (three decisions that are subject to the right of advice and 3.2 decisions that are subject to the right of veto). It shows, further, that in practice an average of 63 per cent of both types of decision are submitted to the works council.

It is remarkably that the decisions subject to the right of *advice*, relating to major business decisions in the economic–organizational sphere, are submitted to the works council at a ratio equal to decisions subject to the right of *veto*, which are decisions in the sphere of social management or personnel administration. A probable explanation is the difference in importance between the right of veto and that of advice. For management, social matters may be easier to discuss with the works council than economic–organizational issues, but there is a greater obstacle to submitting decisions on social issues to the works council in that these decisions—unlike economic–organizational decisions—can be vetoed by the works council. These figures represent overall average values, though. For an individual company the annual number of decisions, as well as the percentage of decisions submitted to the works council, may deviate considerably. Further analysis on this point reveals that the annual number of decisions per company varies from one or a few to over thirty. More interesting to know, however, is that in only 31 per cent of the companies virtually all decisions that come up are submitted to the works council, in 31 per cent the majority of the decisions, and that in 38 per cent of these companies the majority of the decisions are not submitted to the works council.

---

[4] As to the public sector (national, provincial, and municipal) this picture is confirmed by recent research by Tolman *et al.*, (1986). In the near future the first research will be done into the functioning of works councils in small business companies.

With regard to the results of the use of the rights of advice and of veto, the works councils seem, on the face of it, to be reasonably successful (see Table 20.1). This table makes clear that decisions that are subject to the right of advice are regularly influenced (amended or even withdrawn) by the works council in about 40 per cent of the companies; decisions subject to the right of veto in over 50 per cent. It should perhaps be noticed that there are only slight differences in the opinions of works council members and managers. Although the table shows that there are also a great number of companies in which decisions are not actively influenced by the works council—especially decisions that are subject to the right of advice—it gives an impression of the works council's hold on management decision making. If we look at the influence the works council has in the company, specified for the various areas of management, this influence appears to be greatest in the sphere of social and personnel management, whereas in other areas the influence is only limited (in the production–technical and organizational fields) or practically non–existent (in the economic and commercial areas). This clearly fits with the importance of the works council's rights in the various areas of management and with the data on the results of the use of these rights as produced above.

Table 20.1 Results of the use of the rights of advice and of veto

	Right of advice (%)		Right of veto (%)	
	Works councillors	Managers	Works councillors	Managers
Decisions regularly amended or withdrawn in compliance with works council's wishes	41	39	57	49
Almost all decisions supported by works council: no amendments or withdrawals	45	54	29	40
No information/unknown	14	7	14	11
Total N = 189	100	100	100	100

Table 20.2 gives an overview of the works council's influence by areas of management, based on the opinions of both works council members and managers. It is striking that those opinions are to a large degree alike and that the managers in some cases attribute more influence to the works council than the works council members themselves do. As these figures—again—represent overall average values, they can be complemented by the facts that, according to both works council members and managers, the works council has no (great) influence on any area of management in about 45 per cent of the companies, in 35 per cent it has influence in the sphere of social and personnel management only, and in 20 per cent the works council also has influence in other areas.

Table 20.2   Influence of the works council by areas of management

	Works councillors (%)			Managers (%)		
	Much	Moderate	None	Much	Moderate	None
Financial–economic	3	24	72	3	15	80
Commercial	5	18	64	3	16	70
Production–technical	13	50	29	14	41	41
Organization	7	53	38	11	52	34
Social and personnel	41	47	9	58	35	4
(Total N = 189)						

If the influence of the works council in general is compared with that of other bodies within or outside the company, it appears that—in the opinion of both the works councillors and the managers—in all areas of management this influence is smaller than that of the staff and the executives, but in all areas of management, including the conditions of employment, greater than that of trade unions. In comparison with the supervisory board, the works council has more influence on social and personnel matters, but less influence in other areas of management.

If we compare these research results with similar data of ten years ago, we can observe that, generally speaking, the position of the works council, in terms of quality, has improved. The picture that emerged at that time of the functioning of works councils (Hövels and Nas, 1976) may be summarized as follows: the dominant position of the chairman (i.e. the manager), who in most cases drew up the agenda, prevented subjects from coming up and meant that strategic matters were raised only marginally, etc., as a result of which the works council seldom or never succeeded in becoming involved in key issues of management, let alone exerted any influence on them. In comparison, in the present situation there is more equality in the relationship between works council and manager, certainly in matters such as drawing up the agenda, deciding whether or not to discuss certain subjects, etc. It can also be said that the works council has succeeded in taking a place—if a modest one—in the interplay of forces within the company, with the proviso that its greatest strength is traditionally in the area of social management, that its influence on issues of general management and control and the production–technical management is gradually increasing, but that the works council's involvement in financial–economic and commercial management (traditionally an established management prerogative) does not amount to much (at least not yet).

Explanations

In trying to account for the development of employees' representation in The Netherlands as outlined above, we can look for links using an explanatory model (see Fig. 20.2) bearing on democratization in organizations, developed by Lammers (1985*a*: 488). In view of our objective, namely, to find an explanation for the relatively strong rise of employees' representation in The Netherlands in the 1980s, the relation between the top of the model (the various developments and circumstances) and the two blocks at the left side (formal and actual participation) is of particular interest. We will therefore in this context not concern ourselves with the other parts of the model.

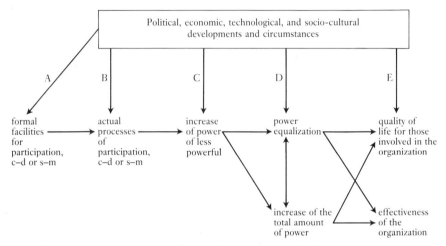

Fig. 20.2 Explanatory model of democratization in organizations

c-d = co-determination
s-m = self-management
Source: Lammers, 1985*a*

With regard to the developments and circumstances, we want to make a distinction between economic, technological, and socio-cultural developments and circumstances on the one hand and political developments and circumstances (including legislation) on the other. The latter factor we then want to regard as a 'dependent variable'—for it, too is an institutionalized factor apart from and reacting to the other developments and circumstances—which results in the model as represented in Fig. 20.3. From this Figure it appears that formal regulations on participation are the result of political decisions which are converted into legislation. Both politics and formal regulations themselves are constantly influenced by economic, technological, and socio-cultural developments and circumstances. The same goes for actual participation, which, in its turn, is closely bound up with the formal regulations on participation. It goes without saying that this is a much simplified model. From earlier studies it is known, for example, that both actual and formal participation are also influenced by other factors, such as

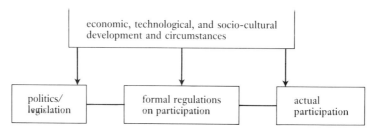

Fig. 20.3 Explanatory model development formal and actual participation

the attitude of the trade unions (Teulings, 1984; Looise, 1985). For our purpose this model will suffice, though. In addition, from extensive international research (IDE, 1981) the relation between formal (*de jure*) and actual (*de facto*) participation emerged as the strongest.[5]

We will now—in reverse order—look at the various parts of Fig. 20.3 and try to establish what the main factors that influenced the developments mentioned were.

Actual participation

By means of an outline of the development of employees' representation in quantity and in quality, in the preceding section an attempt was made to give an impression of the situation with regard to actual participation. In the first place a clear growth of employees' representation—resulting from changes in legislation and similar regulations—was noticed. This is further evidence of the strong relation between formal and actual participation. It was, furthermore, noticed that there are large differences from one company to another with regard to the constitution as well as to the functioning of employees' representation. The question that presents itself now is why, in spite of equal regulations on formal participation, actual participation practices vary so much.

From our research it appears that explanations for using rights or otherwise are not to be found in economic or technological developments and circumstances in the first place, but in particular in socio-cultural developments and circumstances, such as: the attitude of the company towards regulations in the social sphere, the attitude of the manager towards the works council, the attitude of the works council (including its willingness to use means of power), the expertise of the works council, the zest of the employees for works council activities, as well as the degree to which the works council has external contact (especially with the unions). These factors appear to determine the works council's functioning in a general sense. It is

---

[5] The IDE research team comes to the following conclusion on this matter: 'Our findings suggest that industrial democracy is mainly conditioned by the socio-political environment and the institutional, normative set-up of the organization, rather than determined by any other factor' (IDE, 1981: 8).

difficult to indicate, though, to what extent these socio-cultural factors underwent a development that influences (or influenced) the functioning of employees' representation. The most plausible developments that can be thought of in this connection are a more professional attitude of the management (weighing up more rationally the pros and cons of consultation) and the higher level of education (possibly also increased awareness) of employees and works council members.

Apart from that, employees' representation is influenced by economic and technological developments and circumstances in an indirect way, namely in those cases that affect the number of jobs in the company. Our research shows that such a situation often induces the works council to take a more active attitude in the consultations with the manager and, conversely, the manager may also see it as a reason to step up the contacts with the works council so as to have the changes to be carried through accepted and implemented as smoothly as possible. Since virtually all companies have in the past few years been confronted with the necessity for economic and/or technological reorganization, this may have produced a stimulating effect towards actually practising employees' representation. This is contrary to the restraining effect of economic and technological developments mentioned in the introduction to this volume.

Formal participation and politics

This last remark can be said to bear especially on the establishment of regulations on participation in the formal sense. But it is also possible to observe in our country a clearly contrary development. The question is, therefore, how it was possible that such drastic regulations were established in a period of severe economic recession and under a centre right government.

The first explanation often mentioned in this connection (by Lammers, 1985*b*, amongst others) is that legislation and other formal regulations lag behind various other developments. In Fig. 20.3 this effect is clearly visible. Politics and legislation themselves are also influenced by economic, technological, etc. developments, but on account of their institutional and bureaucratic nature it takes some time before the influences they undergo result in new regulations. In The Netherlands this phenomenon of 'institutional inertia' is clearly observable in the amendment to the Works Councils Act as well as in the establishment of the other regulations. Amending the Works Councils Act had been advocated since 1972. This led in the mid-1970s—under a centre left government—to the first concrete steps towards amendment, which was finally effected in 1979. A comparable course of events is observable where the amendment or introduction of the other regulations is concerned.

The institutional inertia of politics and legislation thus seems to offer a plausible explanation for the coming about of the formal regulations on employees' representation in The Netherlands in the late 1970s and the early 1980s. They should be seen as a—somewhat late—effect of the 'democratization wave' of the early 1970s. This explanation becomes less convincing, however, if the (additional) question is raised why the various regulations were carried through in spite of the economic, political, etc. conditions, which had meanwhile changed dramatically. It is true that new regulations require a long time to prepare but revoking them or not carrying them through may be decided on at very short notice. Several instances of this can be found in Dutch socio-economic politics.[6] The fact that this was not the fate of the regulations applying to participation suggests that other factors were involved, accounting for their being drafted and, especially, for their being carried through.

One of those explanations—and probably the most important—must be sought in the decentralization process which since the late 1970s has been going on within the Dutch industrial relations system. The principal advocates of decentralization have from the beginning been the employers' associations, at a later stage supported by the government. It was seen as a major instrument for coping with the economic recession, ranking with such matters as greater flexibility, deregulation, behaving more in accordance with the market, etc. Since decentralization would lead especially to an intensification of consultation practices at company level, further extension of (the rights of) employees representation could hardly be opposed. In addition, an effort had to be made to obtain the trade unions' co-operation in the decentralization policy—which they were traditionally not very keen on. The only possibility of achieving this was a 'swap', with the strengthening of employees' representation, for which the unions had made out a case.

It may be wondered, incidentally, to what degree the employers' associations and the government were not also after drastically curbing the power of the trade unions. Considering the structurally weak position of the Dutch unions at company level, it could be anticipated that decentralization of consultations between employers and employees in combination with a simultaneous strengthening of employees' representation would cause problems—in particular in the form of disputes over competence. In the meantime, such problems did to some degree indeed arise.[7]

On the one hand, however, it would be going too far, on the other it would be a shortcoming, if we were to explain the development mentioned above as resulting from one brilliant comprehensive plan of the employers' associations and the government. It is obvious that the tendency to decentralization—which occurs in other countries, too—is a result of economic (small-scale enterprises, revaluation of entrepreneurship), technological (microelectronics, computerization) as well as

---

[6] Examples are the withdrawal of bills on trade union activities within the companies and on the right of complaint for individual employees, as well as the drastic amendment on relatively very short notice of the legislation on the social security system.

[7] Problems in the relations between employees' representatives and the unions have thus far shown themselves in frequent disputes over competence relating to the introduction of a shorter working week and—to a lesser degree—to issues of remuneration and reorganization.

socio-cultural (individualization, greater consciousness, and emancipation) developments. And so the paradoxical situation occurred that employers' associations in their plea for decentralization were supporting the further development of employees' representation, which they had previously always rejected, and the trade unions, for their part, were confronted with a development they had always asked for, but did not wish to materialize at that moment. All in all, there was no reason for the government—politics—to stop the implementation of further regulations on employees' representation.

Further development of employees' representation: two theories

In order to be able to say anything about the future development of employees' representation in The Netherlands, some remarks should be made about the development of participation in general first. Two theories of this development can be discerned, namely, the replacement or substitution theory and the 'stairway' theory. We will deal briefly with each of these theories, so as to try to draw some conclusions about the future development of employees' representation.

The substitution theory

The approach of the development of participation based on the substitution theory is to a great extent similar to the cyclical perspective in the development of participation mentioned in the introduction to this volume. This means that this development is assumed to progress in waves, dependent on—and determined by—other external factors (especially economic circumstances). A significant difference or addition in this theory, however, is the idea that the various waves in which the development of participation manifests itself do not always concern the same form of participation, but that in the course of time a shift in the forms of participation takes place. This development could be visualized as in Fig. 20.4.[8]

The keynote in the substitution theory is that any form of participation comes up gradually during a longer period, then grows in extent and force, reaches its height and subsequently declines again, in quantity as well as in quality, and possibly disappears altogether in the long run. Meanwhile, however, a new form of participation has developed, being able to take over a number of functions from the preceding form if in another way. On balance this need not have serious consequences for the development of participation, although in the course of time no structural strengthening, merely a shift from more collective to more individual forms occurs.

Applied to the Dutch situation, at first sight the substitution theory seems to

---

[8] The best-known form of direct (group) participation of employees in The Netherlands is so-called job consultation—regular consultations between supervisors and employees about the work in each group or department. This job consultation occurs on a fairly large scale. Moreover, in the last few years new forms of direct (group) participation have arisen, e.g. in the form of Quality Circles, and autonomous work groups.

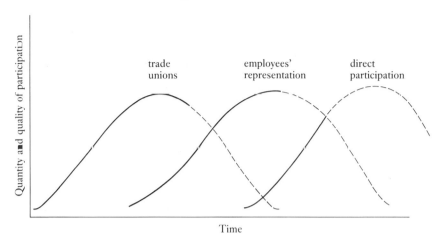

Fig. 20.4 Development of participation according to the substitution theory

First wave = participation by means of trade unions
Second wave = participation by employees' representation
Third wave = possible future wave relating to new forms of participation (e.g. direct (group) participation of employees)

hold true. Thus the stages of development of the various forms of participation can be sketched as in Table 20.3. At this moment little concrete can be said about the end of the height of employees' representation, or about further development of forms of direct participation. What *can* be said, though, is that an increased interest in the latter is observable. Moreover, a clear retrogression, in quantity as well as in quality, of the position of the unions can also be observed. For the adherents of the substitution theory these developments are evidence that their propositions are correct (Van Gorkum, 1982; De Vries, 1985; Bolweg, 1986).

Table 20.3 Development stages: trade unions, employees' representation, and direct participation in The Netherlands

	Trade union power	Employees' representation	Direct participation
Rise	1900–1960	1920–1970	1960–2000
Height	1960–1980	1970–1990(?)	2000–2020(?)
Decline	from 1980	from 2000(?)	from 2020(?)

Although on the strength of the data above some substitution indeed seems to take place, it may be doubted whether it will continue in the future as is supposed in the theory. It is clear, after all, that within the various forms of participation different functions are performed which can only partly be taken over by other forms. Thus the functions of unions can only be taken over by employees' representation where trade union activities at company level are concerned, and not, or hardly at all, where activities of national and industry-wide scope are concerned. The same goes for taking over functions of employees' representation by task-based participation. The answer to the question to what extent will (further) substitution take place in the near future is to a great degree determined by the further course of the decentralization process. In the case of full decentralization the significance of talks at the central level and at the level of the industries is eliminated and with it the functions of the trade unions at these levels. Under such circumstances it is conceivable that the functions of the unions may be taken over in their entirety by employees' representation. However, it is not very likely that such extreme decentralization will take place, for a need for co-ordination at the central level and at the level of industries will remain. Consequently, a number of the functions of the unions at these levels, which cannot be taken over by employees' representation, will also be preserved, although possibly different from and fewer than those in the past. This means also that the substitution theory—at least in its extreme form—cannot be maintained. This brings us to the second theory on the development of participation, the stairway theory.

The stairway theory

This theory also allows for a cyclical development of participation, but an evolutionary perspective is added to it. Schematically, the picture is as in Fig. 20.5. This Figure shows that here, too, the development of participation takes place in a number of waves, each wave representing another form of participation. Contrary to the preceding model (Fig. 20.4), however, one wave does not replace the other, but goes on where the other left off. There is therefore no continual substitution of one form of participation by another, but, rather, supplementation of collective aspects (promoted by the trade unions) with organizational aspects, and those subsequently with more individual aspects (dealt with by the works councils and in direct participation, respectively). In the long run this might result in the increase (in quantity and in quality) of participation as a whole, though moments of temporary retrogression of certain elements of participation are not impossible.

Support of the ideas of the stairway theory can be found in the fact that—at least in the Dutch situation, but probably elsewhere, too—the trade unions played an important part in the development of employees' representation, both in the formal and in the actual sense. In addition, the research of Teulings (1981) found that employees' representation could function well only if it was willing to use means of power from time to time, and this, in its turn, was possible only with sufficient support from the unions. Our own research also suggests this, though less strongly than Teulings's. As a matter of fact, it appears from our research that works councils can achieve results in consultations in two ways, namely, by being

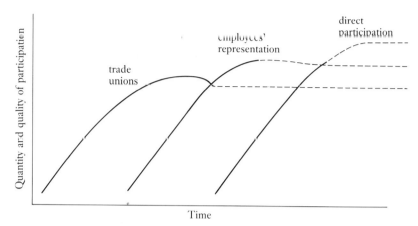

Fig. 20.5 Development of participation according to the stairway theory

recognized by and having a good relationship with the manager, and by maintaining good external contacts, especially with the unions. Since, in the first case, a works council is strongly dependent on the manager's attitude, it remains important to have the second possibility to fall back on.

The foregoing implies that strong trade unions are not only important for the creation of employees' representation—after which it could be left to its own devices—but also play a vital part in its further development and indeed in its (day-to-day) functioning. Given the existence of various regulations, it is probable that employees' representation can also be constituted without the unions' support and even that certain results can be achieved. However, contact with and support from the unions are a *sine qua non* for actual influence on strategic business decisions over a longer period.[9]

An important condition is, though, that in the future, too, the trade unions are able and willing to continue to support employees' representation and that employees' representatives, in their turn, are willing to co-operate with the unions. A further aggravation of the current disputes about competence can eventually only work out unfavourably for both parties and consequently also for the entire development of participation. Mutual acceptance may, on the other hand, have the result that the position of the trade unions remains stable in the long run, that employees' representation is further strengthened, especially in quality, and that it prevents the substitution theory—as a kind of 'self-fulfilling prophecy'—from becoming a reality.

---

[9] A similar relation is possible between direct participation and employees' representation. Research on this point shows that active support from the works council is a necessary condition for the proper functioning of job consultation (Walravens and van Alphen, 1984).

Conclusion

This brings us back, finally, to the position of employees' representation and the question we are concerned with in this contribution, namely, how this position is to be assessed in the present situation as well as with a view to the future. Are we dealing with a development that defies the times, or, on the contrary, with a trend that corresponds entirely with a number of other developments today?

At the beginning of this article it was established that in The Netherlands a considerable growth of employees representation is occurring, especially in quantity, but also—if to a lesser degree—in quality. With regard to the background and causes of this growth it was then observed that these have to be found first and foremost in the establishment or amendment of a number of legal regulations, in their turn the result of the delayed reaction of political bodies and the legislation of external influences (in particular in the socio-cultural sphere) in the 1970s. Furthermore, it was established that the growth of employees' representation corresponds well with the movement towards decentralization which has occurred within our industrial relations from the early 1980s under the influence of economic, technological, and socio-cultural developments. Against this background, we cannot call this a development that defies the times, but rather a trend that is fairly logical in the light of the circumstances.

With a view to the future of employees' representation, the question of to what extent decentralization will continue and what consequences this will have for the position of the trade unions is especially important. At first sight further decentralization—and the attendant further weakening of the unions—seems to offer favourable perspectives for employees' representation. In the long run this advantage will turn out to be illusory, though, since it appears that the proper functioning of employees' representation is dependent on the lasting support of the unions. An important condition for further growth of employees' representation is, therefore, not a weakening but, on the contrary, a strengthening or at least a maintenance of the unions' position.

To conclude, it is to be expected that the development of employees' representation will also be influenced by other means, namely, by the rise of direct participation. By analogy we can also infer that, concerning current problems in the relations between unions and employees' representatives much will depend on what their reactions to the new situation will be: fear of substitution, with consequent withdrawal to existing positions, new disputes over competence, and eventually the risk that what happens is just what one wanted to prevent? Or will they be open to new developments, their own possibilities and limitations, and the advantages of a division of tasks between the various forms, resulting in a strengthening of participation as a whole? For the sake of the future development of both employees' representation and the whole of participation in our country, the latter is to be hoped for.

References

Bolweg, J. F. (1986), 'Minder plaats voor vakbonden in toekomstige onderneming', *Inleiding congres arbeidsverhoudingen* (Amsterdam: Kluwer).

Gorkum, P. H. van (1982), 'OR en vakbond concurrerende machten', *Zeggenschap*, 88.

Hövels, B. W. M. and Nas, P. (1976), *Ondernemingsraden en medezeggenschap: Een vergelijkend onderzoek naar structuur en werkwijze van ondernemingsraden* (Alphen aan den Rijn: Samson).

IDE International Research Group (1981), *Industrial Democracy in Europe* (Oxford: Clarendon Press).

Lammers, C. J. (1985a), 'Organisationele democratie: Literatuurbeschouwing', M & O, *Tijdschrift voor organisatiekunde en sociaal beleid*, 39: 481–501.

—— (1985b), 'Drie krachten: Maatschappij, economie en technologie', *Inleiding Bedrijfssociologische Studiedagen*.

Looise, J. C. (1985), 'Medezeggenschap via de cao: Een verkennende studie', *Tijdschrift voor Arbeidsvraagstukken*, 1(2), 6–20.

—— and Heijink, J. Z. (1986), *De ondernemingsraad en zijn bevoegdheden: Interim-rapport onderzoek ondernemingsraden* (Nijmegen: ITS).

—— and Lang, F. G. M. de (1987), *Ondernemingsraden, bestuurders en besluitvorming: Eindrapport onderzoek ondernemingsraden* (Nijmegen: ITS).

Ministry of Social Affairs and Employment (1972, 1973, 1974, 1977, 1984, 1985, 1987), *Resultaten enquête instelling ondernemingsraden* (The Hague).

Schuit, S. R., Beek, J. M. van der, and Raap, B. K. (1983), *Dutch Business Law* (Deventer: Kluwer).

Smit, F. C. G., and Pelkmans, A. (1985), *Onderzoek praktische toepassing Wet Medezeggenschap Onderwijs* (Nijmegen: ITS).

Teulings, A. W. M. (1981), *Ondernemingsraadpolitiek in Nederland* (Amsterdam: Van Gennep).

—— (1984), 'The Social, Cultural and Political Setting of Industrial Democracy', in B. Wilpert and A. Sorge (eds.), *International Yearbook of Organizational Democracy*, ii (Chichester: Wiley).

Tolman, R. J., Stelt, H. G. van der, and Teulings, A. W. M. (1986), *Nieuwe stijl: Vertegenwoordigend overleg in overheidsorganisatie* (Amsterdam: SORU).

Vries, B. de (1985), 'Hoe verder met het sociaal-economisch beleid?' *Economisch Statistische Berichten*, 70: 792–7.

Walravens, A. H. C. M. and Alphen, N. van (1984), *Medezeggenschap bij DHV: onderzoeksverslag* (The Hague: COP/SER (Commissie Opvoering Produktiviteit/Sociaal Economische Raad)).

21

Does the 38.5-Hour Week Collective Agreement Change the West German System of Co-determination?

RUDI SCHMIDT AND RAINER TRINCZEK

AMONG the big West European nations the Federal Republic of Germany (FRG) distinguishes itself by a remarkably stable system of industrial relations (see the comparative study on Great Britain, Italy, and the FRG, Jacobi *et al.*, 1986). Much has been written about its legally implanted structures, its high degree of 'juridification' (Neal, 1987) and its long tradition, which reaches back into the Weimar Republic. Even more remarkable than the stability itself is the conspicuous fact that this system has indeed made possible considerable improvements for employees, despite a union policy that is not so much based on confrontation but on social partnership.

Throughout the 1960s and early 1970s this policy was the focus of leftist criticism. The DGB (German Federation of Trade Unions) unions were being contrasted with the union movements in Great Britain and the Latin countries where militant strike action had been taken and where, in part, a spectacular penetration of the power structures of companies or even whole branches of industry had been achieved. These successes were usually associated with a closer organizational relationship with the shop floor and only loose ties to the State— quite in contrast to the strategy adopted by the DGB unions. Shop stewards, *commissiones obreras*, and the Turin factory councils (*consiglii di fabbrica*) were set against the West German system of co-determination with its high degree of integration and co-operation, and a change of policy towards anti-capitalist workers' control was demanded.

The spontaneous strikes of 1969 and 1973 in West Germany seemed to support the critics, and the arguments of the union leadership, which said that German workers were not in a worse but rather in a better position than workers in countries with a more militant union policy, were brushed aside as politically narrow-minded.

Since then the situation has changed radically. The beginning of the world-wide economic crisis in the mid-1970s not only marked the turning-point of post-war prosperity but also of the political judgement of the trade unions in Europe, which had reached a level of general political acceptance agreed upon by many critical sociologists at the time. Nowadays British unions not only have to tolerate Thatcherite anti-union policies but have also suffered the sensational defeats of both the miners and the London printers; the French unions are gradually losing ground; and the militant Italian factory councils are, politically speaking, only a shadow of their former selves—at Fiat it is the *padrone* again who has the uncontested say.

Against this changed background, the policy of careful but, nevertheless, determined opposition, in particular by the West German IG Metall (IGM; metal-workers' union) and the IG Druck und Papier (DRUPA; printers' union), in the past years appears quite different. German unions and the system of industrial relations they have helped to shape have become almost exemplary for many a former critic. It has not been ignored that, in times of positive economic development, militant unions which operate mainly in a decentralized way and close to the shop floor are able to maintain a more effective policy in support of members' interests. It had to be acknowledged, however, that in bad times—and in many countries 'bad times' have been the rule for some time now—a differentiated, legally implanted system of a regulated relation of interests between capital and labour—as in the FRG—does provide better protection against what are seen to be exceedingly bold encroachments on the part of the employer (see the comparative study by Bechtle *et al.*, 1985; Heine *et al.*, 1986).

Nevertheless, it has to be pointed out that since 1982, when the Kohl–Genscher Government came into office, this framework of labour protection guaranteed by the State came under pressure. It is a framework which in the past has relieved the West German trade union movement of a considerable number of tasks, and has allowed DGB unions to concentrate on central collective bargaining issues. Thus the present Conservative–Liberal Government appears to have joined the 'international coalition' of governments which pursue a policy of deregulation (Lecher, 1987), which grants more freedom to employers, induces greater flexibility in working conditions, and tries to role back trade union influence in general.

This policy of deregulation at least partially reflects present developments in the economy which are mainly due to the process of a world-wide change in the conditions of production. This process, which is presently being discussed amongst industrial sociologists in Germany and more recently in the Anglo-Saxon countries under such terms as 'new production concepts', 'requalification of labour' (Kern and Schumann, 1984), and 'the end of mass production' (Piore and Sabel, 1984), emanates from increased pressure to adapt to world markets, from continuously accelerating cycles of innovation in product development and manufacture, from a higher turnover of investment capital, and, consequently, from an increase in the flexibility required for the restructuring of production.

The demand for shorter weekly working hours, which was taken up again in

1983 by a number of German unions, was opposed from the very beginning by the employers' demands for greater flexibility with regard to working hours, and for deregulated and differentiated working conditions. The trade unions' campaign had relied not only on the classical arguments for more leisure time and a better quality of life, but also, in the face of high unemployment rates, on the premise that more jobs would be created.

In the course of the negotiations in 1984, the positions of the unions and the employers proved to be incompatible. After an unprecedented political intervention of the Kohl Government in support of the employers' demands, the confrontation of the two camps grew into a major class conflict of a type formerly unknown in West Germany. Measured in terms of working days lost due to strikes and lock-outs, the result was the biggest strike in German post-war history.

The social and political importance of this conflict is mainly due to two factors. First, the metal-workers' union (IGM) and the printers' union (DRUPA) resisted the mighty pressure of the Government and the employers' association by surprisingly being able to mobilize their members, despite the precarious situation of mass unemployment. The unions were successful in convincing their membership that the informal coalition of the right-wing Government and the employers' association had started a 'rolling back' of the whole bargaining system, the historically developed balance of power, and the social and political influence of the unions in general. Although in 1984 the unions were not strong enough to prevent some deregulation and 'flexibilization' of working hours and other working conditions, they proved still to be a relevant factor within the West German political system, able to stem the impending tide of massive deregulation—at least to some extent. Secondly, the unions succeeded in pulling down the barrier of the 40-hour week in a main sector of West German industry, thus opening the way for the move towards the intended 35-hour week. A further step in this direction has since been taken with the 1987 collective agreement in the metal industry, which includes the gradual introduction of the 37-hour week by 1989.

However, the partial success of the unions in 1984 was not to be gained without some major concessions, which may yet initiate considerable changes in the West German system of co-determination.

The 38.5-hour week collective agreement in the West German metal industry and its implementation at plant level

The compromise of 1984 did not, as is usual, consist of forced cuts from otherwise genuine union demands on the employers. Instead, it consisted of the combination of both the union's and the employers' demands into one and the same collective agreement. On the one hand, working hours were reduced by 1.5 hours; on the other hand, a more flexible arrangement of working hours was made possible. For the first time the individual regular weekly working hours (IRWWH) of full-time employees may differ—they may range between 37 and 40 hours a week; on average, none the less, the IRWWH of all employees of a plant may not diverge from the fixed amount of 38.5 hours.

In addition to this, there was an agreement that the 'individual regular weekly working hours . . . may be distributed evenly or unevenly over five working days' and that they must be completed 'by the end of two months'. This clause of the agreement makes it possible to achieve shorter hours in different ways—ranging from several possibilities of shorter daily and weekly hours to the possibility of arranging complete days off for the employee.

With this solution of shorter and yet more flexible working hours, the authority to fix standards, formerly the preserve of the national collective bargaining machinery, had, at least partially, to be delegated to the plant level—a change of the bargaining structure which Wolfgang Streeck (1982) had identified as the necessary consequence of collective agreements on qualitative matters in general. The form the 38.5-hour week should take and the possible flexibility of the working-hour arrangements were to be decided according to the needs of the plant and the politically attainable wishes of those involved in the decision-making process within the plant respectively. The authorized parties, works council (*Betriebsrat*) and management, were to negotiate a collective agreement at plant level, a so-called *Betriebsvereinbarung*.

So far, these *Betriebsvereinbarungen* could only be settled on certain subjects, as laid down precisely in the 1972 Works Constitution Act. Now it was the trade unions and the employers association which handed over some of their genuine bargaining authority to the plant-level bargaining parties—thus, as some critics complained, taking the risk of endangering the carefully balanced two-tier structure of the West German bargaining system.

Bearing these possible and wide-ranging consequences in mind, it is quite understandable why the implementation of the 38.5-hour week at plant level was regarded as a matter of outstanding importance, not only by the parties immediately involved in this process, but also by critical observers of the West German system of industrial relations within the academic community. Three major empirical research projects were initiated on that topic, each of them with a different methodological approach:

- The joint research group of the Forschungsinstitut für Arbeiterbildung (FIAB) and the Wirtschafts- und Sozialwissenschaftliches Institut des DGB (WSI) undertook a quantitative analysis of the *Betriebsvereinbarungen* in the metal industry. The material basis consisted of 3,341 *Betriebsvereinbarungen*, which covered the vast majority of the employees in this industry (Bosch *et al.*, 1986).
- The major approach of the research group of the Institut zur Erforschung

sozialer Chancen (ISO) was the conduct of intensive case studies of the implementation process in several plants (Frerichs *et al.*, 1986). In the course of its empirical work the ISO research group concentrated on the printing industry, where a similar collective agreement had been reached, paying only slight attention to the metal industry which was already being researched by the third group.

• The Research Group for Industrial Sociology at the Institute of Sociology at the University of Erlangen–Nürnberg used a methodological 'mix' when investigating the practical application of the recently negotiated 38.5-hour week collective agreement in the metal industry in the Nürnberg–Fürth–Erlangen area. 103 *Betriebsvereinbarungen* were analysed, which covered almost all the plants in that area, and 38 qualitative case-studies were carried out in those plants which had a work-force of more than 500 employees. The first stage of this project (inquiry period: Oct. 1984–Apr. 1985) focused on the question of how the management and the works council (*Betriebsrat*) were handling the new situation and what the focal points of the arrangements were that had been negotiated in the firms (Schmidt and Trinczek, 1985, 1986*a*). The second stage of the project (inquiry period: Apr.–June 1986) attempted to sum up the practicability of the new working-hour arrangements, and the manner in which they had been handled and accepted by the companies (Schmidt and Trinczek, 1986*b*).

Besides these research projects, an empirically-based diploma thesis was carried out at Berlin University which covered the implementation process of the 38.5-hour week in the West Berlin metal industry (Letschert, 1985).

The major quantitative findings were agreed upon in a rare consensus among the different researchers: the large majority of plants did not make use of the possibility of differentiating the IRWWH of full-time employees between the possible margins of 37 and 40 hours a week (FIAB–WSI: 83.4 per cent of the plants; Research Group, Erlangen: 80 per cent; Letschert: 81.7 per cent). An even smaller proportion of employees in the metal industry were directly affected by differentiated working hours: FIAB–WSI: 5.7 per cent; Research Group, Erlangen: 3.4 per cent; Letschert: 3.9 per cent). Some 55 per cent of the plants chose shorter weekly working hours; roughly 30 per cent made use of the possibility of arranging complete days off and all the others agreed upon some kind of mixed model.

These results were somewhat difficult to interpret. Although some considerable change towards destandardization had obviously taken place, it was sometimes contested whether the findings of the empirical studies were significant enough to support the interpretation of the 38.5-hour week collective agreement as a turning-point in the history of collective bargaining in the FRG. A broad discussion about the potential effects of more flexible working conditions (see e.g. Bosch, 1986;

Mückenberger, 1986) and of shifting negotiating authority from national to plant
level was thereby initiated

On the delegation of negotiation authority of the plant level

The pressure to realize agreements at plant level was one of the most controversial
points of the compromise on working hours with regard to bargaining policies, and
soon after the signing of the 38.5-hour week agreement a controversy arose about
the possible consequences of delegating negotiating authority to the plant level.

For the old leftist critics of a centralized bargaining policy, it seemed sensible to
revitalize the concept of plant-related bargaining policies (*betriebsnahe Tarifpolitik*). This concept had already been discussed at the end of the 1950s, but without
any practical consequences. According to this concept, the plant level was
supposed to gain more weight in relation to the national bargaining level. By
locating the bargaining process closer to the shop floor the *betriebsnahe Tarifpolitik*
was aimed at including the employees to a greater extent in the negotiating process,
thus increasing the strength of unions at the grass roots. If—and this was the hope
of the representatives of this position (a minority)—such an offensive adoption of
the employers' strategy to delegate bargaining authority to the plant level could be
achieved by the unions and the works councils during the implementation phase of
the 38.5-hour week collective agreement, this shift within the bargaining structure
could turn out to be a pyrrhic victory for the employers.

Some of the entrepreneurs had the rarely openly expressed hope that by
delegating bargaining authority to the plant level the strength of the central
'bargaining machine' in West Germany, the IG Metall, might be weakened, as
now the particular interests of the plants would be more strongly enforced. This
would make it more difficult for the union to standardize the interests of the
employees and thus could finally lead to reduced scope for further collective
agreements on (shorter) working hours.

What seemed hopeful to the employers, of course, gave union sceptics reason to
worry. The power of a union is largely dependent on its success in standardizing
the interests of its members as the necessary foundation of any promising collective
bargaining policy. The more differentiated and individualized the working
conditions get, the more difficult the process of intra-union standardization
becomes. Therefore, IG Metall headquarters tried as hard as possible to induce the
works councils to adopt the highly standardized models which had been worked
out by them as the official union recommendation for the in-plant implementation
of the 38.5-hour week agreement.

However, works councils—the representatives of the whole work-force of a
plant and formally not a union body but a legal institution—necessarily have
specific plant-related interests that often oppose the intentions and policies of
'their' union. Therefore, it was not altogether surprising that the IGM was only

partially successful in its campaign, as the results demonstrated. The divergence of opinions between the union and a substantial number of works councils, which resulted in the introduction of many different working-hours models at shop-floor level, sheds some light on the possible long-term effects that the collective agreement of 1984 covering the 38.5-hour week may have for West German industrial relations.

Like any trade union that essentially aims at negotiating industry-wide collective agreements, the IGM has, as a structural problem, to cope with the notorious distance from the shop floor of its highly centralized and effective 'bargaining machine'. At the same time, such an industry-wide bargaining policy has, in comparison with a policy that is mainly centred on the plant, the advantage of consistency, which manifests itself in two respects. On the one hand there is the standardization of the framework within which the firms compete. Such calculable and equal conditions for competition are actually at the core of the interest that employers take in industry-wide bargaining. Proceeding from this 'objective' interest, one may assume that employers have no interest in any unlimited particularization of the bargaining structure, but, rather, in a certain restriction of the standardizing power of the unions. The 38.5-hour week collective agreement seems to be compatible with this wish to weaken the unions' power to shape policies, which, compared on an international level, force supposedly exceedingly unfavourable conditions on German capital interests.

Industry-wide collective bargaining not only sets a standardized framework for the competition between the firms, it also reduces the competition between those dependent on wages and standardizes their living conditions. It is a structural problem for every union movement that a closer interrelation of the bargaining process with the shop floor can only be attained at the cost of this standardization. At any rate, such a policy would run the risk of being unable to maintain the precarious balance between national bargaining and plant bargaining. For, in the case of a shift of the negotiating authority to the plant level, the hitherto fixed and equal conditions of competition become variable quantities which can be influenced by the management again; they are no longer quantities given to the competitor and, accordingly, they can lead to complex and ruinous conflicts in competition.

The effects of a decentralized bargaining structure on the employees' side could be just as critical. The 'plant-centredness' of employees' interests, which, at least to some extent, has necessarily always existed because of the competitive structure of capitalist economies, could increase and become a manifestation of shop floor syndicalism at the expense of industry-wide solidarity by those dependent on wages. Such a policy centred on the plant could possibly endanger employee opportunity, bringing with it processes of differentiation and the destruction of solidarity.

In fact, first signs of these effects of a more decentralized bargaining structure could be observed during the implementation phase of the 38.5-hour week collective agreement. Especially in areas of 'weak' union branch organization, or in cases of works councils with a strong ideology of social partnership, works councils appeared to attach a greater importance to the 'good of the company' as defined by the employers' side, than to the strategic interests of their union. Works councils had often been 'convinced' by the argument of the management that it was only the employers model which represented the required optimal application of the 38.5-hour week agreement. During negotiations these works councils restricted themselves to modifications of the model proposed by the management—in part regardless of whether this would confirm to the ideas of their union, the IG Metall. Consequently, for example, works councils obstinately defended their negotiated agreements over shorter hours in the form of factory closure days, which were rather popular among the employees (i.e. the potential voters of the works councils), against the advice of IGM officers, although such agreements were not permitted according to the legal interpretation of the collective agreement by the union. In the course of these disputes, the legal side of which was never completely clarified, the works councils even quoted some of the arguments set out in the official recommendation from the employers' association. In such cases the definite beginnings of a form of syndicalism, which ultimately undermines the unions' power of standardization, can be observed.

At the same time, these developments confirm the theoretically arrived at conjecture that it is enough for the management, as a rule, to point out the precarious competitive situation of a plant to bind works councils to the common interest of employees and owners of investment capital: the safeguarding of a strong, competitive position of the enterprise. This succeeds even more easily as the realization of this common interest seems to be the prerequisite for both parties to be able to realize sufficiently their particular, competing interests in the capitalist economy: relatively secure jobs, high wages, and humane working conditions on the one hand, profitable use of investment capital on the other.

Despite initial signs of changes within West German industrial relations, the research carried out on the implementation of the 38.5-hour week collective agreement shows that, all in all, until now there have been no substantial problems in integrating the delegation of bargaining authority to the plant level into the existing structure of the West German system of industrial relations. The effects of the 38.5-hour week collective agreement—especially on plant-level industrial relations—which had been anticipated during the run-up to the practical application, showed themselves, as a rule, to have been overestimated. That was mainly due to the surprisingly conservative manner in which the plant-level parties generally handled the potentially innovative collective agreement. One of the major findings of our own research on the subject (Schmidt and Trinczek 1985, 1986a) was that in general neither the management nor the works councils were interested in questioning—in favour of short-term gains—the established 'political culture' of the plant, which in some cases had been tested and kept in a state of balance for decades.

On the political culture of industrial relations between capital and labour at plant level

In almost all the cases examined by us the pattern of the specifically plant-related, plant-developed system of relations between the works council and the management was able to win through against the potentially innovative area of negotiations, introduced by the new national agreement. Interestingly enough, the decision-making parties followed the commonly practised patterns of internal negotiation independently of the measure of controversy which the original demands of both parties might have been expected to bring about—this regardless of whether these patterns were structured to harmonize or conflict.

In the context of these traditional, specifically plant-related standards of normalcy for the relations between the works council and management, it seems right to speak of the 'political culture' of a plant. In doing so an intermediary level of analysis is introduced, a level that is situated between the 'objective' basic conditions of capital–labour relations and concrete action of the subjects involved, a level that seeks to link both structure and action.

According to the result of the research carried through by the authors, this political culture of labour relations at plant level, described as 'shop-floor culture', is of greatest relevance in the analysis of the plant-level industrial relations. Shop-floor culture provides a structure within which the works council and management can act; it provides a framework, so to speak, with the help of which new ideas can be channelled in traditional ways; thus it contributes greatly to the stability of plant-level industrial relations.

The political culture of a plant may be considered to be the sediment of shop-floor power struggles (as in Crozier and Friedberg (1979) with regard to their internally organized 'rules of the game'). The chosen term 'relations between capital and labour' refers to the constitutive structural prerequisites of interaction between management and the employees' representatives, the capital–labour relation represents the structural context in which shop-floor interactive culture is set, and by way of which the interacting parties are, principally, asymmetrically supplied with the resource of power: the defining power, which influences the process of negotiation towards the settlement of concrete shop-floor arrangements is, with regard to these structural prerequisites, distributed unequally between the works council and the management.

This argument, however, says only little about the concrete, plant-related shape of the shop-floor culture and its genesis. The actual political constellation of powers within a plant is, rather, influenced by a number of parameters (e.g. the economic situation of the enterprise, the industrial sector it belongs to, the structure of production and of the product, management practice, the structure of the work-force, the degree of union organization, the social and political awareness of the work-force, etc.), whose relevance can vary depending on the plant. The respective standard of shop-floor relations must be understood as a result of a plant-specific historical process.

In the course of such an economic, political, and social history of the plant an internally accepted definition of 'normal' relations between capital and labour usually develops and finds expression in a set of rules (see Burawoy's 'internal state', 1982: 77 ff.).

In Anglo-Saxon research on industrial relations, questions of the genesis and the practice of such webs of rules are traditionally of central importance. Here, work practices on the shop floor, that is, mainly, the question of job regulation, are usually the focus of relevant studies (see Goodman *et al.*, 1975). Until recently, informal rules (see e.g. Brown, 1972; Hill, 1974; Terry, 1977) have, for several reasons (for example, the relatively low degree of 'juridification' of industrial relations in these countries), enjoyed much more attention under the abbreviation C & P (customs and practice) than in West German industrial sociology (see Dombois, 1980, who, in this regard, is one of the few notable exceptions).

In West German research the wide area of informal structures and rules has only recently been taken into account in a systematic way by sociological analyses of the in-plant social structure. This interest developed when internal processes of decision making were being investigated to a greater extent in empirical analyses, be it decisions regarding the introduction of new technologies (Weltz and Lullies, 1984; Seltz and Hildebrandt, 1985), the reduction of jobs, or the plant's social expenditures (Bechtle *et al.*, 1985; Kotthoff, 1985). The more intensive this research became, the more obvious it became how highly significant the field of informal norms and regulations, largely ignored until recently, is in the area of plant-level industrial relations. It was one of the mutual findings of these more recent studies that certain forms of interaction which have established themselves during many years of almost daily encounters between management and employees' representatives have become traditions that are no longer questioned but have almost become 'institutions' with normative effect: 'Thus . . . custom and practice (C & P) governed behaviour is just as much "structured" as that dictated by "formal rules"' (Wood *et al.*, 1975: 299).

During our own research on the implementation of the 38.5-hour week collective agreement, we, too, encountered this duality of formal and informal structures, which influences the social structure of plant-level industrial relations to a great extent, despite the existence of a highly 'juridificated' system of plant relations. The shop-floor culture seems to be best characterized as a colourful juxtaposition and 'muddle' of formal/informal and procedural/substantive rules. What is given the label of normalcy in the end by this set of rules may vary from plant to plant. It is at this point that the different forms of the political culture of labour relations at plant level are defined. If, for example, the work-force of a plant 'collectively informed itself' at the works council—a process during which employees, similar to strike action, leave their place of work—and if this took place in a plant with industrial relations structured according to the traditional 'social partnership', it would be considered to be a major breach of normal procedures. If the same event took place during important negotiations in a traditionally conflict-ridden plant, it would be considered normal and would only cause half-hearted protests of the management against this putative breach of the content and the spirit of the Works Constitution Act.

The political culture of a plant is reflected in almost all areas of plant-level industrial relations. In co-operative arrangements, for example, the management tends to give the works council more information about the economic affairs of the firm, about future investment plans and their possible effects on the work-force, etc. than the management in conflict-ridden plants typically does.

Informal arrangements between the works council and the management either fill the gaps left by the numerous elastic clauses of the Works Constitution Act or even substitute unequivocal legal sentences. In some firms, where a strong social partnership between the plant-level parties is prevalent, the personnel department informally accepts that the works council vetoes the engagement of non-union members—although that is clearly illegal according to German law.

The developed set of formal and informal rules accepted by both sides indicates that, at least for a limited period, certain areas of conflict have been peacefully settled, inasmuch as 'normal' procedures supported by both parties were successfully established. Those procedures can be called upon whenever needed and can be applied without further question and almost automatically. Thus the area of possible conflict between the employees' representatives and the management is considerably reduced and the range of potential action is limited to a measure that can be calculated and dealt with by all involved.

The established norms of the political culture of a plant thus lead to mutual predictability; they create trust and—to use the terminology of Luhmann's system theory—thereby reduce the complexity of this social situation (Luhmann, 1973). It should be underlined that the political culture of industrial relations at plant level functions properly in this way regardless of the concrete form it takes. As paradoxical as it may seem at first, even an 'offensive, conflict-ridden relationship between works council and management (can be interpreted) as mutual trust' (Kotthoff, 1980: 344). In other words the relationship may be interpreted thus if both parties can rely on the consistently incompatible attitude of the other side—that is 'trust' the other side.

Therefore, once they are negotiated, the standards for internal conflict solution specific to the plant relieve pressure on both parties by establishing a secure framework in which they can act. Accordingly, there is an objective interest in preserving this specific set of rules, an interest that is shared by both the works council and the management. Breaches of these norms bear a risk for the offender; they are taken note of in an extremely sensitive manner, for even the smallest deviation signals that the legitimacy, not only of the rules established but also of the legitimizing procedure itself, is in danger.

The common interest of works council and management in a secure stock of agreed standards of normalcy lends a sometimes, as it seems to outsiders, peculiar stability to the political culture of labour relations at plant level. To a large extent, it was this common interest in stable and calculable relations which led to the rather cautious handling of the 38.5-hour week collective agreement during the implementation phase at plant level. Thus, as the research findings confirm, the existing system of industrial relations was largely able to absorb the pressure to change originating from the metal industry's collective agreement on shorter working hours. Nevertheless, one cannot simply proceed on the assumption that the West German system of co-determination will be able to absorb still more pressure in the case of further deregulation without major problems.

Concentration of capital and its effects on West German industrial relations

Despite the general findings that the West German system of industrial relations has proved its great stability and surprising ability to integrate even a substantial reorganization of bargaining structures, the implementation of the 38.5-hour week agreement threw some light on a slow but gradual change within West German industrial relations, which was given little attention in the discussion about the potential effects of the 38.5-hour week agreement but which, in our opinion, may prove to become one of the most decisive factors of change within the German system of co-determination in the future. This trend, which at present is only indicated, essentially has its cause in the combination of two factors:

1. The concentration of firms of West German industry is constantly increasing (Statistisches Bundesamt, 1985: 261); medium-sized firms of sole proprietorship are also increasingly losing their independence as plants dependent upon an enterprise or on a group become the rule. Whether a plant is an independent unit or dependent upon a group has considerable effects on the policy-making process of the management. Whereas in the case of sole proprietorship, final management decisions can be made at plant level, the essential decisions are made at a supraplant level in the case of enterprises.

Consequently, the works council in a plant that belongs to a larger enterprise is faced with a management that has increasingly less authority and—as was proved during the implementation of the 38.5-hour week collective agreement—a management that, with regard to executive matters, is left with only limited freedom of decision making in internal negotiations (see also Purcell, 1983).

2. In West Germany the classical arenas for employee representation are the sphere of national collective bargaining (with the union) and plant-level consultation and co-determination (with the works council). At the level in between, the level of the enterprise or the holding company, which is becoming increasingly relevant on the employers' side, there is a lack of representation on the employees' side. Relevant bodies for the representation of employee interests in the form of a group works council (*Gesamtbetriebsrat*) have been established by the legislature in the Works Council Act for enterprises and company groups, but they are provided with only little formal authority in comparison with the works councils at plant level; this, in reality, makes it impossible for the *Gesamtbetriebsrat* to force their local branches to adhere to particular policies against their will.

Effective participation at enterprise level is made even more difficult by the fact that the relationship between the different plants of one enterprise is, as a rule, characterized by strong competitive motives, which are, on the one hand, structural and, on the other, sometimes also embellished by the management for reasons of tactics and strategy. As the different local plants compete within their parent company, for example to win the allocation of a 'secure' production line, and, therefore, medium-term job security for their work-force, works councils often become lobbyists for 'their' plants in the supraplant *Gesamtbetriebsrat*. Consequently, it must be questioned whether the *Gesamtbetriebsrat*, which is formally intended to co-ordinate the plant-related works councils, can, in its present shape, effectively fulfil such a function.

If, at this point, one takes up the differentiation made by Walton and McKersie (1965) between 'inter-' and 'intraorganizational bargaining', it may be noted that the structure of interorganizational bargaining between the works council and the management will, in the case of a continuously increasing concentration of firms, shift in favour of the employer's side. The causes for this development, as outlined above, can be found in the different structures of intraorganizational bargaining for employees and employers at the enterprise level. Whereas it is relatively easy for the head office of an enterprise intra-organizationally to standardize procedures for management representatives of the different local plants by means of hierarchical authority, the employees' problem of standardizing their policies on the enterprise level, that is, predominantly the policies of the different works councils at plant level, is much more difficult for structural reasons.

Therefore, the possibility cannot be ruled out that, with an anticipated increasing flexibility of production and working hours within firms, the growing trend towards decentralization of the West German bargaining structure will, in the long run, lead to a weakening of the employees' representation. This is even more valid when considering that the delegation of negotiating authority to the plant-level parties inevitably reduces the importance of the union in industrial relations, but, as a rule, without the works councils gaining in corresponding, actual power at plant level, as the results of our research show.

As a final comment, this does not seem to be the proper moment for 'taking stock' of West German industrial democracy, as we are confronted with a somewhat puzzling situation: there certainly are many signs for possible and even for radical changes of the West German system of industrial relations; but, as this system has proved its surprising ability to integrate new developments without major changes in the past, one, nevertheless, feels reluctant to break out into Cassandra-like cries at present.

References

Bechtle, G., Heine, H., and Schmidt, G. (1985), Ökonomische Krisentendenzen, betriebliche Rationalisierungspolitik und Entwicklung industrieller Beziehungen: Veränderungsimpulse in Italien und in der Bundesrepublik Deutschland: Eine explorative Problemstudie' *Forschungsschwerpunkt 'Zukunft der Arbeit': Arbeitsberichte und Forschungsmaterialien*, 11 (Bielefeld).

Bosch, G. (1986), 'Hat das Normalarbeitsverhältnis eine Zukunft? *WSI-Mitteilungen*, 39: 163–76.

—— Engelhardt, N., Hermann, K., Kurz-Scherf, I., and Seifert, H. (1986), 'Betriebliche Umsetzung der 38,5-Stunden-Woche: Ergebnisse einer Auswertung von Betriebsvereinbarungen aus der Metallindustrie: Zwischenbericht des Projekts 'Umsetzung der Arbeitszeitverkürzung', *WSI-Arbeitsmaterialien*, 12 (Düsseldorf).

Brown, W. (1972), 'A consideration of "Custom and Practice" ', *British Journal of Industrial Relations*, 10: 42–61.

Burawoy, M. (1982), *Manufacturing Consent: Changes in the Labor Process under Monopoly Capitalism* (Chicago, Ill. and London: University of Chicago Press).

Crozier, M. and Friedberg, E. (1979), *Macht und Organisation: Die Zwänge kollektiven Handelns* (Königstein/Ts.: Athenäum).

Dombois, R. (1980), 'Informelle Norm und Interessenvertretung', *Leviathan*, 8: 375–405.

Frerichs, J., Groß, H., and Pekruhl, W. (1986), 'Lernprozesse bei der betrieblichen Umsetzung der Arbeitszeitverkürzung: Erfahrungen aus der Druckindustrie', *WSI-Mitteilungen*, 39: 652–61.

Goodman, J. F. B., Armstrong, E. G. A., Wagner, A., Davis, J. E., and Wood, S. J. (1975), 'Rules in Industrial Relations Theory: a Discussion', *Industrial Relations Journal*, 6: 14–30.

Heine, H., Bechtle, G., and Schmidt, G. (1986), 'Betriebliche Konfliktaustragung in der Krise: Ein deutsch–italienischer Vergleich', *Soziale Welt*, 37: 297–309.

Hill, S. (1974), 'Norms, Groups and Power: The Sociology of Workplace Industrial Relations', *British Journal of Industrial Relations*, 12: 213–35.

Jacobi, O., Jessop, B., Kastendiek, H., and Regini, M. (eds.) (1986), *Economic Crisis, Trade Unions and the State* (London: Croom Helm).

Kern, H. and Schumann, M. (1984), *Das Ende der Arbeitsteilung? Rationalisierung in der industriellen Produktion: Bestandsaufnahme, Trendbestimmung* (Munich: C. H. Beck).

Kotthoff, H. (1980), 'Zur Anwendung des Betriebsverfassungsgesetzes in den Betrieben', in *Jahrbuch für Rechtssoziologie und Rechtstheorie*, (Cologne and Opladen: Westdeutscher Verlag).

—— (1985), 'Kann die Industriesoziologie die betriebliche Sozialordnung ignorieren?', unpublished paper (Saarbrücken).

Lecher, W. (1987), 'Deregulierung der Arbeitsbeziehungen: Gesellschaftliche und gewerkschaftliche Entwicklungen in Großbritannien, den USA, Japan und Frankreich', *Sozial Welt*, 38: 148–65.

Letschert, T. (1985), 'Die Umsetzung der 38,5-Stunden-Woche in der Berliner Metallindustrie', diploma thesis (Berlin).

Luhmann, N. (1973), *Vertrauen: Ein Mechanismus der Reduktion sozialer Komplexität* (Stuttgart: Enke).

Mückenberger, U. (1986), 'Zur Rolle des Normalarbeitsverhältnisses bei der sozialen Umverteilung von Risiken', *Prokla*, 64: 31–45.

Neal, A. C. (1987), 'Co-determination in the Federal Republic of Germany: An External Perspective from the United Kingdom', *British Journal of Industrial Relations*, 25: 227–45.

Piore, M. J. and Sabel, C. F. (1984), *The Second Industrial Divide: Possibilities for Prosperity* (New York: Basic Books).

Purcell, J. (1983), 'The Management of Industrial Relations in the Modern Corporation: Agenda for Research', *British Journal of Industrial Relations*, 21: 1–16.

Schmidt, R. and Trinczek, R. (1985), 'Die betriebliche Umsetzung des Manteltarifvertrags zur $38\frac{1}{2}$-Stunden-Woche in der Metallindustrie der Region Nürnberg/Fürth/Erlangen: Kurzfassung des Projektberichts' (Erlangen: s.a. Frankfurter Rundschau vom 14.1.1986).

—— —— (1986a), 'Erfahrungen und Perspektiven gewerkschaftlicher Arbeitszeitpolitik', *Prokla*, 64: 85–105.

—— —— (1986b), 'Die betriebliche Gestaltung tariflicher Arbeitszeitnormen in der Metallindustrie', *WSI-Mitteilungen*, 39: 641–61.

Seltz, R. and Hildebrandt, H. (1985), 'Produktion, Politik und Kontrolle: Arbeitspolitische Varianten am Beispiel der Einführung von Produktionsplanungs- und Steuerungssystemen im Maschinenbau, in F. Naschold (ed.), *Arbeit und Politik: Gesellschaftliche Regulierung der Arbeit und der sozialen Sicherung* (Frankfurt-on-Main and New York: Campus).

Statistisches Bundesamt (ed.) (1985), *Datenreport 1985: Zahlen und Fakten über die Bundesrepublik Deutschland* (Bonn: Bundeszentrale für politische Bildung).

Streeck, W. (1982), 'Qualitative Demands and the Neo-Corporatist Manageability of Industrial Relations', *British Journal of Industrial Relations*, 19: 149–69.

Terry, M. (1977), 'The Inevitable Growth of Informality', *British Journal of Industrial Relations*, 15: 76–90.

Walton, R. E. and McKersie, R. B. (1965), *A Behavioral Theory of Labor Negotiations: An Analysis of a Social Interaction System* (New York: McGraw-Hill).

Weltz, F. and Lullies, V. (1984), 'Das Konzept der innerbetrieblichen Handlungskonstellation als Instrument der Analyse von Rationalisierungsprozessen in der Verwaltung', in

U. Jürgens and F. Naschold (eds.), *Arbeitspolitik: Materialien zum Zusammenhang von politischer Macht, Kontrolle und betrieblicher Organisation der Arbeit* (Opladen: Westdeutscher Verlag).

Wood, S. J., Wagner, A., Armstrong, E. G. A., Goodman, J. F. B., and Davies, J. E. (1975), 'The "Industrial Relations System" Concept as a Basis for Theory in Industrial Relations, *British Journal of Industrial Relations*, 13: 291–308.

22

Organizational Democracy in West Malaysia: A Case-Study

HING AI YUN

FOR a long time now, the merits and demerits of alternative organizational structures have been debated from both the political and the economic perspective. On the economic plane, questions have referred to prospects of improved efficiency, productivity, and accelerated investments. Political concerns touch on internal patterns of power distribution and how they relate to political structures external to the enterprise.

In Western Europe, where much of the ongoing debate on organizational democracy has taken place, discussion on the subject is more often than not closely associated with problems in the power relations between workers and their managers in industrial firms. However, the case of organizational democracy presented here differs rather sharply from what one could expect if the case was situated in any of the industrialized economies. Instead, it will be shown how this particular model of organizational democracy when realized in the rural context of a newly independent country has succeeded not only in rationalizing agricultural production and raising the standard of living of producers but also in developing collective strength such that producer-members have developed to become a force of political significance.

Study objective and approach

The aim of this study is to investigate whether a particular model of participation can form a transitional stage where learning can accumulate and where the net effect is to encourage greater demand for ever more extensive powers until a conscious and overt confrontation with capital and authority takes place. Or, will participation be essentially co-opting and act only to forestall more radical democratization of the enterprise? Other more specific aspects of participation studied will include its impact on efficiency goals and individual livelihood. In conclusion, political–economic factors will be discussed to show their impact on this particular scheme of industrial democracy. Though the method used here is the case-study, we hope to demonstrate that, peculiarities notwithstanding, case-studies such as this can enable us to draw general conclusions or to hypothesize about various features of participation. Only by carrying out a detailed study of a particular programme for industrial democracy can one draw conclusions as to whether participation will whet the appetite for power among workers or whether it can forestall more radical democratization.

With the increasing frequency and extended spells of recession, the issue of industrial democracy cannot be more urgent or the stakes much higher. Yet, the incidence of joint consultation and worker participation can only be said to be unstable and fluctuating (MacInnes, 1985). Basically, the problem stems from the fact that in capitalist society the interests of the various parties to production are not identical and probably never will be. This divergence of objectives can also be said to account for much of the inefficiency in capitalist firms. Various material incentives, humanization–participation programmes, and diverse forms of direct managerial control have been tried, but to no avail, indicating that labour–capital differences cannot be so simply bridged.

The fact remains that, to maximize efficiency and productivity, wage workers must be willing to exercise constructively their initiative towards improving the firm's performance. In other words, workers should not be expected to do only as they are told, for naked power and the contract alone cannot motivate them to give of their best. To some extent then, the work-force must accept the employer's authority as legitimate before they will work willingly towards achieving company goals. And even if workers have absorbed the ethics of discipline and hard work, management may not always be around to tell them what to do. Management, therefore, faces the problem of developing an appropriate organizational structure which not only draws out the hidden pools of talent and workers' initiative but which also ensures acceptance of management authority and goals.

There is a likelihood that within the capitalist framework some of these problems can be alleviated by resorting to alternative models of organization, but only to the extent that some of the following elements are included within the model programme proposed:

- authority of management is accepted as legitimate;
- actions of direct producers are linked to profits accruing to members;
- some minimum level of social pressure in the form of horizontal control must be present to ensure maximization of individual effort.

But because of difficulties arising from the use of the participative model, we can expect such programmes either to lean towards greater demand for independence or to withdraw completely from most aspects of company affairs. Hopefully, the case-study presented below may be helpful in identifying the dynamics of this particular model of organization.

Data for this study are derived from secondary sources and also from interviews with 200 agricultural producers from four State-run land schemes based on stratified sampling method using housing blocks as strata for sampling. In addition, informal interviews were also held with scheme officers and block leaders.

Case background and history

Malaysia today is still basically an agricultural country with about 20 per cent of the GDP supplied by agriculture, deriving mainly from rubber and palm-oil. And though the proportion of agricultural to total exports has declined drastically (from about half in 1970 to about 20 per cent in 1985) the country is currently the world's leading producer of palm-oil, rubber, cocoa, and pepper. By 1985 about 36 per cent of the labour force were still employed in agricultural production.

More fundamentally relevant here is the fact that the politically dominant ethnic Malays who form just under half of the country's 16.5 million inhabitants constitute the majority (67 per cent) of the rural population. In contrast, the more urbanized Chinese and Indians, who constitute 33 per cent and 12 per cent of the total population, comprise respectively only 23 per cent and 10 per cent of total rural inhabitants. The greater weight of rural votes contributed to the government's assigning top priority to rural development so as to maintain long-term stability.[1] One major strategy of rural development is to create land schemes involving the movements of groups of people into newly opened and previously uncultivated areas.

The case chosen for this study refers to the land schemes managed by the Federal Land Development Authority (FELDA) in Malaysia, which until 1987 had claimed 754,500 hectares from virgin jungle land to settle by July 1987 94,168 landless rural families in about 371 land schemes. FELDA was established on 1 July 1956 as a federal statutory body under Land Development Ordinance No. 20 and administered by a board responsible to the Minister of Land and Regional Development. The reason for choosing this huge enterprise for study is that it is the only case of participatory management in the country that affects a substantial proportion of the population, that is, about 20 per cent of Malaysia's total population of smallholders. It is also conceivable that this particular form of productive organization applied to smallholdings will have wide-ranging consequences if it is translated into general policy. As increasingly large numbers of small farms are incorporated into one form or another of government-managed farms, the cumulative effect of this type of alternative organization may actually help to democratize the country's political process.

As a rough indication of the scale of FELDA's land schemes, their output in relation to the national total is shown in Table 22.1.

[1] It was hoped that by conceding over-representation to the rural voter (ratio of weight shifts as and when it suits the ruling party) rural interests would not be neglected. But, due to spatial concentration of different ethnic groups, this system has been manipulated to the advantage of the Malay component of the ruling party, which holds a two-thirds majority in Parliament.

Table 22.1   Economic significance of FELDA land schemes

Crop	FELDA	Producers Smallholders	Estates	Other state agencies	Total
Rubber (%) (planted hectares) (1984)	11	74	5	10	100
Palm-oil (%) (hectares) (1985)	30	7	51	12	100

A typical scheme comprises about 2,000 hectares of plantation land with enough additional land to accommodate about 400–500 settler families. Each settler is allocated about four hectares of agricultural land and 0.1 hectare for a house lot and for food crops. Settlers are moved in after about three to four years from the time the land has been cleared and planted (by private contractors) with either rubber or oil palms. Settlers are also advanced a subsidy until the trees reach maturity. After five to six years (depending on the crop—five years for palm oil and six years for rubber) settlers are expected to begin repayment to FELDA for capital and management services costs at an interest rate of 6 per cent. After some fifteen years, ownership will be transferred to individual settlers who in most instances are the male heads of households. The scheme is managed as a single entity to ensure the technical efficiency of a large agricultural operation. About 60 per cent of the families are settled in palm-oil schemes and 40 per cent in rubber schemes.

The main objective of FELDA is to improve the living conditions of landless peasants by using modern agricultural techniques and management methods so that, with practice and guidance, peasants can be turned into independent and progressive farmers capable of managing their own affairs. In fact, during the early days of its establishment in 1956 (just prior to Independence in 1957) the spirit of nationalism was strong enough even to suggest that one day these land schemes could be turned over to settlers for total self-administration. Nowadays, this goal is never mentioned at all. Even then, FELDA set about establishing an appropriate administrative and production organization to achieve these lofty aims.

The work group

The most elementary organizational unit in FELDA schemes is that of the block comprising 20–4 families. Families can group themselves based on spontaneous choice, such as religious singing (of Koranic verses) groups, and elect their own block leader. The election of block leaders is held once a year but if block members so desire, they can re-elect another leader if they feel strongly dissatisfied with the conduct of existing leaders. Since block members are most likely to live in close association with one another this seldom happens, as members have intimate knowledge of the leader before they elect him.

The block functions primarily as a work group for the settlers. Under an elected leader and his assistant, members of the block collectively work the land which was individually allotted. All proceeds are then divided up equally among members. The leader and his assistant, who spend most of their time co–ordinating production and marketing the produce, do not have to do their share of planting, harvesting, and maintenance, which will be done by the group. But if these administrators can carry out their production duties in addition to their administrative duties, they will be paid a fixed sum.

The scheme development committee (JKKR)

To encourage democratic participation at every level of administration and management, all settlers automatically belong to the scheme development committee (JKKR) which meets monthly to discuss implementation of policies directed from FELDA headquarters and current problems that arise during the course of work or from community living. Executive committee (Exco) members of the JKKR are elected regularly at the Annual General Meeting for the purpose of allocating various posts to block leaders who qualify to sit on the Exco (see Table 22.2). The JKKR implements its decisions via four bureaux (education and training, social, plantation, and economic), which are in fact sub-committees headed by Exco members of the JKKR. Excos of the JKKR hold their monthly meetings just before that of the main JKKR body.

Table 22.2 Exco of the JKKR

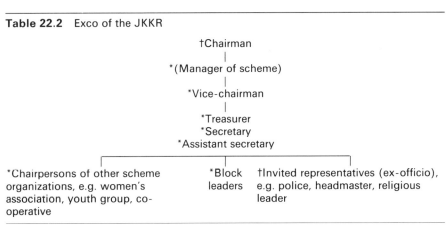

†Chairman
|
*(Manager of scheme)
|
*Vice-chairman
|
*Treasurer
*Secretary
*Assistant secretary

*Chairpersons of other scheme organizations, e.g. women's association, youth group, co-operative

*Block leaders

†Invited representatives (ex-officio), e.g. police, headmaster, religious leader

*Settler representatives
†State representatives

The JKKR was set up primarily to provide settlers with experience and training in the administration and management of the schemes. It was also hoped that the regular joint monthly discussions would facilitate acquisition of problem-solving skills. Because of the automatic membership of settlers, the JKKR would also ensure at least a minimum level of democratic participation by settlers in the running of schemes.

Regional JKKR and the national council

If problems cannot be resolved at the level of the scheme JKKR, they can be referred to the next higher level, the regional JKKR, which constitutes the joint JKKR of schemes grouped under one geographical region. As with the scheme JKKR, which is headed by a technocrat (the scheme manager), the regional JKKR is chaired by a government technocrat (see Table 22.3).

Table 22.3 Participatory scheme

National council
(settler representatives and State technocrats)
|
*Joint regional JKKR
(headed by State technocrat)
|
*Scheme JKKR
(chaired by State)
|
*4 bureaux per scheme
|
*Work groups
|
Individual settlers

---

*Majority representation by settlers

Similarly, issues found to be contentious will be referred to the next highest representative body, the national council of JKKRs which meets once every three months and is made up of both settler representatives and high-level FELDA administrators such as the Director-General of FELDA and his assistant, all regional supervisors and all directors of operations. Settler representatives hold the positions of vice-chairman and assistant secretary of the respective regional JKKRs.

Participatory democracy

Assessment of case-model

At first glance, it appears that the layered structure of decision making (as portrayed in Table 22.3) with settler representation at every level would go far in providing for democratic representation for scheme members, but various factors contribute to frustrating the democratic goals originally promulgated. Not all decisions made by the various committees are binding. FELDA has the final say in that it can veto any decision not to its liking. Fundamental decisions involving choice of crop, work schedule, and form of ownership are handed down from headquarters located in the capital, Kuala Lumpur, whereas the schemes are scattered thousands of miles all over the country. Even the nomination lists for block leaders have to be passed by FELDA prior to election time.

When in 1981 FELDA proposed to change the system of privately held individual plantation land ownership (as opposed to house plot ownership) to that of the share system based on collectively owned land, about 95 per cent of the settlers opposed it. A compromise had to be thought out. But after a widespread show of settler resistance, introduction of the share system was postponed and could only be introduced in January 1985, and even that was limited to new schemes. Up to the end of 1985, 2,878 members had been placed under the share system of ownership.

The old land schemes continued with the existing system of private individual ownership with the result that, after settling their debts to FELDA, some settlers began opting out of the scheme, saying that they wanted to be independent. Since this had just happened recently the Chief Minister of one state warned that the legal implications of the problem were still under scrutiny (the question was whether it was legal for settlers to withdraw their land from the scheme management as they did actually own it and hold legal title to it). He continued that this was an unhealthy trend and should not be allowed 'to spread to the other schemes' (*Berita Harian*, 18 Mar. 1987).

From the above example, it can be said that, though the final veto lies with FELDA, members can still struggle successfully for consideration of their own views. But one can be sure that any compromise or susceptibility on the part of the authorities to give in to settler demands cannot be said to stem directly from the system of formal representation. The resistance shown by massive numbers of settlers and the nature of this resistance are the primary forces responsible for initiating changes or defending against encroachment by FELDA officers. Often, mass dissatisfaction has erupted in the form of violent behaviour such as burning officers' cars, holding officers captive, and even, in extreme cases, murder. At other times, settlers have opted to side with opposition parties and 'deviant' religious organizations ('deviant' only because they are not approved by the State). To avoid having their income deducted by FELDA for loan repayment, it is common for settlers to sell their produce (on the sly) to private agents and not through officially appointed agents even though this is against FELDA rules. This practice was so common at one time and so threatened the flow of repayment of FELDA loans that the FELDA security force was expanded to reduce the occurrence of such offences. To show their serious disapproval, FELDA has in the past taken settlers to court for 'illegal' sale of their produce as this comprises a breach of the contract signed between FELDA and the settlers.

In fact, settlers in one state even set up their own association, which managed to obtain registration from the Registrar of Societies even though it failed to gain recognition from FELDA authorities. The political force represented by such a large number of settlers had, therefore, been put to good use for the achievement of goals denied them by the formal structures set up by FELDA. Because of their political strength, FELDA settlers have become not only the target recruiting ground for various lobby groups such as the opposition parties and the smallholders' associations, but also for the warring factions within the ruling political party (*Star*, 5 Aug. 1981).

It would therefore appear that external political considerations are much more responsible for building up the settlers' strength and bargaining powers than the formal structures of representation set up by the authorities within the land schemes. However, it should be pointed out that these external political considerations could have become crucial and effective in strengthening the hands of the settlers only because the State had gathered together under the modern system of farming and management such large numbers of peasants and placed them under rather homogeneous living conditions and production organization. It was also crucial that producers were not only working together but also living in close proximity. This certainly was fundamental to the enhancement of feelings of solidarity and the development of a strong sense of identity. Ethnic and religious homogeneity (95 per cent of settlers are Malays who are mainly Muslims) further reinforces their sense of solidarity.

It cannot be denied that the FELDA system of production organization and representational structure has provided ample opportunities for training and practice in problem solving and organization of settlers. The confidence generated has certainly contributed towards successful mobilization and organization of settlers by using informal channels to achieve their claims and to resist any encroachment from FELDA authorities. So even when decisions made by the various levels of JKKR are not binding, having the JKKR is itself useful for achieving the aims of members by employing means outside the JKKR structure.

This rather subtle and complicated effect of the JKKR is reflected in the somewhat ambivalent feelings settlers have towards it. When asked if FELDA is playing its role according to the wishes of settlers, 70 per cent said 'yes' while 30 per cent dissented. The size of the dissenting group can be said to be substantial. Their view is that, since all decisions have to be passed by FELDA, how can FELDA have any consideration at all for the views of settlers? Decisions are passed only when it suits the needs of FELDA and its officers.

Even those who initially agree with FELDA's handling of the scheme affairs do not agree that FELDA should continue to dominate the administration of the scheme. Asked the question whether the JKKR could independently and effectively run the schemes without interference from FELDA, 71 per cent of this group suggested that settlers should give it a try, otherwise they would never know if they could independently manage their own scheme. The other 29 per cent were not so sure that the JKKR could be relied upon to run the schemes successfully without any guidance from FELDA. This is because settlers recognize the importance of FELDA guidance, especially in terms of production and marketing of their produce.

Since the JKKR had to refer all decisions and projects to FELDA, their impotence has given rise to conflict with the people they represent, frequently resulting in their alienation. To show the extent of disrespect for the JKKR some settlers even go straight to scheme managers about their problems rather than have them channelled through the JKKR. In fact, less than half (43 per cent) of the settlers are active in the JKKR. Some only contribute in the form of monthly fees they have to pay to finance the JKKR. Some blame this state of affairs on the over concentration of power in a small group of representatives. The more balanced picture is that of disillusionment about time and old age. Block leaders observe that few are healthy or willing enough to give up their time and energy actively to run the affairs of the JKKR. Settlers feel that after two decades there should be an attempt to nurture a second generation of leaders since the original settlers have now reached the age where they cannot do much heavy work. Children of settlers are not qualified to be members of the JKKR as they are not signatories to the contract with FELDA. This in turn disqualifies them from holding important posts on the Exco. Actually, being more educated than their parents (an indication of FELDA's economic success), the younger generation prefer to take up white-collar jobs outside the schemes. In the early days, any call for voluntary labour for community work (such as cleaning the mosque or building security check-points) could successfully draw the mass support needed. Now, it is a problem to raise even half the labour required for a community job. It is therefore not difficult to understand why the same few faces are block leaders, Exco members, or representatives on the regional JKKR. The structure of representation itself may also have contributed to the concentration of representation as only block leaders are qualified to sit as Exco members, and, likewise, settler representation at the regional JKKR is only drawn from the Exco of the scheme JKKR.

However, what settlers want is not total withdrawal from FELDA supervision but a less authoritarian regime. Maybe FELDA could begin by reducing the long list of fines imposed when settlers commit small deviations (Table 22.4 shows the list of fines levied for various petty offences related to work). FELDA could also be more lenient and place less control on alternative 'unapproved' religious activities and not victimize supporters of opposition parties. Settlers want the Government to amend certain clauses in the FELDA Act pertaining to expulsion. This has been used perennially as a threat to any settler who dares to criticize FELDA or the Government. Since its inception, FELDA has forced out 5,000 settlers for committing various offences. After two decades of tutelage, attending seminars and various training programmes, settlers feel it is about time FELDA showed some trust and confidence in the JKKR by giving them more opportunities to make independent decisions.

Even while settlers enjoy berating the JKKR, the latter has actually taken on a symbolic value, representing to settlers their status as independent smallholders and not as wage-workers. So, despite their many criticisms, not all respondents want the JKKR to be abolished. To them, the JKKR is a symbol of their independent status as freeholders. Settler representatives on the Exco, unlike the officers, are also farmers and live among them. Therefore, they can argue with them or quarrel with them when in disagreement. This is based on the expectation that these representatives understand the condition of settlers. The representatives are also uneducated like themselves, so there is no need to sit in fear of them. But there is no room for negotiation with FELDA officers because they can just pull out their book of laws and regulations, thus defeating arguments against them. Yet, a large proportion (88 per cent) do not want to leave the scheme, while only 6 per cent said they are not sure—for they may even be kicked out by FELDA. The other 6 per cent wish to leave soon.

Furthermore, as settlers observed, the number of officers employed in each scheme is not large, usually less than twenty. And, more often than not, this number will be further reduced as the schemes mature and establish their own pattern of decision making and routine organization. In fact, the number of officers is often reduced by half. How can a scheme be run by such a small number of officers and how can they cater to the needs of a few hundred settlers? This is a big problem as a large number of settlers (about half) are illiterate, with the rest having only a few years of primary education.

Finally, according to settlers, abolition of the JKKR will make them appear to be mere wage-labourers on their own farms. Settlers definitely prefer to have the JKKR with all its defects rather than turn their land schemes into some form of private sector plantation employing wage-workers who have no representation at all at any level of management. With the JKKR, settlers feel that at least they are represented by one of themselves, a neighbour of the same status.

Perhaps more striking is FELDA's economic performance. The 1985 *Annual Report* released to Parliament in 1986 discloses some very impressive figures. Capital investments in FELDA corporations, companies, joint-ventures, and settler co-operatives totalled $US110.8 million, of which 69 per cent represent settlers' investments (via monthly deductions from settlers' income). Settlers own 13 per cent of FELDA Corporation (the group) through their co operative, which was initiated by FELDA. (But there is no intention of turning the scheme into a co-operative as this would mean a loss of control for FELDA.) Combined income of the group amounted to $US754.4 million for the same period. Net profit was $US21 million, representing a drop of 28 per cent from that registered for 1984.

Average income for oil-palm settlers for 1985 was $US342 and for rubber schemes income averaged $US162. Rural poverty income level is currently set by

Table 22.4 Fines levied for work negligence

Item of work	Fine/unit ($US)
Failure to weed	
1. around tree trunk	0.19/tree
2. space between trees	0.19/tree
Failure to trim fronds of oil palms	0.19/tree
Failure to trim fronds overhanging roads	1.90/lot
Failure to harvest palm-fruits	0.58/cluster
Premature harvesting	19.00/cluster
Failure to collect scattered fruits	0.19/tree
Failure to apply fertilizer (forgetfulness, carelessness)	0.77/tree
Intentional failure to fertilize trees (indicating rebelliousness)	1.9/branch
Selling of subsidized fertilizers	0.38/lb.
Failure to apply pesticide	0.19/tree

the Government at $US135 per month. On average, the FELDA settler enjoys an income level that is 143 per cent of the average Malay household.

However, the agreement signed between FELDA and the settlers gave FELDA the power to deduct money from settlers' income (from sale of produce made through FELDA's corporations) without written permission from them. Currently, deductions are made for sixteen types of payment including that for meeting loans for purchase of fertilizers, land development, transportation costs, road maintenance, land insurance, and for many social activities. After these monthly deductions have been made, many settlers end up with only the pay-sheet and no money. Settlers have complained that the fertilizers given them (for which deductions have been made) have been found by the local agricultural university to be most unsuitable for their crops. Other items of payment, such as maintenance of roads, should have been borne by the Government instead. Monthly fees are even deducted for membership of the ruling party of which the settlers have no knowledge at all. As a result, settlers feel very confused about the deductions, especially when they are not set out in detail on the pay-sheets. Worst of all, settlers do not know when the deductions will stop or if they will ever stop. With the current pressure of low commodity prices, when income invariably falls below the level of deductions, only 79 per cent of settlers in oil-palm estates can afford to continue their monthly payments compared with 94 per cent in 1984 when income was 28 per cent higher.

Compared to independent smallholders, more settlers in FELDA schemes knew the types of planting materials used and what fertilizers were recommended (Sepien, 1979). However, like smallholders, settlers too were found to have scant knowledge of rubber diseases, their symptoms, effects, and treatment. For instance, FELDA settlers could not differentiate the tretment of root diseases from that of mouldy rot, a disease occurring at the tapping panel. This indicates that

FELDA's management, like that of the commercial plantation, is more concerned with ordering the settlers about to secure job and production quotas regardless of whether or not settlers understand why a certain activity has to be carried out. One result of ignoring the scientific education of settlers is that the cultivator, who actually does the work, is not encouraged to be concerned with improving on existing practices and making innovations, leaving the task of conceptualization to intellectuals working in research stations far removed from the world of production. This presumably explains why, though Malaysia today is at the forefront of rubber and oil-palm research, this is confined mainly to aspects related to biological growth. But, where the labour process is concerned, methods of harvesting oil-palm fruits and tapping rubber-tree latex have remained at the same primitive level as that of the colonial period. Finally, emphasis on short-term production goals can probably be represented as an additional factor contributing to settler alienation and, consequently, further jeopardizing the long term goal of community stability.

Conclusions

Observations from the model of participation discussed go to show that producer participation certainly contributes to improved performance. In organizing landless peasants to work under a modern system of management and methods of production, FELDA has successfully upgraded the productivity of Malaysia's rural producers, who are still essentially freeholders. Currently, the productivity level of unorganized smallholders averages about 1,100 kg of rubber per hectare, while that of the commercial estates is 1,700 kg. The productivity level of FELDA-organized settlers is 1,500 kg, so that the level of FELDA schemes can be said to be nearly on par with that of the commercial estates. Due to the participatory mode of production, FELDA saves on the wages of supervisors as settlers themselves ensure that each block member contributes his share of labour. In addition, since efforts made by work group members are closely associated with income attained, members are motivated to give their best as they themselves will enjoy the fruits of their labour. Linking income to effort still brings good results, though, on the whole the price of their produce is determined by forces outside of their control, that is, by the international commodity market. Economically, the scheme has attained success to a certain extent. The majority of settlers (75 per cent) observed that their situation of life had improved greatly compared to the time before they joined the scheme. Only 7 per cent felt their standard of living had deteriorated while 18 per cent said there was not much difference. Considering that their income is so closely linked to international conditions and the consequence that about half of them had had to take on part-time work when prices dipped to new lows, these views are a good reflection of the economic performance of FELDA.

However, analysis of the political impact of this participation model does not give a straightforward or simple answer, since the unsatisfactory level of participation (taking into consideration the final veto held by FELDA), combined with outside political considerations, has given rise to even more powerful effects than those directly provided for by the formal structure of participation.

First, the formal structure has provided for the settlers to be physically congregated into one community, working and living together under rather homogeneous conditions. As a result, a sense of identity and solidarity has developed, very much reinforced by daily confrontation and struggle with FELDA representatives. Secondly, the system of participation, despite its defects, has no doubt provided many opportunities for learning and practice in problem analysis and thinking up suitable solutions. Still, it is hard not to be struck by how settlers have astutely used their store of accumulated knowledge in approaching outside elements and striking up alliances with oppositional interests to put pressure on the Government to give in to their demands. Finally, if for any reason members needed to be mobilized, the condition of close proximity would certainly facilitate and accelerate any organizational effort. All in all, the interaction of these many factors has greatly enhanced the political force of settlers, a situation which surely could not have been foreseen by the authorities when the model of participation was first mooted. With the help of the National Association of Smallholders, settlers have begun to campaign to replace FELDA with a co-operative controlled by smallholders (*Star*: 10 Aug. 1987).

References

Annual Report (1985), FELDA (Kuala Lumpur).
Berita Harian (1987), 'CM Regrets 29 Settlers Want to Leave Felda' (18 Mar.).
MacInnes, J. (1985), 'Conjuring up Consultation', *British Journal of Industrial Relations*, 23(1).
Sepien, A. (1979), 'Effects of Some Management Proxies and Sociological Factors on Productivity of Rubber Smallholdings in Malaysia', *Southeast Asian Studies*, 17(1).
Star (1987), '50 UMNO Members Join DAP' (5 Aug.). (UMNO = dominant ethnic Malay ruling party, DAP = opposition multiracial party comprising mainly Chinese members.)
——— (1987), 'Scrap Felda, Say Smallholders' (10 Aug.)
——— (1987), 'Settler: We Support "Scrap Felda" Move' (10 Aug.)

Concluding Reflections
Organizational Democracy: Taking Stock

CORNELIS J. LAMMERS AND GYÖRGY SZÉLL

IN our introduction to this volume we wondered what changes in organizational democracy had taken place over the last decades. In these concluding reflections, we will try to answer that question on the basis of the material contained in the foregoing chapters. The authors pay attention to developments which have affected the vicissitudes of various forms of participation, co-determination, and self-management in recent years. Thus, their analyses can be used for another look at the hypotheses we formulated in our introduction more than a year ago concerning the role of different forces with respect to the fate of organizational democracy. Finally, we propose to evaluate the main conclusions with an eye to the future.

Changes in the level and/or pattern of organizational democracy

As will be obvious from the tone of our introduction, we expected to find a reversal since the late 1970s of the processes of democratization that originated in the 1960s. However, in the contributions to this volume we encountered hardly any evidence of an overall tendency towards the breaking down of the democratizing process in Western work organizations. On the contrary, several authors observe that some forms of participation or co-determination have spread further or gained in strength.

Lawler (Ch. 7) notes that participative management was more preached than practiced in the USA before 1980, but has become much more a reality in many American firms in recent years. Strauss (Ch. 18), reporting on the unionized sector of US industry, also discerns a certain diffusion of participation closely linked to concession bargaining. And Russell (Ch. 4), in his survey of the effects of Employee Stock Ownership Plans (ESOPs) on organizational democracy, estimates that in about a quarter of the firms with ESOP arrangements, employees experienced a moderate increase in participation.

In France we notice a similar trend. Bernoux (Ch. 19) describes how experimentation with new forms of work organization sprang up in the decade after 1969 and was later succeeded by a wave of Japanese-style Quality Circles. Furthermore, new legislation (the Auroux Laws of 1982) instigated a series of measures to stimulate group shop-floor consultation sponsored by employers and unions. Tixier (Ch. 2) discusses the predicaments for unions when participative management becomes the dominant style of management.

Borzeix and Linhart (Ch. 11), however, are rather sceptical. They warn that perhaps the demeanour of the French *patronat* might not really have changed as much as the set of criteria applied by sociological researchers who monitor the theatre of French industrial relations. In other words, the move towards more participation may be in the eye of the beholder! We will come back to this intriguing problem later on, but assume for the present that in France, as in the USA, organizational democracy, if not on the move, is at least not on the wane.

The contributions on the Federal Republic of Germany (FRG) allow us to make some cautious inferences pertaining to the current state of co-determination (*Mitbestimmung*). Hildebrandt (Ch. 15) gives us some results of research bearing on the dilemmas German works councillors face when they try to cope with the complex processes of introducing Computer-Aided Production Planning and Control Systems. Schmidt and Trinczek (Ch. 21) describe how works councils in the metal-working industry handle collective bargaining about working arrangements which have been devolved to the level of the firm; a novel experience for Germany.

In both cases the works council in the FRG is portrayed as a viable institution which, although beset by new exigencies, holds its ground fairly well. This tentative conclusion is to some extent corroborated by Kissler's review of co-determination research (Ch. 6). The author examines the shifting emphases and approaches of social scientists investigating the effectiveness of the system of *Mitbestimmung* since the Second World War. But, as a by-product of his research on the history of co-determination, Kissler also informs us of the outcome of a great number of studies reflecting the functioning of works councils (and other provisions of the system of *Mitbestimmung*) in different eras. If one goes by these findings, one can hardly escape the impression that co-determination in Germany over the decades has proved itself to be quite a vigorous and adaptable institution, generally accepted—by the public, the main political parties, and the principal associations of employers and workers—as part of the German industrial way of life.

Turning now to the situation in some of the smaller countries of north-western Europe, we first look at developments in Norway. Premier Brundtland and her escort in this venture, Qvale (Chs. 8 and 9), strike a rather optimistic note about the development of industrial democracy there. Sustained co-operation between the major associations of business and industry on the one hand, and of labour on the other, were and are active in this field under the auspices of the Government. These joint efforts led first of all to the introduction of employee representatives in supervisory boards (1973), later to work environment reforms (1976), and now to the launching of a new programme to broaden the scope of employee participation and to an improved utilization of human resources. Over the years this Scandinavian industrial democracy programme has been inspired by a group of social scientists who were also responsible for a number of practical experiments, advisory projects, and training programmes.

Looise (Ch. 20) presents research findings which demonstrate an extensive diffusion of works councils and similar representative bodies in The Netherlands over the past ten to fifteen years, from large to small firms, and from industry and commerce to sectors like education, health, and welfare. Furthermore, by using comparative data, he shows that on average works councils are a bit more influential at present than they were ten years ago. None the less, in the eyes of both managers and members of such bodies, works councils—even if nowadays in a somewhat stronger position than in the past—still do not carry much weight. Only with respect to social and personnel affairs do about half of all Dutch works councils have a more or less substantial say. In all other areas of management (financial–economic, commercial, production–technical, and organization) the powers of this institution are, according to players of the representative game themselves, at most 'moderate'.

So much for the inventory of information in recent trends in North America and Western and Central Europe. With respect to Eastern Europe, our volume has only one contribution, by Meier (Ch. 16). This account of the implementation of new technologies in firms in the German Democratic Republic (GDR) indicates that several forms of participation are being tried out there and that at present there are tendencies to extend and strengthen such initiatives. Of course it is hard to know how widespread such efforts at liberalizing the regime of work organizations are in Eastern Europe. None the less, the fact that similar developments have also recently been reported from other quarters in the Eastern bloc (notably Hungary, see e.g. Gustavsen and Héthy, 1986), in all probability means that some progress in this direction is being made, or at least that the authorities in the countries in question find it desirable to promote such initiatives. Either case can be seen as a hopeful sign that the 'cause' of organizational democracy in Eastern Europe is not dead.

Up to now we have only talked about events in conventional, hierarchical organizations. What about developments in democratically constituted organizations? Cornforth (Ch. 3), surveying the research literature on this topic, finds no growing trend in the USA and the UK but a cyclical pattern in the formation of worker co-operatives. While in the early 1970s new ventures of this sort were established primarily to explore more egalitarian ways of living and working together, in the less affluent 1980s co-operatives have been set up mainly to protect employment or to stave off unemployment.

This brings us to the issue raised in our introduction. Does organizational democratization conform to an *evolutionary* or a *cyclical* pattern? What strikes one about the cyclical nature of the emergence of co-operatives, as portrayed by Cornforth, is that the waves do overlap to a considerable extent and differ in character. In other words, the upsurge of the 'next' cycle of co-operatives does not gain momentum after the total eclipse of the preceding one, but coincides with the levelling off, or the gradual decline, of the former wave. Furthermore, the second set of initiatives to realize some sort of co-operative is not simply a replica of the first one, but is guided by other principles or imbued with another spirit.

Interestingly enough, these two features of a peculiar kind of cyclical pattern come to the fore in various other chapters in this collection as well. Looise (Ch. 20) is most articulate about the shape of this process and likens it to a 'stairway', thereby indicating that in his view the trend underlying the cycles represents a discontinuous progress in the direction of more mature forms of organizational democracy. Other authors do not detect a positive long-term 'slope' trend, but a relatively constant 'ground swell' beneath the successive 'waves'. However, since the slope of a trend is hard to measure, and since none of the authors makes a serious effort to do so, we will leave the question of progress aside and content ourselves with the supposition that in modern Western society there may be a relatively constant, or slightly expanding, volume of effort to maintain or renew existing forms of participation, co-determination, or self-management in organizations.

So much for the ground swell; as to the waves, a number of authors allude to a sequence of fashions or types of organizational democracy. In addition to Looise's 'stairway' model from The Netherlands, waves or fashions can be discerned in Bernoux's chapter (19) on France, Qvale and Brundtland on Norway (Ch. 8 and 9), Strauss on the USA (Ch. 18), and Kissler on the FRG (Ch. 6). In all these cases, while the styles of participation à la mode in one period do not disappear in the next one, the limelight shifts to new styles, which then become 'the thing to do'.

Of course, from a strictly scientific point of view, one cannot legitimately generalize from our necessarily limited collection of studies. Nevertheless, until we encounter other evidence, it can do no harm to hypothesize that in most Western societies during the last decade:

- there was no downward trend in organizational democracy initiatives;
- there were definite shifts in opportunities and preferences for specific varieties of participation, co-determination, or self-management.

Proceeding from this analysis, we will now direct our attention to the developments that might have brought about the relative stability in the general level of organizational democracy and the changes in its manifestations.

Developments relevant to continuity and change in organizational democracy

Economic recession

In our introduction we argued that the economic recession and weakening of many trade unions could have led to reduced support for participatory projects and for the functioning of co-determination. However, our contributors do not subscribe to such sombre forebodings.

Apparently the downward trend of the business cycle, often accompanied by the loss of union power, brought about only a comparatively slight set-back to the course of direct and indirect participation, or even had the effect of stimulating such ventures! Perhaps the fact that unions lost strength favoured the decentralization of certain types of collective bargaining so that representative bodies saw their scope of activity enhanced. No doubt, particularly in the case of large companies, managers welcomed the opportunity of freeing themselves from 'outside interference' and happily switched over from professional union negotiators to presumably more malleable representatives coming from their own work-force. At the same time, one may take it that quite a few unions, having to cope with more work and less staff, had no choice but to leave the task of defending firm-specific matters to their active members on the scene.

Moreover, the necessity of improving competitiveness and flexibility may have motivated managements not only to reduce their 'primary' work-force, but also to try to utilize the human resources of their regular employees more intensely by involving them in decision making.

Organizational leaders, certainly in continental Europe, also frequently attempt to legitimize and further such efforts to mobilize their employees by enlisting the co-operation of representative bodies for the projects in question. In other words, because of the hard times falling on organized labour, the unions may have withdrawn some support for schemes for direct and/or indirect participation, but in doing so, may at the same time have released and facilitated initiatives of this sort on the part of management.

Up to now we have grounded our argument on the assumption that on the whole unions tend to back efforts to realize organizational democracy. Of course, this was—and is—not always the case. Union leadership may fear that strongholds of direct or indirect participation may be hard to control, that their militants might be diverted from union goals to alternative avenues of activism, or that employers might get a chance to play off such 'home oppositions' against the unions.

Now, to the extent that unions discourage or oppose the establishment of organizational democracy in one form or another, a decline of union power will imply *ceteris paribus* less resistance to participation experiments and to the invigoration of regular institutions for representation of employee interests at the level of the firm.

Therefore we arrive at the conclusion that the end of economic growth in the West, in spite of, or due to, a decreased level of union activity in this sphere, did not cause a reversal of forms or processes of organizational democracy. What about other than economic developments?

Technological innovation

From several contributions in this book—by Bernoux (Ch. 19), Hildebrandt (Ch. 15), Schmidt and Trinczek (Ch. 21), and Looise (Ch. 20) we gather that the noted boost for participation, which at least counteracted any possible negative effects of the recession, is probably a function of the interaction of economic with technological and/or legislative developments. If today we experience a technological 'explosion', that is to say a series of 'developments along a number of different lines' (Gustavsen and Héthy, 1986: 172), this would certainly increase the chances that even in one and the same sector of industry in one country, organizations encountered quite different problems. Given the varying nature of the complexities, different firms then have to sort out and deal with problems as they see fit on the spot. Consequently, such forms of employee participation as those involving highly skilled technologists[1] and decentralized bargaining at the level of individual firms could very well be the result of the simultaneous occurrence of economic and technological changes.

New legislation

The role of the legislator in enabling certain groups of workers or works councils to avail themselves of new opportunities to promote their interests and/or express their views on the work in, and the policies of, their firms comes to the fore in chapters on France (Bernoux, Ch. 19), The Netherlands (Looise, Ch. 20), and Norway (Qvale and Brundtland, Chs. 8 and 9). In all three cases new or additional provisions were enacted bestowing on those willing and able to have a say in decisions regarding their work, work environment, or the organization in which they are employed, the rights to do so.

Besides extending the range of possibilities for participation, such measures often confer a certain leverage on representative bodies. As Teulings (1987) has shown in the case of The Netherlands, if a works council has the formal right to halt or reverse certain processes of managerial decision making, this implies added means of power for such an organ. Therefore, it seems a reasonable supposition that a certain amplification of legal arrangements for organizational democracy will be effective, especially where firm-specific issues arise in connection with technological innovations or market changes.

Cultural change

As pointed out before, legislation of the kind just discussed frequently originated in the early 1970s and had more to do with the socio-cultural and political climate of those days than with the mood current in the 1980s. However that may be, if values and norms have changed during the past decade so as to favour a reduction in democratization, the question must be asked if, and in what ways, shifts in cultural orientation have affected the course of organizational democracy.

If macrodevelopments over the last decade have not resulted in a reversal of the ground swell of participation, but have had an impact on the nature of successive

---

[1] Called 'end user participation' in Ch. 15 by Hildebrandt and 'users' participation' by Meier (Ch. 16). See also n. 4 in this chapter.

waves, then we must apparently look at these waves for evidence of the influence of cultural changes. Now, we do indeed think that varieties of organizational democracy propagated recently, and the ways in which such ventures are being presented and perceived, bear the stamp of current cultural preferences.

Many years ago one of us distinguished between *structural* and *functional* views of democratization (Lammers, 1973). In the latter case direct or indirect participation is recommended as a means towards efficiency and/or effectiveness. In the former conception, however, democracy is heralded as an end in itself, so that 'structural democratization' means power equalization. Now, obviously, most instances of participation in the reports in this book exemplify the functional rather than the structural view of democratization. If managers want to improve the utilization of their human resources by means of participatory projects, and if they attempt to stimulate and legitimize such efforts by involving works councils in their policies, then organizational democracy, in whatever guise, is seen as a means of furthering efficiency or effectiveness. If employees, their representatives, and unionists co-sponsor such efforts and set out to make a success of them, one may take it that they do so primarily to protect job security, to maintain or improve their working conditions, etc.

In other words, we cannot escape the impression that in the 1980s forms and processes of participation are in the vast majority of cases presented, set up, and evaluated as functional programmes and practices. In the 1970s, however, a fair number of experiments to enhance the 'quality of working life', to further the 'humanization of work', or to democratize systems of organizational governance, were—more often than now—couched in terms of lofty ideals like self-actualization of the employee, workplace democracy, etc. One is led to believe that those who advocated and initiated such reorganizations and projects, or participated therein, regularly paid not just lip-service to such ideals, but actually saw their efforts in the light of these values.

Of course, we should take to heart the advice by Bolle de Bal (Ch. 1) and not confuse the (imputed) 'theoretical' with the 'real' functions. In all likelihood, ventures to establish more egalitarian or more humanitarian forms of organization more often than not meant different things to different people and may have done more good (or harm!) to efficiency and effectiveness rather than bringing nearer the realization of the democratic ideal.

Nevertheless, the wave of rather idealistic attempts at democratization which came into being in the late 1960s gradually subsided and in our estimation was replaced by a new wave of moves to establish and extend participatory forms of organization on a different, more pragmatic footing. Even in the case of production co-operatives (as described by Cornforth, Ch. 3) something of a similar change in 'models' comes to the fore. One will remember that, according to this author, fifteen to twenty years ago such co-operatives were started to provide a democratic alternative to the customary, hierarchical set-up of work organizations. This design, naturally, exhibits the hallmarks of a structural type of undertaking, whereas the model co-operative of recent years—established to secure employment—definitely smacks of the functional type of democratization. Very much the same pair of contrasting types of co-operative enterprise is described in Chapter 13 by Gherardi, Strati, and Turner. In a study of Italian co-operative enterprises they discovered some collectives with a 'foundational' culture and others with a 'coalition' culture, again representing the structural and the functional views of democratization.[2]

Let us round off this discussion of cultural influences by observing that the degree of freedom to experiment with structural democratization is limited anyway and anywhere, but especially in business enterprises and in public authorities. In other sectors (not covered in this volume)—for example universities, churches, voluntary associations, communication agencies, health and welfare organizations—a number of rather radical forms of organizational democracy were introduced around the end of the 1960s. Later on, when the value-climate changed, a backlash set in and reversed the democratization process. This may have resulted in a much heavier toll of discontinued or 'restructured' experiments in participatory democracy and self-management in these spheres than in the core sectors of society.

However that may be, we want to point out that certain classes of organization may be more susceptible to cultural fashions in participation than others. Furthermore, it goes without saying that to characterize the transitions from one 'mix' of types of democratization in the 1970s to another 'mix' in the 1980s in terms of structural versus functional models only is far from satisfactory. Closer scrutiny would probably reveal quite interesting and more subtle differences between sectors and also between nations, in the nature of variations over time of the dominant models and shining examples of organizational democracy.

Summary: an explanatory model of democratization in organizations

Thus far in this chapter we have looked at economic, technological, legislative, and cultural macro-developments to understand and explain continuity and change in patterns of organizational democracy. Fig. 23.1 already used by Looise in his contribution (Ch. 20) helps to clarify the way in which the forces in question operate.

Legislation or other formal arrangements, in themselves the outcome of economic, political, and cultural factors (arrow A), can bring about processes of participation, co-determination, or self-management (arrow 1). However, actions

---

[2] Both types of co-operative were formed in the 1980s. Such a coexistence of varieties reminds us of the fact that a difference between waves does not imply that in one period all ventures in organizational democracy are of this kind, while in an earlier or later period they are all of a different kind. As said before, changes in form or style have to do with altered preferences and changes in frequency-distribution.

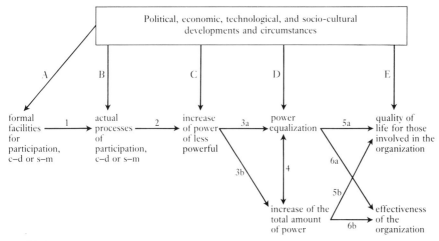

Fig. 23.1 Explanatory model of democratization in organizations

c-d = co-determination
s-m = self-management
Source: Lammers, 1985

and interactions in this sphere are stimulated and shaped only in part by formal prescriptions. Economic, technological, and socio-cultural conditions affect the ways in which, and the extent to which, facilities are used (arrow B). A striking example of unforeseen and unintended ways in which formal provisions may contribute to organizational democracy may be found in the case-study of Hing (Ch. 22). The farmer-members of the (Malaysian) Federal Land Development Authority often enough have their participatory rights curtailed by officials, but, nevertheless, can sometimes indirectly muster political pressure to get their way.

Arrow B also stands for actual processes of participation etc. which arise quite apart from any formal facilities, under the influence of economic or technological developments. The factory occupation studies by Visser (Ch. 14) form a case in point on the meso- or macrolevel, while a phenomenon like 'users' participation' by operators in connection with their work on machinery or automated systems[3] illustrates the fact that one can find instances of informal participation on the microlevel also.

Non-formalized varieties of organizational democracy are not always and not necessarily less durable than formalized ones. 'Covert' participation, as Borzeix and Linhart (Ch. 11) call such processes, is often condoned for quite a while by superiors who feel (rightly or wrongly) that they are free to go along with it or stop it. However, in so far as their subordinates who take part in such practices have some power or can turn to more powerful allies, *they* will tend to consider such

---

[3] See also nn. 1 and 4 in this chapter.

324   *Cornelis J. Lammers and György Széll*

'customs and practices' as 'earned rights'. In such cases one can say—as various authors do—that the participatory practices in question have some durability, since they have become institutionalized. By *institutionalization* we mean that certain patterns of association or interaction have come to be judged by the participants as 'worth while' in the light of certain values (like affluence, efficiency, democracy, or human dignity) and have become the object of collective beliefs and norms.

Institutionalization does not necessarily involve formalization, but no doubt forms of participation and co-determination based on legal regulations or collective bargaining agreements stand an even better chance than informal practices of acquiring such durable qualities over time. At this junction we want to emphasize that, in our view, only those processes of participation, co-determination, or self-management that imply an increase in power for the participants will tend to become institutionalized. People involved in schemes that do not provide them with a real chance to influence decisions in accordance with their interests or views will obviously not attach much value to such practices, let alone defend them. McCarthy (Ch. 10) mentions, as one of the main reasons for people not participating, their experience of 'pseudo-participation'. If people feel they are being manipulated, or if the scheme is merely a sham, they will drop out of it, if possible physically, if not, at least mentally. As Strauss (Ch. 18) puts it in his conclusion, 'The half-life of participation schemes has always been short.'

Therefore, we presume that only those processes of participation, etc., that mean an increase in power for the less powerful participants (arrow 2 in Fig. 23.1) will exhibit the features of an institutionalized practice and can be said to contain at least a minimal degree of organizational democracy. Whether or not efforts at participation, etc., pass the threshold of becoming institutionalized and thereby acquire the status of manifestations of organizational democracy in our sense of the term depends again on a variety of conditions (arrow C). As demonstrated in several reports (for example, by Cornforth, Ch. 3, Turner, Ch. 5, Gherardi, Strati, and Turner. Ch. 13, Abell, Ch. 17, Strauss, Ch. 18, and Hing, Ch. 22) often the backing of external agencies (unions, political parties, special support institutions, the State) is decisive for a project, or even a fully fledged model of some form of organizational democracy, to strike roots and flourish.

Virtually any organization harbours a variety of groups with different interests and/or cultures, as emphasized by Schienstock (Ch. 12) and by Gherardi, Strati, and Turner (Ch. 13). Moreover, as explained in an abstract manner by Bolle de Bal (Ch. 1) and exemplified more concretely in several other contributions, just about any form of participation, co-determination, or self-management will represent different functions for different groups. It follows that the institutionalization of a particular form of organizational democracy will seldom, if ever, come into being due to a consensus about the value(s) it embodies.

We submit that institutionalization of a mode of organizational democracy will generally take place and keep functioning on the basis of a sort of 'agreement to disagree' about its nature and functions. The 'agreement' in such cases consists of an understanding to maintain this or that practice and the joint recognition that the other party may do the right thing for the wrong reason. The 'right thing' is then to observe the rules of the game which have evolved in the course of time and become institutionalized, and to agree that the practice is worthwhile, albeit in the case of the other party for the 'wrong reasons' (that is, in terms of other values and with an eye to functions other than the 'proper' ones).

Schmidt and Trinczek (Ch. 21) account for the capacity of representative bodies to integrate relatively new tasks by bringing forward the idea of a 'political culture' which surrounds transactions in certain German works councils. This concept of a political culture also refers to the institutionalized character of the proceedings. Both management and worker representatives maintain the game of *Mitbestimmung*, and play it according to the time-honoured rules, although the players disagree on the values and functions involved. However, for both parties the system constitutes a convenient, and not too costly, forum to discuss matters of mutual interest, to conduct negotiations, and to settle disputes.

To conclude, we come to the thesis that the continuity of organizational democracy is preserved primarily through the process of institutionalization. We have argued that non-formalized participatory practices can also mature into an institutional pattern, but that, none the less, the bulk of institutionalized varieties of organizational democracy, in all likelihood, are anchored in the law, in collective agreements between employers' associations and unions, or in other formal arrangements (such as management directives). Enough has been said now about trends and developments in the past and present. It is time to turn to the last part of the task we set out to accomplish in this chapter and that is to try and formulate an answer to the question: what can we expect in the years to come? Has organizational democracy a future, and if so, what kind?

The prospects of organizational democracy

The ground swell

Cynics who do not set much store by the scientific methods used by meteorologists claim that, if one makes a weather forecast for tomorrow by simply stating that today's weather conditions will probably continue for another twelve to twenty-four hours, one has a better than fifty-fifty chance of making an accurate prediction. In similar fashion, a sociologist wanting to make a prognosis for a phenomenon like organizational democracy in the years to come cannot go too far wrong if he foresees that present trends are bound to continue.

Actually, in the case of the general course of various forms of organizational democracy, forecasting by simply extrapolating current trends is not a bad idea. After all, when one is dealing with global, long-term processes and not with single events (such as a *coup d'état* or a revolution) or with more specific processes or movements (such as an economy drive in the public sector, a series of industrial conflicts, or the emergence or disappearance of certain types of organization), it appears sensible to make the assumption of continuation unless other relevant developments interfere.

Thus, with respect to the trends we noted in the first part of this chapter—a rather steady ground swell and successive waves of organizational democracy—we must put the question: are there reasons to presume that the developments identified in the second part might gain or lose in strength in the decade to come?

As we noted earlier in this chapter, a fair number of practices of participation or co-determination are formalized and institutionalized. This entails—in the words of Looise (Ch. 20)—a great deal of 'institutional inertia' while, in all likelihood, not only employees and their representatives, but also managements, quite often have some sort of vested interest in such arrangements. The commitment of various parties to these ways of dealing with one another might be the mechanism accountable for what Schienstock (Ch. 12), quoting Herman, calls 'the dynamics of democracy'. Anyway, such proceedings usually exhibit quite a bit of tenacity and will continue unless other powerful forces intervene. This again raises the question of the slope of the general trend. Is an increase or a decrease to be expected due to economic and/or technological changes?

The 'high' and the 'low' road towards democratization

On the whole, these developments are not likely to subside. Therefore, one could perhaps expect an increase in the functional needs for forms of organizational democracy. As indicated in Fig. 23.1, processes of participation, etc. that lead to increased power for the participants (arrow 2)—which we, for that reason, consider as manifestations of 'real' organizational democracy—can bring about either power equalization (arrow 3a) or an increase in the total amount of power (arrow 3b). In the former case, as pointed out before, the democratization process is of the structural variety, in the latter case of the functional variety. A moderate amount of structural democratization can further the quality of working life (arrow 5a) and organizational effectiveness (arrow 6a), but a more drastic power equalization, more often than not, has negative effects.

If democratization is functional, not only by intent but also in fact, this will not necessarily change the hierarchical nature of the organization or the power distribution. In his conclusions Bolle de Bal (Ch. 1) points out that participation can be 'a positive sum game where both sides win if certain conditions are realized', while Schienstock similarly ends his chapter (12) with the observation that 'organizational design measures do not necessarily involve a zero sum play in the relationship between capital and labour'. If the employees concerned become more—and more seriously—involved in decision making, the chances are that this will result in an improvement in the quality and acceptance of proceedings, but their bosses are also likely to benefit from such forms of organizational democracy. In this manner both subordinates and their superiors gain in (joint) power, a process that is correlated with betterment of the quality of working life (arrow 5b) and a heightened level of organizational effectiveness (arrow 6b).

Research evidence shows that the 'route' from efforts to realization of organizational democracy via the 'low road' in Fig. 23.1 (arrows 2 to 3b, 5b, and 6b) is far more potent than the 'high road' (arrows 2 to 3a, 5a, and 6a). In other words, functional democratization, as compared to structural ventures to realize the democratic ideal, far more frequently contribute to an organization which functions well and which is also a more satisfactory place for the employee to work in. This is true not only for direct participation, but for indirect as well (Lammers, 1967; Tannenbaum and Cooke, 1979; Streeck, 1984; Scholl, 1986; Tannenbaum, 1986; Tarrab and D'Aragon, 1986).

Now, if current economic and technological trends continue, the awareness of the potential benefits of functional democratization in organizations may also become part of the common wisdom of managers and their advisers. Who knows, maybe these insights into the advantages of functional forms of organizational democracy will penetrate not only the managerial culture, but also Western culture generally. Is it not conceivable that participative management, semi-autonomous groups, joint consultation, organizational development, users' participation, and kindred forms, will become 'normal' elements of organizational practice, that is to say, part of the normative expectations of our society?

To return to the subject of managers, if a growing percentage of the present and new generations of organizational leaders were to be trained and informed about the human resources which could be mobilized to make their organization more efficient and flexible in response to ongoing technological and market change, this 'ideological' force could then reinforce other tendencies, rendering organizational democracy more common.

Some final considerations

So much for trends that would make one expect a positive slope in the main course of processes of organizational democratization. What about other developments that could have an inhibiting impact on this course? In spite of our optimistic conjecture concerning the possibilities of a more favourable cultural climate for endeavours in the spirit of functional organizational democracy, we must realistically reaffirm what we said earlier about the shift of values endorsing the role of the prominent, strong, decisive leader who tolerates no nonsense. Such notions and the general change in the political climate towards the 'right' do not lead one to expect new legislation or other formal provisions to bolster forms of participation or co-determination in the near future. The trends of deregulation and decentralization in collective bargaining which we discussed render it likely that attempts will even be made here and there to dismantle certain institutionalized forms of organizational democracy. Consequently, at best one may await a certain calm on this front.

Finally, a word about the development of unionism, which could support or inhibit the tendencies discussed earlier. In the past many unions took rather a negative stance with respect to management initiatives in the direction of functional democratization. Therefore, the more 'normal' such forms of participation became in the eyes of managers, the more vehemently would unions try to oppose the initiatives. Perhaps a new unionism is necessary to cope with the new structural challenges in technology and economy. The old formulas for collective bargaining on a centralized level of legal provisions for participation and co-determination no longer suffice. They have to be complemented. The reactions to very different kinds of company and work organization in the context of new technologies and new management strategies require the implementation of direct participation. This demands competence as well. As the 'transparent factory' or 'users' participation'[4] show, the situation is contradictory. It may be a chance for further democratization in organizations, but it may also be a means of integration and more hierarchical control. The future is open. It depends on the individual and collective actors within and outside organizations to achieve more organizational democracy instead of further polarization.

On balance, therefore, we suspect that the positive impulses of an economic and technological nature will be offset to some extent by the negative ones in the sphere of politics, legislation, and labour relations. The slope of the main trend towards organizational democracy could be slightly positive, but in our view is more likely to stabilize around the present level.

Of course, we must emphasize—as we did at the beginning of this chapter—that our observations pertain only to the West. Will the Second and/or Third World witness the growth of some of the new forms of work organization cultivated in their midst or tried out in the West? The few contributions we managed to obtain for this volume on non-Western developments (Ch. 16 by Meier, Ch. 17 by Abell, and Ch. 22 by Hing) do demonstrate the presence and viability of certain participative and co-operative endeavours in the countries in question. However, there is little, if any, evidence contained in these reports on which to ground the

---

[4] Both these terms were used by Hildebrandt in Ch. 15. In Germany, the term 'transparent factory' is used to describe the circumstances that, with the new range of technologies, a vast amount of information on every aspect of a factory's activity, including the activities of the work-force, is now available, thus making it 'transparent'.

The term 'users' or 'end user' participation is applied to technologies which are designed to allow the operator (or end user) to take a meaningful part in the operation rather than to be completely controlled by it.

expectation that major breakthroughs are likely. Moreover, as McCarthy (Ch. 10) stresses in her survey of literature about non-participation, democratic functioning has to be learned not only in the workplace, but also outside work. In other words, if managers and workers are brought up in a society where democracy is not embraced as a value nor practised (at least to some extent) in the family, the school, the polity, or in other major institutions, it is highly unlikely that ideas about participation and co-determination will take root.

As to the chances of large-scale transfer from the West to the Eastern and Southern hemispheres—again there is no reason for optimism. History shows how exceedingly difficult it is to transplant models of industrial democracy from one country to another (see e.g. Ch. 5 by Turner), and how seldom workers take earlier experiences into account. Consequently, it is quite unlikely that the Western examples and models will make the rest of the world safe for organizational democracy.

This implies more inequality of opportunity for working people around the globe to influence the course of their working lives. At the same time we should be aware of the risks of more inequality with respect to organizational democracy in Western society and even within our work organizations. As pointed out before, the mainstream of organizational democracy affects mainly, if not solely, the core employees of primarily large work organizations. The peripheral workers coming from the secondary labour market tend to be deprived of chances to benefit from schemes of participation or co-determination.

Let us finish then our reflections by expressing the hope that these inequalities as to people's rights of participation and co-determination will constitute a new challenge for practitioners as well as scholars to work on in the coming years.

References

Gustavsen, B. and Héthy, L. (1986), 'New Forms of Work Organisation: A European Overview', *Labour and Society*, 11(2): 167–88.
Lammers, C. J. (1967), 'Power and Participation in Decision-Making in Formal Organizations', *The American Journal of Sociology*, 73: 201–16.
—— (1973), 'Two Conceptions of Democratization in Organizations' in E. Pusic (ed.), *Participation and Self-Management*, iv *Proceedings of the First International Sociological Conference on Participation and Self-Management*, Zagreb (reprinted in a slightly different version as 'Self-Management and Participation: Two Conceptions of Democratization in Organizations', *Organization and Administrative Sciences*, 5(4): 17–33 (1974–5).
—— (1985), 'Organisationele Democratie: Literatuurbeschouwing', *M&O, Tijdschrift voor organisatiekunde en sociaal beleid*, 39: 481–501.
Scholl, W. (1986), 'Codetermination and the Quality of Working Life', in R. Stern and S. McCarthy (eds.), *International Yearbook of Organizational Democracy*, iii (Chichester: Wiley).

330   *Cornelis J. Lammers and György Széll*

Streeck, W. (1984), 'Co-determination: The Fourth Decade', in B. Wilpert and A. Sorge (eds.), *International Yearbook of Organizational Democracy*, ii (Chichester: Wiley).

Tannenbaum, A. S. (1986), 'Controversies about Control and Democracy in Organizations', in R. Stern and S. McCarthy (eds.), *International Yearbook of Organizational Democracy*, iii (Chichester: Wiley).

—— and Cooke, R. A. (1979), 'Organizational Control: A Review of Studies Employing the Control Graph Method', in C. J. Lammers and D. J. Hickson (eds.), *Organizations Alike and Unlike: International and Interinstitutional Studies in the Sociology of Organizations* (London: Routledge & Kegan Paul).

Tarrab, G. and D'Aragon, P. (1986), 'Participation in Business: Is it Viable? Under what Circumstances?', in R. Stern and S. McCarthy (eds.), *International Yearbook of Organizational Democracy*, iii (Chichester: Wiley).

Teulings, A. W. M. (1987), 'A Political Bargaining Theory of Co-determination: An Empirical Test for the Dutch System of Organizational Democracy' *Organizational Studies*, 8(1): 1–24.

Name Index

Subject Index

absenteeism, 27, 201, 229, 254, 256
achievement, 14, 24, 148, 159, 308
actor oriented theory, 113, 143
Algeria, 250
alienation, 14, 27, 30, 123, 126, 137, 147, 235, 309, 312
Allied Control Council, 67ff
alternative movement, 91
American *see* USA
anthropology, 114, 155
army, 27, 252
atomization, 14, 20
attitude, 78
Austria, 4
authoritarian personality, 118
autonomous working groups *see* semi-autonomous working groups
autonomy, 24, 27, 31, 34, 134, 138, 144, 146, 152, 169, 230, 253, 269

bank, 44, 46, 210, 216, 235
bargaining *see* collective bargaining
Basque, 45
Belgian/Belgium, 175, 225
Britain/British, 10, 63ff, 173, 178–9, 225, 230, 237, 240, 285–6
British Rochdale, 159
bureaucracy/bureaucratic, 14–15, 23, 27, 32, 277

Canada, 36
capitalist/capitalistic, 123–4, 131, 137, 145ff, 159, 181, 291, 302
Catholic Church, 160, 261
CDU (FRG), 86
CFDT (France), 178, 257, 259, 266
CFTC (France), 266
CGC (France), 266
CGT, 178, 257, 259, 266
Chinese, 303
class conflict, 148, 287
class consciousness, 117
class struggle, 131, 137, 162, 180
CNC, 199
co-management, 185ff, 259, 263
co-operative, 1, 32, 159ff, 170, 180, 210ff, 226, 310, 313, 320, 324

co-operative, industrial, 210ff
co-operative, workers, 10, 38ff, 319
co-ownership, 162
co-determination, 1–2, 4, 9, 63ff, 74ff, 113, 151, 169, 172, 185ff, 226ff, 233, 237, 285ff, 317–18, 320ff, 325–6, 328, 330–1
collective bargaining, 3, 13, 20, 31, 34–5, 41, 65f, 70, 104, 225–6, 262, 265, 287ff, 296–7, 308, 325, 330
communist, 257, 263, 318, 322
competence/competency, 28, 84–5, 101, 169, 189, 197, 201–2, 216, 278, 282–3, 330
competition, 27, 30, 99, 228, 252f, 256, 264, 291
competitive/ness, 2, 96, 132f, 151, 218f, 297, 321
computer/computerized, 21, 27, 96, 134, 136, 139, 185, 197, 228, 251, 278
Computer Integrated Manufacturing (CIM), 186
concession bargaining, 225, 229, 234, 236ff, 240, 224, 317
conciliation, 66, 82
conservative, 286
counter-culture, 138
counter-power, 14
creative/creativity, 28, 32–3, 116, 200

debureaucratization, 11, 14, 20, 23
decentralization/decentralized, 1, 3, 30, 83, 144, 225–6, 278, 281, 283, 286, 291, 297, 321, 330
democracy/democratic, 1, 3, 9, 103, 122–3, 139, 142, 159, 248, 323ff, 328f, 331
democracy, economic, 66, 200
democracy, industrial, 11, 14, 98ff, 103, 130, 133, 155ff, 169, 171ff, 236, 248ff, 264, 298, 301–2, 318, 331
democracy, organizational, 1ff, 9–10, 24, 63, 113, 130, 155, 169, 225ff, 252, 301, 317ff
democracy, participative/participatory, 132–3, 306, 324
democracy, political, 66
democratization, 2–3, 12, 20, 64, 98ff, 121, 142ff, 172, 181, 249, 265, 274, 277, 301–2, 317, 323–4, 328ff
Denmark, 38
deregulation, 120, 278, 286, 296, 330